OVERL
TO EGYPT

On a 1952 BSA Bantam

GORDON G. MAY

To Kay,

all the best,

[signature] John G. May

Editor

JANE GREGORY

NKN
Edinburgh
2013

Rixon Groove

First published in 2012 by
Rixon Groove
PO Box 153, Stockport,
Cheshire, SK6 2EE,
United Kingdom

ISBN: 978-0-9561168-3-3 (Paperback)
ISBN: 978-0-9561168-6-4 (Hardback)

www.overlandtoegypt.co.uk

The publishers thank Mortons Archive (www.mortonsarchive.com)
for their use of the copyrighted photograph of Peggy Iris Thomas on page 6.

To my brilliant and lovely son, Jacques.
Your smiles and laughter swell my heart.

And to Essa Mansori.
You made me feel what it would have
been like to have had a brother.

About This Book

A 1952 BSA 2-stroke motorcycle was unquestionably an anachronistic choice of machine for an overland journey made in 2010. When you're not naturally mechanically talented it could seem to be a somewhat foolish selection. But I've always felt that it's important to do what you have passion for, and in my case, that means riding classic motorcycles, even if keeping them running is a challenge. Although this story could be read as a cautionary tale, for in some ways it is, the richness of the whole experience made it much more than that.

Win Borden* said, "If you wait to do everything until you're sure it's right, you'll probably never do much of anything." This was certainly the case for the first failed ride to Egypt, although I believe by the second attempt, I had done everything imaginable to ensure the bike had as much chance of success as possible. With hindsight, I feel that in both cases the mechanical problems we faced, in a strange way, enhanced the journey and I hope that's a feeling shared by readers of this book. Without doubt, I certainly learned immeasurably from the experiences.

Acknowledgements

First and foremost, my sincere thanks to Derek Thom. Derek recognised that I needed assistance to get a new project launched and not only spent his money to make it possible, but gave his time and encouragement unstintingly. His good humour and keenness meant that I enjoyed every moment we shared together on the project.

Thanks also to the ever enthusiastic and pivotal, Andy Berry, who not only built me an excellent engine, but never made me feel uncomfortable when, day after day, I called him for advice from a succession of far flung places.

The BSA Bantam Club has been very supportive, and I thank in particular club member, Pete Rose, for the time he gave to preparing Peggy and his pertinent tips along the way.

Many companies offered their assistance and provided some excellent equipment which I used on the ride. I was both surprised and pleased by how well people responded to my plans to use such an old motorcycle and their backing was invaluable. I've included a list of them in the final pages of this book, which I hope fellow touring motorcyclists, and Bantam owners, will find a useful resource. I would like to make a special acknowledgement to Debb and Rex of Rex Caunt Racing, who were professional, encouraging and delivered service way beyond the call of duty.

The manuscript for this book was proofread by my oldest friend, writer and editor, Judith Coyle, who I must express my gratitude towards as she always comes to my aid in times of need.

On a personal note, I would also like to thank my parents, Iain and Martha May, for one of their most valuable gifts - that of self-belief. They've unfailingly encouraged me to pursue my dreams and always impressed upon me that I can achieve anything that I set my mind to.

And of course Jane Gregory, an incredible woman, who once again held the fort with our son, Jacques, while I was away. Unselfishly, she employed her spirit, humour and humanity in editing this book and undoubtedly has improved it in every way possible. It's almost impossible to count just how many hours she's contributed, but I'm exceedingly grateful for every one of them. My hope is that in some way I can repay her when she begins to use her exquisite voice to sing professionally again.

While I was on both journeys, I received countless messages of encouragement and support from people following the ride online. Because of the pressures, mostly caused by bike maintenance and the number of hours I spent on the road every day, I simply wasn't able to reply to the hundreds of emails and blog posts I received. However, they did mean an awful lot to me.

Finally, without the ready friendship of people met on both journeys, who gave assistance, hospitality and so generously shared themselves with me, the journey simply wouldn't have been worth making and this book not worth the paper it's printed on. Essa Mansori in particular made an enormous difference to the success of the second ride, but along the way there were literally hundreds of people who smiled, shook my hand, gave their time and made me feel safe and welcome. I hope this book in some way goes to recognise them and show my deep appreciation.

Gordon G. May
December 2011

* There is currently no biographical information available about Win Borden, but this is a popular quote.

My heroine and her two heroes:
Peggy Iris Thomas, Oppy the Bantam
and Matelot the Airedale.
Canada, 1951.

Introduction

"To Egypt... on a Bantam! Are you joking?" Almost without exception this was the response I received when I first told people about my intention to ride to Egypt on a 1952 lightweight 2-stroke BSA. It was inevitably followed by the question, "Why?" which takes quite some explaining.

My first encounter with a BSA Bantam came, rather incongruously, on a Qantas flight from Wellington, New Zealand, to Melbourne, Australia, in 1993. On the way to the airport I'd stopped at a local newsagents to collect my monthly subscription to *The Classic Motorcycle* magazine, which always arrived in New Zealand some six to eight weeks after publication in the UK. Once on the plane, heading out over the white-capped Tasmin Sea, I settled back into my seat and flicked through its pages until I came to a story titled *Friday Afternoon Bantam*.

Up to this point, I knew nothing about the workings of 2-stroke motorcycles and if I'd seen a Bantam before, it certainly hadn't impressed itself into my motorcycling consciousness. But the story of this particular bike, along with some excellent photographs, captivated me. Registered in 1954 as NEL 906, the 125cc D1 Bantam was bought by a man who, until then, had bicycled 10 miles to work and back every day. Unfortunately, the Bantam was what was known as a *Friday Job*, built by 'someone whose body was assembling a component, but whose mind was making plans for a few jars, a bag of fish and chips and a long lie in the next morning.' In this case, a vital component was left out on the assembly line... the condenser. This resulted in very rough and unreliable running and after just 77 miles, the owner pushed it into his garden shed, rationalising that motorcycling wasn't for him, and got back onto his bicycle.

There it sat, like a fly in amber, for the next 39 years. After its owner's death, NEL 906 was passed on to his nephew, an enthusiast who was unable to get it running without the same misfire.

"Probably the crank seals," was the verdict of an expert, but on inspection they proved to be in fair condition, as did the carburettor. It was then that the missing condenser was spotted... there wasn't even a hole drilled into the points backplate for it to be fitted! When resolved, the bike ran reliably and sailed through its MOT despite still wearing the original Dunlop Universal Tyres which, like the rest of the bike, had survived the four decade hibernation with virtually no degeneration. This gave the 1993 magazine tester the rare privilege of riding a 1954 motorcycle boasting barely more than delivery mileage.

The article impressed me, as did the Bantam, which was painted a pale green colour with a yellow panel on its fuel tank. Unlike many other British lightweights of the era, it looked sturdy and practical, to all intents and purposes a proper motorcycle, just made smaller. Lo and behold, two years later, I spotted a D1 advertised for sale in *The Dominion*, Wellington's daily

7

newspaper. It was a later 1957 model but when I went to view it, my now tatty copy of *The Classic Motorcycle* in hand, I found that it looked almost identical to the *Friday Afternoon Bantam*. I immediately bought it and my love affair with BSA's little rooster began.

Over the next three years I rode the bike virtually year round. It proved to be an ideal mount within the city limits, easily able to accelerate at the speed of modern cars on the hilly streets and also cruise comfortably at 40 mph around the harbour and bays that surround the capital. And with such a magnificent coastal vista to take in, there was no need for anything faster. Throughout this period I had a small inner-city factory and a men's clothing shop located in the central business district. The Bantam, light and easy to manoeuvre, was on many occasions left hidden under a stairwell in the factory foyer or bounced up the steps and into the shop for a night, allowing me to go out for the evening and either catch a taxi or walk home. For two weeks it even became the focus of a shop window display, with a selection of colourful shirts and ties spreading from temporary pannier bags. It proved to be a real crowd pleaser too, often stopping people, mostly men, in their tracks as they walked past.

When I moved to the UK in 1999, the Bantam followed in a shipping container squeezed between an assortment of household possessions. But as I initially had nowhere permanent to live, it was stored for at least three years before finally being re-registered for road use. For a while, I tried riding it around Manchester but found the city drivers far less tolerant of our lowly speeds and hand signals than they had been in New Zealand. Moreover, by then I always had a 350 or 500cc classic at hand that was more suitable to the local road conditions and consequently, it was hardly ridden. When in 2004 I urgently needed some cash to fund another motorcycle project, I cast my eye around my garage to see what I could sell. To my regret, the Bantam, along with another lightweight, a 125cc Royal Enfield Model RE, was sold.

In 2008 I rode my 1953 500cc Royal Enfield Bullet from Manchester to Chennai, South India. It was a wonderful journey, made special by the numerous encounters I had with the kind, generous and remarkably hospitable people I met, particularly in Turkey, Iran and Pakistan. But it was not only the ride itself that was so enjoyable... I also gained a great deal of satisfaction from preparing the motorcycle for the trip and after my return, from writing a book about the adventure.

Overland To India was published in December 2008 and in many ways it changed my life. Having given up a well-paid job as the operations director of a hi-tech surveillance company, an industry I loathed and only stuck with because of the company's inspirational MD, I found that I was able to scrape enough of a living together by taking my new book, along with a selection of motorcycle reference books and a few classic bike accessories, to motorcycle shows. During the week I travelled far and wide giving talks about the journey to an assortment of groups, not just motorcyclists, and usually sold a fair number of books at the end of each evening. But what made the biggest difference was the reception the book got from its readers. Their encouragement, kind words and positive feedback gave me the further motivation I needed to dream of more journeys, again on classic bikes, and to write more books too.

During the latter stages of preparations for the ride to India, I struck a problem getting pannier frames modified to fit my bike. As if by divine intervention, I met Derek Thom at the Netley Marsh classic motorcycle *Eurojumble*.

"Need some fittings making?" he asked, when I explained my dilemma. "I'm not called Mr. Bracket for nothing, you know! Let's have a look."

Although the show was 240 miles away from my home, it transpired that we actually lived only 32 miles apart. Over the next two months, Derek, a retired police motorcyclist, welded the pannier frames, created stainless steel brackets to retro-fit indicators and a small fly screen to the bike, and when at the last minute I struggled to get my new carburettor running smoothly (caused by a microscopic hair in the pilot jet housing), spent a whole morning stripping and testing it. Furthermore, as an unexpected bonus, he became a friend, happy to help with the project purely because he wanted to see me succeed.

Roughly a year after my return from India, over a cup of tea at his home near the Cheshire town of Runcorn, we got round to talking about motorcycles, which was nothing unusual.

"So, come on, what's on the agenda Gordon? Where are you going to ride to next?"

"That's the million dollar question," I replied. "I'm pretty broke after the ride to India. The Bullet's in need of quite a lot of work and I don't have another bike that's either suitable or appealing to travel a long way on." I continued. "But I'd love to do a shorter ride on a Bantam. You know I used to have one and regretted selling it. Maybe something like round the coast of Britain or perhaps to a really offbeat place for a lightweight, like Athens or Timbuktu... or better still, the pyramids in Cairo."

Derek's a man who likes to give people a helping hand; it just seems to be an innate part of his character. This is well illustrated by his reason for joining the police. While in his early twenties, working as a research scientist in an ICI laboratory, he needed to leave work for a doctor's appointment. En route, riding his 1973 Triumph Bonneville just a tad over the speed limit, he was stopped by a motorcycle policeman who asked him what the rush was. Derek apologised, admitted he was speeding and explained he was on his way to the doctor's. The officer, who was approaching retirement age, gave Derek a break.

"Off you go," he said. "I'm going to phone the surgery and if I find you've been lying to me you'll get your speeding ticket. If you're telling the truth, I'll let you off this time." On arrival at the surgery, Derek was told by the receptionist that a policeman had phoned and left a message for him along the lines of, "I'll keep my word but keep your speed down in the future." Derek was so impressed by the man's humanity and fairness that within a few months he quit his job and joined the force, where he stayed for the next 26 years.

"I told myself," he explained when first relating his tale to me, "that the kind of policeman I wanted to be was just like the officer who let me off the speeding ticket, fair, honest and always willing to give someone a chance. Oh, yes, and ride motorcycles every day!"

As I mulled over what I'd just said about riding a Bantam to Egypt and wondered how it could possibly happen, Derek spoke.

"I'll tell you what, Gordon. I'll sponsor you to ride to Egypt by providing the bike. At the end of the trip we can work out between us what to do with it, whether I sell it to you or keep it myself. But for now, I'll buy it and help you make it ready for the journey. The rest is up to you."

I could have hugged him!

Preparation

I wasn't alone in using BSA's smallest motorcycle for long journeys. In the 1950s, before the advent of affordable cars and budget air fares, travelling on such a diminutive machine as a Bantam was surprisingly common. The contemporary press regularly featured articles on motorcycle touring and Bantam riders were far from being overshadowed by the owners of larger machines. In 1951, Mr. and Mrs. Wendle Agne from the United States rode a 125cc Bantam over 5,000 miles around France, Germany and Italy, reporting their only problem as one burst tyre. In 1952, Englishman Clifford Hall took his wife on a 14 day tour to Germany and back on a Bantam, covering 2,142 miles on just 14 gallons of petrol. In 1953, Kathleen and Michael Percival, resplendent in pith helmets, took their school age son, Duncan, on a journey the length of East Africa to Cape Town. Their mounts were a pre-war side valve Norton sidecar outfit loaded with provisions and spares and a D1 Bantam for Kathleen. The journey took six months and was an exceptional achievement considering the inhospitable climes they travelled through. As for the Bantam, Kathleen reported it 'looked and behaved as though it had never ventured farther than the Tottenham Court Road... the spring frame made all the difference.' The little BSA even protected her from a leopard when caught alone in the bush at dusk pushing the Bantam 4km towards a farm somewhere north of Mpika, Zambia. Demonstrating remarkable coolness, Kathleen put the bike on its stand, edged round the far side of it, then bashed an empty petrol can as loudly as possible onto the handlebars to scare the crouching animal away!

Also, in 1954, Brenda Collins, a 25-year-old English journalist living in Montreal, decided to embark on a journey to see North America as cheaply as possible. She bought a D1 Bantam, equipped it with a fabric and perspex windshield and a pair of white tassled western-style leather saddle bags, then set off. Her route took her from Montreal west across Canada to Vancouver, south down the Pacific coast to San Diego, east along the Mexican border and southern states en route to Jacksonville, then finally north to New York and ultimately Boston. Living on $2 a day, the plucky traveller managed in excess of 10,000 miles in just ninety days.

But without doubt the most famous Bantam journey of them all was made by a 25-year-old English woman from Ewell, near Epsom in southern England. Her name was Peggy Iris Thomas.

Miss Thomas bought her Bantam, a rigid-framed 125cc D1, in 1950. She immediately named it Oppy after its registration number, OPE 811. With no previous riding experience, she learned to handle it on the dealership forecourt then, three weeks later, passed her driving test. Within a month she set off on a 4,500 mile camping tour around Scandinavia accompanied by her Australian friend, Prudence Beggs. A 4 page article on their journey was printed in *The Motor Cycle* magazine of 8 March 1951 and this was soon followed by BSA advertisements featuring Oppy and the two young women.

However, Miss Thomas's most famous journey was an 18 month, 14,000 mile epic in North America. She took her 60lb Airedale puppy, Matelot, along, ensconced in a large tin box secured to the Bantam's parcel rack. Starting in Halifax, Nova Scotia, with only $60 in funds, the pair traversed Canada to Vancouver on the Pacific coast then headed south down the west coast of the United States through Seattle, San Francisco and Los Angeles. After riding across the arid states of Arizona and New Mexico, they crossed into Mexico and travelled as far south as Mexico City before heading for the Atlantic coast and the port of Veracruz, from where they caught a steamer to New Orleans. After an extended stay on the Florida Quays, the journey ended with a ride north to New York. Along the way Miss Thomas wild camped, crossed mountains and deserts, lost the cat-chasing Matelot several times, encountered black and grizzly bears and had numerous breakdowns, tumbles and trials including her beloved Bantam catching fire. To pay her way she worked in a fruit orchard, ice cream parlour, a woodmill and for a short but exhausting time, simultaneously held down a night job as a typist in the Canadian Pacific telegraph office and day job as a secretary.

As well as her clothes, a tent, cooking equipment, food for a growing dog and herself plus tools and spare parts, Miss Thomas carried a typewriter with which to write a book about the adventure. Released in 1953 in the United States as *Gasoline Gypsy*, it was published in the UK a year later under the title *A Ride In The Sun*.

Both titles have long been out of print and are very hard to find, but in 2005 I finally managed to pick up a well worn ex-library edition for £100. It's a story of true adventure and courage undertaken by someone with a positive and open-minded view of the world and its people. Perhaps in some ways it simply reflects the optimism of the immediate post war years but the book and Miss Thomas absolutely capture the essence of joyful, freewheeling, independent travel. It's also written from a motorcyclist's perspective, which means that the problems and highlights of riding and maintaing a motorcycle on such an arduous journey are discussed and even celebrated. Straightaway it became one of my favourite reads and several times I devoured it from cover to cover, captivated by the obvious courage and intrepid spirit of the writer.

For some time Derek and I discussed the most suitable Bantam for the job. In my opinion, the style of the original D1 is the most eye pleasing model and I reasoned that using one would tie in nicely with my initiation to Bantams via NEL 906, my own New Zealand mount and, of course, Miss Thomas's bike, Oppy. But I wasn't so sure that a standard 125cc D1, with its three speed gearbox, would be suitable, especially for crossing the Alps. Derek immediately understood my rationale.

"I've seen how much luggage you carry, Gordon. It's not just a fourth gear that you want... you need some more grunt."

I posed the question, "Do you think it's possible to retro fit a later model 175cc engine into a D1?"

After a short amount of research time on the internet we had our answer. The simple mounting layout of the BSA power unit, secured by just four short bolts, had remained unchanged right through the production life of the model from 1948 to 1971.

It didn't take long to locate a suitable donor engine, which turned up on eBay a few days later. It was advertised by a small Scottish restorer, Rob, as a freshly rebuilt 1968 D14/4 engine, and cost £300.

"Do you know of any D1 Bantams for sale?" I'd asked Rob on the phone. "Preferably a plunger suspension type, not the early rigid."

To my surprise, his answer was affirmative.

"I have a friend in Glasgow, Jim, with one. I actually did some work on the bike a couple of years ago and sold it to him. It's a runner, but I don't think he's had the chance to ride it much and now needs the space in his garage." He continued keenly, "It's a 1952 model and as far as I remember from its old log book, has been in Scotland all of its life. I bought it from a guy in Glasgow who'd had it on display in the lounge of his tenement flat for years."

Rob promised to follow up on the Scottish Bantam. The next morning, two photos of a green D1 popped into my email inbox along with a message that said it was available for £1,000. Derek readily agreed to the purchase and we snapped it up.

A week later we had both the bike and the surrogate engine at Derek's home.

"Go on, take it for a spin before we swap the engines over," he encouraged me.

I hopped on and after firing up the motor on the second kick, enthusiastically set off. The bike accelerated briskly but didn't feel very willing above 35mph, which in the circumstances wasn't a real concern. More importantly, it handled well and the suspension and brakes felt solid. The test ride took 20 minutes and I don't think I stopped grinning the whole time.

Derek has countless years of experience keeping bikes on the road, with his current stable including a pair of late '50s AJS and a stunning green Norton ES2. Smack in the middle of restoring a 1946 500cc AJS Model 18, arranged in large gleaming lumps on his lounge carpet, he nevertheless threw himself into the preparation of the Bantam. Our first task was to transplant the 175cc engine, a straightforward job which took under an hour. However, before we could fire it up the electrics needed upgrading from 6 to 12 Volts. As we had everything at hand, including a new coil and battery, that didn't take very long either. With the fuel tank back on, we tried to test the engine. It simply wouldn't go, despite a meaty blue spark emitting from the spark plug electrodes. The crank seemed to be spinning freely but repeated kicks failed to produce even the faintest cough. We whipped the carburettor off and disassembled it, revealing internals coated with white, powdery oxidization.

"Let's just see if that's the cause," said Derek, as he removed a much bigger carburettor from one of his 4-stroke AJS and fastened it onto the Bantam engine.

The first kick produced a colossal roar, with flames spitting backwards from the open carburettor air inlet. I yanked on the throttle cable with my fingers and the engine revved lustily before letting out an almighty flaming backfire.

"That proves a point, eh?" Derek grinned as he cut the ignition. "I think we need to find you a better carburettor!" Half an hour searching through various boxes in his shed produced a suitable replacement.

We spent a couple of very companionable weeks making the bike ready. In this time Derek created an alloy sump guard, a stainless steel battery carrier, brackets to hold a pair of pannier frames in place and fixings to attach the new coil and a 3-phase rectifier. A new pair of tyres were fitted along with a shiny alloy rear sprocket and matching Iwis chain. After attaching a pair of sturdy but lightweight period pannier frames, Derek set about modifying a Royal Enfield sidestand so it would fit on the much smaller Beeza. His handiwork, when we bolted it on, looked indestructible!

The biggest problem proved to be mounting the exhaust system to the substituted engine. The downpipe required for a D14 engine is of a larger diameter than the one needed for a D1. A pattern replacement, made by English firm *Wassels*, was speedily supplied by a Bantam parts vendor, *Bournemouth Bantams*. However, when we offered it up to the bike, we found that its curve ran straight into the D1's footrest. After scratching his chin for a few minutes, Derek came up with a workable, if rather industrial, solution.

"I can't bend the downpipe as it's too thin and will collapse. I'll cut and shut it as much as I can but doubt we'll be able to completely avoid the footrest arm. What I can do is saw the right footpeg in half, weld a piece of round steam pipe into the middle of it, then pass the exhaust through the hole. It won't look pretty but it'll be strong and do the job."

Just hours later it was on the bike.

"Don't worry, Gordon," he said as I inspected his handiwork. "The bike will break before that steam pipe bends."

His cheerful commitment to the project resulted in almost daily words of thanks from me, the day of the fixed exhaust being such a one.

"You don't have to keep saying thanks, Gordon. I'm enjoying it too," he said after one particularly effusive bout of gratitude.

Continuing my research into other Bantam travellers, I found a short article in a 1967 edition of *The Motor Cycle* which related the epic journey of Ralph and Marina Lewis Hall. Amazingly, within a couple of hours of their wedding in Birmingham, the pair set off on their honeymoon... riding a secondhand, £35 D3 Bantam to Australia! The bike was modified by Ralph, a carpenter, who built a luggage system out of plywood. Apart from punctures and broken spokes and an encounter with a Turkish man, already with three wives, who wanted to buy Marina, the eight month journey was reported as being incredibly trouble free.

Then I came upon the tale of Julian Preece, who set off from his home in Northampton for India in October 1985 on a 1966 175cc D7 Bantam. In preparation he'd rebuilt the engine and rubber mounted spare fuel containers onto the rear suspension units. He made it to Turkey but was unable to secure a visa for Iran so turned around and headed for Africa instead, entering via Egypt. He travelled as far south as Bangui in the Central African Republic before turning north west through the Cameroon and Nigeria to Algeria then, after almost seven months, home. It was by no means without problems, with Julian reporting that by the time he crossed the Sahara on the return leg, 'The Bantam's front mudguard stays had sheared and a few spokes had broken, the mechanical noise had become louder than the exhaust noise as the big ends and mains had worn. Both sprockets were almost round and the chain was like elastic; the carburettor was temperamental and began flooding at random. Basically the bike was a wreck, but it still moved forward.'

Sadly, I was unable to track either of these people down for advice. Instead, I managed to speak to a friend, Richard Miller of Bournemouth, who apart from riding a Royal Enfield Bullet from India to the UK in the 1990s and from his home to Cape Town in 2006, had used a Bantam in the Motogiro, an annual 1,000 km competition run over five days in the hilly Tuscany region of Italy. In the event's vintage class, 120 riders take part on bikes of under 175cc that have to be manufactured before 1958.

"Gosh, Gordon, all I can tell you is they can be made reliable, but you might be best to uprate the electrics. On the Motogiro all machines are closely scrutinised for originality on entry so my Bantam's engine was heavily modified but only internally. I certainly wouldn't want to climb those mountains on a stock 125 with just a 3 speed gearbox."

I get a similar response from *Classic Bike* editor, Hugo Wilson, who participated in the 2009 Motogiro on a D1 Bantam.

"I used a D7 engine for its 4 speed gearbox but fitted with the original D1 barrel and head, so it passed scrutiny but rode a lot better than standard. I also used electronic ignition by Rex Caunt, which made it very reliable. My advice would be keep the points cam well lubed, upgrade the electrics to 12 volts and use fully synthetic oil, the best you can get. To be honest, I had a brilliant time on it with no real issues at all. Good luck on your ride."

Finally, while displaying the *Overland To India* Bullet at the *BMF* (British Motorcycle Federation) show in Peterborough, I met a man in his late sixties who introduced himself as John Storey.

"I've ridden over 300,000 miles on my Bantam," he told me when I mentioned my impending trip. I shook his hand in awe, keen to hear more.

"My bike's an ex GPO D1 Bantam that I bought in 1965 for ten quid. It was nearly a decade old then and had already done god knows how many miles."

He dug in his pocket and removed a wad of well thumbed photos that all featured a battered, rather motley looking blue Bantam.

"I call it Project 9, because it's the ninth bike I've owned," he continued as I stared in wonder at the aged photographs. "I know it looks beat up, but I've never really been concerned about appearance, just on it getting me where I'm going."

Over the next quarter of an hour John happily recounted tales of his annual holidays in Europe, where he'd travelled as far and wide as Scandinavia, Yugoslavia and Morocco.

"I've been to so many places and had that many breakdowns, I can fix just about anything with my eyes closed. People used to laugh at me, you know, when I went off every year on my Bantam. Some still do, but I don't care. It suits me and I've never had that much money to spend on luxuries anyway."

Explaining my intended route, I asked for any advice or guidance he could offer.

"You're crossing the Alps. One time, coming down a mountain pass in Switzerland, I set fire to my front brake I was pulling on it so hard and long... nearly killed myself, I did, and had to use my feet to stop us."

Daunting as this sounded, it was no less dire than the next warning.

"Coming down a long hill in Italy I lost my front brake when grease from a leaking front fork got into the hub. That was scary too."

I asked how many miles a day he'd been able to comfortably travel on his bike.

"Well, one day I did 300 miles, and I never go much over thirty. That was travelling from Stockholm to Oslo, but it was too much. Mostly I'm happy doing 150 miles a day, especially as I've got older."

Before we parted, he advised me to check that there was no play in the rear wheel, pack the plungers and forks full of grease and keep my brakes adjusted.

"Let me know how you get on, and yeah, watch out for the police. The last few times I went to Europe I was constantly stopped because the bike looked so rough."

With that, he thrust a piece of paper with his telephone number into my hand and sauntered off. I stood there, absolutely astonished.

However, it seemed that every time I spoke to someone about journeys on Bantams, the name of Peggy Iris Thomas cropped up.

"Wasn't there a lady with a dog that made some epic journey on a Bantam in the 1950s?" or "Years ago I read a book by Peggy Iris Thomas about crossing America on a Bantam. I wish I could find a copy as I'd love to read it again."

For the umpteenth time, I read her book. Shortly afterwards, my thoughts were unexpectedly crystalised during a phone call with Derek.

"You know, you're going to have to give the bike a name," he had said towards the end of a conversation about strengthening the rear mudguard, then after a moment's thought added, "How about Berty Bantam?"

"No," I replied, surprising myself as I continued without really knowing what was coming out of my mouth next.

"There's only one name that I'd want to call it... Peggy!"

"Of course, after Peggy Iris Thomas... yeah, it has to be, really, doesn't it," he concurred.

With the Bantam's moniker now firmly set, I managed to track down a series of magazine articles published in Britain between 1951 and 1952 that had great photos of Miss Thomas, an extremely photogenic Matelot and a crazily overladen Oppy. How wonderful it would be, I thought, to be able to find her if she's still alive, tell her about my forthcoming journey and ask for any pearls of wisdom. I knew it was a long shot, as a rough calculation based on her probable age during the war when she joined the WRNS (Women's Royal Naval Service) indicated she was most likely born in 1925 or 1926, making her approximately 84 years old in 2009. Nonetheless, I set about my search with gusto, telling myself that such a spirited, enterprising character had every chance of living into her eighties and well beyond.

With no previous experience of finding missing people, I began with internet searches. This resulted in nothing beyond a few references to her book and journey. I then subscribed to a service that offered to 'Search for people, businesses and places in the UK.' This immediately brought up a list of over a hundred women called Peggy or Margaret Thomas. I ignored all those with a middle initial other than an 'I' and set to work phoning. Nearly 60 calls later I'd exhausted the list but without any joy. The nearest I came was when an obviously elderly lady, one of the few Peggy I Thomas's, answered the phone.

"Yes dear, I'm Peggy Thomas."

I asked if she was Peggy *Iris* Thomas.

"What did you say? You'll have to speak up as I'm 85 and don't hear very well."

"Are you Peggy *Iris* Thomas" I repeated, my heart beating loudly.

"No, my middle name's Irene, not Iris," came the reply. I told her about Miss Thomas and my search in somewhat fortissimo tones, which she seemed to enjoy hearing, before I disappointedly ended the call.

A week or so later I began to search for authors, reasoning that someone who wrote one book may very well write another, albeit on a different subject. Almost straight away I came across a website for the Redland Park United Reformed Church in Bristol. On a page called Church History was a picture of a grey haired lady. My eyes nearly popped out of my head... her hairstyle and cheekbones were so redolent of the young Miss Thomas. My joy turned to despair as I read the words next to the photograph. 'Archivist Peggy Thomas, who died in December 2009 aged 93, had a unique knowledge of the church. She joined Redland Park aged ten in 1926 and experienced the war years when the original church was bombed. Her history of the church is still available.'

A name and number was provided for anyone who wished to order her book. I immediately dialled it.

"Did she write another book? No, I don't think so," replied the rather baffled sounding woman who answered the phone.

I persisted, mentioning motorcycles.

"Our Peggy... a biker. I think not!" My explanations about a journey across Canada and the United States in the early 1950s produced an even more emphatic response.

"I'm certain she lived the whole of her life in this area and the history of our church was all that she wrote. Sorry I can't help you more, unless of course you'd like to buy her book?"

My hopes dashed, I concluded my research into authors then moved onto obituaries. After a couple of long days' work this resulted in sore eyes from staring at the computer screen and scanning old newspaper reports but not a mention of Miss Thomas.

Next I tried a new angle of attack. Throughout *A Ride In The Sun*, Miss Thomas referred to a young Danish civil engineer that she met while on her first Bantam ride to Scandinavia. Their romance blossomed during the 18 month American odyssey, with Carl-Erik sending letters, a reel to reel tape recording (which she rather embarrassingly had to listen to in front of two sound engineers at a Vancouver radio station as that was only only place with suitable equipment), and eventually a proposal of marriage accompanied by an engagement ring. Somewhat mortifyingly, Miss Thomas lost the engagement ring in Mexico but nevertheless, at the end of the book, the plan was to sail from New York to Denmark to marry Carl-Erik.

I'd already searched the Danish online telephone directory for Peggy Thomas at the start of my quest. There had been none. I'd also tried a general search for Peggy. None of them had the middle name *Iris*, but as well as the *Peggy Sue American Car Club of Denmark*, which sounded rather fascinating, fourteen had no middle names. Over a two week period I called them all. Those that could speak English politely informed me I had the wrong number and those who only spoke Danish didn't need to tell me they were not the Peggy I sought. Going back to basics, I scoured the pages of *A Ride In The Sun* for a clue to Carl-Erik's surname. Despite becoming Miss Thomas's fiancé, he's mentioned surprisingly few times and no family name was apparent. I typed Carl-Erik into the online phone book and got over 1,000 hits. I quickly gave up on that one... I had as much chance of finding him as searching for a John Paul, Michael Peter or something similar in the UK! With the date of my departure rapidly approaching, time became an issue and the search was put on the back burner.

Two months before the journey, Peggy was ready for her first road trials.

Everything seemed to be going well... brighter lights and the new hearty electric air horn, which replaced the old honk honk rubber squeeze type fitted as standard in 1952, worked brilliantly. All the new fabrications, including a small flyscreen, again assembled by the maestro of brackets, felt solid and free from rattles. Most importantly, the 175cc power unit started first or second kick, usually without choke, and would quickly establish a steady rhythm.

I set off on our first outing with a great deal of excitement, hoping to clock up a good 50 miles around the Peak District. All seemed to be going swimmingly well and I was more than happy with the upgrade in power. The extra gear also proved ideal, especially when climbing up some of the steep hills at the edge of the national park. But alarmingly, each time I clocked up 8 to 10 miles the engine began to accelerate of its own volition, reaching a crescendo of such a screeching intensity that I felt sure self-destruction was imminent and had to switch off the ignition. Some time later, when it cooled down, I could set off again only to find that twenty minutes later the same abhorrent auto-acceleration would return.

Derek drove to my home and we spent countless hours tweaking the carburettor and making sure no air could be leaking in around the intake manifold. The problem improved somewhat but was never completely eradicated.

I described the issue to Kev Cherrett of *Bournemouth Bantams* on the phone. At that time, as well as selling Bantam spares, his company offered a restoration service.

"Why don't you bring it down and I'll have a look at it. I'll have her running sweetly in no time," he suggested. It was just the kind of help we needed.

With less than three weeks to go to my planned departure, I loaded Peggy onto a bike trailer and drove 230 miles to Kev's unit on a small industrial estate a few miles north of Bournemouth. Wasting no time, he hopped on and took her for a ride. On his return, still sitting on the bike but bending over to adjust the air screw with a screwdriver, he pronounced,

"Nothing wrong with that, she's just hunting a bit." Right on cue, as he slowly decreased then increased the tickover, the engine raced off into the all too familiar self-generated mayhem, reaching a fever pitch of revs within a few seconds. Switching off the ignition didn't work... it still hammered along at horrific speeds.

"Stall it!" I shouted above the din, pressing Kev's foot down with my own boot to slam the engine into gear. Peggy jerked forward and the cacophony of tortured whirring metal ceased.

"Sorry," pronounced Kev, "your crank seals have gone. They often harden when they get old, letting air in. I've had one before where the engine raced like that. Replacing them is all you can do. You'll have to leave it with me."

I folded the collapsible trailer into my car boot and set off for home feeling a mixture of despondency and relief... the problem was a big one but at least the fault had been diagnosed and could be remedied.

Four days later I returned, thanked Kev profusely as I loaded Peggy back onto the trailer, and agreed to call in on him en route to Egypt in just two weeks time.

As with my ride to India, I'd worked out the countries I wanted to pass through but not which roads I would follow nor where I would end each day's travels. My initial plan was to ride through France, Switzerland and across northern Italy before turning due south and heading down the Adriatic coast towards Greece. After that, a ferry to southern Turkey followed by a ride through Syria and Jordan then ultimately into Egypt. All I needed were visas for Syria and Egypt, both of which were straightforward to arrange by post with the respective embassies in London.

The return journey was rather more problematic. Libyan entry requirements seemed to change whimsically but for quite a few years it had been necessary to organise a guide to accompany you before a visa would be issued by the authorities. I tried several Libya based tour companies online but none were keen to work with a lone traveller... the rule of thumb seemed to be that a group of at least four was required. Then I came across the website of *Temehu*, which offered comprehensive travel information for Libya as well as visa and guide services. I sent an email with my probable dates of travel and requested a quote. Within a day I had a reply. Yes, they were happy to help organise the visa and again yes, they would be delighted to supply a guide for seven days. The cost was 585 euros, which included his accommodation and food and he would even have his own vehicle, which was a relief as I had no hope of carrying a pillion! I signed up without hesitation.

The first part of the visa process went smoothly. Five weeks before my departure I emailed a copy of my passport to *Temehu* and received back all the supporting documents I required, which I took to the *Libyan People's Bureau* in Ennismore Gardens in London. In a rather austere room, I joined several would-be travellers, some of whom were engaged in heated debates with staff as to why their visa applications were held up, or in one instance, had been declined. Sitting on a hard plastic chair in front of the counter where a member of staff carefully questioned applicants about their travel plans, I spoke to a woman in a hushed voice.

"This is my second attempt," she began. "I've no idea why it was rejected before, something to do with my sponsors. I'm due to fly there in two days' time, a mixture of business and holiday, but they still won't confirm if I'll be given a visa."

It all sounded rather worrying. When my number was eventually called, I approached the counter and as humbly and civilly as possible presented my paperwork, including the required six months' worth of bank statements to prove my solvency. Everything was taken, stamped, then inserted into a folder.

"Into the next room, please," the formidable agent commanded.

I went where he indicated and was motioned to a desk. There followed questions about my reasons for visiting Libya to which I simply replied leisure and cultural interests. Next came questions about my occupation. I've long learned that the two answers to avoid at all costs are 'author' and 'journalist'.

"Website designer," I replied, which to a large extent was true as I do build my own.

I was then photographed and had my fingerprints taken. Holy Mackerel!

"We'll post your passport back to you," I was told before being ushered to the door.

The remainder of my paperwork fell into place quite quickly. I was delighted to find that adding Peggy to my existing classic motorcycle insurance policy, with the superb Carole Nash, cost a mere £22. The Bantam's Carnet de Passages en Douane, effectively a temporary import license with punitive penalties for failing to leave a country without either your vehicle or having the carnet stamped, was efficiently taken care of by the RAC. As with my Royal Enfield, it was easy to declare the value of the Bantam as a low amount, which was a real boon as Egypt has the highest import duty rate of 800%... for more than the first time this made me glad not to be the owner of a shiny, new and obviously expensive machine.

Much of the travel equipment I'd used on the ride to India was in excellent condition and easily reusable on this venture. However, this time I decided I'd have to camp more in order to keep costs down. In very quick time I had the support of UK outdoor equipment manufacturer, Vango, who supplied a compact, lightweight tent and sleeping bag; Multimat, who provided an inflatable sleeping mat that could be used in temperatures as low as -60 degrees and Primus, who contributed one of their incredible *Ominifuel* stoves. Not only could it be run on diesel and aviation fuel, it was equally content to burn a mixture of unleaded petrol and 2-stroke motorcycle oil. Perfect!

One of Derek's hobbies is to have a stand at a number of select classic bike autojumbles. I'm sure he buys almost as much as he sells but it means he usually has an eclectic assortment of old motorcycle parts stored in boxes in his shed. Unselfishly, he sorted out a number of spares I might need, including a coil, alternator stator, sets of points and assorted nuts and bolts. *Bournemouth Bantams* was able to fill in many of the gaps in my spares list, including clutch plates and springs, along with the loan of a clutch extractor tool. I bought six litres of high quality 2-stroke oil which I hoped would get me most of the way there and more spark plugs than even the most pessimistic 2-stroke rider could possibly envisage I would need.

One person I certainly wanted to visit at the beginning of the ride was John Garner of Redditch. I first met John at a small classic motorcycle show in the Midlands where I had a trade stand. I complimented him on his motorcycle, a striking pre-war BSA Gold Star that looked very well used.

"I've had it a long time," he replied. "I'm nearly 80 but I can still ride it comfortably. I see you're interested in Bantams," he continued, pointing to the book I'd been reading before he approached my stall, Peter Henshaw's *BSA Bantam Bible*. "I'm mentioned in that book, as well as Owen Wright's Bantam book. As a young apprentice at BSA I was sent out to road test the very first prototype Bantam."

As it was a quiet show set in the grounds of a church hall, we had plenty of time to talk. John's tale was incredible.

"You know that BSA, along with several other motorcycle manufacturers, were given the bike's blueprints as war reparations?" he began. "It was originally a DKW design, called the RT 125. Well, when the German bike arrived at the BSA factory in 1947 we had to copy the engine, although to suit British riders we swapped the gear change and kickstart to the right and brake pedal to the left. In effect, the design was a mirror image, although we also changed the carb to an Amal and used a Lucas generator. After the development engines were bench tested and a few final alterations made, one of them was put back into the DKW frame and I was sent out on it."

In awe, I listened to John's story of riding that very first Bantam. As BSA eventually built over 400,000 of the model, making it by far the all time best selling British motorcycle, it was like experiencing first hand some unique and extraordinary moment in motorcycling history.

"I rode up Bwlch-Y-Groes, the highest mountain road in Wales, three times on it. It nipped up a couple of times too, but I made it back. When we took the head off, the piston was scored and a ring was stuck but despite that it had kept going."

Not long afterwards, John's career at BSA took a turn in another direction and he moved away from the Bantam project, which saw the model launched to export markets in mid-1948 and to the British public at the Earls Court Show in November of the same year.

"The engines were built in Redditch, at the Studley Road factory," he added, "and rest of the bike assembled at the giant Small Heath BSA works in Birmingham. I still live in Redditch, although the factory was demolished decades ago."

I outlined my journey on Peggy and asked if it would be possible to meet John in Redditch en route.

"I'd love to see where the factory was," I explained.

"There's nothing much to see, except rows of houses, but I'll gladly take you there."

A date was fixed and John even willingly agreed to ride his old Gold Star, creating a much anticipated first day to the adventure.

As always before a long journey, it takes me almost as much time to organise my affairs, mostly relating to my home and business ticking over satisfactorily during my absence, as it does to make preparations for the trip itself. For weeks I had lists that were sub lists of other lists and for a while each of them seemed to get longer rather than shorter despite concerted efforts to the contrary. But being perfectly organised wasn't the biggest concern. My family, Jane and Jacques, were my greatest anxiety.

For a long time I didn't mention my plans. There is a well known saying, 'It is easier to ask for forgiveness than it is to get permission'. I wasn't consciously aware of deliberately implementing this strategy, believing that the longer Jane knew about the journey, the more time she would have to worry and to conceal the information from Jacques. By many standards we have a strange relationship but it is underpinned by love and respect. A dedicated mother to her children, Jane's concern when it comes to my travels is always for Jacques' well being. Justifications I've made in the past, to the effect that many men and women have to travel for work, often for months on end, are always rebuffed because Jacques' is undeniably adversely affected by my times away. Yet at the same time this is somewhat ameliorated by the understanding that I, like Jane, have to make choices and do what is necessary to make my own life work. Undoubtedly, she genuinely wants me to follow my dreams... it's just that the price is often a high one to pay.

When, two weeks prior to leaving, I finally revealed my ambitions to ride to Egypt and write another book, her response was one of anger for leaving the announcement so late. I'd felt caught between the devil and the deep blue sea... leave it too late and I'm disrespectful, raise the subject too early and I'll be guilty of inflicting months of unnecessary stress. In the end I did leave it too late and in an attempt to make good, offered to postpone the trip for eight months. To her great credit, after a night's sleep, Jane told me to continue making my plans.

"Just make sure you get back safely for your son's sake," she had stipulated.

During the last few days there were still many things to do to the bike. I'd bought a pair of bar end indicators, mostly for riding through Europe, which needed fitting and wiring in. I had also become increasingly worried about the amount of weight I would be carrying over the rear wheel, both in terms of its effect on handling and for the integrity of the wheel itself. Although I would be taking nothing like the weight Miss Thomas lugged around, her experiences of Oppy's rear wheel collapsing three times served as a stark warning.

On my last visit to Derek, he dug out some stainless tubing and began welding together a pair of front luggage racks. They looked like engine crash bars but were actually intended to carry a couple of bags of heavy items, such as tools and spare parts, in a position that was low down and in front of the bike's centre of gravity. Construction and fitting took most of the morning. When complete, Derek stood back and admired his handiwork.

"You know what they remind me of, Gordon?" he chuckled. "Wallace and Gromit's ladders!" ... And he was right, they did.

"Well that's it, I reckon," I replied once we'd stopped laughing. "There's nothing left to do but ride her."

Before I travelled home, Derek suggested a short run to check all the work we'd done functioned properly. Unearthing a 500cc AJS from the back of his garage, we rapidly donned our riding gear and set off. To my relief, all the last minute modifications seemed to have worked and I was able to buzz along at 45mph in the wake of the booming AJS exhaust. Most importantly, the engine accelerated only when I opened the throttle and not of its own accord. In a few miles we came to a halt at a grassy area in front of the graceful arch of the Silver Jubilee Bridge, which spans the Manchester Ship Canal. After taking some photos for posterity, we came to say our final farewells. As Derek shook my hand, I told him not to worry, that I'd look after his motorcycle.

"I expect that bike to come back with battle scars all over it... in fact, I don't want to ever see it looking like this again. It should be covered in muck and oil and look as tho' it's really been through it." Enough said!

The final impediment to the journey's timely commencement proved to be the Libyan visa. In 2001, a former Libyan intelligence officer, Abdelbaset al-Megrahi, had been found guilty of the bombing of *Pan Am* flight 103, which crashed into the Scottish town of Lockerbie in December 1988. In July 2009, after two failed appeals, Megrahi asked to be released from jail on compassionate grounds as he was suffering from terminal prostate cancer. The debate became a hot topic on British television and in the newspapers. The Scottish Parliament was even recalled from its summer break to question the Scottish Secretary of Justice on the matter. During this period, my passport resided in the Libyan embassy and my increasingly nervous phonecalls to ask for an update were greeted with little more than a metaphorical shrug. On the 20th August, Megrahi was released on humanitarian grounds and quickly flew home to Libya. Two days later, to great relief, my passport arrived by special delivery.

I immediately scanned the visa and emailed it to *Temehu*.

'They have made a mistake,' came an urgent reply. 'Instead of making the start date of your visa 24 September, they have made it the end date. If you can get here in time, we will be able to extend it once you are inside the country. But if you don't reach the Libya - Egypt border by that date, I'm afraid there is nothing we can do.'

Rather than acting as a deterrent, it gave me an added incentive to succeed. Bizarrely and almost contrarily, visiting Libya now seemed equally as important as reaching Egypt itself.

First Ride

Saying goodbye to Jane and Jacques the night before departure, I'd joked, "If Peggy only knew what lies in store for her, I'm sure she'd keel over and expire!" It was undeniably a case of many a true word spoken in jest.

In the morning, already an hour behind schedule, I'd left the task of filling up the Bantam's fuel tank until last. Next to her sat two 5 litre cans brimming with petrol that I'd bought a couple of days previously. Around 10am, I carefully poured one and a half of them down a funnel into her tank, then added the appropriate amount of 2-stroke oil. It was a brand I'd never used before but was promoted as being specially formulated for classic vehicles. The result was catastrophic. Unbeknown to me, the oil, a heavy straight 40, sank straight to the bottom. After giving Peggy a quick shake to help mix it, I replaced the tank bag, donned my riding garb then kicked her over. With clouds of smoke, she spluttered into life, coughed painfully as though suffering from chronic bronchitis, then expired.

For 15 minutes I kicked and cursed, scratched my head and kicked again. Nothing happened apart from me getting very hot and bothered. The plug, when I removed it, was slippery with oil. Another twenty minutes of labour and Peggy finally restarted. The billowing exhaust smoke inside my garage was asphyxiating, but its production was short lived as the engine soon gasped and cut out. The problem turned out to be the oil... or to be more precise, the manner in which I'd used it. With all previous 2-stroke oils, I'd simply relied on it efficiently mixing itself with the petrol. For years I'd applied the same basic mixing technique as today, nothing more complicated than jiggling the machine from side to side for a few seconds when it was first added. However, this new 'specialist' oil was an altogether different beast, as when I eventually looked it up on the manufacturer's website, I learnt that it should be thoroughly mixed with the fuel before being poured into the tank.

I should have paid more attention to the experience of Miss Thomas, who wrote when riding towards Mexico, 'Oppy's lubrication system works directly from the tank, and this entails the messy job of mixing a heavy grade oil with every gallon of petrol. The trick of shaking petrol and oil thoroughly together resembles the making of a milkshake. I had a special little tin for doing it and an old spoon to see that the job was well done. Whenever I was too lazy or too clean to bother with this messy job I always regretted it, for then the heavy oil sank into my carburettor and clogged up the whole engine.'

Sometime after lunch, I drained the tank, drove to a petrol station to refill my cans with fresh fuel, and started all over again with some cheap mineral 2-stroke oil from *Halfords* which was, to all intents and purposes, self-mixing. At 3.15pm, fully kitted out in wet weather gear, I eventually set off for Egypt in the middle of a very heavy rain shower. After just half a mile, with rain bouncing high off the road, the engine surged, cut out and surged again. Then it stopped.

We came to an embarrassing halt at the entrance to a *Morrison's* supermarket car park. I tried kicking her over but got absolutely no response. A push on the horn button, which didn't even produce a murmur, revealed the fault. Three fruitless hours trying to get the bike started had drained the battery and our short ride, with headlight aglow and sat nav on, had sucked the last bit of juice out of it. I pushed Peggy home... the ignominy!

It took nearly four hours to fully recharge the battery, by which time it seemed imprudent to set off riding in rain and darkness with a potentially weak charging system. I phoned John Garner in Redditch and the team from *Sprockets Unlimited*, who were due to put me up for the night, and, with many apologies, cancelled. Instead, I ate a peculiar dinner of instant camping food in my flat and gave Jacques, to his delight, an unexpected game of rough and tumble. As I lay in my sleeping bag on an unmade bed, worrying about what the following day might hold, I told myself that things could only get better.

At 7am the next morning, determined to get back on track, I prepared to set off again. The recharged battery and better oil mix did the trick as after three swift kicks, Peggy settled into her usual steady 2-stroke beat. My stomach was in knots for the first few miles as I waited for something else to go wrong... the engine to run rough or cut out, the luggage to shift or maybe some part of the frame fracture under the load I'd piled onto it. But nothing untoward happened, Peggy unwaveringly got on with the job at hand. Indeed, she pulled so strongly, including taking hills in top gear, that after the first hour I began to relax a little and even smile.

Our route took us down the A34 then through the centre of Birmingham, which appeared pointlessly over-regulated by traffic lights. Eventually free of the city, we at last found open country roads. South of Stratford-upon-Avon, I considered stopping for petrol. We'd travelled around 115 miles and although I expected to get roughly 150 from a full tank, it seemed wise to fill up and maybe grab a sandwich at the same time. Within moments of these thoughts, while tackling a steep incline, Peggy cut out, stranding us on a busy, narrow, A-road. Fearing the worst, I hopped onto the thin verge and with my back pressed into bushes, checked the battery by pushing the horn. It emitted a strong honk. With cars blasting past just inches away from Peggy's handlebars, I opened the petrol cap and peered inside... the tank was bone dry. Deciding there was nothing for it but to push, I set off uphill as the *Garmin* indicated the closest petrol station was in that direction. Before I'd covered more than 10 metres, a large touring BMW pulled in ahead and its rider, a man roughly my own age, removed his helmet and asked if he could help. I confessed to my blunder with more than a little embarrassment, but as there was nothing to be done, he gave me an encouraging pat on the shoulder, wished me well and departed. I continued to push.

Ten minutes later the BMW returned and its rider, Neil McGee of Rugby, produced a 2 litre petrol can from between his legs. He'd bought it specially and filled it with fuel.

"When I saw how far you had to push, I had to do something to help," he said. "It can be my way of helping you get to Egypt." What a gent!

With Peggy's engine humming sweetly, we crossed Salisbury Plain, much of which is used as a training ground for the British Army, passing several ominous 'tank crossing' and 'unexploded bomb' warning signs along the way. Finally, we pulled into the courtyard of the *Bournemouth Bantam's* workshop near Ringwood. Kev's jaw dropped open when he saw how much gear was strapped onto the bike.

"Poor little motorcycle," he said over and over while shaking his head. After giving Peggy a once over, tweaking the carb air screw and adjusting the clutch, he declared her fit for purpose.

Our next stop was south in Bournemouth itself at the house of Chris Gamble of *Rooster Ignitions*. Chris had offered to personally fit a *Rooster Booster* electronic ignition unit to the bike, which to our mutual surprise, took almost two hours, prolonged by quirks in the existing wiring set up, most of which he managed to untangle.

I set off just after dark for my chosen campsite, *Grundy's Farm*, which was roughly 9 miles to the north. Within 5 miles, while riding under streetlamps in a surprisingly busy village, the engine missed a beat, lunged forward, missed again then cut out. The headlight, when I peered over the handlebars, emitted little more light than a glow worm would manage and a push of the horn button produced zero response. Quickly turning the lights off, I waited for a minute then attempted cranking the engine over. It caught but needed constant revving to keep it alive. It seemed highly unlikely I could push the fully laden Bantam the remaining 4 miles and I also thought it improbable that the RAC, should I call them out, would be able to charge the battery long enough to get us going with lights again. In a tight spot, I decided there was nothing for it but to wait for a car to pass in our direction and follow its taillights as closely as possible.

Riding along dark country roads without lights was something I'd never imagined doing and I felt both nervous and unhappy as I pursued a series of three different cars. Thankfully, due to their moderate speed and the sat nav, which I'd reset to run off its own internal battery, we made it safely to the almost hidden campsite turn off... with great relief!

Just after 10pm, I knocked on the office door and asked where I could pitch my tent.

The owner, Mr Pitt, informed me that he once owned a BSA C10 but now raced 200mph Maclaren-engined Formula 2 cars for fun. Intrigued by the Bantam, which he could see in the light from his lounge window, he instantly offered to charge the battery overnight. Pitching my tent on a small patch of lawn under an apple tree, I reflected on the 238 miles we'd covered and the help we'd been given. It had certainly been a memorable day.

The feeling that luck was starting to favour us continued in the morning, as on rising at 5am, I found the battery and charger neatly laid out beside Peggy. My packing routine, still unpractised, took too long and to avoid waking other campers, I had to push Peggy away from the campsite. Halfway down the track I began to run beside her as time was getting short. When safely out of earshot, I attempted to fire her up. Fortunately, she responded impeccably and off we roared on an invigorating 12 mile race to catch the 7.30am ferry from Poole. Close to Bournemouth, Peggy stopped dead. With my heart in my mouth, I leapt off and frantically searched for the problem. After 30 seconds I had it fixed... even for a mechanical ninny like me, a wire hanging loosely beside the cylinder was hard to miss. We boarded the ferry 40 minutes before it sailed.

Three hours later, upon arriving in France, I quickly fell into the routine of riding on the right. Heading in an easterly direction, my aim was to skirt round the south of Paris, follow a trajectory north of Dijon then cross into Switzerland. I left Cherbourg with both optimism and a sense of calm, but the long steep hills which surround the port city took their toll on Peggy and within an hour she began to struggle, misfiring while climbing and popping and banging when travelling downhill. At the crest of a long, slow incline, I took a break, buying a baguette at a service station before inspecting the spark plug. Whiskers had developed on the electrodes and the gap, which I'd carefully checked at home, had widened.

A replacement produced an immediate improvement, and as the sun emerged and warmed my back, we rode round the Caen ring road. Busy with fast moving traffic, this was a frightening experience, especially when two overtaking British caravans, that both misjudged our lowly speed, came within an inch of sideswiping us.

I developed two new techniques for monitoring the bike's performance. My gloved left hand placed on the cylinder became our engine temperature gauge. Leaning over and counting out loud whilst riding, a benchmark was established of nine seconds before it became too hot and I had to remove my hand. Any less than that and I began to worry. As for a charging system meter, that became the horn button, and I fell into the habit of tooting it every ten minutes or so to make sure the battery was holding its charge. Obviously, technology exists on more modern machines that automatically carries out these checks and warns of problems, but my little routines gave me a modicum of reassurance and in any case seemed quaintly appropriate for a machine of Peggy's era.

After the 15 hour marathon of the ride to Bournemouth, day three had been a case of putting some miles on the clock without exhausting myself. We rode through Écouves Forest in dimming light and then called it a day at the small city of Alençon having clocked up 168 miles. Quickly finding a campsite, it was good to cover the Bantam up, pitch the tent, pump my *Primus* stove and make dinner.

Everything changed for the worse on day four. Tracking east in golden summer sunshine, following a minor road, the D955, through a region of heavy agriculture, my heart for once felt carefree. I rounded a bend and came up short behind a large, modern tractor that was pulling a clattering trailer. After a minute tailing it, we cornered another bend and ahead lay a long straight, the perfect opportunity to overtake. Swinging out, I accelerated hard and simultaneously beeped the horn to alert the farmer. The resulting sound was faint and tonally flat, signalling that the battery was not charging. Within two minutes, Peggy began to misfire and I was forced to come to a halt under a large overhanging tree. The tractor, to my embarrassment, rumbled inexorably past a few moments later.

Horizons Unlimited, the website for motorcycle travellers, have produced an excellent series of DVDs called *Achievable Dream: The Motorcycle Adventure Travel Guide*. Parked under the tree, with no way of charging the battery, I recalled an interview with a couple of round-the-world travellers in one of the films. Their philosophy, they had said, when either experiencing a breakdown or crash, was to say to each other, 'I wonder who we're going to meet today, because we're certainly not getting out of this situation without any help.' I decided to adopt the same approach, looking down the road with the positive expectation that this was a chance to meet someone new.

In a short time, an approaching car slowed then came to a halt next to us. Out stepped Fabrice, a genial Frenchman with smiling eyes. With my schoolboy French, his equally challenged English and a great deal of hand waving, I was eventually able to communicate that I needed the battery charging. Promising to return, he drove off to his farm, a small distance away. In the meantime I set about swapping Peggy's alternator stator for the spare I was carrying. Twenty minutes later, Fabrice arrived driving a miniature tractor. With a flourish, he produced a set of jump leads from between his feet! After more animated and convoluted communications, I was able to more thoroughly convey the simplicities of the Bantam's ancient workings. He left with my compact battery charger and battery to begin the charging process while I worked on the alternator repair.

That completed, I freewheeled Peggy downhill to the buildings that Fabrice had pointed out. The part restored farmstead was a couple of hundred years old and, with the aid of his parents, Fabrice was in the process of modifying it to a home rather than a working farm. After a drink and a guided tour, I determined there was enough charge in the battery to get the Bantam going. It seemed sensible to check that the new stator was working correctly before setting off properly again, so following Fabrice, we travelled to the commune of Brou where he knew the owner of the town's only garage.

Pulling up in the forecourt, I was introduced to the manager, who soon found me a voltmeter. Fabrice, who had to return to his work, said farewell. I measured the voltage across the battery terminals, went for a spin, then returned and remeasured it. There was a slight increase in the charge.

Delighted to be back in business, I returned the voltmeter then prepared to continue on my way. Peggy wouldn't start. The horn and lights worked, but no spark was being produced at the plug. Then I noticed that the red flashing LED on the side of the electronic ignition box was unlit... the unit, possibly because of something I did when checking the electrics, was dead.

I spent the next two hours rewiring the bike, digging deep into my memory banks to remember all that Chris had done in Bournemouth and reversing the process. It was very stressful. Part way through my labours, I was approached by a local who offered to put me in touch with the town's classic motorcycle enthusiast should my endeavours fail.

"I will be here for half an hour, but after that, this is my cell number," he had said, offering me a piece of paper. "He is the only person I know who likes old bikes. He has many."

"Is your car in the garage to be serviced?" I asked, curious as to why he'd been hanging around the forecourt for so long.

"Oh no, I also collect old vehicles, mostly World War Two tanks. One of my friends is bringing my American White M3 Half Track here. He's been working on the engine and it's nearly out of petrol."

As sure as eggs are eggs, ten minutes later, while I was crouching beside Peggy reconnecting wiring to the points and condenser, I heard a distant rumbling that soon grew to thundering proportions. Looking up, I stared as the relic from the Normandy landings trundled to a halt beside the petrol pumps. Drab green with single white stars on its bonnet and sides, the blockish, menacing vehicle was covered in fuel cans, spades, rope and ammo boxes. Even more intimidating was the .50-caliber Browning machine gun mounted on top of the driver's cab. I watched in amazement as they started to fuel it up, not stopping until the round figure of 200 litres showed on the petrol pump gauge! At Peggy's rate of consumption, approximately 14 miles per litre, I estimated that was possibly enough to get us from here to the Egyptian border.

"How long will that last?" I asked the owner, who was on his way back from paying.

"Oh, this is good compared to my tanks... two hundred and fifty kilometres, perhaps a little more."

Blimey.

Having completed my tasks, I cranked Peggy over with bated breath and was stunned when on the second kick, she actually worked. Furthermore, after a short spin, the battery continued to show an increased charge. I again handed back the voltmeter, noting to always carry one in the future, and departed the garage with my sincere thanks. Despite only clocking up a meagre 69 miles, I decided to cut my losses as it was already after 6pm. Brou has a small municipal campsite beside a lake so I opted to head there for the night. I soon found it but the reception had already closed. Undeterred, I leaned Peggy over, pushed her under the barrier and set up camp beside a small row of caravans.

After belatedly paying my pitch fees, I departed the following morning into a solid wall of rain, which although not hard, was dense in a misty kind of way. It slowed our advancement towards Dijon considerably. Lunch was a cheese sandwich bought from a *pâtisserie* in a village south of the forest of Fontainebleau. Chilled to the bone, I ate it on the doorstep of a closed shop for protection from the continuing drizzle. Back on Peggy, at the outskirts of the next village, I noticed that the exhaust note was becoming progressively louder. Pausing at traffic lights, I looked down and saw, to my horror, that the exhaust securing ring had fully unwound itself and, completely detached from the cylinder, the exhaust header pipe was oscillating freely... no wonder it had sounded so noisy. Parking up, I searched in vain through my tool bags for the correct C spanner to reattach it. After ten minutes, becoming increasingly sodden, I gave up, guessing that I'd left it behind on my garage floor. I didn't have a hammer either, as there was only so much that I could encumber poor Peggy with, so I had to forage around in the garden of a nearby derelict house until I found a suitable stone to use. Then with a screwdriver, I attempted to hammer the ring back on.

All of my screwdrivers, it transpired, were too large for me to get their points positioned at the optimal angle, resulting in slow progress and a couple of scuffed knuckles. To my rescue came Pascal, a man in his forties with a beard and a very long pony tail. He parked his battered old VéloSoleX moped, still a common sight in rural France, and squatted down next to me. Quickly ascertaining the issues of scale that I was experiencing with my improvised tools, he produced a smaller screwdriver from his pocket which turned out to be the perfect length. Trustingly holding it in place whilst I thumped it with the rock, we soon had the exhaust secured. Standing up and stretching our backs, we attempted further communication, in pidgin English and French, about where I was from and my destination.

"*Vous allez en Egypte?... l'Egypte!*" he stammered. He looked at Peggy, then me, grabbed hold of my hand and began the most complicated handshaking procedure I've ever participated in. The routine included several variations of strangely positioned thumbs, wrists, knuckles and palms and all the time, Pascal grinned and repeated, "*l'Egypte!*"

Half an hour later, in the next town, I stopped at a *supermarché* for petrol as their fuel always seems to be significantly cheaper than branded petrol stations. Whilst filling up, I looked over towards the entrance and there, emerging with a carrier bag in one hand, was Pascal! We waved, then he hopped onto his moped and rode off. Ten minutes afterwards, passing through the town centre, I was surprised to again see my new friend, and this time he was waiting for me. He jumped into the road, flagging me down. Coming to a rapid stop, I found myself at the entrance of a moped repair shop. Pascal gesticulated that this was where he took his bike for repair and within a few moments had borrowed a C spanner from the mechanic so that we could make a more thorough job of tightening the exhaust ring. After another round of almost impossible to follow or keep up with handshakes, we said farewell.

We'd only ridden a soaking 178 miles by the end of the fifth day, and again found a municipal campsite to pitch up, this time at Troyes. Falling asleep on the hard ground, I reasoned that progress may have been stilted, but I'd been blessed with the help of two incredibly genuine and friendly Frenchmen.

It felt essential that I reach Switzerland the next day, as the cumulative effect of Peggy's troubles was putting pressure on our chances of making Libya ahead of my visa expiry date. The weather was much brighter and warmer and the string of minor roads that we took were quite lovely to swoop along, but soon after lunch, Peggy began to run harshly and became hot... five seconds was the most I could keep my hand on the cylinder without risking first degree burns. Judging that carburetion had to be at fault, I set to adjusting the air/fuel mixture, a process that entailed several short runs to check the effects on the spark plug. But when that failed to make any difference, I had to spend much more time stripping the carburettor to clean it, then fitting a new gasket.

During the afternoon, a heavy rain front washed in again and for reasons unknown, this seemed to suit the Bantam better. Dressed in waterproofs and rubber mitts, I slowly snaked through an attractive labyrinth of narrow streets in the old city of Besançon, the birthplace of Victor Hugo. The city, which is enveloped within a large U-bend in the Doubs River, proved to be hard to navigate and worse still, to exit to the east, we had to join the E23 which began quite unexpectedly to climb the side of a very steep hill. Pinned in by a rock face on our right, with an ever mounting queue of traffic trapped behind us, I was forced to push Peggy much harder than I'd have liked, revving as strongly as possible between second and third gears for a good ten minutes. It was a tremendous relief to reach the top and let our long tail of following vehicles overtake. When the road, no longer constricted by the side of the hill, broadened to become a dual carriageway, I took the first opportunity to give her a break, pulling in at a leafy rest area. To my horror, as we came to a halt, the engine began to accelerate all by itself... the uncontrollable acceleration that had plagued the first few weeks of the surrogate engine's life had returned!

Once she was thoroughly cooled I set off again, but after stopping for petrol, found that the problem persisted, indeed, I was forced to kill the engine by savagely stalling it to avoid the red lining revs resulting in major damage. The racing engine, if it proved to be failed crank seals again, would spell the end of the journey, so rather worriedly I phoned Kev to ask for guidance. His suggestion was to recheck the seal between the carburettor and the inlet tract, making double sure no air could be getting in by smearing silicone around the outside.

An hour later with the job done and darkness rapidly advancing, I typed the co-ordinates of a campsite into the sat nav and very nervously set off. Thankfully, following eerie country lanes that led mostly downhill, the engine behaved itself and the charging system coped with the drain of full headlights.

Torch in mouth, I pitched my tent on a small campsite outside the village of Ornans in lashing rain, exhausted after the day's 167 mile trek.

I had low expectations the following morning when again, in pouring conditions, I prepared to leave.

"See you soon," shouted the attendant with a cheery wave as I exited the campsite gate. "That might be a lot sooner than you think," I shouted back. Thankfully the irony was lost on him.

To my complete surprise, Peggy ran wonderfully, the constant, face-stinging rain again our unexpected ally. We climbed non-stop, ascending 850 metres in just under 12km. When we paused at the top, I was nothing short of incredulous that she was still going so strongly. Without further delay, we motored to the Swiss frontier some 40 miles to the east. As Switzerland isn't in the EU, we were halted at the frontier by a tall, serious looking officer who asked for my passport. Extracting it from inside layers of waterproofs and warm clothing was a bit of a wriggly affair, but after a check on his computer, which we passed, it was handed back and we were allowed to leave. As I set off, exiting the large concrete canopy suspended across the road that had protected us from the elements during the entry process, I glanced in my mirrors and watched the guard. Standing in the middle of the road with arms folded and legs astride, he was looking in a rather bemused way at the receding rear of the oily, overladen Bantam.

They used to say that all roads lead to Rome, but in Switzerland they seem to lead to Berne. I had wanted to avoid the city but, after weaving our way around a number of hillsides and country lanes in a futile attempt to bypass it, we were inescapably drawn into its vortex. Near the centre, progress was arrested by a series of traffic lights and I became fretful that Peggy would overheat again. Then we wound up in a one-way system where ahead, past more traffic lights, I could see that the road was closed by major roadworks. In desperation I cut the engine, dismounted, and sweatily pushed the little Beeza a good half kilometre along the pavement... to the astonished looks of several pedestrians.

"Harley Davidson?" asked a spiky lad dressed in punk rock gear who walked alongside us for a while. At least he made me laugh!

When I finally relocated the route south, it lead straight onto a motorway. The approach road, which was only metres long, made it impossible for us to turn around so with considerable trepidation, I powered on, accelerating to our fastest speed yet... all of 45mph. For the next 19km Peggy maintained this heady pace.

"Go on, girl. You can do it," I shouted at her as cars and trucks tore past. She did, valiantly, and without over-revving too. However, I was immensely grateful to exit and join a lakeshore road.

For 7 miles we followed the shoreline of Lake Brienz, whose milky, turquoise waters appeared intensified by the backdrop of dark, towering mountains. In time, we drew up at one of many roadside campsites just ahead of the quaint resort town of Interlaken, where it cost as much to pitch my tent as it does to stay in many English budget hotels. But it was worth it... with a brisk breeze whipping off the lake, there was just enough time before nightfall to get the tent dry and cook a warming meal while watching a distant rowing boat bobbing across the water. Illuminated by the ascending moon, the lake and snow capped mountains resembled a watercolour painting. In the warmth and comfort of my sleeping bag, rather than being despondent about the insufficient number of miles we'd travelled, just 119, I tried instead to focus on the positives of the day, with no breakdowns and a well behaved engine top of the list.

Conscious that in the past my tinkerings had often caused as many problems as they'd cured, there were nonetheless several essentials that had to be tended to so in the morning Peggy received some maintenance before we left Interlaken. I cleaned the horn terminals and spruced up the spark plug, the cylinder head was torqued down and the rear exhaust clamp and lower front engine bolts tightened. The kickstart proved to be loose on its splines and my attempts to tighten it were ineffective. Feeling sure it would eventually fail if left unattended, I removed it and set off around the campsite to see if I could borrow a hammer. Approaching a large tent that was occupied by four Dutchmen travelling in a rusty orange VW campervan, I asked,

"Excuse me.... do you speak English?" I received a couple of encouraging nods so continued.

"Do you have a hammer or mallet I can borrow please?"

"You have a problem with your wife?" someone asked.

"You could say that!" I answered.

A hammer was produced and the kickstart quickly beaten into shape.

Once underway, we followed the lakeside for a while then began to climb. As one hairpin bend led to another, it became incrementally more difficult to keep our revs up, an essential for the little 2-stroker. After half a kilometre we were forced into 2nd gear. A cluster of modern bikes roared past, their multicoloured leather clad riders taking the racing line round a series of sharp bends then charging up a long straight, clearly visible along the edge of the mountainside. By contrast, the best we could manage was 20mph and it felt as though I was thrashing the life out of the engine to maintain even that.

I rounded a particularly tight hairpin and incredibly, the road became even steeper, illustrated by the sat nav altimeter which showed our height increasing at more than a metre a second. I was forced into 1st gear and tho' I tried to rev and change up to 2nd, the gradient was simply too steep and I had drop back down to 1st almost immediately. Droning on in this way at an average of 10mph for roughly half an hour, I stopped at a view point to let the pitiable motor cool, finding it hard to believe that it'd taken such punishment and survived. When, 10 minutes later, I attempted to resume our upwards journey, the incline was simply too steep. Even when slipping the clutch and revving like billy-o, we were unable to get going. The only solution I could think of was to turn around, descend to the last hairpin and spin round in a sharp U-turn. With our revs now sufficiently built up, we could recommence our buzzing 1st gear ascent.

At 2,160 metres, we crossed the Grimsel Pass and began to descend.

"You've done it, girl!" I shouted, walloping Peggy's tank with my left hand. But almost immediately the next challenge came when I had to slow her down on a wickedly precipitous descent. Until this point I'd been surprised by how well the brakes had performed, but with no engine braking to speak of, I had to ride with the front and rear brakes constantly full-on. The front brake lever pulled almost flat to the bars, I somehow slid us round hairpin bends, my right foot acting as a third brake. Having descended 700 metres, I began to smell burning from the front of the bike. Coming to a complete standstill proved to be a mighty task, but eventually we weaved to a stop and I dismounted to inspect the front wheel. The paint on the brake plate was starting to blister and burn and felt as hot to the touch as the cylinder head. With John Storey's warnings in my head I wedged the bike against a crash barrier and waited for everything to cool thoroughly before completing our descent.

After a sandwich in Andermatt, a village of cobbled streets and steep-roofed wooden houses from which an assortment of large flags fluttered, we tackled the day's second big climb, over the Oberalp Pass at 2,050 metres. This went much more smoothly and, thanks to less hairpins and a flatter incline, we were able to maintain 2nd gear the whole way. Descending was a gentler experience too as I confidently breezed along the sides of stunning meadows bedecked with delicate alpine wildflowers. There were lone farms, herds of cattle with clanking cowbells munching on the lush grasses, villages perched on mountainsides and icy, brilliantly clear rivers. The 'Swissness' of it all got me into the mood for a spot of amateur yodelling, which thankfully couldn't be heard above Peggy's engine, not that there was anyone around to listen.

At 6pm, 105 miles from our journey's start, we arrived at a campsite in Chur, a township overshadowed on all sides by massive, pointed mountains. Hearing our approach, the receptionist leapt through her office door and waved me on, issuing swift instructions.

"Hurry, make your camp now. Come back and pay later."

I looked heavenwards to where she was pointing. Large thunderclouds were advancing from the north and a torrential downpour appeared imminent. I rushed to get the tent up, threw my belongings inside and just got the cover onto Peggy as the thunder, lightning and pummelling rain began.

Frustratingly, it was almost midday by the time we exited Chur, thanks to a restless night on rocky ground and a petrol leak which needed fixing. Whilst I was on my knees beginning the repair, the German cyclist who'd camped next to us came to say goodbye. In the course of our conversation, he mentioned we would be travelling in the same direction that day, crossing the Albula Pass at 2,350 metres.

"We will have to climb sixteen hundred metres to get there," he said with a certain masochistic relish. I'd already passed many cyclists on the mountain roads and the ones I'd spoken with all seemed to take great pleasure in riding up the highest passes... I'd found it exhausting enough astride a 175cc engine!

The climb turned out to be much like the previous day's first ascent, a taxing process of continually shifting from 1st to 2nd gears with the briefest of bursts into 3rd. The wooded hillsides and meadows were remarkably eye catching up to around 2,000 metres, then the scenery became barren and quite wild. We passed two unforgettable glaciers on the way up and reached the summit just a couple of hundred metres below the snow line, passing at least a dozen cyclists on the way. Sadly, I wasn't able to identify our neighbour on the way up and couldn't hang around for long as the wind temperature was bitterly cold.

"It's all downhill from here," I yelled to Peggy as we skirted past St. Moritz and turned due south for the Italian border. Then I noticed a road sign which proclaimed 'Bernina Pass Open' and after the promise of no more mountains, felt I'd somewhat stitched Peggy up as we began another arduous climb to 2,330 metres. Fortunately, it proved to be the most enjoyable by far, the road on the upside resembling little more than a twisting lane that wound through pine forests until finally emerging onto a bare, rocky plateau.

Towards the end of our equally pleasurable descent, we came upon an Alpine train, the *Bernina Express*, as it entered the town of Brusio. Like us, it had departed from Chur and after a halt in St. Moritz, was heading for Tirano in Italy. Its four hour journey, also over the Bernina Pass, although hardly ever visible from the road, makes it the highest adhesion railway route in Europe. Unable to overtake, we followed it down the middle of the main road, a stressful experience as I feared getting our front wheel caught in the slippery metal rail tracks. When it finally pulled into a picturesque station, several passengers waved to us as we eased past.

In contrast to the heights of the Bernina, the last miles of Switzerland were baking hot and I had to stop to remove some layers... for the last few days I'd worn almost every item of clothing I had with me heaped under my waterproofs. Finally we came upon the Italian frontier post and pulled up next to a border guard. Expecting a similar inquisition to the one we'd received on our arrival in Switzerland, I was delighted when he simply smiled and waved us through with a cheerful "*Prego*".

"We're in Italy, Peggs" I called out, feeling wonderfully proud of her.

She had triumphed over four alpine passes, each well in excess of 2,000 metres, and was running sweetly, well, as sweetly as any tinny, oily old 2-stroking Beeza could. After a sedate climb into the peripheral hills of the Dolomites, we stopped for the night at a campsite outside the village of Edolo, having progressed 105 miles. There, thanks to a delivery boy on a Vespa, I had the pleasure of eating my very first, but certainly not last, Italian pizza.

Sitting beside my tent, which was still in shadow as the morning sun hadn't cleared the surrounding peaks, I crunched my way through a bowl of muesli while watching another touring cyclist emerge from his featherweight tent and begin packing it away. Jan, a Dutchman nearing the end of a month in northern Italy, came over and told me there was just one more pass to climb before we were clear of the mountains. This was music to my ears as I'd hoped, by this time, to be making my way towards the Albanian border, more than 1,000 kilometres south east of Edolo.

Passo del Tonale, situated at 1,830 metres, was easily surmounted thanks to a shallow upslope. Being Sunday, there seemed to be more motorcycles on the roads than cars, with Ducati and Triumph sports bikes especially popular. In comparison to their peacock riders, dressed in the most striking and fashionable racing leathers I'd ever seen, I looked more like a vagabond. They all rode like Valentino Rossi too, although somewhat to the surprise of one group, I quickly caught up with them when they stopped at a petrol station 15 kilometres along the road.

First heading east, then south towards the city of Trento, Peggy continued to accelerate energetically for such a heavily loaded machine and remained comfortable, good for at least three hours before I needed to take a break. Handling was excellent too and on tight corners I repeatedly scraped the side of my boot or footrest onto the ground. Despite the many setbacks, I found myself thoroughly enjoying the Bantam-touring experience.

I stopped for a bread and cheese lunch at the bottom of the pass. Relaxing beside a stream and watching a solitary kingfisher diving off the branch of a nearby tree, I gave Peggy plenty of time to cool down. For no discernible reason, when we resumed there was a sudden degradation in performance. Rough running and a hunting engine began almost straight away. After 20 miserable miles I paused at the outskirts of a village. The engine popped, banged and generally sounded poorly. Moreover, it kept going when I turned off the ignition switch. I removed the carburettor and fitted yet another new gasket, applying an extra thick glob of sealant, but nothing changed. Wearily, we limped on for half an hour before I gave in and parked for the night at a roadside motel on the edge of the village of Grigno, the first time on the journey that I'd slept in a proper bed. It offered a degree of comfort while I considered our next move.

The first two hours of the following morning were spent with the carb off again, sealing with silicone every joint that could possibly be causing an air leak. I also replaced the slide, needle and main jets just in case one of them was the culprit. But when we departed, with the roads empty due to a public holiday, things continued to deteriorate. The engine just could not run smoothly. It juddered and rattled so badly that it became almost impossible to stay in gear with the throttle closed.

I phoned *Bournemouth Bantams* for further advice. Kev suggested that the cylinder base or head gasket may have blown. Parked on a side street, I blew a solution of washing up liquid and water round all the joints using a straw I'd begged from a *McDonalds*. With the motor ticking over, the base gasket appeared airtight but I thought there were slight traces of bubbles around the cylinder head. Within an hour I had it changed, giving the head and piston crown a much needed decoke at the same time. While it was off, I checked the piston for play... it appeared free to turn about 5 or 6mm, which seemed rather excessive, but all I could do was hope that a worn small end wasn't the cause of the rattle.

Nonetheless, I set off with renewed hope. It was soon dashed. If anything, Peggy's performance was even worse. With night fast approaching, I headed 40 kilometres to the coast and searched for a campsite. Entering the popular tourist resort of Bibione, I felt deeply ashamed to be riding a motorcycle that was running so badly. At every set of traffic lights, roundabout or pedestrian crossing people stared at us, doubtless wondering what the screeching commotion could possibly be. When I finally climbed off at the *Il Tridente Tourist Camp*, the engine was smouldering hot. Pitching my tent in the dark and climbing into my sleeping bag, I felt extremely low.

Bibione has many 4 and 5 star hotels plus a couple of luxury, beachside family campsites with all the amenities imaginable. The receptionist, when I booked in for another night, issued me with an electronic pass and all manner of instructions, including a strict warning to observe the noise curfew between 1pm and 3pm every day. This, I was informed, was so that campers could take a siesta. When I asked for more information about the town, I was told that in the height of summer, there are upwards of 35,000 deckchairs and sun-loungers on the local beaches. Struth! After a double shot of caffeine in the bar, I decided to take the day off, hoping to clear my mind, consider our options and find some inspiration in the pages of my *Haynes* workshop manual.

In the afternoon, deep in contemplation, I went for a walk and plonked myself down on the beach. Staring out to sea, I spent at least an hour drifting off into a world of my own. Eventually, I looked around and for the first time took in the appearance of my fellow *Il Tridente* guests. All had the full gamut of seaside paraphernalia with them, including sun umbrellas, windbreaks, vast squares of colourful towelling, beach balls, footballs, volleyballs, kites, model boats, remote controlled aircraft, noisy children! Some of the women were topless but the majority sported smart swimwear. To the last one, they were well tanned, their bodies glistening with sun oil. I, in sharp contrast, had a pocket size camping towel, my trousers rolled to my knees, my nose and forehead caked in thick white sunblock and my brown arms and neck outshone by my lily white legs and torso... I was only short of a knotted hanky on my head! Feeling greatly out of place, I got up and padded to the waterline to dip my feet in the sea. As I glanced down at the shoes and socks in my right hand and thought what a sight I must make amongst all the stylish Italian and German holidaymakers around me, I began to belly laugh.

'Don't take everything so seriously, Gordie,' I told myself as I wiped tears from my eyes.

I returned to my tent with my spirits lightened and my mind made up to try and find a local mechanic the next day. I'd been surprised by how modern the motorcycles and scooters were in Italy. Indeed, I'd only seen a couple of classically styled Piaggios on the road in the previous three days. An old-school Vespa mechanic skilled in the art of maintaining 2-stroke engines seemed my best hope.

As I cranked Peggy over the following morning, I anxiously muttered through half closed lips,

"Please forgive me if you get another thrashing today."

The gatekeeper kindly drew a sketch indicating the locations of Bibione's two mechanics, telling me that he thought they did general repairs to everything, including cars, motorcycles, scooters and boats. Luck came our way at the first one I tried. In halting English, the receptionist explained that a semi-retired engineer who fixed old Italian motorcycles for a hobby lived in a village just 8 kilometres to the north. I headed there immediately and soon found his inconspicuous workrooms to one side of the main road.

A balding man dressed in shorts opened the door when he heard my approach and with a smile introduced himself as Luigi. As he didn't speak English and my command of Italian stretched no further than the three essentials - hello, goodbye and thank you - I attempted to describe the symptoms and my efforts to remedy them by imitating screaming engine sounds, using words I hoped would be common international motorcycling parlance, like "cylinder head gasket", and even desperately drew pictures in the dust on his pathway. Quite a palaver!

Over his shoulder I spotted a long row of gleaming Italian classics and, noting the glint in my eyes, he invited me inside to view them. I quickly ascertained that Italian bikes were his speciality and that he was quite unfamiliar with British motorcycles. A beautiful Moto Guzzi Falcone, his current restoration project, was proudly uncovered and a single-seat helicopter nestled in the workshop corner, which I eventually understood he'd built from scratch. I was very impressed. Without further ado, he grabbed a handful of tools and began working his way around the Bantam.

With the tank off, he replaced the HT lead, plug cap and spark plug from my box of spares. However, when the still hot engine was put to the test, it showed no noticeable improvement. By then it was lunchtime and I was given to understand that he was expected at home by his wife. He closed the workshop door but left it unlocked and, as we parted, indicated I should remove the carburettor after I'd had lunch.

I made my way to the village's only café, which also doubled as a bar and lively meeting point for local men. When I entered, most of them were enjoying a lunchtime glass of wine and engaged in loud, animated conversation. All heads turned my way and an immediate silence ensued, the stuff of comedy... or horror films. I put on my biggest smile and headed to the bar. Thankfully, normality returned to the room and the barman swiftly produced a much needed *espresso*. I went to sit by the window and was brought a superb toasted sandwich with layers of cheese, pickled artichoke and red pepper, then relaxed for a while simply soaking up the lively Italian banter, noting the mounting number of *Raboso* bottles that were being quaffed by the increasingly friendly patrons.

Some time later, back at Luigi's, I removed the carburettor and meticulously cleaned off all the gasket sealant. The engineer returned just as I'd finished and examined the carburettor flange. He secured it in a vice and began to file it down, showing me where it was bowed while he worked. He also indicated that the carburettor body was worn and slightly bellowed but with exaggerated shrugs, we came to the mutual conclusion that there was nothing we could do about it.

When all was refitted, Peggy started first kick but even though the engine was cold, it still seemed to be racing. Like so many times before, when we turned off the electrics it continued to run. Off came the tank again and Luigi began to examine the wiring. His concern, he demonstrated, was that the connections to the coil, which he thought were incorrect, might be a contributing factor. In spite of a feeling that this was possibly a red herring, as the switch had appeared to function correctly thus far, I decided to continue to give Luigi a fair go at tackling the problem his way. Beavering around in his workroom, he quickly fabricated a new switch panel and inserted a second switch into it, which he connected directly in line with the coil. All the while, under his breath, he muttered something which I gleaned to be to the effect of, "Why is it that these British bikes have to be positive earth when everything else in the world is negative!"

When we were finally done, I started the bike and Luigi adjusted the carb's air screw until satisfied with the tickover speed. I had to agree that she sounded great, turning over with a steady beat and responding crisply to twists of the throttle. I packed everything away and awaited my bill to be written out. It came to 40 euros, which for about 3½ hours work, a switch and a couple of custom-made parts, seemed extremely reasonable.

I thanked Luigi profusely with a strong handshake and departed. Once clear of the village and heading back in the direction of Bibione, I opened Peggy up. Acceleration was sharp and we were soon up to our usual 40mph cruising speed. I slowed for a roundabout... there was no hunting. Hurrah! I grinned widely, daring to think that maybe my fears of blown crank seals were unfounded after all. In my head I began planning our early morning departure for Slovenia, Croatia, Albania…

We travelled at a constant 40mph for the next 6 kilometres and then I closed the throttle on the approach to another roundabout. The vibrating, uncontrollable revs immediately returned. I felt sickened to the core as I rode the last few kilometres to the campsite. Pulling up before the gates, I shut the throttle off and selected neutral. The engine chugged heavily then began to gain speed, becoming faster and faster until it took off, still with the throttle closed, into manic revving. I fumbled, frantically searching for Luigi's new engine kill switch whilst the piston continued going hammer and tongs. At last it stopped. With my heart pounding, I dismounted and pushed Peggy the last hundred metres towards our tent. I put her on the side stand and checked the engine temperature. It was spitting hot. When she'd cooled sufficiently, I covered her up.

Much of the following day was spent on the internet and telephone, seeking advice and guidance. I received many knowledgeable emails and blog posts from people with valid and useful suggestions for curing the problems. However, as the symptoms had developed to the point of being identical to those previously experienced in the UK a few weeks before departure, it seemed reasonable, if painful, to conclude that the crank seals had indeed once again failed.

I decided we needed expert help and telephoned my motorcycle insurer, Carole Nash, as European breakdown cover was included in my insurance package. They sympathetically took down all my details, and after a few hours, which I'd spent pacing along the beach, called back with the only viable solution: recovery to a specialist motorcycle shop.

Feeling well and truly cut down to size, I was met by a recovery van at 9am sharp the next morning. With Peggy strapped into the back, we were driven 35 kilometres to the small historic town of Portogruaro. I had no idea what the garage we were being taken to could do to help, but had been told on the telephone that they were experts in old British bikes.

Anxious to check them out when we arrived, I leapt from the van before it came to a complete halt. Entering the workshop, called *Moto Roberto Pasqualotto*, I instantly spotted a stripped-down BSA M20 on one workbench and a beautifully restored T160 Bonneville on another. In a showroom adjoining the workshop were a gorgeous 1951 Norton Dominator, a Triumph Trident and... a 1971 BSA Bantam Bushman. On the wall, stretching from floor to ceiling, hung a faded but genuine 1960's BSA distributor's poster. It felt like I'd struck gold!

The garage owner, Roberto, and his friend and customer, Renato, who it transpired owned the Bushman, introduced themselves. Fortunately, Renato could speak excellent English and was able to act as translator. He told me that Roberto had learnt his craft under Les Williams in the UK and was a perfectionist. Despite my protests that no further confirmation of his credentials was required, I was then shown into the engineering area at the back of the workshop which, packed full of neatly aligned lathes and machinery, was spotlessly clean.

At the first opportunity I described Peggy's symptoms and the repairs that I'd already tried. Roberto asked me to start her up then got down onto his hands and knees and attentively listened to the engine. He stood up and headed off in search of the appropriate tools. Returning a couple of minutes later, he stripped off the primary cover and removed the alternator stator. Then he grabbed hold of the rotor and tugged. It moved easily backwards and forwards, pulling the crankshaft with it.

Renato translated the verdict.

"The crank is very loose inside the bearings. See how much lateral movement there is. Your crank seals are ruined and will need replacing, but Roberto believes with this amount of movement they will blow again within 500 kilometres."

The news got worse.

"He can strip the engine and rebuild it correctly with new bearings and seals, but the movement will probably have caused stresses that have damaged the con rod, piston and bore. It may be that the crank itself will need restoring. Including getting parts, it might take twenty days or more to completely rebuild the engine and get you on your journey again."

It was a bitter pill to swallow. I sat outside and racked my brain for alternatives but could come up with none. If I had been on a round-the-world journey or had 18 months ahead of me like Miss Thomas, I would certainly have entrusted Roberto to do a superb job with the rebuild. However, I didn't have a spare three weeks to tack onto the end of the ride, especially as I was already one week behind my schedule. Furthermore, there was now no hope of being able to enter Libya and of completing my circular route back to England, as my visa would be weeks out of date. The news spelled the end of the journey.

On the phone, Roberto reported to the recovery agents in Italy and wheels were set in motion. I spent the rest of the day in the excellent company of Roberto, his delightful wife, Nada, and Renato. In the evening, with all my belongings itemised and repacked, I patted Peggy's tank and said *"au revoir."* She was to be picked up by the insurer's collection vehicle and returned to the UK in approximately three weeks. Renato then drove me to a hotel adjacent to the Piazza della Repubblica where we dined together, my disappointment and deep sense of failure somewhat ameliorated by his companionship... and some fine red wine.

Sixteen days after departing, having ridden Peggy 1,407 miles, I took a taxi to Treviso Airport and caught a flight back to the UK. Staring out of the window, I watched our approach to England as the whole of south east Kent, from the nuclear power station at Dungeness to the historic harbour at Whitstable, appeared without the blemish of a single cloud. Flying over the Thames barrier, we followed the M1 north for a while then tracked east, with Stoke-on-Trent's football ground, the Britannia Stadium, an easily identified landmark. As we flew above the M6 on a course for Manchester Airport, the numbness I'd felt throughout the flight dissipated. The experience of failing for the first time on a motorcycle journey was a deeply humbling one. But as we made our final approach to the runway, I reflected that Bantam riding was great fun and despite the long list of problems that had beset us, I remained highly impressed by what such a diminutive and antiquated 2-stroke motorcycle could achieve, with crossing the Alps a case in point. My determination to have another crack at the ride to Egypt solidified.

Switzerland, 2009.

Inbetween Times

Peggy arrived at Derek's house a couple of weeks after my return, shoehorned into a trailer with an assortment of modern sports and touring bikes that had either crashed or broken down while on European trips.

"You should have seen her squashed in next to a new BMW GS and a Ducati Monster that'd been in a head-on collision," said Derek down the phone one October morning.

"And I've got a bone to pick with you. Do you know how much all your luggage weighed?"

"Er, no," I replied, wincing in anticipation of the answer.

"Forty eight kilos," he exclaimed. "You could be arrested for cruelty to Bantams!"

I didn't have the heart to tell him that I'd also brought 15 kilos back on the flight with me, although in my defence, the D14 Bantam was designed to carry a pillion, many of whom would have undoubtedly weighed more than a measly 63kg.

Collecting Peggy a couple of days later, I took her straight to Andy Berry's so we could drop the engine out and start the rebuild.

"The Phantom Bantam," he declared when I pulled up outside his garage doors. "Let's get her inside and see what we're dealing with."

I first met Andy in 2001 when I launched *The Bullet-In* magazine, indeed, one of his bikes featured in the inaugural issue. From then on, as well as providing endless technical advice for readers, he patiently allowed me to photograph every single step of the restoration of a 1951 350 Bullet engine and stoically endured my endless and, occasionally, pea-brained questions.

Andy is one of the most upbeat people I know. He lives and breaths classic motorcycles, especially their engines. Although Royal Enfields are his true passion, with over 90 rebuilds chalked up, he's worked on everything from Egli Vincents to Triumph twins. His forte is making them go fast - very fast - which he does using a mixture of precision engineering, the methodical application of the fundamental principles of engine tuning, years of experience and a touch of magic. He even has cams ground to his own profile so that he can squeeze the absolute ultimate out of an engine. For my ride to India, Andy applied all of these skills and used the very best components to build the engine for reliability rather than speed, making it as bullet proof as is possible for an old push rod single. I bitterly regretted not taking the Bantam engine to him before the first attempt of riding to Egypt... money was tight, but this proved to be a false economy of huge proportions. Lesson learned.

In no time we had the motor out and on his work bench. Half an hour later it was in a hundred pieces.

"Look at the play on that crankshaft," he uttered in dismay. "And those crankseals have had it too... they look ancient."

Andy is a perfectionist and will never re-use a part unless it's in perfect condition or he knows it's an item that's not prone to excessive wear. We soon had a substantial inventory of requirements, with a new crank assembly top of the list. Recommendations led to Peter Savage, a 2-stroke engine specialist, who was tasked to modify Peggy's flywheels to accept a larger crank pin into which he would fit a heavy duty MZ con rod. Peter's repertoire of enhanced Bantam parts also included a strengthened clutch outer cover, as Peggy's had warped, and a redesigned points backplate that incorporated reliable car points and condenser. We parceled our existing crank up and had it in the post to him in a jiff.

Rex Caunt Racing of Earl Shilton near Leicester, who'd previously been recommended by Hugo Wilson, produce a gold mine of practical and performance parts for Bantams, often manufactured using modern high grade materials. Andy immediately suggested we go to him for new crank seals made from much more flexible Viton rubber, as well as a complete new set of engine and gearbox bearings. However, being in many ways a traditionalist, he felt it would be better to fit an original Hepolite piston, which were renowned for quality, rather than a modern Suzuki equivalent from Rex. I got on the phone to the enigmatic 'Bantam John', who promised to dig one out for me and get it in the post. Finally, we replaced Derek's worn carburettor with a new Amal 626 MK1 Concentric carburettor from the UK manufacturers, *The Amal Carburettor Company*. With a 'stay-up' float and brass slide, it would ensure reliable, maintenance-free carburation for a relatively small outlay.

With everything for the rebuild set in motion it was time to address some of the other issues that had arisen on the first journey. My 'to do' list, in no particular order, read:

A replacement set of higher handlebars. (The trials bars I'd used previously were angled too far back for long-distance comfort).

Upgrade luggage straps. (I had used four Rok Straps on the first ride, which worked brilliantly, but also a number of bungees and ratchet straps which ate up time and never felt completely secure).

A sidestand for the right hand side of the bike. (The continental road camber completely negated my left mounted sidestand unless I turned the bike around every time I wanted to park).

A spare fuel container for mixing petrol and oil and a proper measuring jug. (For a better and more accurate fuel/oil mixture).

A more robust and reliable charging system. (A major weakness on the first ride).

Stay in cheap hotels and guest houses. (I love camping but didn't meet many local people at the campsites I'd stayed at, which tended to be in out-of-the-way places).

Reverse the route. (In order to optimise my chances of reaching Libya).

Most were straightforward to address, with the right hand sidestand the most challenging but Mr. Bracket, ever willing, once again stepped into the breach with that one!

During an autojumble at Kempton Park in late October 2009, I was approached by a man who introduced himself as Tony East, Secretary of the Isle of Man section of the VMCC (Vintage Motorcycle Club).

"If we fly you over and put you up for the night, would you come and give us a talk about your ride to India?" he'd enquired.

Is the Pope a catholic? The following January I caught a flight from Manchester to Ronaldsway Airport, where Tony, who'd developed a large and successful motorcycle related business in the UK before retiring to the Isle of Man, met me. After a meal in a Douglas restaurant, we followed part of the hallowed 37 mile TT circuit en route to his home, *The Old Vicarage* in Kirk Michael. And what a treat he had in store for me, for Tony has turned his extensive classic motorcycle collection into a private museum.

"We're open throughout the summer and during the TTs, of course, but only by appointment in winter," he explained as we entered the main hall, "which means you've got the place to yourself."

With Tony keenly relating the history behind some of the gleaming machines, I stared in reverence along the lines of classic British machinery, a miscellany of the exotic and the ordinary, all in outstanding condition. Ahead were a row of Amaranth red Triumph Speed Twins, parked across from a brace of Vincents and a line of purposeful and sleek looking silver tanked Nortons. Historic motorcycling nirvana!

In the extensive grounds of the museum is a handful of cottages where guests can stay, plus a number of outhouses and garages that are home to even more motorcycles including trials machines, lightweights and bikes awaiting restoration, as well as a fine collection of memorabilia. In one of these buildings I came to a halt beside a pair of D1 Bantams, both of which looked completely unrestored.

"This one," said Tony, avid as ever to share information, "is a bit special. It was actually stored in a man's shed for forty years, with only seventy miles on the clock, before his nephew put it back on the road in 1993. We got it from him about four years ago with only 900 miles on it."

My jaw dropped. The bike was NEL 906, the very wellspring of my fascination with Bantams!

I animatedly related my tale to Tony, who was obviously delighted.

"Let me think, I had to put new tyres on it, as the old ones were pretty ropey, but apart from that it's exactly as it was when it left the factory. I even have the original tool roll and owner's manual that came with it and somewhere in the office are the first owner's HP agreement and insurance certificate."

I sat, elated, on the bike's pristine sprung saddle.

"When you've done the ride to Egypt, come and give us a talk about that journey too," said Tony, who could see my sincere attachment to his little mist green exhibit. "I'll make sure it's on the road and you can take it for a spin if you like." I was on cloud nine!

Motivated by the bond I'd built with Peggy on the first ride, I resumed my dedicated search for the real Miss Thomas, committing day after day of concentrated time to the hunt. My best break came from tracking down the publisher of *A Ride In The Sun*. The original company, *Hodder & Stoughton*, had been acquired by another bigger publisher but I managed to trace the right person in that company to speak to.

"The last known address we have is from 1979 in Copenhagen," I was told. "But we can't give it to you because of our privacy rules, I'm sorry."

I asked if she could tell me the name of the author when they last had contact.

"Okay. Why not... it's Peggy Iris *Sorensen*."

I almost leapt for joy at this point and after repeated thanks, got straight back onto the online Danish phone book. I instantly found four Margaret Sorensens but each of my calls resulted in polite apologies. However, able to narrow my search for her husband by now entering his surname, a much more manageable list of 30 names, a mixture of Carl and Karl Eriks, emerged on my computer screen when I keyed in my request. Diligently I phoned them all. It took almost 2 weeks to speak to everyone but in the end, exasperated, I had to concede defeat.

Sometime later, in desperation, I set about reading through a list of every Sorensen in Denmark, a formidable task. Roughly half way I spotted a man called Johnny Thomas Sorensen... could this be the son of Carl-Erik and Miss Thomas, I wondered, who'd been given both their names? I dialed the listed mobile number and spoke with a amiable young man who sadly informed me that Thomas was just a man's name, not the maiden name of his mother. I didn't keep track of how much time I put into these pursuits but it ate up hours a day for a couple of months, until I simply had to put Miss Thomas out of mind and concentrate fully on making the second ride more successful.

With the engine now made good by Andy, including the installation of a new high output alternator, uprating the remainder of the electrics was my next task. I removed both wheels from Peggy, washed her chassis as thoroughly as possible and when dry, carried her up two flights of steps to my first floor flat. Propped against the wall in my bedroom, I soldered new terminals onto every connector and made Luigi's switch more secure. New fuses were inserted onto the wiring loom and all the old wiring from the defunct electronic ignition unit removed. At the end I stood back and admired my work, feeling that if anything did go amiss again, I'd certainly know where to start fixing it. In no time I had the wheels and mudguards back on and Peggy was once more beginning to resemble a motorcycle.

Derek visited a few days later and spent almost an hour adding then grinding down layers of weld on the centrestand so that it would hold the bike securely rather than only partially clearing the rear wheel off the ground. Once it was reattached to Peggy, we heaved the engine into place and tightened everything up. Finally, she was pushed out of the flat and, holding onto the front brake lever with all my might while Derek took control of her rear, we bounced her down the stairs and back onto solid ground. Within a week I took her for an MOT test which she passed with flying colours, although I'm as sure as can be that while I read a newspaper for 20 minutes in the garage office, Peggy sat untouched in a dark corner of the workshop... she was neither fired up nor were the electrics switched on!

Six months before the first ride I'd joined the *BSA Bantam Owners Club*, a lively and friendly organisation with around 800 members. One of their area representatives, Pete Rose of Southport in Lancashire, sent me a couple of emails wishing me luck and offering any assistance should I need it. I met Pete by chance a few months later, along with his bubbly girlfriend Margaret, at a motorcycle show in Uttoxeter.

"I'm serious," he said as we shook hands. "I've built up lots of Bantams over the years so if you need any help then just give me a shout."

Pete drives vans for his living but had previously worked as a motorcycle mechanic. His passion was Bantams and he obviously knew the model inside out. His latest projects included restoring a D1 for his dad and a 'back to bare metal' job on his own 1969 Bushman, which was just about to get re-registered for the road. One of my concerns was for Peggy's front forks as they'd begun to ooze grease when descending from the Bernina Pass in Switzerland. I gave him a call and asked if he'd cast his expert eye over them.

"No worries," he replied without hesitation. "I'm free on New Year's Day if you want to come over. We'll strip 'em down and see what's needed."

On a piercingly cold morning, mercifully not suffering from a hangover, I once again loaded Peggy onto my trailer and headed for the seaside.

"I don't have much space, but Margaret lives in the retirement home where she's the manager. There's a large utility room we can use there," he'd suggested when we made our final arrangements.

Well wrapped up against the icy wind, Pete and Margaret were waiting for my arrival. Once we had Peggy safely in the room, surrounded by washing machines, Margaret left to check on her charges. She reappeared with a steaming mug of tea and in her rich northern accent declared the immortal words,

"Hey... I've just told 'em we've got a living legend in our laundry!"

We cracked up laughing.

The forks were off within 10 minutes, exposing worn seals and a badly scored main tube on the left fork. Wiping his long hair from his eyes and donning a pair of John Lennon-style glasses, Pete examined the leg.

"Looks to me like the wrong size grease nipple's been on there for a long time. You can see how much damage it's done by constantly rubbing on the tube."

I looked on, nodding quietly and praying that it could be saved.

"I'll take it away and dress it up. Back in an hour," said Pete, disappearing out of the door before you could say Jack Robinson.

Feeling rather lost, I wandered over to see Margaret in her flat. Immediately I was handed a huge chunk of chocolate cake and a large cup of coffee, then, when Pete failed to reappear, asked if I'd like to go on a tour of the building. Margaret is obviously very fond of her residents and over the next hour knocked on several doors so that I could be introduced to some of them.

"You're riding a motorcycle to Egypt, dear... what on earth for?" was asked more than once.

Pete arrived back nearly two and a half hours later.

"Sorry, Gordon, couldn't get the blasted fork spring off the tube. Had to resort to some strong arm tactics in the end!"

During the remainder of the afternoon the forks were reassembled with new seals, Pete giving me step-by-step instructions as we progressed so that I'd be able to do it in the future if necessary.

"See, it's a piece of cake," he said with a cheery grin when the front wheel was back in place and I sat on Peggy. Bouncing up and down with the front brake hard on produced the smoothest fork action I've ever experienced on a Bantam. Excellent!

With the new engine in, the forks refurbished and the electrics ironed out, I began to feel more confident. Now top of the list was running in the engine and I set myself a modest target of 500 miles to do this. The first ride was to visit Andy, some 40 miles north west of my home, on a wintry Monday in February. Without using the M60 motorway it was hard to stay away from slow city traffic, making a far from ideal start for the new engine. Indeed, departing the umpteenth set of lights in Manchester city centre, I felt a tightening of the engine which didn't bode well. On reaching Andy's, he took the bike for a short blast then spent some time tweaking the carburettor settings and double checking the ignition timing.

"Nothing wrong with that," he pronounced.

I voiced my concerns that it may have nipped up at the start of the ride, so we removed the downpipe and peered up the exhaust port with a torch.

"Looks OK to me Gordon, " he reported. "Can't see any shiny marks or gouges. Just take it easy and let her cool from time to time."

From Preston I cautiously rode north to visit friends in Lancaster, Judith and Ed Coyle. Judith is my oldest and dearest friend and furthermore the person who first encouraged me to write. Indeed, she was my editor during the two and a half years that I ran The Bullet-In and, on reflection, I'm sure I would never have dared attempt it without her support and guidance. I'd not seen them for several months and a visit seemed a great opportunity to put some miles on Peggy as well as catching up. After I removed my waterproofs and had the usual round of welcoming hugs, Judith made a confession.

"I'll tell you what, Gordon, I'm really glad I've met Peggy. To be honest, from your descriptions I've been quite worried about you, imagining you're embarking on some perilous trek on little more than a moped. Now I can see it's a real motorbike I'll be far less concerned."

What I'd failed to calculate was where to leave the Bantam overnight, as the front door of their artisan style terraced cottage, located in a part of Lancaster close to the city centre, opens more or less onto the pavement and has no access to the rear garden.

"Bring her in, Gordon," they both said without hesitation.

We tried, first twisting the handlebars to the left, then the right but despite our best efforts Wallace and Gromit's ladders appeared to be just an inch too wide. Next we tried reversing her in, but after further sweating and cursing, failed.

"Give me a minute," I announced, retreating to the kerb then unearthing an adjustable spanner from my pocket. Under the bemused scrutiny of curious pedestrians, I hastily whipped off the offending luggage rails and tried again. This time she slipped through the doorway and into the lounge, where I parked her under the watchful eye of their faintly growling terrier, Pip.

Further journeys included a bitterly cold ride almost fully laden over the High Peak to the Derbyshire spa town of Buxton. Most encouragingly, on a long steep climb over blustery moorland still covered in a crust of glittering frozen snow, Peggy pulled solidly at 30mph in third gear for close to half an hour. She never missed a beat. I also tested her on a couple of farm tracks near my home, dodging cow pats and bouncing along patchy, broken tarmac. The forks coped brilliantly, as did the rear plunger units which Derek and I had stripped and re-greased. But most importantly, the closer I got to the magic 500 mile mark, the more my confidence in the engine, and consequently my optimism for the ride, grew.

Throughout this interim period I kept in regular touch with *Temehu*. Two months before my departure, which was set for late April, I asked them, with some trepidation, when I should make a return journey to the Libyan Embassy. A reply came back almost immediately.

'Dear Gordon, entry regulations have changed once again. Now it is possible to collect your visa at the Tunisian border. Just confirm you are running to schedule a week before your arrival and we will have everything set in place, including one of our representatives to meet you.' Phew!

My new route was to ride through France to northern Italy from where I'd catch a ferry to Tunisia. D-day had been carefully selected from the classic motorcycling calender to immediately follow the enormous Stafford *International Classic Motorcycle Show*, an event that was simply too big for me to be able to afford to miss. The organisers, *Classic Bike Shows*, kindly offered to make a space for Peggy so that she could be displayed fully laden, although in practice, her numerous bags were all stuffed full of bubble wrap, their real contents neatly arranged in piles on my lounge floor.

As ever the show was packed out, with more than 25,000 visitors attending over the course of the weekend. Peggy attracted lots of attention with many people coming to my stand to wish me luck and just as many to laugh about what appeared to them to be a preposterous amount of baggage... if only they knew how little it weighed that day! I felt uplifted by everyone's good wishes, for as well as the general public, Andy, Pete and Derek all attended the show and took the time to give some eleventh hour encouragement. So did a large number of my fellow traders, which came as something of a surprise. There's generally a very good camaraderie between stallholders, many of whom meet up weekend after weekend at motorcycle events all over the country. But as a relative newcomer, I was uncertain if anyone outside of the friends I'd made even knew of my impending travels. When the last of the show goers left the building on the Sunday afternoon, I packed up my stand then retrieved Peggy from her space next to the organiser's desk. As I wheeled her across the fast emptying hall to where Derek was waiting to attach an extra bracket for the troublesome second sidestand, I received slaps on the back, handshakes and several calls of "*Bon voyage,*" and "Take care... come back safely," from people whose names I didn't even know. The genuineness of their support was quite overwhelming.

Back home, as I prepared to leave, I reflected on the last few months. The indignity of arriving back in the UK without Peggy, after a topsy-turvy 2 week journey, now seemed a long way behind me. My disappointment had evaporated with the hugely enjoyable process of preparing the bike and I was itching to be on the road again. It took a couple of hours to pack my bags and load them onto Peggy in the garage, leaving the rest of the last day for Jane and Jacques.

Jane had remained stoic throughout these intervening months and Jacques, who'd been elated by my early return in 2009, seemed more perturbed about me missing his forthcoming birthday than the length of time I would be away. We'd organised an early birthday party for him, but it had a strained feel to it.

"I've got a good idea for your next book... Overland To Huddersfield!" my son declared, citing the Yorkshire town less than 40 miles away where his cousin lives. It said it all really.

But still, the open road beckoned...

Second Ride

Day 1, Manchester to Kingswinford, UK.
60 miles.

Peggy sits in my garage ready for the off. Surprisingly there's nothing left to do. My luggage has been strapped on since the show at Stafford, the petrol tank was filled yesterday and all my riding gear is neatly laid out for me to step straight into. As on previous journeys, I've already said farewell to my loved ones, thus avoiding further upset for them or tears distracting me from riding safely. I lock the garage then return to my flat for a last minute check. There's one phone message from Jane:

"We love you. Take lots of care." I'm too choked to phone back.

Today is the most carefully planned day of the whole journey. My first scheduled stop is to have lunch with a friend, Keith Batten and his delightful wife Juliet, who's known to all as 'Chooch'. Keith runs quirkily named *Pig Farmer Bike Magazines*, which supplies motorcycle magazines from the 1930s onwards to customers around the world. Curiously, he isn't a pig farmer, however his home does house a menagerie of domestic pets, including the chickens that will hopefully provide fresh eggs for our lunch.

Keith lives in the West Midlands town of Kingswinford which is practically en route to my next stop at Redditch. There I've arranged to meet John Garner, who has kindly offered to lead me to the housing estate where the old Bantam factory used to be. Finally, I'll ride a few miles south east of Evesham to spend the night with Jane and John of *Sprockets Unlimited*. Despite my non-show on the first ride to Egypt, Jane has promised 'take two' of her vegetarian chilli dish for me.

I make a note of the mileage shown on the speedo: 30,773 miles. Next comes the new starting routine for the rebuilt engine and replacement carburettor: turn on the fuel, tickle the carb until it floods, open the choke fully, prod the kickstarter 3 times to ensure the engine is primed, switch on the electrics and give the kickstart a swinging kick. To my delight, it catches immediately. I rev vigorously for 10 seconds then turn the choke lever to the closed position. The little 2-stroke motor instantly settles into a steady if somewhat 'poppy' rhythm.

I set off with the lightness of spirit that so often accompanies enthusiasm and optimism. Peggy's running better than she ever has, my luggage feels secure and evenly balanced and I'm confident that I haven't overlooked anything important, either for the journey or at home. To top it all, the sun is shining. Egypt here we come!

Our route takes us past Romiley where Jacques and Jane live. Unable to face riding past the end of their lane, I break off from the course suggested by my sat nav and head along a backroad for Poynton then onto the Silk Road to Macclesfield. I like this Cheshire market town. In its heyday it was the world's largest producer of silk and has no less than four museums dedicated to the craft. It's also a regular stop on the West Coast Mainline train route from London to Manchester, so my association with it has always involved a feeling of being on the move, either to or from home.

After Macclesfield I ride alongside the twinkling Rudyard reservoir, pass through the town of Leek then head south east on the A528 in the direction of Stone. The road is a pleasure... long sweeping bends with swooping undulations that rapidly climb then drop, giving great views of the lush surrounding countryside. A more perfect start to the journey I can't imagine. I pat the Bantam's fuel tank.

"This time girl," I say, grinning from ear to ear.

I decide to stop and give Peggy a rest, bearing in mind that I should do this every 40 miles or so. A lay-by soon appears on my left. Pulling up, I turn off the engine and wander around eating a chocolate bar. After 10 minutes I become impatient. The bike is running beautifully and I see little reason to delay further, so press on.

At a large roundabout, I take the exit for Wolverhampton then begin to accelerate crisply up a long incline. Unexpectedly, there are a couple of short, sharp tugs on the rear chain. It's a slightly unsettling feeling as the sensation is one I'm not familiar with. 'Must remember to check the chain tension,' is my first mental note of the journey.

A couple of miles further on the A449 becomes a dual carriageway. There are few cars on the road and I feel relaxed cruising at 40mph in top gear. Ahead is a roundabout where the road intersects with the more major A5. Signs warn me of the approaching junction and caution me to slow. On a Bantam that's unnecessary until the last moment, especially as the road is gently climbing uphill, so I press on. Without warning, the rear wheel locks up solid. Simultaneously, there's a stomach-churning whirring sound as the piston comes to a graunching halt and the engine cuts out. I instinctively haul in the clutch. The engine's seized!

We coast to a halt 10 metres ahead of the roundabout. I leap off, drag Peggy onto the grass verge, pull her onto the centrestand then walk away feeling utterly despondent. I've never seized an engine before but know that what I've just experienced is serious.

Digging out my mobile, I call Andy Berry, painfully describing the two tugs I had felt together with the sickening sound and sensation of the seizure. He's gobsmacked by my news.

"Those two jerks on your rear chain were a warning the engine was nipping up," he explains. "What do you feel when you kick it over?"

"The kickstart turns without any resistance. There's no compression at all," I reply.

"Take off the head and barrel then have a look at the piston," he suggests. "If you're lucky it'll have just nipped up at the exhaust port. You might be able to dress the piston with some wet and dry paper and clean any melted aluminium off the inside of the cylinder in the same way."

We say goodbye... for now. I immediately phone Keith and explain my predicament. Without hesitation he offers to pick me up in his van.

"It might take an hour though," he warns. "The van hasn't been unloaded since the Stafford Show. There must be five thousand magazines crammed in from floor to ceiling. I'll unload them then come and rescue you."

With time to kill until his arrival, I get started on checking out the severity of the seizure. It only takes a few minutes to remove the petrol tank, cylinder head and barrel. I look around the piston, then phone Andy again.

"It's not good," I start. "The piston is badly marked on four corners and the rings are thoroughly welded into their grooves. The only positive is that the barrel has just a few light silver marks and they feel raised rather than scored."

"You'll have to use your spare piston," he replies. "Clean the barrel lightly with fine wet and dry, making sure you rub in diagonal directions. Also, test the clearance on the new piston. The piston you seized had 4,000th of an inch clearance, which is already a bit more than the factory tolerance. It might be necessary to get it honed, maybe to as much as 5,000th."

I hang up, tidy up as best I can then sit on the grass beside the stricken Bantam. Thoughts of precision honing, piston clearances in thousands of an inch and my already ruined timetable confusingly dart around in my head. After all my careful preparation, I feel gutted to have encountered such a major problem within hours of my start.

Before I become too maudlin, Keith arrives in his van. He's a calm, stable character who generally sees the bright side of things, partly, I suspect, as a result of suffering a life-threatening heart attack while in his early 30s. We load Peggy into the back of the van and strap her into place. I climb into the front beside Jack, Keith's very excitable dog, who leaps onto my knees in recognition and immediately covers my face in slobber. Things can only get better!

We drive a slow 15 miles through central Wolverhampton, reaching the Batten home around 3pm. Keith quickly helps me unload Peggy then sets off to collect his two sons, Elliott and Joseph, from school. Setting about work on the barrel, I soon eradicate any obvious signs of the seizure. Next is the search for my spare piston which is not something I ever seriously thought I'd have to use. I try it in the barrel but struggle to fit a 4000th of an inch feeler gauge between it and the cylinder liner, so telephone the ever patient Andy for a third time. Between us we come to the conclusion that the barrel will definitely need to be professionally honed to create the required clearance.

Keith returns from the school run and I explain the prognosis.

"That's not a problem," he responds to my amazement. "One of my best mates, Rob, is an ace mechanic. He works in a Yamaha dealership but his hobby is restoring classic Yamaha engines. He's a perfectionist. Honestly, you won't find anyone better to do the job."

So convenient a solution seems highly unlikely at such short notice. Keith whips out his mobile phone, presses a couple of keys and is soon in deep conversation, pacing around in ever widening circles. Phrases like "...seized, yeah, a big one... really, Egypt!... got to be tonight," drift over towards me. Within a couple of minutes he's sorted it.

"Let's get going," he says, giving me a big slap on my back. "Rob's work is nearly 60 miles south, in Cheltenham. He's cleared it with his boss. He can keep the workshop open late and do your barrel."

We set off in congested rush hour traffic, skirt around Birmingham then join the M5 motorway. Nearly an hour and a half later we pull up outside *Skellerns Motorcycles*. I walk past the showroom and enter the workshop, carefully picking my way around rows of relatively new motorcycles which are in for service. As soon as I see Rob walk towards me with his hand outstretched to shake mine, I realise we've met previously at motorcycle shows.

He diligently checks the diameter of my new, genuine BSA piston with a dial caliper. Multiple areas inside of the barrel receive the same treatment.

"It's actually already on 5,000th of an inch," Rob proclaims. "Your feeler gauge just can't flex well enough for you to get an accurate reading." Nevertheless, he does think it's worth giving the cylinder a hone.

"Whoever honed it previously has done a superb job," he says, "but I'll just take the lightest amount off it to make sure there are no snotty bits of piston left. It'll also help your new piston rings to bed in."

While Rob sets up his honing equipment, we discuss possible causes of the seizure.

"The guy who built the engine, Andy Berry, thinks I should have stuck with mineral oil instead of switching to synthetic," I tell him, adding that we'd stopped at a bike shop en route for me to stock up on *Rock Oil* mineral oil.

"It's possible on an old bike like a Bantam," Rob concedes, "but to be fair, synthetic oils are superior and shouldn't have caused this. What kind of petrol were you using?"

I name a well known brand.

"I filled up with their Super 98 Octane yesterday."

Rob looks knowingly at me, then Keith.

"I'm not surprised to hear that. There've been a few bikes in here recently with seized pistons. The word is that biofuel's being mixed in with super unleaded and old or highly tuned motorcycles just don't like it."

With my high compression D14 Bantam piston, it's important to use high octane fuel. The news that I should avoid one of the biggest international brands is not good.

Rob sets to honing the cylinder while a colleague pours a constant stream of oil down the barrel. He's meticulous, expertly working his way around the steel liner then putting a chamfer on the inner rim of the cylinder bottom to help ease it over the new piston. Finally, he deftly grinds smooth the edges of the cylinder ports, which he feels are a bit crudely cast. In all, the job takes half an hour.

Rob dips the barrel into a degreasing solution then hands it over to me.

"Wash it thoroughly in *Fairy Liquid*," he instructs. "Rinse it, give it a wipe dry, then immediately spray it with WD40. Dish-washing liquid has a very high salt content that'll help clean it, but the cast iron barrel will be covered in a film of rust within minutes of drying out if you don't protect it."

Rob won't accept any payment for his time or services, telling me there's nothing he would like more than to hear that the old 2-stroker makes it to Egypt. I leave feeling encouraged and extremely grateful.

We arrive back in Kingswinford at 9.30pm. I follow Rob's washing instructions to the 'T', then join Keith in his garage. The first job is to remove the old piston. We wedge the con rod securely with blocks of wood and try to press the gudgeon pin out. It won't budge.

"How many pistons have you changed?" Keith enquires.

"This one!" I tell him. "But I've watched Andy do them before."

Keith confesses this is a first for him too.

"Blind leading the blind," he laughs.

We find a piece of dowel lying around that's almost a perfect fit for the gudgeon pin. While Keith adds further support to the piston, I set about trying to drift the offending pin out from the small end bearing. It's well and truly stuck. We both get hot and sticky, trying to apply as much force as possible without breaking the con rod or damaging the big end.

I consult one of several manuals I'm carrying on the journey.

"It says to heat up the piston with a hot towel."

"I don't think that'll do it. It's locked solid," answers Keith.

He rummages on a couple of shelves then returns with an electric paint stripper and a pair of leather gloves. I nod my approval.

Within moments of switching it on the heating elements at the gun's nozzle begin to glow red. Keith points it first at the piston crown then around the skirt close to the gudgeon pin. After 30 seconds he drops the gun, grabs hold of the now very hot piston and shouts,

"Knock it out quick before my hands burn!"

I fumble the dowel into position and give it a solid tap. The gudgeon pin flies out, landing on the floor with a ping. Keith lifts off the piston, looking relieved.

Following the instructions in my manual, I lightly oil the inside of the small end bearing and the new gudgeon pin. Keith holds the replacement piston in position while I line up the new pin and attempt to press it in. It moves a couple of millimeters then jams. I lightly tap it with the hammer. It doesn't move at all... talk about an interference fit!

"I know," says Keith. "We'll heat the piston up first then you knock it home." He sets to work with the heater gun, then once again repeats the operation. I press in the gudgeon pin and give it a tap. It moves half way into the hole then sticks.

"Hit it harder," says Keith in a pained voice. The scalding piston is cooking his fingers.

"It won't move," I say in exasperation.

It won't come back out either. We're forced to let everything cool then reapply heat to the piston to free the jammed pin.

"Let's freeze the pin first," suggests Keith.

It makes perfect sense. I walk through a dark garden, enter the kitchen and pop the gudgeon pin into the back of the deep freeze. A few minutes later I run back to the garage with it sticking icily to my palm. Keith has been heating the piston for quite a while.

"This time," he says, as I wipe oil on the pin and centre it on the piston, "thump it hard and don't stop until it's all the way through."

It makes the edge of the small end on the first tap. The second tap eases it further.

"Don't stop... keep going," shouts Keith. I give it a third and fourth hit, but the heat from the piston has transferred sufficiently to cause the pin to expand and we're stuck again.

It takes half an hour to carefully extract it and start the cooling and heating processes all over again. This time I give it a heavy knock then keep pressing with the hammer.

"Again, again!" encourages Keith.

I do and am rewarded with a yelp of joy from the other side of the engine.

"Okay, okay, we've done it. It's butted up against the circlip," Keith pronounces jubilantly.

We both collapse in a state of relief.

It's already midnight but we're by no means finished. I carefully apply gasket sealant to the top of the crankcase and bottom of the barrel. Keith lowers the cylinder base gasket into position then hovers the cylinder over the piston. My job is to compress each of the three piston rings whilst Keith lowers the barrel over them. I'm quite nervous, as the rings are brittle and I'd hate to break one.

It should be a 5 minute job. It takes us nearly an hour. The rings slip round in their grooves, jam against the cylinder and pop back out each time we try to level the barrel to manoeuvre it squarely over the next ring. We curse, strain and curse more as the heavy barrel tires our hands and arms and the silicone sealant begins to set hard. It's a performance that Laurel and Hardy would have been proud of.

Finally, Keith finds a method that works. He stands high above the bike, looking down the bore. It helps him line the cylinder and piston up more accurately. Eventually it goes over the last ring. I set about removing what cured silicone I can from the metal surfaces without damaging the gasket, then reapply a new film.

At 1.15am it's done. Although our work is untested, Peggy is miraculously ready for the off tomorrow.

"Thanks mate," I say to Keith, who looks pleased as Punch. "I can't imagine how I would have got this done on my own."

Exhausted but strangely satisfied, we shake hands and congratulate ourselves on our successful, if somewhat inept, accomplishment.

"If that engine makes it to Egypt after me and you have worked on it I'll eat my hat!" declares Keith.

I hope he's wrong.

Ready for the off, day 2. Keith, Juliet and Jack, Kingswinford.

Day 2, Kingswinford to Oxford, UK.
93 miles.

The Batten household rises early and breakfast is a family affair. Juliet makes porridge and, specially for me, a pot of fresh coffee. The sun shines through their dining room window and inspite of our labours late into the night, or maybe because of them, there's a distinct feeling of aliveness at our shared achievement.

"Do you reckon it'll start?" Keith asks as he crunches his toast.

"First time, without a doubt," I reply, with as much gusto as I can muster.

Peggy doesn't disappoint...she starts first kick. We look at each other in disbelief... it's nothing short of miraculous! I hurriedly put on my riding gear and set off on a test ride with Jack chasing my rear tyre, barking furiously. To my amazement I'm too nervous to ride. The dread of another seizure is petrifying and I have to stop within a couple of hundred metres or so, heart pounding with anxiety. Keith takes over. He's never ridden a British bike before but tells me most of his past motorcycles were Japanese 2-strokes so not to worry. He rides the Bantam 4 miles and returns with the happy verdict,

"There's nothing wrong with that!"

Juliet and Keith both hug me as I pick up my crash helmet ready to leave. Their conviction that I'll make it to Egypt gives me renewed confidence.

"Send us a postcard," they shout as I depart.

Unfortunately I hit early morning hold ups in many of the small towns that have been all but absorbed into Birmingham. Numerous sets of traffic lights, often at the top of steep hills, compound the problem. I'm constantly on tenterhooks, my left hand glued to the clutch lever awaiting the grisly sound of another seizure. It aches, as do my shoulders and neck, from tension. I so desperately want to get the trip back on schedule but feel I have no option but to stop every 5 to 8 miles to let the engine cool. The new piston has clearance aplenty but the rings need to bed in well and Andy's advice is to take it easy for the first 100 miles.

Bypassing Bromsgrove, I follow roadsigns for Redditch. I was due to meet John Garner here yesterday but sadly, he's unable to reschedule a family commitment this morning. I drive towards the town centre, turning off the main Bromsgrove highway to head down Hewell Road. It's a journey, or in some ways a pilgrimage, I've made several times before. Roughly half way along this unremarkable road is an industrial estate with several old buildings at the roadside. One has a large slate roof in a poor state of repair. Indeed, it hasn't been touched since the 1960s. Still visible, although now very faded, are two rows of white letters each at least two metres high. They spell out the name 'ROYAL ENFIELD'. It's the site of the once great Royal Enfield motorcycle and bicycle factory. Although the vast majority of it has been bulldozed and replaced with new structures, this former office building, evident on many photographs from the early part of the 20th Century until the company's sad demise in 1967, has somehow survived. I come to a halt and, staying in my saddle, spend a couple of minutes staring at the roof. The Bullet I rode to India originated from here, as did a couple of other old bikes currently in my garage. I hope these last vestiges of a once proud motorcycling industry can remain preserved.

My next stop is for a cup of tea at a lakeside café in the Arrow Valley Country Park, which is also a nostalgic place for me. In July 2003 an event was held in this park called *Redditch Revisited*. Organised by the *Royal Enfield Owners Club*, more than a thousand Royal Enfield motorcycles and a crowd of around 4,000 people gathered for a day celebrating all things Enfield. It was a huge success.

In 2007, I decided to launch a series of motorcycle shows called *Motorcycling Big Days Out*, incorporating many of the elements that made that 2003 Redditch event such a crowd pleaser. The first bash was to be staged here in the Arrow Valley Park and was called *The Royal Enfield Big Day Out*, followed a month later by *The Triumph Big Day Out*, a show held in Meriden where Triumph motorcycles were manufactured between 1942 and 1983.

I worked flat out for 4 months, wanting people not only to have a wonderful day but also the chance to learn first hand about the motorcycles and the history of each company. I hired venues, booked an expensive advertising campaign, bought a large marquee and rented seating for 130 people along with a large projector screen and a PA system to facilitate a series of talks and lectures from former factory workers, local historians and technical experts. At Redditch there were new Indian-made Royal Enfield motorcycles available for test rides and also a notable speaker from the Indian factory. Likewise at Meriden, a guest speaker from the resurgent Triumph company at Hinckley attended along with a display of the makers' range of bikes, which included a model launched only two days before the event.

Ten gazebos were lined up down one side of Arrow Valley Park, with exhibits of competition motorcycles, development prototypes, Royal Enfield bicycles, lawnmowers, static engines and a Royal Enfield powered Berkeley sports car. At Meriden there were contributions from two museums and even the world's oldest and seldom seen Triumph, dating from 1902. A large display of images spanning the history of each company plus an open-air art gallery of sales literature and contemporary advertisements was arranged. Specialist traders and autojumblers selling marque-related goods were booked. At Redditch, one unique trader even travelled from the Isle of Skye to sell her historic advertising prints. Finally there were the bikes. First time round, I wasn't sure if I could attract the thousand plus machines that had caused such a stir in 2003, but I certainly hoped enough would be parked up to make it a feast for the eyes of all attendees. Mmm... it's quite a stirring memory.

I sit in the cafe, unable to see Peggy but sure she's safe in the quiet car park. I sip my tea and think about how it all went.

We started setting up at Redditch on a sunny Thursday afternoon two days ahead of the event. It rained heavily all night and continued relentlessly all day Friday. Preparing the showground under a blanket of intense, driving rain was exhausting and, as puddles of water grew into larger pools and eventually swamped fields, became thoroughly disheartening. I was assisted by my family and a band of hard-working, loyal friends, but got so far behind schedule that I was forced to work through Friday night without sleep, dragging generators across the fields and setting up the bike areas in the small hours... and still it rained!

We were rushing around completing finishing touches when the gates opened to the public. Although parts of the showground were waterlogged, the rain, thankfully, stopped. Sadly, many riders stayed away as the bad weather continued in other parts of the country. This was, after all, the summer when Britain experienced unparalleled flooding, with many areas suffering severe weather related damage, and numerous outdoor events, including long-established county agricultural shows, were cancelled. The Met Office later declared 2007 the wettest summer since records began 240 years earlier.

In spite of this, around 450 Royal Enfield motorcycles did attend the Redditch show. The marquee was packed for each of the seven lectures. Traders and autojumblers reported excellent sales and the onsite catering, which I had also organised with the help of friends, was a great success. Unfortunately, and most likely because of the appalling weather in the build up to the show, the general public failed to arrive in significant numbers. By the time I took the gate receipts to the bank night safe, I knew I was looking at a pretty substantial loss.

Meriden, a month later, was also blighted by the weather. While Redditch at least dried out during the course of the day, the Triumph show had to be moved to an adjoining field at the last minute due to general flooding. In the build up to the event, with further atrocious weather forecast, I could have cancelled the show and claimed on my insurance. Deep down I knew this was never really on the cards.... I'm not one to throw in the towel easily. Maybe enthusiasm overrode caution but I didn't want to disappoint the many people who were set to come. Somewhat predictably, it absolutely threw it down from midday onwards and once again, attendance suffered terribly, including many traders and specialist display contributors who either phoned to withdraw at the last minute or simply didn't show up.

There's no doubt there were things I didn't get quite right, for example, several people did take issue with having to pay an admission fee, perhaps failing to understand the enormous costs involved in setting up such a show. One man became so irate at being asked to pay £5 at Redditch that he rode hard at my gate staff who had to jump for safety out of his way!

It had been my intention to do two shows the following year, the *BSA Big Day Out* and *The Norton Big Day Out*, with each event repeating every two years. After the Meriden washout I spent a lot of time reflecting on the experience, reviewing the £18,000 loss... and licking my wounds from the disappointment. In the end I found myself with a clear choice for the year ahead; did I want to risk my last savings and possibly further failures in another gamble with the British summer weather, or would I rather ride my motorcycle to India. The latter won hands down and as a further consequence, I now find myself battling my way to Egypt... again!

Stirring from my reverie, I check Peggy over then head south towards Evesham and a hastily rescheduled lunch appointment in Badsey with John and Jane. The couple live in an old converted barn down a long rutted farm track. I stand on the Bantam's footpegs trying to take the strain off the frame. The rear dampers bottom out on a baked earth mound just as the front wheel kicks sideways off a sizeable rock. I absorb the jolt then reset the bike's course before we clip more rocks on the side of a field. The new handlebars work a treat, allowing me to stand comfortably and have total control of the motorcycle. My mind becomes completely absorbed in the riding challenge, a welcome break from the anxieties of the last day and a half.

The couple welcome me into their home. I had hoped to meet their pets, a pair of giant Norwegian Forest cats called Toby and Milo, but Jane tells me they are out hunting for rabbits, their favourite meal. As I enter the lounge, the television news is on.

"Look at this," says John excitedly. "Gordon Brown has probably just cost himself the General Election!"

Indeed, the news doesn't bode well for the incumbent PM. Apparently, Mr. Brown left a TV company's lapel microphone switched on while being driven away from a 'meet the public' session. With a certain comic irony, he's clearly heard calling a 65-year-old lady, who says she has been a life-long Labour voter, a bigot and is then shown humbly apologising. It makes compulsive viewing, though for me there's the feeling that all the hoopla of the build up to the election, to be held in 6 days time, will soon be literally behind me as I hope to be somewhere in North Africa on polling day.

Jane makes me a couple of toasted cheese sandwiches.

"Sorry," she says. "When you phoned to say you couldn't make it last night I bunged some meat into the veggie chilli I'd made for you... and then we ate it all!"

I laugh, glad that nothing was wasted. Fortunately, last night's apple crumble has survived and I gladly wolf down a large bowlful while on the TV, Premier Brown continues to try to dig himself out of an ever-deepening hole.

John and Jane have been in business as *Sprockets Unlimited* since 1985, supplying chains and sprockets for motorcycles of all ages, though most events they attend with their mobile trade stand are classic bike related. They kindly provided me with a top quality *Iwis* drive chain for Peggy, along with new gearbox and rear wheel sprockets and a replacement primary chain. Only a few weeks ago I'd downgeared the Bantam, which means that my rear chain is now a half link too long. We'd agreed that shortening it could wait until this visit.

After my second bowl of crumble and ice cream, we wheel Peggy into a barn and park her next to John's bike. I must confess I'm surprised by his choice of machine. John has very long greying hair and adorns a faded and obviously well loved black leather bike jacket like a second skin. I always had him down as an old-school rocker, riding the same well-oiled and nurtured BSA A10 or 1960's Triumph Bonneville for the last 30 years or so. The bike in his barn serves as a good reminder not to pre-judge people... it's an ultra modern Suzuki GSX1300R, heralded at its launch in 1999 as the world's fastest production motorcycle.

"Nah," exclaims John when I reveal my misconception. With a cheeky grin and a wink, he points to Peggy and adds, "I can't be doing with all that wasted time fixing problems by the side of the road. With this I can ride as fast as I want and as far as I want without ever having to worry about anything going wrong. Japanese bikes overtook the British industry for good reasons, you know!"

He gets under way, deftly removing the Bantam's chain, then disappears into a work room to remove the surplus link while I go round Peggy checking all her fastenings are secure. Returning in no time, he soon has the chain back in place. He vanishes once more and this time reappears clutching a vernier gauge.

"Might as well do the job right," he says, using it to measure the rear wheel snail adjusters so that they are precisely equidistant on each side of the bike. Once done, I tighten the wheel lock nuts, reconnect the rear brake rod and set it to what I think is the correct position.

"Can you lift the rear of the bike, please John, so I can test the brakes are adjusted properly?" I ask. He looks a little daunted at raising Peggy and all her luggage off the ground, but nonetheless gives it a go.

"It's not as heavy as it looks," he says in surprise.

"That's what I keep telling everyone," I respond with a smile.

The wheel won't turn. I loosen the rear brake rod, assuming I've tightened it too far, but it remains locked solid.

John lowers Peggy to the ground and I stand up, puzzled. I walk round the back of the bike and take a close look at the rear wheel from the opposite side.

"Aha," I say. "The tyre is pressed hard against the mudguard on this side and has acres of room on the drive side." In fact, there's no doubt that the wheel's sitting in the frame at an odd angle.

John is confounded. He gets down on his knees and remeasures the chain adjusters with his vernier.

"I don't understand," he says. "They're in an absolutely identical position on both sides."

"Yes, but this is an old BSA, it's most likely had a wonky frame from new... the best of early 1950's low cost mass production! I guess we can't trust the wheel to sit true by taking measurements... we'll have to align it by sight to the frame and mudguard, not to the adjusters."

John, a perfectionist in his work, shakes his head as I make the changes with my spanner. Soon the wheel is spinning freely again.

"British bikes...!" he says. We both laugh.

With little chance of reaching my intended destination, Folkestone, tonight, I depart Badsey hoping to find a campsite as far south of London as possible. However, now I'm on open roads and not constricted by heavy town traffic, I notice that engine performance has deteriorated. I stop frequently. First I alter the carburettor air screw position several times. With no improvement I reseal the carburettor flange with a new gasket and silicone sealant. On further stops I check the spark plug, holding it high and trying to interpret its colour before making more adjustments to the carburettor needle jet position. All is fine when the engine is relatively cool but within a couple of miles, once hot, it severely pops and bangs on the overrun. Nothing I alter seems to make any difference. Indeed, for the bike to run at all I have to have the air screw fully closed, which seems wrong.

The poor running engine and having to repeatedly fiddle with the carburettor eats away at time. I give up on either getting anywhere near London tonight or catching my *Eurotunnel* train to France tomorrow morning. Stopping again to consult my map, I assess the options for somewhere to stay. It will soon be dark and, after little sleep last night and an almost equally stressful day today, sound slumber seems essential.

I notice how near I am to Oxford and remember staying at the Oxford Youth Hostel on the first night of my ride to India. Somewhere both familiar and comfortable, where possibly I can work on the bike in the morning, is an ideal solution so I immediately reprogramme the sat nav to divert there.

The last few miles are an ordeal. I have to run a gauntlet of fast trucks and impatient cars along the A34. Forced to ride rapidly, around 45mph, to avoid being smacked into by the speeding trucks that tailgate us, Peggy really struggles. A grotesque image of the engine seizing, this time with a fully loaded articulated lorry just 2 feet from my rear wheel, burns itself into my consciousness. It spurs me on to push the bike harder. The engine starts pinking... it's nerve racking. At last I see the exit slip road for central Oxford. I gratefully take it and immediately slow down, relieved to have a engine that still runs. Backfiring horribly, we lurch towards a roundabout. Poor, poor Peggy!

We limp into the city centre and locate the sanctuary of the modern Youth Hostel which nestles beside the railway station. I feel utterly drained by the last few miles of the ride. Thankfully, there are still beds available and equally as importantly, space for the Bantam in the secure rear courtyard.

Grabbing a quick shower, I scoot down to the restaurant before it closes. After the meal, I long to turn in and drift off into the oblivion of a world with no fears of engine seizures and another failed trip. But I'm determined not to be beaten and spend the next 2 hours on the telephone, first to Andy, then Derek, Keith and Rob. All offer advice that makes sense and seems to be congruent.

With a plan of action for the morning, I retire.

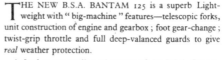

Day 3, Oxford to East Grinstead, UK.
93 miles.

My alarm rouses me at 7am. I was the only occupant in a pleasantly furnished six bed dorm when I turned in. There are now four other men in the room, all deeply asleep, so I tiptoe around, getting myself dressed and emptying my ample locker which is full to bursting with motorcycling gear. I'm very self conscious of all the rustling and scraping noises I make, but my roommates, probably well attuned to youth hostel life, sleep on.

The first hour and a half is spent working on the Bantam. The consensus of opinion last night was that the base gasket must have blown, a result of being gunged up with cured silicone whilst Keith and I struggled to fit the barrel. To rectify it, I attempt to put a bead of silicone around the bottom of the cylinder. I can make a tidy job of both sides, but the back and front are quite tricky to access. I get as much black gasket sealant on my clothes as I do on the engine. Despite my best efforts, it's 11am before I don my waterproofs and depart.

There initially seems to be an improvement and we buzz merrily along leafy Oxfordshire lanes in light rain. As the sun peaks through the heavy blanket of clouds, the drizzle lifts and, assisted by flat roads, we ride for a dozen or so very pleasant miles. Then, at the top of a hill, I notice the engine start to pink and performance begin to drop. I revert to yesterday's miserable pattern of stop-start riding, trying to either eliminate any obvious problems or make subtle improvements. After each halt in a series of damp lay-bys or muddy tractor entrances to fields, we manage a couple of miles of decent riding before engine performance wanes and I once more look for a place to park up.

My plan is to skirt around London on the outside of the M25 orbital motorway, passing first through Henley on Thames. I stop on the far side of its grand 16th Century, arched stone bridge which spans the river Thames. Digging out my mobile phone, I call Jane, who's pleased to hear from me but concerned by my continued troubles.

Jane is a highly accomplished singer who studied at the Royal College of Music for five years plus a further year in Germany on a scholarship. She has, quite simply, the most beautiful voice I've ever heard... which isn't just natural bias. Her rendition of the *Pie Jesu* segment of Andrew Lloyd Webber's *Requiem Mass*, that she premiered internationally, literally moves me to tears each time I hear it.

"Didn't you once tell me you'd sung at the Henley Regatta?" I ask her.

"Oh, yes," she answers, "years ago... Jonathan Dove was my accompanist. We did some lighter repertoire, Cole Porter, Gershwin, that sort of thing. Why do you ask?"

I explain that I'm standing at the edge of the Henley Bridge close to where the Regatta is held. Her singing forgotten, she becomes enthusiastic,

"I just remember being spellbound by Andrew Logan's beautiful, sparkling sculpture of Pegasus which had been placed by the water's edge. It was fabulous... absolutely magical."

Strangely enough, I'd seen a similar 'Logan' Pegasus in the middle of a roundabout close to Keith's in Kingswinford. I didn't know what it was at the time but had thought its spangly, glittering form quite magnificent too. It strikes me as a rather poetic coincidence.

Leaving Henley behind, we strike across country towards Bracknell and Woking, with the frequency of stops and my calls to Andy increasing rapidly. On his instructions I do a series of 'plug chops', which involves riding at a particular throttle setting and, when clear of traffic, hauling in the clutch and concurrently switching off the ignition. This is no easy feat on Peggy as the ignition switch, which is situated on the frame behind my right leg, can only be accessed by my right (throttle) hand. In the space of an hour I do three tests in this way, at 1/8, 1/4 and 1/2 throttle openings. After each stop I remove the burning hot spark plug, examine its colour and report back to Andy. We're unable to come to a diagnosis of the problem. The plug was a healthy chocolate brown colour when running the engine in. It still is.

There is one place I'd hoped to visit en route to the coast, Box Hill. But with Peggy struggling so much I'm in two minds about risking an unnecessary steep climb. In the end, as I'm so close, I decide it would be a shame to miss it. Afterall, I tell myself, I'm supposed to be enjoying this ride!

Box Hill is a popular vantage point on the Surrey Hills looking towards the South Downs. As well as being the setting of a famous scene in Jane Austen's novel, Emma, it is also something of a Mecca for motorcyclists, bicyclists and walkers. I first heard about it in the 1980s when a band I saw at The Reading Rock Festival, the wackily named Dumpy's Rusty Nuts, performed the song Boxhill or Bust. It also features in a Richard Thompson song I've subsequently heard on the radio, called 1952 Vincent Black Lightning. Off the A24, a tight lane called The Zig Zag Road winds its way to the summit where there's a National Trust Visitor Centre and café. I push Peggy hard, determined to reach the top in one go. Despite protesting with a noisy, chugging engine, I steer her round a couple of tight hairpin bends and soon pull into the car park.

A few other motorcycles, all modern except for a 1960's Triumph, are parked against a wooden barrier. There are quite a few cars and several picnic tables around which people are taking in the view as they eat. I feel confused about where I should park, not wanting to have to answer too many questions about Peggy, why she's heaped with so much luggage and the sensitive subject of our destination, which at the moment seems a long, long way away. I halt some distance from the other bikes and set to work cleaning my spark plug and putting my largest pilot jet in the carburettor.

The Triumph owner wanders over and asks if he can help. With hope, I ask if he knows anything about 2-stroke carburation.

'Two things only," he replies. "Sod-all and nothing!"

We both laugh then he asks where I'm heading. I can't bring myself to say Egypt, so I tell a half truth.

"Folkestone," I reply.

He wishes me luck then departs to join a couple of his friends who are preparing to leave. I soon follow.

By late afternoon Peggy is just about unrideable. She kangaroos awkwardly as soon as I close the throttle and pinks on the flat or under load when climbing hills. My rainsuit is brilliant for keeping me dry and warm, but on a muggy, wet day like today, it acts like a pressure cooker, especially when I stop to work on the bike. The whole experience is wretched.

On the phone, Andy suggests replacing the cylinder base gasket. I've already used my only spare so we decide I should remove the old one and try making a better, if temporary, seal using silicone. However, as I've just about emptied a whole tube of the stuff in the last 48 hours, I'll need to buy more before I can attempt any remedial work. A search on my sat nav for the nearest Halford's car parts superstore directs me due south to Crawley, quite a long way off my intended easterly route to Folkestone. I feel I have no option but to divert.

I locate the Halford's in a large shopping complex in the centre of Crawley, purchase some more gasket sealant then ask to speak to the shop manager. A smartly dressed man arrives at the checkout. I explain my predicament and ask if he minds me doing the work under an overhang in front of his shopfront window.

"Not at all, be my guest," he cheerfully responds.

At the last minute I remember I'll need to buy some degreaser to clean all the surfaces thoroughly before applying the new sealant and ask him to direct me to the relevant isle.

"Don't worry about it, we have a half-used can in the back office," he replies. "I'll bring it out to you." What excellent service!

I set about things. Loathe to completely remove the barrel as I can't imagine getting it back over those tricky piston rings on my own, I work with it raised a couple of inches by jamming the end of my stubby hammer between the bottom fin and the crankcases. The existing gasket is translucent, like rice paper, and burnt to a crisp in places... a sure sign of culpability.

I pick and scratch with my fingernails, trying to remove all the pieces of scorched gasket paper and silicone without any of it falling into the crank. It's not easy, especially as the silicone stretches stringily then whips back into position like a rubber band time and again. Eventually I get it as clean as possible, then wipe both top and bottom faces with a cloth sprayed with degreasant. Finally, I use my little finger to smear my best attempt at an even layer of new silicone into the gap to create a fresh seal.

After tightening down the cylinder head and replacing the tank and seat, there's nothing to do but pace around for half an hour waiting for the silicone to cure. I'm back on the road at 7.40pm, still 68 miles short of my bed for the night in Folkestone. The first mile, which is mostly around flat town streets, is fine. Then I join a dual carriageway on a long steep hill. As soon as we begin to climb, the pinking, surging and banging return with a vengeance. It's hard to believe that Peggy is running so badly... it feels as if she's about to explode. I slow as I approach a junction on the outskirts of East Grinstead. The engine chugs terribly, making a clamorous dung! dung! dung! dung! dung! sound. I halt at a red traffic signal. Peggy stalls. Pushing her to the roadside, I stand feeling utterly dejected then step back a few paces, looking at her and shaking my head.

Suddenly I remember the episode of *Fawlty Towers* where Basil's car, a badly abused orange Austin 1100, breaks down.

"I'll count to three," he shouts. "One... two... three. Right, that's it... I've had enough!" He leaps out of the car in uncontrollable rage. "You can't say I haven't warned you," he hollers, furiously waving his finger at the defunct vehicle. "Well this is it, I'm going to give you a dammed good thrashing!" Basil disappears from view, returning a few moments later with a leafy branch freshly ripped from a nearby tree which he uses to frenetically beat the car bonnet and windscreen.

I have no intention of giving Peggy such belligerent treatment, indeed, I feel sorry for her having to endure such a gruelling and difficult ordeal. But thinking about Basil's impotent wrath, and the brilliant comic genius of actor John Cleese, helps me to laugh at myself and the situation I find myself in.

Peggy starts after a few kicks and we crawl into the car park of a brightly lit *Premier Inn*, conveniently just 100 metres past the lights. The sign outside advertises £29 rooms and there's even an adjacent pub restaurant. Perfect. I wearily go in and ask for a room.

"That'll be £71 please, sir," says the receptionist.

Open-mouthed, I point through the glass doorway to the £29 sign.

"I'm afraid that's the internet price and you'll have to book at least three weeks in advance to get that rate."

It's not the best news and I'm far from happy given my present circumstances. The receptionist, however, is a helpful gentleman. When I ask if he knows anywhere in the locality with rooms at roughly half that price, he consults a notebook and without hesitation phones a number.

"Will £35 be OK?" he asks, holding his hand against the phone.

"Sure... great," I quickly reply.

He reserves me a room, then even takes the trouble to walk out of the building and onto the main road to direct me to the Bed and Breakfast he's just booked for me. It's only 300 metres away. I shake his hand, hugely grateful for the humanity he's shown... with my spirits so close to rock bottom, his kindness means an awful lot.

The bed and breakfast is an odd place, seemingly frequented by a mixture of itinerant construction workers and travellers looking for budget accommodation close to Gatwick airport. My tiny room, the last available, is box like, but it's clean and the manager is friendly, allowing me to park Peggy in the safest courtyard spot next to his lounge window.

I phone my friends Tony and Jan in Folkestone, tell them not to wait up for me, then head back to the *Premier Inn* restaurant where I slowly chomp through a meal, reflecting on what has been a thoroughly grim day. An hour later I lie in my bed, talking to Jane on the phone. I've been unable to find internet access so she goes online and, for a second time, postpones my *Eurotunnel* crossing.

"You know what you've got to do?" she says, "Live each minute fully and try not to be too stressed about things going wrong. Get yourself into that flow you always have when you travel, then you'll be in the right place, with the right people, for things to go right."

It's just the advice I need.

Day 4, East Grinstead to Folkestone, UK.
67 miles.

The B&B owners, Robin and Dee, rush around serving breakfast to a packed dining room. Half way through my second round of toast and coffee, I have a chat with Robin about the bike and its problems. My request to use his courtyard to make repairs is immediately granted. This time I'm determined to really take my time over the job, with making a new paper gasket a priority. I don't have an old one to use as a pattern, let alone any gasket paper, so it isn't going to be easy but I'm game to give it a go. On the strength of last night's performance, I plainly need to do something if we're ever to reach the Channel... in many ways it feels like today will be a make or break day for the whole journey.

Before getting started, I decide to order a couple of pukka gasket sets as a back up. I've used several parts suppliers for the bike, but on a hunch, call *Rex Caunt Racing*. The phone is answered by Rex's lovely American wife, Debb, who takes my order and confirms the gasket sets can be sent straightaway to Folkestone.

"I'll check with our courier, but I'm certain I can get them there before 9am, even on a Saturday morning," Debb says in her usual sunny way.

Towards the end of our conversation, she suddenly adds,

"Let me phone Rex at the workshop and see if he has any ideas for you."

A few minutes later Rex calls me back. I describe the seizure and the terrible running I've subsequently experienced. Ever a gentleman, Rex politely begins,

"If you don't mind me saying so, Gordon, I think your D14 piston might be too high compression for the job you're trying to do." My ears prick up as it's not something Andy, Derek or I ever considered.

"I'm especially concerned by the pinking you're having," he continues. "Maybe you can try lowering the compression just a little using two cylinder head gaskets."

It's an excellent idea.

Next I ask Robin where the nearest stationers is so that I can buy some good quality paper to fabricate my temporary gasket. He disappears into the back office, returning a couple of minutes later with a selection of papers for me to use. I settle for some thick, satin-finish photographic paper which I feel is the most suitable.

Using the cylinder head as a rough guide, I cut out a large circle then spend the next thirty minutes shaping further small holes and curves into the improvised gasket, trying to make it fit as perfectly as possible. The flaw in my endeavours is that I'm still unprepared to risk completely removing the barrel singlehanded which means I have to cut slits into the paper to allow it to fit around the engine studs. Some air will inevitably be able to move through these cuts so my only hope is that lashings of silicone will help form a make-do seal. After a final fitting, I stand upright, ease my aching back and knees and examine what I'm left with. A work of art it will never be, but fingers crossed, it'll do the job for the rest of today.

Once sealed in place with silicone, I set to work on the cylinder head. The gaskets are made from pressed aluminium alloy. I had two at the start of the journey, both of which have already been used. On inspection, they seem in pretty good shape, so I give them a gentle cleaning with a damp cloth impregnated with oven cleaner, courtesy of Robin, then apply a fine layer of silicone. Following Rex's advice, I affix both under the cylinder head.

It's nearly 1pm by the time we get under way. Skirting around the edges of East Grinstead town centre, we head out into an area of open farmland. The miles tick by... 2 miles, 4 miles, 6 miles. Peggy certainly sounds quieter and although she still chugs a little when slowing down, is far more manageable than yesterday, thank heavens.

Pinking returns after 9 miles, but only when climbing steep hills. On the flat the engine seems to be coping well. I stop on the edge of a farm track to check the colour of the spark plug and give Andy an update.

"Why not try retarding the ignition a little?" he suggests. I know we checked the timing on my last visit to him but it has to be worth a go.

Just as I finish, a rusty old van brakes hard and comes to a halt a little way in front of us. A wiry man emerges dressed in shorts, wellington boots and a sou'wester hat.

"Well blow me, there's a Bantam under all those bags!" he exclaims. "Having trouble?"

I give an outline of the last few days and my current tweak to the timing.

"I've got a few old bikes," he tells me, "but no 2-strokes. I've just finished building a Triton out of a T120 engine and a featherbed frame. It goes like stink." He also lists a few other fast machines in his collection before shocking me by saying. "Not bad for eighty four, eh?"

"Blimey," I reply. "It certainly gives me hope!"

Before we say our farewells, he digs out paper and pencil from his van's glovebox and begins writing on it.

"I live on a farm just a few miles down the road. Here's my phone number. If you get stuck, ring me. Don't go paying for a hotel for the night... I've a caravan in the farmyard you can doss down in."

With that, we shake hands. I kick Peggy back into life and accelerate away.

The sun comes out as we enter Kent. We roar through Royal Tonbridge Wells then make our way towards Ashford. On the town's inner ring road, my thoughts shift to its famous WWI tank, which sits under a purpose built canopy at the edge of a pedestrian precinct. It's a 1916 MK IV tank, one of only eight remaining in the world out of 2,636 originally built. In 1919, 265 First World War tanks were presented to towns and cities around the British Isles, including this one to Ashford. It's now the only one that remains outside of museums, with the majority melted down for their iron during the Second World War. It's thought that the Ashford tank survived because in 1929 it had its rear cut off and its internals removed before being converted into an electricity sub station!

My memories of it, from when I lived in this area in the 1980s, are as an incomplete wreck covered in graffiti. I was delighted to read that it had recently been restored, so peel off from the traffic jam that is Ashford at 5pm on a Bank Holiday weekend Friday and drive along a small one way street until I find it. The restoration is superb. Not only has the back been replaced so that it's indistinguishable from the original main section, but the tank has been repainted, including the addition of its original WWI divisional markings.

Feeling refreshed by my stop beside the curious relic, I rejoin the ring road, looking for the old southbound A20. The congestion is worrying in the circumstances but Peggy steadfastly keeps going. Nervously, I stop at a series of traffic lights, impatient to be moving again as the heat from her engine builds, radiating uncomfortably on the inside of my legs. Once finally back onto open roads, I realise how strong the wind has become, fortuitously blowing from behind, pushing us faster towards our destination.

We enter Hythe almost opposite its renowned railway station, a terminus on the *Romney, Hythe and Dymchurch Railway,* which with 15" gauge tracks was for more than half of the 20th Century the smallest public railway in the world. Its steam engines are still in full use, not just for tourists but for local passengers. I stand tall on Peggy's footpegs as we ride round a bend that curves towards the sea front, but sadly catch no sight of the smoke or steam that would suggest there's a vintage train in the station.

A bus pulls out in front of us at the base of Sandgate Hill, costing us all our momentum. It crawls up the steep incline, drops off a passenger at a point where it's impossible for us to pass, then recommences its painfully slow ascent, all the while blasting me with lungfuls of diesel fumes. We round the summit with Peggy pinking loudly. Fearing imminent seizure, I make a hasty right turn and come to a stop on the cliff tops. The wind howls in from the sea, almost blowing Peggy off her centrestand, so for most of our 15 minute break I place myself on her landward side, bracing us both against great gusts. Looking out over the Channel, I wonder if we'll even get to France, let alone Egypt.

I ride through Folkestone then head along the Alkham Valley road to the refuge of the home of my dear friends, Tony and Jan Henry. This is where I stayed on the second night of my ride to India and it remains one of my most treasured memories of that whole journey. There was no safe roadside parking, so I rode across a field of wheat stubble to the back of their garden. Plans to leave my Royal Enfield in the field overnight were thwarted by neighbours announcing they were having a summer party and it was needed for car parking. Tony thought about the problem, disappeared into his garden shed for a minute before emerging with a chainsaw, gloves and goggles. In what was an unquestionable measure of true friendship, he chain-sawed a bike-sized hole in the garden hedge enabling me to park my motorcycle safely in their garden. I know from our recent phone conversations that the hole has been freshly trimmed in readiness for my arrival and Tony's promised to place an old wooden door over a small ditch to make my access even easier.

The farm gate is open and I ride straight through. At this time of year, the field is full of green shoots, some 18 inches high, so I'm forced to hug the edges, trying desperately not to damage any of the crop. It's not easy. There's precious little gap between the hedge that borders the field and the first row of vegetation. Furthermore, the furrows are deep and uneven, causing Peggy to weave from side to side. I stand on the footrests, trying to maintain my balance but occasionally have to stamp my boot down to prevent falling off as we bounce and bump our way forward, the beleaguered Bantam engine all the while revving hard in 1st gear. Turning the final tight corner, I power straight over the promised wooden door and through the hawthorn hedge, its branches whipping my face and tugging at my sleeves and saddlebags.

Stopping sharply, I hop off and inspect Peggy. The frame and wheels are mercifully in one piece despite their battering, and the engine, although yet again labouring and sounding ominously loud, is still ticking over. I look downwards... great clods of earth and grass are jammed into the engine sump guard, footrests and centrestand. Before I clean them up, Tony comes running out of the house and throws his arms around me in a huge bear hug.

"Great to see you mate," he says. "I knew you'd make it!"

We're soon joined by Jan, who also wraps her arms around me. Although at this point I have no idea at all if I'll be able to remedy Peggy's problems and progress any further, it feels so good to be in the bosom of my caring and loyal friends that for the first time in four days I relax.

Day 5, Folkestone, UK.
21 miles.

The courier arrives with a small jiffy bag containing three gasket kits.

"Is that it?" Tony asks. "I was expecting half an engine to show up."

I'm eager to get started. Tony prepares an area of decking around one of his garden summerhouses, Badger's End, so that there's a measure of shelter under a canopy should the menacing black clouds produce rain. This time I fully remove the barrel, Tony tending to the open crankcase with a large rag should any of the rings break. It all comes off fine.

I spend the next hour carefully picking and scraping all the gunk off the barrel, head and crankcase, buoyed with the optimism afforded by new gaskets. It's funny to think that only four days ago I didn't have a clue how to do this on a Bantam, yet now work with a measure of confidence, sure I can put everything back together again. I remember Jane mirthfully recalling that over the years she'd learnt about the ins and outs of car engines as a result of driving a string of beloved old VW Beetles which regularly broke down. Seems I'm in a similar situation - a case of learning mechanics by default!

Perhaps I've over-stressed to Tony the difficulties Keith and I experienced in getting the piston inside the barrel at Kingswinford. He looks very serious as he holds the lump of cast iron in his hands, his body braced to take the strain. Slowly I ease each set of rings into the cylinder. Following Keith's method of looking down the barrel as he works, Tony does a sterling job. All three rings locate in under five minutes... Keith will never believe it! This time I've not made the mistake of putting any sealant on the gasket in advance, so by the time I do this and tighten the barrel and head, complete with two new alloy gaskets, I'm feeling pretty happy with the whole thing. Tony looks mightily relieved.

In spite of all this, I'm still very anxious when, after a long break for lunch, we wheel Peggy out of the garden and onto the road. She fires up second kick and I set off. Within a couple of minutes she begins to labour under load on a long but gentle incline. Feeling thoroughly sick, I get off and tweak the carb air screw which is set very rich. The rough running vanishes so I hop back on and nervously continue. The next 20 miles are just about the best I've done on her, which in the circumstances is astonishing. I head up Spitfire Hill towards Hawkinge. The village is famous for its involvement in the Battle of Britain, with RAF Hawkinge the nearest fighter squadron to France. There's little remaining of the old aerodrome which has largely been covered by a new housing estate, but a small museum, the *Kent Battle of Britain Museum*, has survived. A collection of aeroplanes are housed there, including a Messershmidt ME109, a Hurricane and a Spitfire. I'm so thrilled Peggy is running properly that I shout "Tally Ho!" over and over as I ride past.

In a state of suspended tension, we take the old Canterbury road. The

Bantam is pulling beautifully, running smoothly without a trace of any troublesome pinking or kangarooing. Acceleration is sharp and hills are easily conquered in 3rd or 4th gear. After about 10 miles, I stop to let the engine cool, praying that this time there'll be no deterioration in performance when I set off again. Twenty minutes later I kick her over and head back towards Folkestone. She sounds and feels as good, if not better, than she ever has, so it is with exhilaration that I blast along the Alkham Valley road, roaring past Tony and Jan's house at over 50mph. On the far side of the village I stop, make a U-turn and return to my friends feeling overjoyed. The ride is back on!

There are only three pre-booked elements on the ride to Egypt... crossing the Channel, the ferry to Tunisia and my scheduled entry into Libya. My *Eurotunnel* reservation has proved incredibly easy and cheap to amend online but I'm very concerned about the ferry crossing from Genoa in Northern Italy to Tunisia, which sails on Wednesday at 4pm. Based on my experience of getting from Manchester to Folkestone, it seems inconceivable that I could ride Peggy 800 plus miles to Genoa in under four days. However, should I reschedule, the next available sailing is three days later, a delay which could prove problematic at the Libyan border. Looking at my map, I hum and ha about Peggy's capabilities. I get as far as calling the Italian ferry office to change my booking but hang up before anyone answers and decide to give it a go, reasoning that if I encounter more problems in France, I can always attempt changing our sailing at the last minute. Online, I decide to plump for tomorrow's earliest *Eurotunnel* crossing which leaves at 8am.

Tony and Jan have tickets to see comedian, Jimmy Carr, this evening so we arrange to meet up after the show for a drink. On impulse, I decide to look up a couple of old friends. Catching a lift into Folkestone, I walk the short distance to the home of Ray and Lynn Fielding whom I haven't seen in almost ten years. Ray was my first ever flatmate after leaving home and we shared a flat for almost six months before he moved out and Tony moved in. He was 33 and I was 20, but I clearly remember thinking of him as an old man and recollect saying to him, "How does it feel to be so old?". As we reminisce, we laugh hard, as he's about to celebrate his 60th birthday. I restrain from asking the question a second time.

Lynn is now retired and the couple's living area has been completely taken over by her new hobby. Lining the walls are several bookshelves, filing cabinets, workstations and a computer terminal all dedicated to the art of 3D greeting card making. Her work is meticulous and the finished product both striking and beautiful. There are hundreds of different designs including some stylishly themed on vintage racing motorcycles which she proudly shows me.

"I wish you'd been with me in East Grinstead yesterday, Lynn," I tell her. "You could have made a perfect gasket and saved me a lot of stress."

Later, I head back into Folkestone town centre then along the Old High Street, a quaint, narrow lane that steeply winds downhill to the seafront. The harbour once flourished as a small fishing port and a busy ferry terminal, complete with passenger railway access. Indeed, the *Venice Simplon Orient Express*, on its way from London to Venice, regularly rolled into the harbour, across its breakwater and onto waiting boats. Sadly, the last ferry sailed in 2000, the fishing industry is seriously in decline and the once thriving traditional English seaside resort, with its amusement arcades and rollercoaster rides, is now flattened to wasteland. It makes a gloomy sight, especially under the sodium glow of street lights.

Walking uphill from the shore brings me to the town's famous cliff top promenade,*The Leas*. Accompanied by the cries of seagulls, I stroll along its wide walkway to the *Leas Cliff Hall* concert venue and enter the small glass-walled foyer and café which is the only part of the building that protrudes above ground. The café's closed but I can hear muffled echoes of hearty laughter drifting up a wide stairwell from the subterranean auditorium, indicating that the Jimmy Carr show is still in progress. A solitary commissionaire is on duty so I ask if it's okay to sit and wait for my friends.

"Be my guest," he replies with a smile and a broad sweep of his hand.

He's a smartly dressed man, probably in his sixties, and is engrossed in his newspaper crossword. I spark up a conversation, explaining that I once lived in Folkestone and how fond I am of the place.

"I'm a migrant too," he tells me. "originally from the East End of London. I used to come to Folkestone on seaside holidays as a boy in the 1950s and early 60s. It was brilliant, so much going on."

I'm keen to hear more of his memories, especially having just walked past the sad remnant of the town's former entertainment centre, the Rotunda.

"We'd arrive on special day trip trains, the *seaside trains* we called them. Anyway, I had such good times on those holidays, I moved here in the 1970s. It was still popular then, but package holidays, cheap flights and all that have killed it off."

He does, however, have some hope for the future.

"There's been a lot of money put into the old part of the town, which looks really good now, and there's some great plans for redevelopment along the seafront, but we're told that work will only start after the recession ends."

On that note, I hear loud applause, immediately followed by the sound of doors crashing open. Quickly, I shake hands with the doorman as a wave of cheerful looking faces floods up the stairs.

"We've laughed so much," says Jan. "It hurts to smile."

We walk to a nearby pub for a drink then catch a taxi back to the Alkham Valley for a nightcap. Tony and I sit together on a settee chatting about times past until eventually the conversation drifts to this morning's work on Peggy. He shakes his head slowly while sipping his Bushmills and says with incredulity,

"I can't believe a small piece of oddly shaped brown paper has made all the difference between a machine that was unrideable and one that's running perfectly… it's just a bit of paper for heavens sake!"

Day 6, Folkestone to Berry Au Bac, France.
182 miles.

The rain is falling steadily when I rise at dawn, which makes loading the BSA an unpleasant task. Tony gets up at 6am to share a plunger of coffee and help push Peggy silently out of the garden. We say farewell at the roadside, which I find strangely upsetting... it's much less emotional when I quietly slip away on my own.

I arrive at the *Eurotunnel* check-in a few miles north of Folkestone in increasingly heavy rain. It's quite chilly, so I'm wearing just about all the spare clothes I've got underneath my waterproofs. The man shepherding the queues of cars signals me to stop, then does a double take at my bike.

"That's never a Bantam is it? Blimey... my first bike was a D10. It was forever breaking down!" As motorcycles are the last vehicles to be put onto the train, I have a longer wait than everyone else so take cover in an empty bus shelter. The attendant joins me, recounting stories of his old bike and the number of different ways it let him down... most encouraging! Nonetheless, he's tickled pink to see the old Beeza start first kick and wishes me luck as I remount and ride onto the train.

It's still teeming down as we disembark. I have to concentrate so hard on staying safe, peering through a veiled curtain of grey precipitation, that there's really no time to worry about how the bike's running. Thankfully, Sunday morning France is quiet and there's little traffic to contend with as I negotiate my way around Calais' slippery streets in search of petrol before heading out into the countryside.

The first of several road signs gives directions to war graves from the Battle of the Somme. I've read a few books about First World War trench warfare, with Remarque's *All Quiet On The Western Front* and Sebastian Faulks's *Birdsong* giving the most chilling descriptions. There were more than a million casualties on the Somme between July and November 1916, with 60,000 British troops injured or killed on just the first day of the offensive. Unprepared for this, I slow Peggy to a halt, lean forward onto my tankbag and give it some thought. It doesn't take me long. Although the cemeteries are only a few miles off my route, I can't help thinking that it would be somewhat ghoulish to go, and doubtless very distressing too. I ride on.

My lunch stop is a plain roadside cafe where I sit at a red formica-topped table, dripping waterproofs pulled off my chest and loosely tied around my waist. Rising to pay the bill, I guiltily notice that a puddle of no small proportions has formed around my feet and the seat is soaked, as is the adjoining chair on which I'd placed my helmet and gloves. Making my apologies, I leave. Outside, the rain has mercifully ceased so I take a few minutes to check Peggy over. The exhaust has worked loose at the head, which is easily remedied, but all else seems fine... remarkably.

Fuel range is roughly 120 miles from the Bantam's 7 litre tank. Although this is an improvement on the 105 miles per tank I averaged on the first attempt, it still means refuelling stops are never far away. By early afternoon I know I'm getting low and begin to search for a petrol station. This should be easy because at the press of a button my Garmin will quickly show me the nearest dozen. The first one it points me towards, an Esso garage, is shut. Similarly the next, an Elf. I waste more than half an hour diverting off my south easterly route, trekking round another three closed stations. It's not just the petrol stations that are closed for business, the village and town streets I ride along are all but deserted too. Fretting that I'll soon run out, I divert even further off route, riding into the large town of Arras. Finally, there's a Total station that's open. When I remove the petrol cap and peer into the tank, it's bone dry... I must have been running on fumes for the last couple of minutes!

Back on the road, with my spare 5 litre fuel can full to the brim, the sun comes out. Although perfectly straight, the highway rises and falls steeply, but Peggy's on song, climbing and descending faultlessly. It's such a good feeling to ride a healthy bike that, for at least half an hour, I merrily sing the Buddy Holly song, *Peggy Sue*, with extra emphasis on the Peggy bit.

Approaching my path from the west, I notice a large storm moving in. The towering cumulonimbus clouds are a menacing oily black colour, yet above and to the east, the blue spring skies are crystal clear. Riding hard, I aim to scuttle through before it hits. Just as it seems we'll miss it, a bend in the road turns ten degrees to the right, leading us inevitably towards its fringes. Instead of rain, I'm hit by a barrage of hailstones the size of marbles... not much fun with an open face helmet. There's no choice but to keep riding or we'll become entirely engulfed. The sharp ice crystals bounce high off the road, making vision and going conditions treacherous and it suddenly becomes so dark that I can only define oncoming cars by their full beam headlights. We take a real battering, the hailstones noisily striking Peggy's petrol tank, headlight and mudguards. My cheeks, nose and lips are pummelled and the sound is distractingly intense as it bounces off the top of my crash helmet. It's a struggle to stay focused as the icy blows continuously make me flinch and blink, resulting in an arduously long and very painful five minutes ride. When we finally get clear, I stop to catch my breath. Fishing a soggy tissue out of my pocket, I wipe the water from my face... it comes away stained red from two cuts inflicted by the hail.

Today's destination is the cathedral city of Reims. Feeling weary, I count down the remaining distance on a succession of signposts. With just 32km to run, I glance at the handlebars and notice that the BSM (Battery Status Monitor), a new addition to help me keep an eye on the charging system, is slowly flashing red. This is not good news as it signifies that the battery isn't charging properly. Leaning forward, I immediately turn off the headlight and look for somewhere to park up. A layby comes into view on the opposite side of the road, so I swing over and brake to a sharp stop. Praying that the problem is nothing worse than loose wiring, I work my way around the bike, checking all electrical connections. Everything seems to be in order, but I remove the terminals from the battery to give them a wipe before replacing them tightly. Kicking Peggy over, I'm instantly rewarded with a solid bright green colour on the monitor. Eureka... the battery's charging again!

To my dismay, a couple of kilometres on, the slow flashing red returns and no amount of wire fiddling by the side of the road seems to remedy it. Looking at my clock, I guess there must be under two hours of daylight left. How long Peggy can keep running with an uncharged battery is impossible to know, but I suspect that even without lights, the ignition coil will drain it in under a quarter of an hour. In a state of trepidation I set off again, urgently in need of accommodation before the engine cuts out.

Ten minutes later, some 20km short of Reims, I enter the village of Berry Au Bac and straightaway spot a large modern motel, the *Logis Des Nations*. With a wave of relief, I pull into its empty courtyard. I haven't reached Reims but at least I'm not stranded at the side of the road in fading light. The reception room is open but there doesn't appear to be anyone around. I loiter aimlessly for a few minutes, wondering how I'm supposed to check in, then see a British hire van pull up outside. The driver, a well-spoken Englishman, is obviously in a more alert state than I am. After saying hello, he reads a sign on the office wall, extracts a mobile phone from his jeans pocket and without hesitation dials a number. A few sentences of quick-fire French later, he tells me someone will be with us in ten minutes. I wander back outside to Peggy but feel too drained to tackle the charging problem right now. It'll have to wait until the morning.

As promised, a man soon arrives in an expensive looking Range Rover. After checking in my fellow traveller, (who's elegantly managed to jump the queue), he introduces himself to me as Sebastian, the manager, and shows me to a room. It's small but well furnished and reasonably priced to boot. I nod and agree to take it... as if I were in any position to refuse, then wheel Peggy round the building, chaining her up to a post next to my window.

Back at the reception, Sebastian is preparing to leave. In school-boy French I ask where the nearest restaurant is. His English is only marginally better than my French, but it's clear from his demeanor that I'm out of luck. The village's only eating place, just 200 metres along the road, is closed on Sundays. The nearest alternative is 6 kilometres away and I seriously doubt Peggy has enough juice left in her battery for a round trip. With a combination of hand gestures and Franglais, I explain my predicament, finishing by asking if there's a supermarket that is closer. This also draws a blank.

"No problem," says Sebastian. "I bring food from the restaurant. Please give me five euros." I can't believe my good fortune when even my request for the meal to be vegetarian produces a similarly phlegmatic response.

"It's OK, please wait."

Within half an hour he returns, producing a substantial wooden tray from the front seat of his car. I stare at the offering, amazed by its size as well as touched by his kindness in getting it for me. On the tray are a large plate with three salads, two chunks of deliciously pungent soft cheese, a long stick of French bread, a waffle-like dessert dripping in lemon and raspberry sauces and sprinkled with *Smarties*, a bottle of mineral water and a bottle of local beer. I'm almost lost for words and find myself shaking my host's hand for a very long time in sheer gratitude. He just smiles, no doubt recognising the look of appreciation on my face... and quite likely wishing I'd release his hand from its gripped captivity.

Bringing a chair out of the room into the relaxing twilight, I eat my feast beside Peggy. The label on the beer bottle indicates that it has been brewed using *methode champenoise*, which, considering I'm now in the Champagne region of France, seems pleasantly appropriate. As I melt deeper into my seat, I sip the refreshing and surprisingly potent brew. Once replete, I take a short walk around the village which, like everywhere I've passed through today, resembles a ghost town. All the houses are silent, their aged windows and doors covered by faded wooden shutters, The local shops and restaurant are so heavily boarded up, they appear as if they're permanently closed. Following a circular route, I come to a small civic hall that doubles as a library. Grandly engraved into the stone across the front of the building are three words: *Liberté, Fraternité, Egalité*. I don't need to be fluent in French to work out what these fine sentiments mean: freedom, brotherhood and equality. Wandering back to the motel I begin to muse on the way things sometimes work out. I'd felt glum and drained on arrival but after some human kindness, a good meal and a positive walk, I actually feel glad that I wound up in this sleepy little place.

Retiring early, I set my alarm for a dawn start tomorrow. With luck, the charging problem will be easily remedied and I'll be on my way again. If I can improve even slightly on today's pace, there's a definite chance I'll make that ferry.

Day 7, Reims to Dijon, France.
188 miles.

I'm up with the birds, groggily rechecking all Peggy's wiring and connections. An hour later, finding no obvious faults, I kick her over and am delighted to see the BSM turn from yellow to solid green. It's not apparent what I've done that's got the system charging again, but I'm nevertheless chuffed to be under way without further delay. Rather than bypassing Reims, I head for its centre as I've some happy memories of a visit there when younger. Despite the low clouds and damp atmosphere, from at least 10 kilometres away the magnificent *Notre-Dame de Reims* cathedral dominates the city skyline. By the time I reach it through a seemingly endless string of temporary traffic lights and streets closed for roadworks, the BSM is flashing red again. Agh!

Unable to bring myself to attend to the problem immediately, I park outside a café that doubles as a boutique champagne retailer, and order a double *espresso* at a pavement table. Staring at the 13th century cathedral, where the kings of France were once crowned, my mind begins to reminisce about the first time I saw it.

In 1986, working as a low paid auxiliary nurse, I spent a very colourful ten days hitchhiking around north western Europe on a shoestring summer holiday, which included an impromptu stop at Reims. An obliging car driver dropped me off in its centre, not far from the spot where I now sit sipping my coffee. Within moments, I ran into a bunch of six lighthearted young men, all school friends from Majorca, who were spending their summer holidays travelling on bargain Eurorail train tickets prior to starting university in the autumn. As they were carrying rucksacks and collectively studying a map, I approached them to ask if they happened to be heading for a campsite and if so, could I tag along. As it transpired, the group were travelling on an even tighter budget than me, sleeping under the stars in fields and parks as a matter of course.

They were terrifically hospitable and without hesitation, suggested I join them for the night, sleeping in the nearby central park. Once there, we placed our backpacks into a large pile and sat around in the warm evening sunshine, eating bread, cheese and tomatoes and swigging coarse red wine from their traditional leather bota bags. It was wonderful. After our meal, in what was obviously a regular nightly routine, two of the lads were assigned to look after the luggage whilst the rest had the chance to go off and explore. That night's bag guards encouraged me to leave my backpack with them and head off with the others, which, with intuitive trust, I did.

We wandered up a series of wide boulevards, heading for the cathedral which was gloriously illuminated for a tourist 'sound and light' show. Stopping at a café bar in the lee of the colourful spectacle, I was soon drawn into conversation by an engaging and highly sensual woman whom I judged to be a couple of years older than me. Her English was on a par with my basic French, but we somehow struck up so much of a rapport that my camping companions began to give me surreptitious winks and furtive thumbs ups. Flattered by her attention and with all the testosterone of a 22-year-old coursing through my veins, I readily agreed to accompany her when it was time to leave, hardly believing my luck.

We walked along empty streets, heading, I assumed, for her home. During the course of our conversation I'd not been able to establish her work, only that it had something to do with money. I'd surmised that she must be employed in a bank or possibly work as an accountant. Suddenly, to my utter dismay, we wound up at the doorstep of a rather disreputable looking hotel where I was sweetly asked for payment for her services. The nature of her employment finally dawned on me! I felt thoroughly gutted as I hastily backed away. Not only was the illusion of being desired by such a delightful and alluring woman shattered, I also felt terribly guilty that she'd wasted two hours of hard work on someone who had neither the finances nor the propensity to pay.

Back at the park, the lads were awake, lying in their sleeping bags and chatting. They too had been fooled by the young woman's appearance and demeanor and laughed mercilessly when I recounted my tale. Eventually, one by one, we had fallen asleep.

As I finish my coffee, the nostalgic trip back to my youth ends and I look over to the poor Bantam. Getting up, I push her to the edge of the cathedral, and, as misty rain begins to drift in, attempt to retackle the charging problem. My first guess is that the combined regulator-rectifier, which allows only a predetermined amount of voltage to go to the battery, has failed. I rummage in my saddlebags for a few minutes and eventually locate the spare. Replacing it under the saddle is a fiddly job and I feel quite sad at having to dissect the wiring I'd so painstakingly tidied up during the winter. That completed, I fire her up but the BSM persistently continues to flash red.

The only other possible cause that springs to mind is the alternator, which would be disappointing as I recently fitted a new one. I take my time carefully removing it then mount the spare in its place, which is the same one I'd used on the first ride when the original BSA unit failed. This, however, brings me up against a stumbling block... there's one extra wire on the spare stator and I don't know which two to twist together to make the right connection. I phone Derek, but he's not at home, so send his mobile a 'help' text message.

A couple approach. The man is obviously intrigued by the Bantam, peering closely at the inside of my alternator.

"Do you need any help?" he asks. He goes on to tell me he rides classic racing Hondas and is fascinated by all things motor sport. Indeed, that very morning he'd taken his wife, who at this point smiles indulgently, to see the defunct pit lanes at the famous Riems-Gueux circuit.

"Formula One races were held there until the mid '60s, and there used to be a Reims 12-hour endurance race too, which both Stirling Moss and Graham Hill won," he explains. "Motorcycle Grand Prix were raced there as well. Geoff Duke won in '53 in his first season on a Gilera. The pit lanes are great, you really should go. Walking along them is like stepping back in time, even the old advertising signs are still in place."

I'm fascinated, but can't really relax and enjoy the conversation as we're already half a day behind schedule and catching the ferry to Tunisia is beginning to seem more improbable by the minute. Unfortunately, the man can't help my wiring dilemma as electrics are not his forte. He wishes me *Bon voyage* just as my mobile beebs with a reply from Derek. It reads: 'Phoned around. We all think you can combine any 2 wires. Good luck.'

Taking pot luck, I join the connections up and start the bike again. Infuriatingly, there's still no change to the BSM's red light. As a last resort I phone Paul Goff in Buckinghamshire, England. Specialising in electrical components for classic bikes, Paul is one of the traders I frequently see at shows and he supplied the regulator-rectifiers, the new stator and a host of other small electrical components used on Peggy, including the BSM. At first he's rather bewildered by the problems I'm experiencing, but soon recovers.

"Of course, what you're not considering is that the BSM itself could be faulty."

That silences me. He continues,

"Kick it over and turn on your headlight. Rev the engine and watch the headlamp bulb. If it goes brighter when you rev and dims when you close the throttle, the battery is charging."

I do it while he's on the line.

"I'll be blowed, Paul," I tell him. "It's doing just what you said."

"Sorry mate," he confirms. "The BSM's had it."

I hang up feeling a measure of consolation at having identified the issue as non-threatening, though somewhat cheesed off at the amount of time I've spent chasing my tail.

The shenanigans with the electrics have eaten hours out of the day and by the time I've replaced the original stator, tidied everything up and repacked the bike, it's after half past two. I leave Reims in constant drizzle, which pretty much matches my mood. Clear of the city and on the open road again, with Peggy riding true despite the faulty warning gauge, I find some fortitude and reason that I'll simply have to ride long stretches to make up for lost time... thankful that my bum's at least on a pain-relieving gel pad!

I'm aided by a strong tail wind. It blows us up hills in top gear and at one point the sat nav shows Peggy's tipping 75, (kmph, not mph, but still fast for a heavily laden old 2-stroker). The BSM continues to flash slow red but the engine runs faultlessly, the lights are on and every time I check, the horn toots loudly. After 7pm I have the roads to myself. They're straight for as far as the eye can see, with huge dips which conjure up images of riding the never-ending tail of an enormous Loch Ness Monster. In the soft half-light, speeding alongside fields of rape seed which radiate an almost luminous yellow, I grin profusely, experiencing my first real sense of contentment since we began.

By the time we reach the outskirts of Dijon, the capital of the Burgundy region, it's after 9pm and almost dark. There's probably a Youth Hostel in the city centre but I don't have the energy to go trailing around in search of it. At a large roundabout there are several signposts for business hotels. The Holiday Inn and Ramada are well outside my budget, but there's also a sign for a Formula One motel, which I've read is part of a cheap and cheerful French chain. Without pausing for thought, I follow the signs through several junctions and roundabouts, pulling up at the entrance within 10 minutes. Today's mileage reads 188 miles, which is more than yesterday, and in the circumstances, a minor miracle.

I lug my gear in relays into the motel. A young woman who checks in behind me is given the room opposite mine. She stops fiddling with the electronic keypad that locks her door and stares first at the mound of bags I've amassed in the hallway, then at my spare tyre. Feigning an incredulous tone she asks.

"Is the rest of your motorcycle folded away inside your bags?"

Everything in the motel is made from plastic. The beds have plastic frames and the floors are a strange kind of easy-clean linoleum. Food is available in plastic bags from a vending machine with a handy microwave adjacent. Most things appear to be automated, like self-cleaning showers and toilets that flush themselves once you exit. Pay-as-you-go Wi Fi is obviously obtainable... it's all very 21st century.

I'm too wiped to go out, content to shower, eat a bag of my camping food, phone home then turn in. Drifting off to sleep, I can't help but think that tomorrow I'm going to have to coax Peggy into covering more distance than she's ever gone in one day and only hope that it doesn't break her again.

Day 8, Dijon to Briançon, France.
260 miles.

In the morning light, Peggy looks grimy and uncared for as I remove her cover, the result of many hours riding in heavy rain since landing in France. I take a certain pride in keeping my motorcycles clean but learnt a valuable lesson when riding to India. I had the Enfield jet washed four times in the course of that journey and on my return to the UK discovered that the pressurised water had driven sand and grit into the gearbox, brakes and wheel bearings. It's quite a perverse feeling, for me at least, to feel virtuous about keeping the Bantam mucky.

On the road good and early, I'm grateful again to be assisted by a powerful tail wind which relentlessly steamrolls us ahead. So potent is its force that I cruise at 70kmph with the throttle closed and the engine ticking over. After some time it dawns on me that this is dangerous for a 2-stroke engine as it's being starved of vital lubrication delivered with the petrol. I open the throttle on the straights, pushing an impressive if somewhat reckless 76kmph, comforted in the knowledge that I'm helping prevent an engine seizure. There are mile after mile of vineyards heading towards Lyon which this early in the spring look windswept and lifeless. Soon I see signs for the E60 east to Besançon which runs across my current route at right angles. This is the road that we took towards Switzerland last September! Pulling up at the intersection with it, I sigh, remembering with mixed feelings what an intense struggle that whole journey was. Rather unwanted, the French proverb, *plus ça change, plus c'est la même chose - the more things change, the more they stay the same,* finds its way into my mind. I forcibly dismiss it and ride straight ahead.

Indeed, my confidence in the Bantam is steadily growing. Although she pops a bit on overrun and the exhaust occasionally works loose at the head (the increasing noise level acts as a surefire warning sign), she steadfastly eats away the miles, hour after hour. I'm also impressed by the patience of French car and truck drivers. In my mirrors I see them sitting a prudent distance behind us, waiting for an opportunity to safely overtake. Where possible, I ease in towards the verge and wave the vehicles through. Almost without exception, the drivers either wave, toot their horns or flash their indicators in appreciation. This consistent level of consideration and courtesy is something I find sadly lacking in the UK. I can't help wondering if the French are more familiar with and thus tolerant of slow motorcyclists and moped riders... or maybe it's simply that they're generally more laid back.

Peeling off a long stretch of dual carriageway, I stop for lunch at a large, faceless service station. Around the entrance of the cafeteria are roughly 20 Harley Davidsons with their riders and several female pillion passengers milling around them, doubtless, like me, trying to stretch their legs and simultaneously get warm. Each has a huge embroidered Harley Davidson patch which completely dominates the back of their jacket, proclaiming membership of a Belgian *Harley Owners Group*. Many appear quite flamboyant with colourful headscarves, tassles on their jacket sleeves and interesting (in a couple of cases garishly colourful) hair and beard weaves. The bikes are a mixture of styles too, some in normal road trim while others are chopped or heavily customised. Parking Peggy on her sidestand next to the long line of American metal, I head straight for the café. Through the window, as I munch predictably on croissants and cheese, I see practically the whole group gather around the little Beeza, inspecting, pointing, and in a few cases laughing at the amount of luggage she's carrying. A couple look towards me. They smile and wave and I reciprocate. As I prepare to leave, discreetly sweeping an excessive amount of pastry crumbs from the tabletop into a napkin, I hear one of the group loudly calling the others to mount up. There's a terrific rumble as all the bikes depart at once, heading north on what, I assume from the conspicuous absence of luggage, will be a very long ride back to Belgium. No wonder they laughed at the sight of Peggy!

We arrive at Grenoble a couple of hours later. I'm thrilled by our progress... already 170 miles covered and it's only 3.30pm. Following the route suggested by my sat nav, I take the main road straight through the heart of the city. It's traffic light hell! There are scores of the blessed things, often with only 20 or 30 metres between them and I can see row upon row of forbidding red and enticing green lights stretching away into the distance. Their apparent lack of synchronisation is infuriating and no matter how hard I try, find it impossible to race through two consecutive sets at green. The constant stop-start crawl between junctions and pedestrian crossings takes an age and Peggy gets seriously hot, so much so that her gears become clunky and just about unselectable. Neutral is impossible to find. It takes nearly an hour and a half to escape and accelerate unhindered on the open road again.

Traffic thins then all but disappears as we begin to climb into the Alps. I've changed my mind several times already about which route I'll take to Genoa. My original idea was to make a long dogleg, heading straight for Marseilles then following the coastline through Cannes and Nice. Part of the appeal was that I've never visited the Côte d'Azur, but just as importantly, this direction would avoid me hauling Peggy over slow and taxing Alpine passes. Losing so much time in the UK forced my first rethink. For a while I'd toyed with taking the E25, an incredible trans-European highway that runs from the Hook of Holland right to Genoa (and then across the islands of Corsica and Sardinia before terminating in Palermo, Sicily). The biggest benefit would be that it goes through the Mont Blanc Tunnel which would save an awful lot of time and effort climbing over the Alps. Somewhere around Dijon I came to my senses. The Mont Blanc Tunnel would be a real timesaver but it's accessed on both sides by busy, fast motorways which I know would be dangerous on slow old Peggy. The route I finally settle on, the D1091 to Briançon then on to Turin in Italy via Susa, is often part of the Tour de France circuit and was originally used by the Roman armies of Pompey and Julius Caesar to conquer Gaul. It's even thought that Hannibal may have marched his war elephants this way in 218BC. To be in such prestigious company surely makes it worth taking.

It's 7.30pm before I reach 1,000 metres. Stopping to let Peggy cool, I eat a muesli bar and check the map. Italy is tantalisingly close, approximately 50 kilometres due east. I set off briskly but as the ascent steepens, have to resort to a lowly 20mph in 2nd gear. I smile… the new piston and rings must be thoroughly bedded in by now.

The sun has well and truly set as I reach the unfortunately named village of La Grave. It could be worse... on my map I've spotted a village 50 miles due south of Grenoble called 'Die'. La Grave at first appears deserted, with the wooden houses and a couple of small hotels that line the main road shuttered and dark. I approach the only sign of life, a local walking his dog, and ask how far it is to the summit. He tells me Col du Lautaret is just over 2,000 metres high and approximately 10 kilometres east. We're only at 1,500 metres yet it's bitter cold. Since arriving in France, I've worn every stitch of clothing I have, including two pairs of socks, my waterproof suit and rubber over-mitts. Shivering, I get going without further delay.

The rocky and barren surroundings immediately give way to an exquisite alpine vista. In the blue moonlight, an awesome spectacle of snow crested mountains, forested valleys and dramatic rocky escarpments opens up to our right. The road's verges are an oily white colour with dirty caked snow still unmelted from the winter. There are clusters of stones and rocks scattered across the road from small landslides and, apart from the familiar *put put put* of Peggy's engine, it is silent. Only one car has passed me in the last hour and that was a sturdy 4x4. I ask myself out loud what on earth I'm doing up here on my own at this time of night, close to freezing, on, of all things, an old Bantam. But I know the answer is innately within me and despite being intensely focused on the job in hand, find myself laughing cheerily, my heart full of joy at doing what I love.

A 500 metre climb doesn't sound much but Peggy rapidly loses power. I've read that as oxygen thins with altitude, so the main jet in the carburettor needs to be made smaller, rebalancing the air fuel mixture. My main jet is suitable for use up to 3,000 feet and approaching the summit of the pass I'm at almost 7,000 feet. To change the jetting would take at least 20 minutes, and in the sub zero air temperature and imminent pitch darkness, is not a viable option. I halt, dig a screwdriver out of my tankbag and tweak the carburettor air screw to weaken the mixture. The results are not what I expect. The engine struggles to start. I rev hard but can't keep it running... it cuts out. I return the air screw to its original position and, revving furiously, lurch forward. A couple of tight hairpin bends reduce us to a first gear crawl and to get round them and continue the ascent, I rev even harder, slipping the clutch mercilessly to keep the engine running. Without warning, an unlit hotel appears out of the gloom by the roadside and a sign indicates we've made the summit. I don't even pause to savour the moment, desperately keen to lose some height and restore normal running conditions. Peggy, nevertheless, gets a couple of well deserved pats on the fuel tank.

The road has several long straights interspersed with occasional tight bends. We scoot downhill, my sat nav altimeter winding down like the depth gauge of a submarine in an emergency dive. It takes less than twenty minutes to descend to 1,200 metres and the quiet resort village of Briançon. With help from a lone walker, I locate the railway station and pull up behind the Hotel de Paris. The accommodation is fairly basic but reasonably priced. Within 15 minutes I've lugged everything up to my room and covered Peggy for the night.

Returning to the reception with my passport to fill in the registration form, I seize the opportunity of quizzing the young receptionist about my route to the Italian border.

"There are two routes I can take," I tell her, Garmin in hand. "One goes south east in a fairly direct route to Genoa. The other is a more major but less direct route, heading north east then onto Turin. Which will be the best?"

She rummages in a drawer and produces a huge topographical map, which she unfolds then refolds to find the area I'll be travelling through.

"Look," she says. "There are three very high passes on the south east route but only one on the way to Turin, Col de Montgenèvre at 1,850 metres."

Another 600 metre climb in the morning is not good news, but at least I know the challenge that lies ahead and can prepare accordingly. Just as importantly, I haven't plumped for the shorter route proposed by my sat nav... with three passes to cross I'm certain there would have been no chance of reaching Genoa in time. Topographical maps are added to my mental checklist for future journeys.

I walk to a Chinese restaurant, seemingly the only place still open. Sitting at a quiet corner table there's time to reflect on the day. We've covered 260 miles and, apart from the torturous last few hundred metres climb to the Col du Lautaret, it's been trouble free... who would have believed it? I've certainly had my doubts, riding with my left hand permanently locked onto the clutch lever in anticipation of imminent seizure ever since leaving Kingswinford on day two of the ride. Now, as at the start of the journey, I really feel that getting to Egypt is possible. Back at the hotel I set both my alarms for 6 hours time, determined not to be beaten on the last day of the charge across Europe.

Day 9, Briançon to Genoa, Italy.
182 miles.

The beeping alarms of my cellphone and watch erupt into life simultaneously at 6am. I'm breakfasted, the bike loaded and off by 7.15am. Most unexpectedly, an almost impenetrable curtain of rain is lashing down.

Once under way, it's hard to see very far ahead even though I'm climbing slowly in only first and second gears. My face is protected by an elasticated skiing muff plus a pair of Mk9 Halcyon flying goggles. They usually cope well in the wet, but riding into such intense rain and at these altitudes, both my spectacles and goggles constantly mist. The deluge is so dense that it's impossible to guess what's more than 20 feet ahead but I'm conscious, all the time, of the hard rocky face of the mountain to my right and the scary plummet to oblivion beyond the barrier on my left.

We plod on. At 1,500 metres the stinging on my face lessens as the precipitation eases. Any relief is short lived... almost in slow motion, my brain works out that it's snowing! Using my left hand as a constant windscreen wiper for my goggles, we continue up the mountain. At 1,600 metres the snow starts to lie on the road. By 1,700 metres, its surface is completely white. Apprehensive but unshakably determined to reach the pass, I ride as close to the rockface as possible.

At 1,800 metres, it's virtual whiteout. I have to ride with my goggles up and glasses tightly held between my pursed lips. Snow is already a good two or three inches deep on the road. This close to the summit I reason it would be just as tricky to turn around and descend, so keep going, desperately trying to keep my grip on the handlebars relaxed and my pace steady. The sky is still dark but the weak light of dawn is supplemented by an ethereal pale radiance created by the thickening snow. We've been on the road for nearly 30 minutes and haven't seen a vehicle heading in either direction. Even the comforting sound of Peggy's exhaust is muffled by the blanket of giant snowflakes that surrounds us, heightening my intense feeling of isolation.

It's amazing that my skinny tyres can grip at all. I keep my revs as constant as possible and gently ease my way onto the Col de Montgenèvre, the mountain pass. It's completely deserted. With the snow a good four inches deep, the road and a small roundabout are only just discernible by the outline of large stones that mark its edges. It is much windier here, the snow turning into a blizzard across the summit. I pick my way gingerly on the top flat stretch then mercifully begin to descend. Ahead I see a tunnel, shelter from the storm.

'No one will believe this', I think... even I can't believe I'm riding in these conditions. It's totally nuts! In normal circumstances, I wouldn't attempt it in a car, let alone on a 58 year old lightweight 2-stroker. In an instant, I decide to stop to take a photograph.

I lightly touch the brakes. Peggy goes sideways underneath me as both wheels lose traction. It's so sudden and swift that I hardly feel it happen. I'm left standing in the road but fall over in a sort of delayed synchronicity as soon as I try to move. I could have only been doing 10mph in a straight line so the fall, although unexpected, was quite gentle and somewhat farcical. It's a real struggle to stand the bike up as my feet keep slipping from underneath me and I'm blinded by the snow hitting my eyes. Breathing heavily from stress as much as exertion, I eventually get her righted but on this steep, slippery downhill slope can't manage to park her on either centre or sidestands. I give up trying, somehow get a leg over the saddle without falling over again and slither downhill to the sanctuary of the tunnel using both my feet as stabilisers.

Under the orange lights of the tunnel I park up and inspect the Bantam. Damage seems minimal as the saddlebags on the back of the bike have absorbed the bulk of the impact without harm. The bars that hold my luggage at the front are badly bent on one side, but I manage to lever them back far enough with my boot to give enough clearance for my left foot to comfortably operate the footbrake. Thankfully, she starts first kick. Reasoning that I must lose altitude fast to get out of the snow and stand any chance of catching my ferry, I'm soon under way again. Emerging from the shelter of the tunnel, I tentatively continue, my feet acting like skis. It's preposterous... I'll be in the Sahara in two days time!

Five minutes later I meet a bright yellow and red snow plough, its revolving safety lights creating eerie patterns in the billowing snow. I daren't try to brake again and will certainly not ride against the barrier which is now on my right... even through the whopping snowflakes that veil my vision beyond a few feet, I can tell there's an awfully long drop right next to it. Exceptional circumstances, I think, as I steer to the wrong side of the road and in a somewhat wobbly fashion hold my ground in the face of the oncoming plough. The driver quickly grasps what I'm doing and steers to my right, trundling past me on its way to the top. I continue to descend on the left of the road, using the lane it has cleared, my boots still hovering an inch above the icy tarmac in case of another slip. At 1,500 metres precisely, as though by the flick of a switch, the snow vanishes and rain starts again.

.... It doesn't stop! It takes another hour to get clear of the mountains. On the plains, I head for Turin then continue east towards Asti, the Piedmont town famous for its *Spumante* sparkling wine, and Alessandria. The rain pummels me relentlessly and for long stretches my view ahead is grey and misty. At times it's so heavy that it bounces high off the road, which is itself awash, and cars that overtake me throw up such dense plumes of water that my vision is completely obscured. I repeatedly hit sharp potholes and manhole covers that are hidden by water. Over and over I tell myself to take care, to be cautious and anticipate the actions of others... when I can see them. In Alessandria city centre I ride through great pools, with dirty sewer enriched water washing over my feet on the footpegs. Cars, which unlike my motorcycle are unable to pick the best route, go through water higher than their door sills. Their spray and wake drench me. And still there's no let up from the heavens.

A lot of people have told me that a Bantam is simply too unreliable to take on a long journey. After my problems last year and on the first few days of this ride, I was just about ready to concede that they were right. Today I see the results of all the preparation that went into the bike. Despite some rough running caused by the volume of water being sucked in through the air filter, Peggy continues valiantly on, never once faltering.

The Garmin begins to show signs of water under its screen and malfunctions, repeatedly commanding me to plug it into a USB device. My overmitts start to leak and water that has travelled down the front of my wetsuit from the neck collects rather uncomfortably around my crotch. I even take a wrong turn due to the rain obscuring signs around roadworks, and have to travel two scary 5 kilometre stretches on the Autostrada just to get back to the same city roadworks and my correct turn.

It's 2pm when I finally clear Alessandria's outer limits. Genoa is 65 kilometres south and there are two hours to reach the ferry. The road starts to climb. This is completely unexpected… another mountain range! I stop and consult my map. The Ligurian Apennines appear to be more like a series of rambling high hills than the icy peaks I've recently crossed, but it's a setback nonetheless. Blinded by rain, I press on. Traffic is agonisingly slow around hillside towns and the roads treacherous. 2.50pm, 29 kilometres to go. I begin to descend on lanes resembling fast flowing streams, hitting Genoa's outskirts at 3.20pm with 17 kilometres remaining. At long last the deluge abates and in the distance I can even see patches of blue sky. I follow signs for the city centre and harbour, but take the wrong turn for the port. Instead of reaching the seafront, I motor past it on a high overpass, looking down at a colourful line of ferries and cruise ships tantalisingly moored at the docks. To my left and ahead is a view of grand old buildings stacked up steep hillsides and in the distance a stretch of the city's famed old walls. After 4 stressful kilometres I take the first exit, do an illegal U-turn and track back. 3.50pm, 3 kilometres left. I enter the port and am waved straight through to the queue for the Grandi Navi MS Splendid, a colossal ferry, at 3.57pm.

Without pause for thought, I grab my tank bag and hightail it to the ticket office. Despite the warnings on my reservation that all check-in and immigration formalities must be complete by 4pm, there are still quite a few people milling around at various stages of the departure process. There's no queue at the ticket window or immigration and within 10 minutes I have my boarding pass and customs clearance to leave Italy. Walking back to the Bantam in a trance, I strip off my waterproofs and jacket then sit near Peggy on a curbstone, my sodden clothes steaming in the warm afternoon sun.

I look across at row upon row of vehicles heading for North Africa. There are Land Rovers and Landcruisers heavily modified for the desert, complete with industrial grade roofracks carrying complete sets of spare tyres, sand ladders and army surplus jerry cans full of extra fuel and water. A couple of RVs tow trailers packed with dirt bikes, the name of an adventure tour company plastered all over them. More fascinating are the beat up, ludicrously overladen jalopies, mostly converted minibuses and pick up trucks, used by transcontinental traders and entrepreneurs to export a veritable medley of goods. Without exception they are so hideously overweight that the rear wheels have just about disappeared into their arches. I definitely don't want to get stuck behind them in the Tunisian customs hall! There are a few glossy BMW and KTM adventure motorcycles in the line too, their sophistication, engineering finesse and imposing size making Peggy appear like a wreck.

The sense of excitement in the air infuses me. All of a sudden the tension of our race from Folkestone vanishes... we've made it! My face erupts into a huge smile and I'm engulfed by a feeling of great joy which ameliorates the discomfort of my stiff muscles and aching stomach, reminders that I've ridden all day with only two brief stops for petrol. My Scottish parents sometimes call me 'Last Minute Jock' as I often cut things a bit fine, but I've really surpassed myself on this one.

Walking over to Peggy, I pat her affectionately on the tank and quietly, so no-one thinks I've lost my marbles, thank her. Within minutes the lines of vehicles begin to board. To my immense pride, Peggy starts with the lightest prod of her kickstarter and I glowingly steer her up the loading ramp onto the ferry. Aided by a couple of other motorcyclists, I secure her to several anchor points with a spagetti-like swathe of oily old ratchet straps then carry everything up to my cabin in relays.

After a shower and some lighthearted negotiations with my three Tunisian room mates over who gets the bottom bunks, I head for a deck top café. The ship is well out of the port and heading south through the Lingurian Sea as I make my way through a bowl of pasta. Transfixed, I watch the Italian news on a giant TV screen. First it shows dramatic footage of floods, with cars wading through roads that resemble large ponds, cancelled railway services as a result of washed-out tracks and a series of traffic accidents caused by the treacherous conditions. Then come images from the Alpine passes - blizzards, snowploughs and abandoned cars. I'm riveted... it's the story of our day! I end the evening with a glass of cheap red wine with which I quietly toast Peggy, valiant conquerer of storms.

Day 10, Tunis, Tunisia.
12 miles.

I sleep for ten solid hours, woken only by my roommates' ablutions inside the small corner cupboard which houses a shower, toilet and sink. Spending a few minutes lying in my bunk, I plan some maintenance for Peggy in Tunis, then head out to a decktop café for breakfast. We passed Corsica during the night and are now tracking parallel to Sardinia across the intensely dark blue sea. The crystal clear sky is punctuated by two white fluffy clouds that drift over the grassy hills of the nearby island and in pleasurable contrast to the last few days, I sit back and relax deeply into my seat.

In the main reception area a screen shows a map of our route, informing passengers about speed (in knots and kilometres per hour), distance covered and time left to run. It's fascinating. So far we've covered nearly half the 853km distance at an average speed of 38kmph. I ponder on the time it would probably take Peggy to ride this far and guess at three days. Obviously, consistency of speed makes all the difference, there being no need to stop for the toilet, sleep, tightening exhaust header pipes and certainly no Grenoble-like traffic light system.

As the ship clears the southern tip of Sardinia, the swell in the Mediterranean becomes far bigger and I begin to feel a little green around the gills. "Look at the horizon," I mutter to myself, and decide to take some photos of the rapidly disappearing island. Back in the cabin searching for my camera, I spend a few minutes with the friendly Tunisian man, Kefla, to whom I relinquished my bottom bunk last night due to his arthritic knees. He speaks only a little English and French and my Arabic vocabulary spans roughly fifteen words, but nevertheless we communicate quite effectively. He's intrigued by all my motorcycling gear and asks where I'm going. I list the countries.... Tunisia, Libya, Egypt, Jordan, Syria, Turkey etc. He blows his cheeks out making a puffing sound then asks if I'm travelling on my own.

"Yes," I reply, keeping my words as simple as possible. "But it's okay. Arab men are good men."

He nods, then says, "You treat Arab man with respect, he treat you like a brother." I agree, as this has always been my experience. "But you treat Arab man not good, and... phhiiit!" The sound he makes, a sharp, truncated exhalation between pursed lips is accompanied by a dismissive, chopping swing of his rigid hand, making clear the consequences of disrespect. Very edifying. I smile and nod my understanding, then we warmly shake hands.

The ship's crew is largely made up of young Filipinos led by a smaller number of Italian officers. As I head towards a midship restaurant for lunch, a smartly dressed Italian seaman stops and addresses me in heavily stilted English.

"You have BSA Bantam?"

"Yes, that's me," I cheerfully reply

"I have BSA 441 Victor," he tells me. I know that's a fast motorcross bike from the 1960s but have never seen one.

"I buy in England and ride to my home in Milano," he adds.

"Excellent, " I say, shaking his hand.

"I want to ask you," he continues, "how your two stroke moto ride in Africa. It's too hot, no?"

Now that's the 64 million dollar question! I shrug my shoulders and raise the palms of my hands upwards as we laugh together.

In the afternoon I wander towards my favourite place onboard, the stern deck, which is accessed via the defunct swimming pool area in which are placed twenty or so tables. Each one is crowded with Tunisian men drinking *espresso*, smoking and loudly engaging in debate and banter. The noise of their impassioned Arabic conversations rings around the outside of the ship, creating an exotic buzz. I meet a Swiss couple, Thomas and Marion. They're on a two week vacation from work and have ridden their bike from Switzerland to Genoa virtually non-stop on motorways in order to maximise their time exploring Tunisia. Over a cup of coffee, we study a guidebook and come to the same conclusion about a hotel that seems a good bet as it's close to the old city and has a courtyard large enough to park our bikes. We agree to ride there together.

My anticipation and excitement builds when I see a hazy hint of the Tunisian shoreline... Africa! It seems to take an age for the crew to turn the ship around and reverse into Halq al Wad port, finally docking at 4.30pm. Along with the handful of other bikers that are onboard, I free my motorcycle from its moorings, load her up and wait to be released. Once off the ship, I ride into line next to Thomas and Marion, who are on a huge and well travelled *BMW R1200GS Adventure* complete with large *Zega* alloy panniers and a host of other *Touratech* accessories.

Tunisian immigration is well organised and Peggy is only given a cursory glance. Far more time is spent filling in forms and registering my GPS with the police than on checking the motorcycle. However, to my delight the words *BSA Bantam moto* are now immortalised in my passport next to the entry visa. Excellent!

We exit the disembarkation compound around 6pm. The sun dips low in the sky, casting long golden shadows across the road and the air is clean and hot, although thankfully not stifling. Mixed with the salty smell of the sea is another sweeter, less familiar aroma.

"Africa!" I say to Peggy loudly, vigorously slapping her tank as we follow the huge BMW. "You're in Africa, Peggs. Can you believe it?"

We take turns to lead the way on the long causeway that heads towards the city centre. Once there, we're halted by a traffic policeman at a roundabout. I shout to Thomas,

"I was worried you'd blow your engine up trying to keep apace with me."

He laughs, "I was revving real hard trying to keep up with the Bantam, but you were just too fast!"

We quickly find the Grand Hotel De France, a charming establishment on a side street close to the medina. As promised in the guidebook, it has faded colonial splendour aplenty. After we secure two rooms for the night, Thomas rides his BMW up a step and through the hotel foyer to a large ante-room where it will spend the night. I go a little further along the street and mount the pavement via a conveniently broken kerb. Cutting my engine, I push the little Bantam over the step and quietly through the reception, aware that asphyxiating blue smoke would not be appreciated by either staff or guests.

My room has old wooden beds covered in crisp white cotton sheets and blankets, a large ornate wash basin with an ancient mirror above it and an archaic porcelain bidet. There's an old fireplace and even an antique coat stand, which I use to dry my washing. The floor is completely covered in worn but colourful tiles laid in a complex geometric pattern. Best of all is the tall window. It's protected by heavy wooden shutters that, when opened. reveal a tiny balcony overlooking a small inner courtyard with trees and planters. Not bad for about 20 euros a night.

I meet up later with Thomas and Marion and head out to explore the medina. Within five minutes we stand underneath the imposing Bab El Bhar gate, an enormous arch left stranded when its adjoining fortified walls were flattened. We plunge into the narrow alleyways of the medina and are immediately surrounded by the tightly packed, brightly lit shops and vibrant stalls of a souk. The atmosphere is alive with boisterous cries from traders,

"Hey, you want new shoes/bag/carpets/postcards...?"

It seems that a great deal of the items for sale are crafts and souvenirs for tourists. Because the three of us appear to be the only foreigners left at this time of night, we get plenty of attention and offers from the shopkeepers. As we delve deeper into the maze of back alleys and covered walkways, many of the shops are closed or closing, their shutters rattling down around us as street sweepers move in and start their work. The old city, now a *UNESCO World Heritage Site*, is home to a long list of palaces, mausoleums, monuments and mosques, along with a multitude of old houses. Pleasingly, our unpremeditated route brings us to the Al-Zaytuna mosque, a beautiful structure of ancient columns and old stone walls that dates back to 732AD. The mosque is home to one of the oldest universities in Islam and through an open gate we see a group of worshippers sitting at prayer.

After a budget dinner of spicy couscous in a small restaurant alive with the chatter of local men, we enter a dark and atmospheric tea house. The night ends splendidly with a glass of *thé à la menthe*, a traditional black tea with fresh mint leaves. Not long after, I drift off to sleep feeling wonderfully unwound and full of anticipation for tomorrow's ride.

Day 11, Tunis to Sousse, Tunisia.
86 miles.

Thomas and Marion are fed, packed and ready to depart by the time I surface. They drink a second round of coffee while I eat breakfast, then, after swapping addresses and offering encouraging words about Peggy's chances of success, they push their hulk of a motorcycle through the reception area and onto the street. They're heading south to a yet undecided destination.

Today is Jacques's eighth birthday. I desperately want to phone him on *Skype* (the cheap computer based video/phone service) before he goes out for the day but there seems to be a dearth of internet café s in Tunis. It takes more than half an hour, including two wild goose chases, to locate one, thanks in the end to a kind traffic policeman who leads me to its unsignposted entrance. Access is via a dusty alleyway, with the room squirrelled away on the third floor of what resembles a derelict office building. I'm quite hot and stressed by the time I get myself seated, a state of mind that's not helped by the failure of three consecutive webcams. The excitement in Jacques's distant voice turns to frustration and disappointment each time I call out,

"Can you see me this time?... No I can't see you either."

Finally, we manage to distinguish each other's faces via a fourth computer, but sod's law prevails. A slow connection speed results in the picture continually freezing. Jacques misses me and is very upset that I'm not there to share his birthday. He runs away from the computer screen and doesn't return. Switching off the frustratingly useless webcam, I talk, pictureless, with Jane. She's furious about the hurt my absence is causing Jacques and in no uncertain terms gives me a protracted and thorough bollocking. Eventually, after a partial reconciliation in which I tell her how much I love her and Jacques, we hang up.

I'm about to switch off the computer when I notice a *Yahoo* news screen reporting yesterday's British general election which resulted in a hung parliament. Out of curiosity I click a video clip interview of Conservative party leader, David Cameron, but can't bear to listen to his rhetoric and within moments pull off my headphones, tossing them onto the desk. His voice continues to boom at maximum volume from unnoticed speakers placed either side of the computer. I hurriedly close the video clip, then glance around. There are at least 20 other people squeezed into the room, a couple of whom are looking at me. As if to confirm something that my brain has already begun to deduce, I click the *Skype* test button. A shrill ring tone followed by,

"Hello, welcome to *Skype* call testing service..." issues loudly forth.

"Oh god," I whimper, realising that the entire and intensely personal conversation, including Jane's colourful language and the proclamation of my love, has been broadcast full blast to the entire internet café. With all the dignity I can muster, I gather my possessions, pay and exit post-haste.

Tunis is a seductive city. Under shady trees I drink an *espresso* at a pavement cafe on the main thoroughfare, Avenue Habib Bourguiba, then meander along several back streets in search of my hotel. Lined with crumbling colonial architecture and aged wrought iron work, the bustling lanes are alive with the smells of olive and fish shops. I pause for a moment to take in the hubbub of a vividly colourful flower market. Tunisians seem very relaxed and, atypical for the centre of a capital city, have time to stop, chat, and in my case, give further directions... I'd completely lost my bearings charging from pillar to post in my search for an internet café.

On the dot of midday I check out of my room and spend a couple of hours doing all the bike maintenance I'd planned on the ferry, including comprehensively straightening the bent luggage bars. To say the Bantam has been ridden hard all the way from Calais, I'm really pleased by how little she seems to have suffered. I then repack my bags, with waterproofs, overmitts and all warm clothing consigned to the bottom... fingers crossed.

We set off at 2pm. Once off the main boulevards, the city's narrow streets are jammed with traffic, mostly held up by pedestrians that use the roads as an extension of the pavement. It takes roughly 45 minutes to clear the capital and hit a good clear stretch of tarmac, but when I try to accelerate freely in 3rd and 4th gear, Peggy responds lamely. The engine feels woolly, as if the choke were partly open. Reasoning that it may be running too rich for the warmer North African climate, I stop, take the top off the carburettor and in under 2 minutes, return the needle jet to its middle groove, the original factory setting. There's an instant improvement. I might just be getting the hang of this Bantam malarkey, methinks. Oh, how we should never temp fate.

National Highway 1 travels in a south easterly direction. It's mostly single carriageway and very popular with large, lumbering trucks. Unfortunately, they all seem able to go just one or two kmph faster than us and being constantly overtaken makes for a white knuckle ride of thundering wheels and stinking hot, buffeting air currents. Once ahead, they often swing back over to our side of the road too rapidly, catch the verge and shower dust, sand and stones over us. Perilous in a completely different way are young Tunisian moped riders. Astride battered and patched-together machines, mostly French Motobécanes or Peugeots with tiny 30cc 2-stroke engines, they unpredictably weave from side to side paying scant attention to other motorists. I give a wide berth to these clapped out, buzzing wrecks as I overtake them, cautious of the loose parts which not only rattle threateningly but in some cases are actually hanging off. Unbelievably, on several occasions they instantly respond to us by trying to race with Peggy. I can see them in my mirrors, wild looks on their faces as they painfully rev their engines almost to the point of destruction. Although distracting, it's in good spirit... the goal nothing more than the chance to pull alongside and give a smile or a wave.

I stop for fuel at a busy petrol station popular with these moped daredevils... there are at least 10 in the queue to buy small quantities of a red liquid I presume to be ready-mixed fuel and oil. I decide that it's better to continue mixing my own with the oil I'm carrying, but take a few minutes to further indulge in moped-watching. Pedalling furiously to get them going, their cavalier riders launch themselves onto the busy road seemingly without a care in the world.

Tearing myself away from the spectacle of several near misses, I set about buying petrol. There are no signs with fuel octane ratings and I can't make myself understood by the men who try to assist me. Several attempts at finger-writing 95, 97 and 98 on the dusty sides of the pumps followed by questioning shrugs produces nothing but incomprehension and, ultimately, giggles from the attendants. In the end, I opt for *Super Sans Plomb*, which I hope means super (high octane) unleaded (without *plomb*), then rejoin the highway.

Less than 3 miles later, Peggy begins to make a chattering noise. I stop and try tightening the exhaust, but it doesn't resolve. The hotter the engine gets, the worse the noise and vibration become. Rather worried, I have to stop for twenty minutes to let it cool. Reasoning that the new petrol has to be at fault, I retard the ignition a fraction on the points backplate in the hope this will reduce the pinking. There's some improvement... the knocking is still bad but takes longer to begin from a cool start and doesn't feel as terminal as before. I stop and move the points backplate again. It's now just about as retarded as I dare make it which produces another marginal improvement but I'm far from being out of the woods as the engine still sounds distinctly poorly. The words of John P. Mitchell, who rode a 1928 Norton from Algeria to Tunisia in the late 1930s, come to mind. Needing petrol immediately upon disembarkation from a steamer ship in Algiers, he wrote, 'I filled up with the world's worst petrol. What an anvil chorus I had later!'

Over 2 hours are wasted in my attempts to cure the fault so, with heavy rain clouds fast approaching from the sea and nightfall less than an hour away, I make a dash for Sousse, the search for higher octane petrol my top priority for tomorrow morning. Once in the city centre, we limp round the grand exterior of the medina, its ancient sand coloured, rampart-topped stone walls magnificent in the amber post sunset glow. Along a cramped one-way street not far from the main square I find a small hotel. Sitting on a stool outside a nearby shop, a man leaps to his feet and bounces over to me as I dismount.

"Beautiful moto!" he exclaims. "What is it?" BSA draws a blank, so I try again in my best pigeon English,

"Bee... ess.... aah." It's to no avail, but undeterred, he's keen for more information.

"500cc?" he asks. It's hard to stop myself laughing as I give him the low down.

The man, Mohammed, turns out to be a valuable ally, first keeping an eye on Peggy when I go into the hotel to enquire about room rates, then cheerfully leading me a few blocks north to an underground car park where I can safely store the bike. His questions continue en route,

"How many cylinders, three or four?" I pat him on the back as I warmly tell him there's just one... my newfound friend obviously thinks that all foreigners' motorcycles must be big and powerful.

The garage's wizened night watchman, Hassan, promises to take good care of the Bantam. He's also delighted to meet someone travelling from the UK.

"My son lives in London. He's married to an English woman. Only last year I visited them," he tells me with pride.

"Tottenham Hotspur!" he chants as an afterthought.

I'm then invited for a coffee in the morning with promises to show me photographs of his family. Despite my concerns about Peggy, I readily agree, infected by his hospitality and general bonhomie.

The amphitheatre of El Djem.

Day 12, Sousse to El Djem, Tunisia.
57 miles.

Breakfast is served in the empty hotel dining room which is little more than an extension of the reception area. The surly, ruddy-faced night manager doubles up as waiter.

"*Bon appetite*," he mutters as he plonks a plate in front of me. On it is a single small french bread stick with unappealing dollops of some runny jam and butter. He returns carrying a cup of insipid instant coffee. Feeling like Oliver Twist requesting more gruel, I turn round a few moments later to ask if there is anything else and catch him groping the bottom of the (much younger) lady who's 'prepared' my breakfast. I hold his gaze as he glares uncomfortably at me. Unable to vent his annoyance on a guest, he marches to the open door, waves a fist and shouts abuse at three hapless schoolboys who happen to be walking past. Basil Fawlty once again coming to mind, I leave without further ado, shaking my head at the innate comedy of life.

Coffee with Hassan is an altogether different experience. He generously sends out for *espresso*, which tastes as potent as rocket fuel... maybe I should try Peggy on some! After a pleasant time viewing family snaps on his mobile phone, we walk over to the far side of the garage where, to my surprise, he draws back a large sliding door revealing the Sousse seafront. With the sound of waves gently lapping against the seawall, I uncover the Bantam and set about checking the ignition timing. I have a small plunger-type tool that screws into the spark plug hole and indicates when the engine reaches top dead centre (TDC). There are lines etched down the sides of the plunger every millimeter, allowing the timing of the ignition spark to be set to a defined point before the piston reaches the top of its stroke. That's the theory. In practice, the marks on the tool are so thick and closely spaced that it's impossible to accurately discern when the plunger is sitting 1.5mm below the point of TDC. When the piston is in its optimal position, the contact breaker points should just be breaking open, an occurrence which is checked and adjusted by placing a single self-rolling cigarette paper between them! Despite the seriousness of my engine's malady, I can't help but smile at the basic nature of the tools.

When this task is complete to an accuracy factor of 'there or thereabouts', I spend some more time checking the spark plug, the carburettor and all ignition wiring connections. Everything seems fine. Now for the cursed petrol. Saying farewell to Hassan, I load up hastily at my hotel then hightail it to the nearest fuel station. On this occasion it's a Shell, which I hope will guarantee a tankful of high octane. The forecourt manager quickly grasps that I want my petrol tank drained. This is efficiently achieved by one of the attendants using an empty 5 litre oil can. Again, there's a distinct absence of information on the pumps. I repeatedly ask for *Super* and after another round of confusion about *essence sans plomb* and *essence ordinaire*, not to mention *hulle*, which it gradually dawns on me is oil, the forecourt manager points to an innocuous looking pump and tells me it is *quatre-vingt-dix-huit* (98 octane)... hurrah! I fill the tank to the brim and set off, keen to make serious progress. I'm expected at the Libyan border, some 350 miles away, in less than 48 hours.

The first 10 kilometres are heaven, with Peggy gliding along the empty roads quite delightfully. Passing through a village, I slow for a roundabout. Without warning and in the space of just a couple of hundred metres, the awful engine vibrations and knocking sounds return with a vengeance. So much for 98 Super... it feels like I'm running on diesel! I spy a small motorcycle repair business by the roadside. Better still, the mechanic is diligently working away at a 2-stroke scooter engine as I pull up. Looking up from his labours, he gives Peggy a measured appraisal, stretches, then walks out through the open doorway asking me a question in Arabic.

"*Parlez vous Anglais... Français?*" receives a rapid shake of his head. I kick Peggy over so that he can hear the engine, but he just looks at me blankly. Digging a notebook out of my tank bag, I draw sketches of a barrel, piston, and representations of TDC. With increasing frenzy, I attempt to describe pre-ignition by making all kinds of clicking noises to accompany my sketches. I even try to draw a proper timing disc in the hope that he will have one to perfectly set the ignition timing. Rather pleased with my artwork, which makes perfect sense to me, I become growingly bewildered by the dumbfounded expression on his face. I point at my pictures again and again, trying to describe my needs. Eventually, he shakes his head and walks back towards his shop door where he turns and stands, in apparent bemusement, leaving me to ride off feeling mightily frustrated by the encounter.

It's not long before it becomes impossible to ride further without fear of blowing up the engine, which is now sizzling. The surrounding countryside is stony and dusty but scraggy olive trees somehow manage to grow in rows at regular intervals. Selecting one close to the roadside, I steer Peggy under its welcoming shadow and spend the next hour doing further checks. This includes the coil and HT lead and changing the condenser. Kicking the little Beeza over, I jump as she a backfires loudly and immediately cuts out. Groaning to myself, I have the feeling I'm making matters worse rather than better so decide to put the old condenser back in. The engine starts first kick and runs perfectly. Drawing a big X on the faulty condenser with a marker pen, I toss it into my tank bag, glad to be carrying enough spares for it not to be an issue.

The fix is superficial. My afternoon comprises riding 10 kilometres then letting Peggy cool for twenty minutes before doing another 10 kilometre stretch. She runs beautifully for the first five minutes of each stint then the painful shuddering resumes. On the third or fourth occasion, I'm forced stop in the middle of nowhere. The surrounding fields are devoid of life and there's no shelter from the direct heat of the afternoon sun. Sitting on a mound of baked earth and stones, I see the slow moving silhouette of a man emerge from the heat haze. As he approaches, it becomes apparent that he's very old and walks with a stick. He's dressed in battered leather sandals, slate grey baggy pants and a long cocoa brown suit jacket. Resplendent on the top of his head is a threadbare, carmine fez. Without a word, he perches next to me. I smile at his weather-beaten face and proffer my hand, which he shakes strongly. This simple gesture seems to open the floodgates because he starts talking in sing song Arabic, delivering a monologue of foreign sounds that's beguiling to listen to. I nod and smile for at least ten minutes before he finally comes to a halt.

His left hand is missing its first two fingers. I point and ask what happened. Smiling broadly, he launches into another lengthy tale. While he recounts his story, a shepherd drives a flock of lanky, long-eared sheep down the middle of the road, enthusiastically assisted by an energetic sheepdog. The heat, the problems with my motorcycle and my worries of not reaching the Libyan border in time evaporate as I absorb the wonder of this moment... it is, for me, the kind of experience that makes travel magical. As I prepare to depart, the man stands, gently puts his arms around my shoulders and hugs me, planting a kiss on my cheek in the process. My western upbringing makes it difficult to reciprocate, but I know it's a gesture of brotherhood and ride on feeling moved by the deeply human encounter.

Rippling into view like a mirage on the horizon appears the giant 3rd Century Roman amphitheatre of El Djem. I see it from miles away, the hot distance creating an impression that it's floating above the middle of the highway. At a fork in the road on the outskirts of the small, modern town that surrounds it, is another fuel station, an Agip. Doubtful if it will make any difference, I drain my tank once again and fill up with the only petrol on offer, *essence sans plomb*, then ride the last few kilometres into El Djem. The amphitheatre, the third largest in the Roman Empire, is in remarkable shape considering the number of battles that have raged around it over the centuries. Parking in a courtyard at its entrance I wander around the enormous outer walls, staring up at tiers of grand colonnades. Unfortunately, I've arrived just a few minutes after closing time and feel somewhat thwarted at missing the chance to act out the gladiator in me.

Instead, I take a rake of photos of Peggy against the imposing backdrop then head for the open road. Within a few minutes she starts to struggle again, rattling and buzzing noisily. There's little choice but to turn around and head back to the town to find accommodation. As I ride, it occurs to me that I've possibly been barking up the wrong tree for the last couple of days, my powers of mechanical deduction being as limited as they are. What if the Tunisian petrol is good, I think, and it's simply that the Bantam needs a decoke? An excessive build up of carbon could cause pinking. A phone call to Andy Berry for advice is imperative.

To my dismay, the town's only hotel is boarded up but following the advice of a policeman, I slowly backtrack 5 kilometres to a barely occupied resort hotel, the Ksar el Jem, that I'd ridden past earlier without noticing. Set in expansive grounds down a dirt lane of considerable length, I see a large number of cabins spread out amongst well irrigated gardens, giving it the feel of a desert oasis. The pool may be empty and the furnishings worn and tired, but it's a bed for the night and a shady place to work on the Bantam tomorrow morning.

After dinner, I try using my laptop with the hotel's Wi-Fi but fail to get a connection. Thirty fruitless minutes later, I swap my computer for riding gear, kick Peggy over and set off for El Djem along pitch dark roads. Dreading a seizure at night, it's a relief to eventually find the town's small internet café. I phone Andy and update him with my tale of woe.

"It's most likely bad petrol," he says. "Engines designed to run on high-octane leaded, like your 14/4 motor, really suffer with rubbish fuel. But a decoke's a must. If there's a build up of carbon on the crown of the piston it'll soon glow with heat causing the fuel to ignite too early." I'm nervous about disturbing the cylinder base gasket and the consequences of that but Andy tells me to take my time and put the engine in gear while I'm scraping the carbon off.

"Keep me posted," he says as we end the call.

Next I email *Temehu*, explaining the problems and the likelihood that I'll be a day or two late at the border. Finally, I phone Jane, who despite being concerned about Peggy's running problems, roars with laughter about our very public exchange in the Tunis internet cafe. Our shared mirth lightens my mood considerably. It's nearly 10pm when I finish and the café manager, Mustafa, who's kept a watchful eye on Peggy for me, parks himself on an adjoining chair for a chat. He tells me he has two degrees in marketing from Tunis university, one of which is in tourism marketing. He's a bright, positive and friendly young man, frustrated by the lack of opportunities in his country, especially after the events of September 11 and the kidnapping of two Austrian tourists, later released, in February 2008, both of which had a big impact on tourist numbers. We talk about more jolly things, including his love of football, seemingly the *lingua-franca* of young Tunisian men. My passion for cricket draws a complete blank.

In the cool evening air, I ride back to the hotel, guiding Peggy along a walkway lined with red flowering hibiscus highlighted by ground-level lighting, the atmosphere heavy with the intoxicating scent of honeysuckle. Securing her in a small courtyard in front of my room door, I reflect on the day. The meagre distance I've covered and the challenge that faces me if I can't resolve the engine's problems are easily outweighed by the encounters I've had with Tunisians, who have once again wowed me with their ready friendship and hospitality.

Day 13, El Djem to Mahares, Tunisia.
66 miles.

Sometimes, when I remember to get my mindset right, I imagine that I can expand time. It's a belief thing, which of course the slightest doubt will scupper, but when it works, I can get an inordinate amount done in what I would normally regard as an impossibly short amount of time. Leaping from bed with crackling energy and my time-expansion mode set to go, I launch into Peggy's decoke with the conviction that I'll have it done in an hour and be on the road within two, allowing the gasket sealant plenty of time to cure.

Five minutes and the saddle, petrol tank and cylinder head are off, revealing a jet black crusty layer of rock-hard carbon on the crown of the piston and top of the combustion chamber. I set to work with the best tool I can find for the task. It's the rounded end of my home-made spark plug spanner handle, a present from Derek prior to departing for India. Chipping away at the caked coke, while trying to avoid scoring the alloy surface it's keyed onto, is tough going. My fingernails, already grubby, soon resemble a coal miner's... in my past life as a swanky clothing shop owner in New Zealand they would have horrified me. Now they just go with the territory. Once the worst is removed, some fine wet and dry paper smoothes off the remaining rough surfaces. With this filthy job done, I feel quite optimistic that there'll be an improvement in performance, aware that the particularly thick deposits around the spark plug could quite possibly have been the source of all Peggy's problems.

Everything is rebuilt in 55 minutes. Cheered by the outcome and the success of my time warp, I grab breakfast then briskly load the little Bantam. By 10.15am we're on the road that bypasses El Djem and prepared for a very long day in the saddle. Within a few kilometres, it becomes obvious that my efforts have been in vain. Disheartened, I stop and sit beside the rippling heat of the bike engine, head in hands.

We're soon back to the routine of 10 kilometre spurts followed by 20 minute cooling breaks. To add insult to injury, a gusting headwind makes the engine's struggle feel even more difficult, although it's counterbalanced by reducing the amount of time I have to wait for its temperature to drop from melting hot to touchable.

The first major habitation we come to is the city of Sfax. A road sign tells me it's twinned with Grenoble in France, which is one of those pleasant sort of coincidences. However, a quick check in the *Lonely Planet Tunisia* guidebook reveals that it is a large industrial centre, specialising in processing phosphates and iron ore. I'd love to simply swing onto the ring road and give it a wide berth, but am swayed into giving my petrol fetish one last indulgence.

Traffic in Sfax is treacherous, the worst since Tunis. Cars join the main road from the right without pausing. The same happens at roundabouts where no one seems to give way, forcibly edging into the line of cars and trucks that are already circulating. This coerces me into either swerving around them, or more sensibly, letting them through. Red traffic lights serve only as a method to make vehicles slow down, not stop. Unfailingly, the leading driver glances left and right, then just goes for it, irrespective of what he sees! The next in line follows immediately with a knock-on effect on all behind. I have to concentrate so hard, glaring into the sun, that my head starts to ache. Rather than battling on, I turn around, ease my way past a truck that has just shed most of its load of oranges across the road, and head back towards the bypass.

Renegotiating a roundabout, I catch sight of three fuel stations in a line just off to the right. Perfect. I try each in turn and to my surprise, find that every attendant speaks enough English to discuss my obsession with low-grade fuel and the poor running of the bike. They assure me there's no such thing as 98 Octane in Tunisia… the '*Super Sans Plomb*' I've been buying is nothing but standard 95 Unleaded. Rather than feeling angry at the misguidance I've received over the past few days, I'm relieved to at least be able to give up my search and make the most of what is available. In one final try, I choose to drain the small amount of petrol that remains in my tank and fill up with Total, reasoning that another well-known brand has to be worth a go. It's not a good decision, indeed, it's the most awful fuel yet, making the poor Beeza engine pink and judder horribly almost instantly. Within 5 kilometers I'm forced to pull up.

Time passes slowly as I stop and start, pushing the engine to the limit before pulling in the clutch, switching off the ignition and letting her coast as far as possible to a standstill. A couple of times I have to rest up without shade. My watch, which includes a thermometer function, tells me it's 33 degrees… thank goodness there's a wind and I have plenty of water. Food, however is a problem and my diminishing supply of muesli bars is being guzzled at an alarming rate. Eventually, I reach the coastal highway, route P1, which tracks in a south easterly direction along the grey-looking Gulf of Gabes. In the distance, I notice an enormous tree overhanging my side of the road. It's the first shade I've spotted in the last hour. As I get closer, a small fruit stand comes into view that's been set up by a local farmer who routinely risks his life stepping out into the road in an attempt to flag down passing motorists.

I need no such persuasion, eager for both sustenance and respite from the afternoon sun. The makeshift stand is lined with cartons of fruit so gloriously colourful that, highlighted against the surrounding brown hues of baked soil and sand, they resemble an artist's palate. For a couple of dinars, I feast on apricots, strawberries, a large peach and three nectarines. With juice running down my fingers and chin, I contentedly sit beside Peggy, watching the pained and rather dangerous efforts of my host to drum up more custom.

Our next stint is less than 5 kilometers. Spotting another substantial tree, this time on the coast side of the highway, we pull over. Re-energised by the last stop, I tinker with the ignition timing and points as the sharp breeze cools the cylinder to a reasonable level. After 20 minutes, I turn on the ignition and kick the bike over. The engine revs momentarily, backfires then dies. The same happens on each repeated and increasingly anxious stab of the kickstarter. I pause, turn off the fuel in case I've flooded the carburettor and try again. This time there's not even a short burst of life. The engine simply won't start.

John Lennon said, "Life's what happens while you are busy making other plans." This was certainly the case during the months of build up to the journey as I ran from pillar to post trying to make a living, get ready for the ride and have time with my family. Three hours by the roadside and nothing's going to plan again! However this time, among these unfamiliar surroundings and totally engrossed in my motorcycle, I feel completely and wonderfully in the moment. It's paradoxically splendid. The rest of the world, with its everyday struggles, has shrunk to insignificance.

I change the points. I check the timing. Three condensers are given a go, all to no avail. In the end, with dust and sand swirling around me, I strip the carburettor, blowing down each and every orifice in its internal workings as mightily as possible. When it's reassembled, sealed back into place and primed, I get the same loud roar followed by the same backfire followed by... silence. Moving Peggy and all my bags and tools a few feet in order to keep us in the slowly moving shade of the descending sun, I sit on the gravel eating yet another muesli bar. The running battle of ants versus dung beetles is in full cry around me. Fascinated, I watch an ant gamely carrying a defeated beetle at least four times its size on its back, an incredible feat. There's a rumble and the ground trembles. Out of nowhere, a freight train trundles past at a snail's pace just a couple of metres beyond my tree. I hadn't even noticed the lines!

Intermittently, my work and cogitations are pleasantly interrupted by a succession of moped riders who stop to ask what I'm doing. Only a couple can speak any English and few hang about for more than a couple of minutes once they've established that I'm okay. Checking my watch, I realise it's already past 5pm and begin to wonder how we're going to get out of this one. There are no obvious villages or towns in sight and I don't fancy pushing Peggy for miles. I look around, assessing the surrounding countryside for a suitable place to camp out of sight from passing traffic. The dunes that separate the road from the sea, approximately one kilometre away, look a good bet, but that entails getting Peggy over the railway. Across the road looks an easier option, with a parched plantation of olive trees in the distance potentially offering good shelter if I can muster the energy to push the bike uphill across a bare and dusty field. Whichever, I'm sure there has to be a simple remedy to Peggy's problems, something so obvious that even a mechanical numpty like me can resolve it given a few more hours.

I decide to try changing the coil and HT lead. As I gather my tools, a scooter comes to a halt... well, I guess it was once a scooter. The whole front half of the bike is missing, revealing a battered, warped skeleton and tangle of colored wires that somehow connect to the exposed rear-wheel mounted engine. The rider beams at me with open friendliness and asks in French if I need help.

"*Merci*," I reply. "*Un hôtel, s'il vous plaît*," I add as a joke.

"*Sans problème, à deux kilomètres*," he says pointing down the road. I look at him in dumbfounded silence. It's completely empty as far as the eye can see.

Gathering my wits, I point to Peggy.

"*Kaput*," I say.

"*Mécano, mon ami*," he smiles, producing a mobile phone from his tracksuit pants pocket and dialling a number. He conducts a quick conversation, hangs up and says, "*dix minutes*," while gently waving his hands downwards to suggest I relax and wait.

Gathering my tools together, I start repacking, in complete trust of my new ally who perches on his scooter puffing a cigarette. Just as I finish, a large white Peugeot van slows, does a U-turn and stops beside us. The driver's door flies open and a highly energetic man dressed in colourful Enduro riding clothes and an orange and black KTM baseball cap hops down and springs over the short distance to us.

"Ahhh... a BSA!" he exclaims. "Where are you going? Can I take you to the hotel?" Without pausing for breath he introduces himself as Moncef, a Tunisian biker who lived in Amsterdam for many years, which is where he learned to speak English with a charming Dutch accent that makes a lot of 'sssch' sounds. Flinging open the van's two rear doors, he reveals a tall KTM off-road bike with exceedingly long front suspension, then tells me he regularly competes in the Tunisia Cup Enduro event. He'd just returned home from an afternoon practicing on the nearby dunes when he received the phone call about us. Peggy is quickly loaded into the van next to his machine and after the briefest of drives - the hotel is just over the horizon on the outskirts of the unseen town of Mahares - wheeled out into the courtyard of a smart hotel with surprisingly reasonable room rates. I fumble in my pocket for some money to pay Moncef for his time and fuel. He firmly shakes his head, saying in English with his Dutch accent,

"We are bikers. Sssholidarity!"

Grimy, tired and half cooked by too many hours in the sun, I nevertheless believe I'll get to the root of the starting problem tomorrow... it has to be something really basic. Refreshed by a power shower, I check out the hotel restaurant. A waiter, dapper in a penguin suit, solemnly hands me a menu. One glance at the price of the main courses and I beat a hasty retreat. The cheapest meal is more than the cost of my room for the night! Exiting the hotel compound, where the gatekeeper promises to watch over Peggy, I head for the town centre, wandering along the Mahares cornice. Like the whole experience of arriving here, the cornice is a very pleasant surprise with several sculptures lining the seafront, including a striking, tall statue of an iron man that resembles a cross between the Statue of Liberty and Wicker Man. I find a relaxed café with a menu that includes freshly squeezed orange juice and pizza from a wood-fired oven. While I wait at an outside table, a motorbike zooms past, swings around then comes to a screaming halt next to me. Of course, it's Moncef, this time piloting a Suzuki Hiyabusa rocket ship, the only big and fast motorcycle I've seen since arriving in Tunisia. We talk bikes for a while before I walk back to the hotel and enjoy a cold beer on my balcony. At this point I have absolutely no idea what tomorrow will bring, but like that ant, I'm determined to get Peggy to our destination whatever is required.

Spanners out... again.

Day 14, Mahares to Matmata, Tunisia.
90 miles.

Like every other morning in Tunisia thus far, once breakfast's finished I launch straight into spannering. The front courtyard of the hotel offers no real shade from a dazzling sun that's already high in the sky. The best I can do is seek partial refuge by squeezing Peggy tightly against a potted palm, which creates a hazy leaf pattern along the top of her mudguards, tank and seat.

The first hour is spent re-stripping and cleaning the carburettor. Reasoning that just one grain of sand could block a jet or one of the feed passages, I purse my lips against various parts of its body and blow 'til I'm red in the face and dizzy. I also have a go at the points back plate, which needs to isolate the points from earthing. The ignition timing gets plenty of attention too. After each alteration or change I try the engine, but nothing works. The hotel's owner, who's half Tunisian and half Belgian, comes out to have a chat. I explain how miserable Peggy's performance became as soon as I filled up with Tunisian fuel.

"This is typical," he says. "Even modern new cars can have problems. The benzine quality here is very bad." It's edifying, but doesn't resolve my immediate problem.

A few minutes after he retires to the air-conditioned luxury of his office, a smart waiter brings me a large bottle of chilled mineral water dripping with condensation, a frosted glass filled with ice and a slice of lime. All are beautifully presented with a white linen napkin on a silver tray, compliments of the management. Wedging myself under a different potted palm from Peggy's, I swipe sticky flies off my arms and forehead for at least the hundredth time and glug back the icy water whilst considering the next move... it'll soon be time to check out of my room. Then I remember that last night, just before Moncef liberated me from the roadside, I had been about to change the HT lead. It takes only a moment to locate a spare length conveniently placed in the first saddlebag I open, screw the existing plug cap onto it and without any real hope, kick the bike over. Peggy vigorously fires up and immediately settles into a constant tickover. All these hours of toil and it only needed a few minutes to change a faulty HT cable... I don't know whether to laugh or cry.

I shower, load up and motor to last night's cafe to grab a quick lunch, then fill up with the local Star brand of fuel. It's 1.15pm before we depart Mahares. Heading out into busy traffic, I slow for a roundabout at the edge of town. Peggy coughs, cuts out then refuses to start. In sheer exasperation, I look to the heavens and shout out, "What now?" I put her on her stand and am about to start the long list of checks thoroughly engrained into my consciousness when it dawns on me I didn't turn the petrol tap back on after filling up. It's the easiest fix of the journey to date!

The further south we travel, the dustier the air becomes. On both sides of the road lie dry, baked plains. Some areas are planted with olives trees but increasingly there is scrubby desert. A strong tailwind helps push me along, 'though the shock waves of air that rock us from oncoming northbound trucks are seriously frightening. I have to desperately hang onto Peggy's handlebars to struggle through the turbulence. With an element of insult to injury, these blasts also carry a shower of sand and my face gets a thorough exfoliation.

Our first run is 14 kilometres but this rapidly declines to 10 then 6 kilometre bursts before the vibrations start. It's like riding a cement mixer. Initially I continue to fiddle with the ignition timing to see if further retardations make any difference but eventually give up, simply relaxing beside Peggy and absorbing the surroundings whilst she cools.

Each village we pass through seems to specialise in one form of commerce or another, however, those that deal in sheep are not easy for me to stomach. At these places there are many roadside traders, each with a headless, half skinned carcass hanging from a pole. Tethered around them are the forlorn living, miserably awaiting their turn for the chop. A thickly smoking barbeque sizzles alongside each establishment filling the air with the strong smell of mutton kebabs. I ride through as quickly as possible, no matter how hot and rough running the Bantam's engine might be.

The highlight of the afternoon is undoubtably my meeting with four teenagers who are hitchhiking in the opposite direction. They cross the road to where I sit, taking what shade there is under the large steel sign that heralds our arrival at another village. One produces a large bag of apricots which he passes around. Our attempts at communication are stilted, but the sweet fruit produces a few minutes of shared happiness. The lads smile and laugh with their eyes, as thrilled by the whole thing as I am. Suddenly, the tallest jumps up at the sight of an approaching truck and successfully flags it down. Within seconds, after four informal handshakes, our brief but uplifting encounter is over.

Last night I was forced to telephone the agency that have arranged my Libyan visa to confirm that I'll be a couple of days late reaching the border. All my hopes are pinned on reaching Libya, as everyone tells me the fuel there is high octane... in fact they've even said that leaded petrol may still be available.

We reach the city of Gabes around 5.30pm and make yet another fuel stop. By now I'm resigned to accept whatever's in the pumps, but ask nonetheless for 'super benzine'. The well-spoken attendant indicates that they only have regular unleaded.

"But," he adds, "you can buy Libyan super by the roadside. It looks very green." At this point he disappears into a small workshop, where a mechanic labours underneath a battered car, and returns with a plastic water bottle half full of pea green liquid.

"Smell," he instructs, thrusting the open top under my nose. "This is smuggled Libyan petrol, so much better than here in Tunisia."

Although I pride myself on having become something of a gasoline aficionado, I can discern no difference in the aroma but earnestly nod in agreement all the same.

"Can I buy it, please?" I'm so desperate for any chance to make Peggy run normally that I have to stop myself from clasping my hands together and begging for it!

The attendant tells me the fuel belongs to his boss, who uses it in his personal car.

"Wait, I will ask him."

He walks across the forecourt to where two businessmen are deeply engrossed in a conversation. After gaining the attention of the older one, he avidly describes my request to purchase the petrol. The owner looks my way, waves, then nods his consent.

"There is no charge," say the attendant a few moments later. "The boss says it is a gift to you."

I gratefully pour it into my tank, then fill up my 5 litre fuel can with regular pump petrol which I'll use later. Finally, when the owner ends his conversation, I walk over and thank him profusely for his generosity, aware that he'll never be able to grasp just how much his litre of black-market benzine means to me.

It would be ideal to reach Medenine, some 80 kilometres south east, today but at this late stage it will now entail riding for several hours in the dark. Instead, after studying my map, I change plans and head in the direction of Matmata, only 40 kilometres due south. The village is famous for its Troglodyte pit homes and also for being used by George Lucas in the first Star Wars movie. Several scenes from *Monty Python's Life of Brian* were also shot in the locale.

My route follows an empty back road, the shorter but less travelled way. The surrounding countryside becomes stony barren desert, a couple of isolated houses the only signs of human settlement. After 9 kilometres, Peggy begins her all too familiar shake and rattle. We pull over... so much for the super benzine! Removing my helmet and gloves, I sit beside her, surprisingly content to do nothing except imbibe the changing colours of the sky as the sun accelerates towards the horizon. Bright orange becomes ruby red in just ten glorious minutes. The emptiness of the silent milieu is so utterly calming that I lose track of time and have to literally jolt myself back into action, spraying water from my Camelbak reservoir onto the engine to speed up its cooling.

I love the ride, despite Peggy's propensity for vibrating like a dumper truck after the first five minutes or so. The road, which gently rises and falls, is devoid of all other traffic as I motor along happily, a cooling breeze in my face and a purple glow on the western horizon. On the final approaches to Matmata the landscape, practically indiscernible in the beam of Peggy's headlight, changes dramatically. The gentle undulations transform into a steep, twisting ascent, reducing us to third then second gear as we press on round blind corners, me praying constantly that the plagued engine doesn't self-destruct. Now pitch black, it's a relief to finally round a tight right-hand bend and see our destination dimly lit up below. We descend to the souq of Matmata, a collection of open fronted shops where small clusters of men sit, talking and drinking under pale single light bulbs. There's no street lighting and the shop fronts are all powered, it would seem, by a lone generator which drones somewhere nearby.

The array of hotels on offer, all advertised by a jumbled assortment of hand painted signs on each street corner, is mind-boggling. After a couple of false starts, we pull up outside one with a locked courtyard. The hotel offers half board accommodation only.

"Be quick please," instructs the manager, after ten steely minutes skillfully negotiating a room rate with me. "The restaurant closes very soon."

I sit down and wait at a table next to a large and deliciously cool looking swimming pool, which compared to my usual rough-it accommodation represents an incongruous opulence for me. Having showed up late and then requested vegetarian food, my expectations of the meal are low. Soon I'm presented with a large basket of crusty bread and a tasty salad. I wolf down every morsel, wipe my mouth on a napkin and make ready to leave the table. As I begin to stand, the waiter appears with three generously heaped full size dinner plates. It's my main course and appears to comprise a dollop of everything in the kitchen that isn't meat. Obliged to make an effort, not least to get my money's worth, I eat as much as I can cram in, plus dessert. Absolutely full to bursting, I'm barely able to walk to my room let alone contemplate a swim. Practicalities of the journey, however, require that I wash Peggy's air filters followed by my goggles, then put the sat nav on charge before I can finally crash out for the night.

Day 15, Matmata to Ben Gardane, Tunisia.
93 miles.

I decide to visit the *Star Wars* set. Cheesy, I know, but Jacques is massively into the films. He plays for hours at a time with *Star Wars* action figures and spacecraft. Recently, he also began to covet *Star Wars Lego*... not the new, readily available sets, but the rare and subsequently expensive items produced years ago. This he justifies by revealing that he's not just a boy, he's a collector! I convince myself the visit is for him.

Five subterranean homes have been joined together to form the Hotel Sidi Driss. One of these homes was extensively used as a set in the 1977 *Star Wars* movie. I descend a flight of stone steps into the hotel. It's a basic affair and at this early time of day no-one's around, including at the simple reception desk. An overhead sign leads me to the film set, parts of which are instantly recognisable like the entrance to the bar that Luke and Obi-Wan Kenobi visit when they first meet Hans Solo and Chewbacca. Up close, the space age pipes and weird fittings mounted onto the surrounding walls look very Heath Robinson, but step back a few paces and you can see how effective they are. It all feels quite surreal. I'd been reticent about even visiting Matmata, planning to give the tourist hot spot a wide berth. Now I'm surprisingly glad I didn't.

The silence is broken by voices, loud with anticipation, coming down the approach tunnel. Looking up I see a coach load of European tourists arrive. In under a minute at least 40 of them converge in the small, confined space. With great excitement, people pose eagerly for photos. I help out, two cameras around my neck as I snap pictures of French, then Swedish couples at the top of a flight of steps hewn out of the sides of the dwelling. Taking my turn, I climb to the top and grin like the Cheshire Cat... for Jacques, of course. As I emerge back to ground level, the coach is preparing to leave whilst simultaneously the next one pulls up disgorging another camera-laden, chattering crowd.

Wandering along the much quieter main street, I search for an internet cafe. In an area of empty land adjacent to a street corner sit four regal, cud chewing camels looking unselfconsciously impressive in their ornately embroidered saddles. Their drivers hunker in a small inward-facing circle, smoking and talking quietly. Passing them, I begin to cross the road, guessing they must be waiting for the arrival of a tour party because they pay me no attention whatsoever. As I reach the opposite pavement, a rusty and dented powder blue pick-up truck travels at speed towards me. I'm transfixed by the sight of its load. Unsecured by ropes, a donkey is planted squarely in the cargo bay, its long ears held strangely erect against the headwind and a look of unadulterated pleasure on its face. I laugh out loud, realising that its body language and expression remind me of dogs, including the cartoon variety, that poke their heads through open car windows, revelling in the sensation of rushing air and speed. As the truck blasts past, the donkey lets out an enormous and very long bray, which I interpret as a sound of sheer joy... brilliant!

It's the usual round of calls from the internet café. I tell Derek,

"I can hardly go five miles before it feels like she's about to self-destruct."

"Do you think you'll have to give up and ship her home?" he asks in a rather bleak tone.

"Never! If it came to that, I'd have to fix the bike and set off all over again. It'd be like a BSA version of *Groundhog Day*. No... making it to the Libyan border means that there's only one more country to cross to get to Egypt and by then it's got to be easier to go forward than to come back, whatever happens. You know Derek, I'll strap that blooming bike to my back and carry it over the border if I have to."

As I set off, the gods seem to be smiling on me for with my resolve spoken out loud, I experience some of the best motorcycling to date. The desert is formed around rocky escarpments, with soft-toned layers of sediment showing on some of the crumbling hillsides that border the road. Peggy's on song, accelerating sweetly uphill, then sweeping at speed around perfectly proportioned bends that allow us to lean well over, before descending onto long straight sections. The appalling engine racket seems to have vanished! Twisting the throttle open again, we race up a steep hill, just keeping enough revs to reach the summit without changing down. Blissful.

Ahead is a roundabout, a small cluster of palms at its edges. I slow, looking for a signpost but fail to find one, so choose the exit which seems to head in roughly the right direction. The road soon deteriorates, becoming potholed and gravelly. A couple of kilometres on we enter a small village, Techine. It proves to be a smaller version of Matmata, with several pit homes but none of the posh hotels or restaurants. Under a tree sit a group of local men playing dominoes on a creaky wooden table. As I come to a halt, so do their jovial conversations... they all but freeze and stare at me.

I point in the direction I'm heading,

"Medenine?"

The men laugh unanimously, some shaking their heads and pointing back in the direction I've come, signalling I should then take a right at the roundabout.

I turn back and take the suggested exit. The road ahead climbs steeply, then twists and twines around rocky hills. My sat nav shows 19 kilometres since we started this morning... a record. We descend at full speed, corner a tight bend, then start climbing again. Half way up the hill, without any warning, the motor begins to knock and shake.

We stop at the top and I look around at mile upon mile of stony yellow and red landscape, punctuated only by a few lone palm trees. It appears desolate and empty yet incredibly beautiful. Peggy's engine ripples with heat as I put a sunhat on my head, smooth the stony ground with my boot and sink down beside her. Surveying the surrounding hills, I remember *Monty Python* actor Michael Palin's visit to these parts when, in 2002, he made the BBC documentary, *Sahara*. In his book of the same name he mentions revisiting the scene of the *Life of Brian* crucifixion which was filmed in 1978: 'I find myself standing above the village of El Haddej, almost 23 years to the day since I hung on one of two dozen crosses, tapping my feet and singing *Always Look on the Bright Side of Life*.' As the crow flies I can only be a few miles from El Haddej. Looking at Peggy, and with absolute certainty that no-one can be within earshot, I burst into the song, singing the same chorus line over and over again at the top of my voice. Sardonic or not in my predicament, it's therapeutic.

Back into our regular stop start routine, we ride through several Berber villages, evident only by large signs on their outskirts saying 'Berber Village. Welcome'. The road begins to climb very high and it takes ten boneshaking minutes to reach the summit as Peggy struggles deplorably in the heat. At the top is a small café precariously clinging to the edge of a giant cliff. I bounce along its track and park up to admire the view, which is utterly breathtaking. There's one other vehicle, a car driven by a young European man. He seems to be accompanied by an elderly Tunisian in Arab dress, who is, to all intents and purposes, walking around in ever decreasing circles.

The man, Pieter from the Netherlands, is very friendly and after admiring the Bantam, tells me the tale of his trip.

"I'm touring around for two weeks with my girlfriend in a hire car," he says, pointing to the café where I can just make out the shape of a seated woman.

"We'd been in Tunisia for a couple of days when we met this man in the street and he helped find us somewhere to stay. He's quite incredible actually, speaks five languages and is very well read." I look across at the man, who has stopped his contemplative circling and gives me a toothy grin.

Pieter continues,

"We had dinner with him, as he was so interesting. The next morning, he was waiting at our hotel reception and asked if he could be our guide for the day, for free. He just wanted to be helpful to us. After that, he asked if he could travel with us, being a guide and interpreter. His family are grown up and departed, and I think he lives alone. He's travelled with us for a week now and he's great, a bit odd at times, but it's made our trip really special. He won't accept any money, won't even let us pay for a hotel room for him... just sleeps in the car or outside in the open. He meditates and practices yoga, and is... er... very, very wise. It's like having our own personal Yoda with us."

Farewells said, I set off again. Peggy loses power almost immediately and I'm on tenterhooks that she's about to seize up. It gets to the point where I can only ride 5 kilometres at a time before being forced to stop. At the first opportunity I put several litres of supposedly smuggled pea-green Libyan fuel into the tank but it makes absolutely no difference.

It's dark before we're within reach of our destination, Ben Gardane. At what I hope will be our last cooling stop, I spend a further ten minutes trying to improve on the engine's running. This time, in the light provided by a couple of houses, I fit a new condenser. All day I've tweaked this and adjusted that, just in case there's an answer to Peggy's problems which isn't actually petrol related.

Cranking the engine and getting under way again, an awful misfire develops, with the Bantam unable to accelerate without missing or backfiring. I remove the points cover and set off once more. Looking down, showers of sparks appear to be shooting off the contact breakers like a Guy Fawkes night sparkler! I halt. We're in the middle of nowhere with no moon, zero light pollution and I can't see a foot in front of me without my torch. Sand eddies whip down the road, driven by a gusting wind. Replacing the original condenser, torch in mouth, whilst being thoroughly gritted is fiddly and infuriating... but does solve the sparking and misfire instantly.

Ben Gardane is a bit of a one horse town. We limp into its centre and pull up outside the first hotel. It occupies the first and second floors of the building, but the young man who acts as night manager... as well as bellboy, receptionist and cleaner, quickly remedies our need for safe parking.

"This is my family's hotel. Our house is behind it. Please, push your moto round the back and I will meet you there. We can lock it in our courtyard for the night."

That resolved, I head for food then phone Andy to see if he's got any more suggestions. I've rung him every day for the last week and am concerned that he may be getting a bit fed up with my repeated requests for support. Nothing could be further from the truth... he's desperate to know how we're getting on, frustrated by the problems and keen to share his experience.

"What does the spark look like?" he asks.

"Bright blue, fat," I answer.

"How about the coil? Have you checked the HT lead is secure against it? Is it leaking at all?"

I tell him there's a bit of black gunge around the point where the HT lead fits.

"Change it, Gordon. That's the insulation oozing out of the coil, probably caused by heat."

Then it's straight to bed. I have to be at the Libyan border, 30 kilometers away, by 9am tomorrow. Setting the alarm for 6am, I doze off with plans to swap the coil in my mind, and not only fingers, but toes crossed tightly too.

Day 16, Ben Gardane to Zuara, Libya.
49 miles.

Ben Gardane is silent and dark and, not for the first time, I'm glad to have the means to make my own breakfast thanks to a water filter, powdered milk and plenty of muesli. Feeling rather guilty, I wake the night manager who groggily unlocks the gate to his home then wheels Peggy out. Illuminated by the light of a golden dawn, I remove both saddle and petrol tank in a sandy back street. As the air temperature intensifies and sweat pours down my face, I grapple with changing the coil. My spare is much larger than the original and won't fit either onto the securing bracket or into the space that's formed between the two lower halves of the petrol tank.

In New Zealand, a piece of simple but extensively used farming equipment, No. 8 gauge fencing wire, has become the symbol of national pride in Kiwi ingenuity and adaptability. It's commonly said that New Zealanders can create or fix anything using it. While preparing for the trip, in lieu of the real thing, I cadged a short rolled length of similar diameter wire from my father. When all else, including cable ties, fails to securely attach the new coil, I remember dad's wire and use it to successfully suspend the oversize unit from the original bracket. In New Zealand vernacular, 'Good as gold!'

Peggy is encrusted with fine red sand that's bonded to a grungy film of oil. I can't contemplate washing her... where would I begin? However I do feel compelled to carry out some general maintenance so it's almost 9.30am when we set off, precisely the time I'm supposed to meet my Libyan escort some 30 kilometres away. It soon becomes evident that the leaking coil hadn't been the issue and the ride to the frontier is a nightmare. If Peggy's performance over the last couple of days could be compared with a cement mixer, this morning it feels more like sitting on a pneumatic drill. She loses power and can only manage 25kmph on the flat before juddering abominably. It's as though I'm destroying my motorcycle... but the pressure's on to get to the border today as there are strict limitations on entering the country. Despondent, I'm forced to take a break half way, finding shade under a small acacia tree that's somehow struggled into life at the roadside.

Stressed by the fear that the guide will give up on me, assuming I'm not coming, I recall motorcycle travel paragon Ted Simon who rode along this road twice. The first time was with a Triumph Tiger in 1974, on the journey that resulted in his seminal book, *Jupiter's Travels*. The second was in 2000, at the inspiring age of 70, when he retraced his first trip around the world. On that second transit, the Libyan travel agency that arranged his visa told him it wasn't necessary to be met at the border by a guide. However, the Libyan immigration authorities saw it differently and sent him packing. But for the fortuitous intervention of a German tour party and their Libyan guide, he'd have been forced to return to Tunisia and, as it was, spent a long six hours waiting at the frontier.

After ten stifling minutes during which the air fails to stir and the engine's temperature stays red hot, I revert to lightly spraying water onto the crankcase, then eventually the barrel and cylinder head. Hissing steam rises off Peggy and my heart misses a beat in case I crack something. Caught in a dilemma between missing my guide and seizing the engine solid. we continue to the border at a torturous crawl.

For reasons I fail to understand, exiting Tunisia is protracted, and in the circumstances, extremely frustrating. Uniformed men walk away with my passport, returning twenty minutes later apparently without any progress being made. A plain clothes policeman questions me about where I've been and where I intend to travel after Libya. His incisive, unemotional questions and blank expression while listening to my answers are quite unnerving. The sat nav, which had been the focus of attention on entering the country, isn't even mentioned and much of the questioning seems to centre around the amount of money I have. I feign a complete lack of understanding, trying to remain calm as I sense that any attempt to speed up the officialdom will only result in further delays.

I'm finally released around midday and gratefully ride the short distance to the booths that mark the entrance to Libya. In truth, I have grave reservations about using the services of a guide. It seems extremely decadent to have such one-to-one attention but my concerns go much deeper. I'm used to travelling on my own, relishing the opportunities and synchronicities that emerge from having the freedom to intuitively respond to any situation as it occurs. It has also been my experience that I meet and connect with people at a less superficial level when on my own, as I've always believed that strangers are more open to, not to mention less intimidated by, a lone traveller. I've allowed myself seven days to cross Libya and don't want to be caught in an inflexible plan or worst still, be dictated to by my guide. And then there's Peggy... goodness knows what the escort will make of her! Even though I informed the agency that she was old and slow, as I park up I can't help wondering if he'll withdraw his services once confronted with our running problems.

The immigration officer, crisply dressed in a white t-shirt, navy uniform and matching beret with two jaunty tassels hanging from it, looks more like a sailor than a member of a border control force on the edge of the Sahara desert. He flicks through my passport until he finds last year's visa. Looking up, he fixes me with a steady stare, then calls for an English-speaking supervisor to join us.

"Your visa has expired," I'm told.

I begin to explain that a guide with documentation for a new visa should be waiting for me, but stop when I notice a man dressed in jeans and a casual short-sleeved shirt running towards us.

"Hello. I am Essa," the man says as he slows to a halt and warmly shakes my hand. Before I can apologise for my own late arrival, he continues,

"Sorry I wasn't here to greet you. There is a group of Italian police motorcyclists over there. They cannot find their interpreter, so I have been asked to help them complete their paperwork. Please wait ten minutes then I will be free from them." He hands a thick pile of official-looking documents to a third immigration officer, whom he introduces as Mr. Ali, then rushes off again. Mr. Ali speaks no English but gestures for me to follow him. We walk to a police car and get in. As soon as the engine starts, ice-cold air conditioning hits me. In comparison to the sweltering heat outside, it's like sitting in a commercial blast freezer.

As Mr. Ali begins to drive, I look back but already Peggy is out of sight. I've no idea where I'm being taken or why and my concerns grow as we leave the border compound behind and set off along the main road to Tripoli. Before the sweat on my clothes turns to ice, the car comes to a rapid halt next to a bank. Mr. Ali has brought me to change money while I'm waiting for Essa... what splendid service! Unfortunately, Sterling is not accepted, only euros or dollars, both of which I have in limited amounts and want to keep in reserve. An obliging Mr. Ali simply shrugs his shoulders, smiles and motions me to return to his mobile ice-box.

Back in the compound, I wander over to the Italian party. Lined up in almost perfect symmetry are nine pristine blue and white Honda Transalps and a huge BMW. Milling around them are their riders, all immaculately dressed in spotless matching rally suits. There are two support vehicles, a fully kitted out long-wheelbase transit van and an open top pick-up truck, both of which are plastered in advertising logos. According to the large map and information panel on the sides of each vehicle, they represent *Moto for Peace,* a police organised charity overlanding from Rome to Cape Town. The side of the van proclaims, in both Italian and English, 'Moto for Peace is an Italian State Police Association whose international motorbike rallies seek to enhance police professional experiences and co-operation by pursuing multi-partner humanitarian goals on the ground and engendering police goodwill and solidarity.' It seems the group, as well as meeting police forces in every country they pass through, are raising funds for a charity operating in Ethiopia.

Essa joins me as they mount up.

"Okay. I'm done. They are going to Tripoli now for meetings with Gaddafi's son and also with senior policemen."

We look on as four Libyan police out-riders dressed in spotless white uniforms with matching leather gauntlets, pudding basin crash helmets and white goggles, appear from behind the immigration hall and form the vanguard of the convoy. Next come two troop carriers of heavily armed Libyan soldiers that tag onto the back of the line, followed by two ambulances and a police car. One of the Italian support crew stands up in the pick-up. a professional looking TV camera on his shoulder and a second, with an equally impressive camera, jumps onto the back of one of the bikes. It's all very organised and high powered, resembling a presidential motorcade more than a group of touring bikers. They set off at speed, sirens wailing and blue lights flashing.

"They are closing the road to Tripoli for them," says Essa, shaking his head and laughing.

Back to the matter at hand, he vigorously launches into the procedures required to clear my entrance into Libya. Once my passport is stamped, he hustles around purchasing road insurance, has my carnet filled in then arranges the hire of a Libyan number plate which I secure over my own with a few strips of gaffer tape. I can't believe the speed at which Essa is able to achieve all these tasks, smoothing his way forward with smiles, handshakes and laughter.

"They all know me very well here," he confides.

In under an hour we're ready to exit the compound. Following Essa's suggestion, I remove all the luggage from Peggy and load it into the boot and backseat of his car. As I work, I try to explain Peggy's predicament to him. He takes it all in his stride.

"Nothing is a problem," he says. "Your motorcycle is not what I expected, but I like it very much. Anyway, it is my duty to help you."

While wriggling into my back protector and jacket, I look towards the now empty immigration and customs halls then upwards at the national flag which gently flutters on a towering white pole. It's mightily unusual, a solid shade of pine green with no inscriptions or symbols. As I kick Peggy over and climb onto the saddle, my face creases into a huge grin... we're in Libya!

We travel a couple of kilometres to a petrol station where the tank is drained. Essa's quite happy to pay for everything until I can find somewhere to exchange money, not that the cost of fuel is going to impoverish me... 1 euro buys 10 litres! It's by far the cheapest petrol I've ever heard of. Essa tells the attendant about my issues with Tunisian benzine. The man answers in rapid Arabic then dips his fingers in the drained fuel and analyses the result by rubbing them together. After a moment he sniffs inside the empty tank.

"Kerosene," he announces with distaste.

A short conversation ensues then Essa tells me he thinks my petrol has been doctored with cheaper and much lower octane kerosene, which is generally used as heating and cooking fuel. After all the hassles in Tunisia, nothing would surprise me.

We leave the station and to avoid the main Tripoli highway, head along the quiet coast road towards Zuara. Despite the fresh Libyan petrol, Peggy quickly gets hot, pinks and recommences her ghastly shuddering. Feeling somewhat disconsolate I stop beside a tree. Essa, who's been leading the way in his car, makes a U-turn and joins me, completely unperturbed that his charge's bike is practically unrideable.

"The city of Zuara is just 20 kilometres further. Once your engine cools, we will find lunch there at a very good restaurant I know, then we can make a plan of what you need to do to repair your motorcycle."

He gives me an encouraging pat on the shoulder. My fears of being stuck with an inflexible and dictatorial guide are evaporating quickly... in fact it's a great relief to have his support.

Some time later, over a rejuvenating couscous lunch, we discuss our options.

"If you want, I can hire a truck to drive us to Tripoli," suggests Essa. "Or if you prefer, I can find somewhere to stay here tonight and you can try fixing it."

I decide on the latter, with access to an internet café high on the list of priorities.

Essa leads me around three shops that offer an internet service before we find one that has a working connection.

"This is typical in Libya," he explains. "In the middle of the day it's often hard to get a connection. But that will soon change because the government has begun a huge project to bring high-speed broadband into the country. Fibre optic cables are being laid all the way from Dubai to here!"

Looking around the dusty, empty streets of this Berber fishing port, thousands of miles of desert away from the UAE, such a thing seems incredible. After some delay I reach Andy on his mobile phone. His disgust at one of his engines being mistreated reverberates down the line.

"Kerosene! That's the same as paraffin, isn't it? For God's sake! That's what you'd use to clean an engine, not to run it."

I struggle to find words to respond.

"Sorry, but you're going to have to lift the barrel and look at the piston and bore. It really does sound like it's been getting melting hot and nipping up, which it would do on a kerosene mix," is his verdict.

We locate a budget hotel and the kind manager finds me a sheltered corner of his back yard to work on Peggy, even damping down the dusty floor first with water. Essa looks on with interest as the cylinder head and barrel come off. On first inspection things don't seem too bad. There are a few scars down the side of the piston but these are quite light and would hopefully smooth out with some wet and dry paper. The bore looks fine with just a couple of faint marks where the edges of the piston rings have been. I inspect the rings. The top one is jagged but free. The bottom one has a sharp edge and is thoroughly welded into its groove in the area of the exhaust port. It's game over for piston number two and this time I haven't got a spare.

For someone who has no experience of motorcycle mechanics whatsoever, Essa immediately grasps the severity of the problem and helps me wheel Peggy into a lockable shed. I feel strangely philosophical about the damage as it certainly explains a lot. It's probable that the seizure occurred on the ride from Tunis with my first tankful of petrol. At least I now know what I'm dealing with, and moreover, it's not insurmountable.

Retiring to a nearby café, Essa asks,

"Time for a new plan?"

"A replacement piston might take days to arrive from the UK, not to mention getting it through customs. Maybe we should go to Tripoli and wait."

"I agree, Tripoli would be best," he says. In a flash he makes three short calls from his mobile.

"A man will meet us at the hotel to arrange transporting your motorbike. I don't think it will be expensive," he reports.

Essa is certainly a man of action. Within ten minutes a driver arrives at the hotel and quickly measures both Peggy and the cargo bay of his Toyota pick-up. It's a comfortable fit. Essa also bargains a good price... 45 dinah (about £20) for the man to meet us early tomorrow morning and drive Peggy 110km to Tripoli.

I spend part of the evening on the internet, running through my options with Andy and sending an email request to Rex Caunt in England for a new piston to be dispatched by courier. Even though Essa's family live not very far away, he stays with me for dinner. The small pizza parlour, with only four bar stools and a narrow shelf to eat at, make quite simply the best pizza I can ever remember eating. Fresh, creamy buffalo mozzarella and sun dried tomatoes... heavenly. My comment to Essa that it's better than any pizza I've eaten in Italy is immediately relayed to the two staff. They're tickled pink and each heartily shakes my hand.

An enormous cockroach has taken up residence in my hotel room. Easily the size of my thumb and speedy, it takes quite some time to evict it. Piling the flimsy mattresses and blankets from two beds onto one in an attempt to alleviate the discomfort of uneven bedboards, I fall into a troubled sleep, wondering just how difficult it's going be to get a BSA piston into the Great Socialist People's Libyan Arab Jamahiriya.

Day 17, Zuara to Tripoli, Libya.
69 miles by truck.

It takes me so long to fall asleep that when the alarm wakes me I feel like a zombie. During the night the unforgiving bed boards have played havoc with my spine, my body's unbearably itchy and my right hand and shoulder throb painfully. Opening the curtains, I inspect myself with growing horror... I'm covered in bites! Some are big and bright red with opaque centres, clearly the work of mosquitos, but the majority are formed in tight clusters of small red swellings making fleas the culprits. Worst affected is my right index finger which, as the result of 22 of these bites, is extremely swollen. My right buttock is altogether another matter. The blotchy bites are in straight lines... bed bugs I suspect. It's a pointless exercise but with somewhat morbid fascination, I meticulously count every bite I can find. There are 92 in total. I've obviously been the night's feast for a multitude of beasties.

Essa waits in the hotel lobby clutching armfuls of brown paper bags containing our breakfast. We walk into the neighbouring café and order coffee to accompany our food. With sticky fingers and lips, we devour almond and chocolate croissants soaked in honey, fresh fruit salad and a smoothie-like drink made from ripe dates and bananas. It's a delectable concoction and goes a long way towards raising my spirits.

Peggy's efficiently loaded into the waiting pick-up truck. The driver has thoughtfully brought ratchet ties and a coiled length of rope of enough girth to moor ships, which he expertly uses to lash the little Bantam securely upright. Following in Essa's car, we begin our journey to Tripoli, chasing after the truck at between 120 and 130kmph, which is probably the fastest the little Beeza has travelled in its whole 57 years of existence. Nonetheless, I feel troubled that I'm not riding the Bantam which, despite all her problems, I've grown to love. My spirits sink further as I ruminate on my goal which was to ride her overland to Egypt, not travel behind as a passenger in the sophisticated comfort of a car. Then I remember Miss Thomas, who was rescued from the roadside on many occasions by an unusual assortment of wagons and trucks. Indeed once, on the way from New Orleans to Alabama, Oppy had developed magneto problems and she found herself surrounded by barrels of shrimps in the back of a fish lorry. The memory cheers me up tremendously.

The outer suburbs of Tripoli are nondescript and traffic is heavy, so much so that we have to do a couple of U-turns in order to make any headway. The pick-up eventually indicates and comes to a sharp halt at the edge of a pedestrian precinct. We unload Peggy and pay the driver, including a tip for the length of time it's taken him to battle the congestion en route. He's chuffed.

"Come this way, Gordon," says Essa. "I think you will like this hotel... it has character and no fleas. Bring your motorcycle so we can ask for parking."

I bounce Peggy onto the pavement then, following Essa, push her among scores of pedestrians. We stop at a door which opens straight onto a staircase leading to the first floor hotel reception. Essa bounds up the stairs in search of the manager, who exclaims in surprise when he descends and sees Peggy.

"It's a Hitler bike!" he shouts with obvious pleasure. This is certainly the oddest description of a classic British motorcycle that I've ever heard and I'm rather dumbstruck. Essa explains,

"It looks like the kind of motorcycle the German army used when they occupied Libya in the Second World War. There were lots of them left behind at the end of the war and everyone calls them Hitler bikes."

Considering the Bantam's DKW pre-war German heritage and its adoption by BSA as a part of war reparations, it's a darkly fitting term.

The manager tells us they have a sister hotel further along the street where Peggy can be safely stored. Leading the way, he even helps lift her up three steps so she can be parked in a quiet marble-floored hallway behind the hotel's restaurant. I lock her and cover her up, confident she'll be safe under the watchful eye of Colonel Gaddafi who looks down from a framed picture on the wall.

After an exceptionally good lunch at one of Essa's favourite haunts, the buzzing *Mat'am Obaya* restaurant, he leads me to an internet café to check for a response from Rex Caunt. I'm quite anxious, as getting the right size piston sent by courier is imperative and I'm not sure what sizes are available or how fast anything can be shipped. There are two emails, both asking me to phone urgently.

Debb answers the phone, full of enthusiasm and friendliness. Despite a confusing echo on the line, she clearly relays Rex's suggestion that I use a D7 Bantam piston as it's flat-topped and will give lower compression than the domed D14 pistons I've been using to date. This, she explains, should help counteract low-grade petrol. I instantly agree.

"In that case we're going to send you two pistons," says Debb, "plus a couple of spare gudgeon pins and circlips as well as two more gasket sets. Let's get you going again... you've got to complete that journey!"

Once my contact details in Tripoli are confirmed, Debb tells me they'll arrange TNT international freight that day, even if it means Rex driving into their nearest city, Leicester, to get the parcel sent.

"And don't go reading me your credit card number out loud in an internet café," she adds. "Sort it out when you get back to the UK. And have a great and safe ride."

This wonderful solution to my problem takes just five minutes to convey over a Skype phone and I feel a lump in my throat at the kindness and support of Rex and Debb, people I've never met but who have now, twice, swiftly and generously responded to my calls for help.

As I sit in the internet café catching up on various things, two Italian motorcyclists from the group I saw yesterday at the border arrive. They use computers at opposing ends of the packed room. The one nearest me gets into a heated conversation via his PC. As his voice rises, I make out the words "ferry" and "Wadi Halfa". There's obviously a problem with the group's Lake Nasser ferry connection between Egypt and Sudan. He begins to shout, then pulls off his headphones and throws them onto the computer table in temper. Jumping up from his chair, which flies backwards, he stands in the middle of the floor and dramatically relays the outcome of his conversation to his companion *fortissimo*. His arms and hands fly around in wild gestures as his strained voice quickens. It's quite a spectacle, more Italian football player being refused a penalty than level-headed policeman.

After a few minutes I'm ready to leave and approach the man to say "hello", mentioning I'd seen him at the border yesterday when my guide had helped his group. He puts out his hand to shake mine.

"I am Paulo, from Interpol, Rome," he says. It's not what I expected to hear. The response that leaps into my mind is:

"I am Clouseau, Sûreté, Paris," but I just can't get the words out and instead mumble my real name and say farewell.

Packing Essa off to visit friends, the remainder of the afternoon and evening are spent absorbing the atmosphere of Tripoli's old walled city. At sunset I walk around the preserved Roman arch of Marcus Aurelius which is situated in sunken gardens close to my hotel. The relic is one of only a few remaining pieces of architecture from Tripoli's historic past as the Roman city of Oea. Built in 163AD and showing considerable signs of a tough life, it's still possible to see the goddess Athena riding in a chariot towed by a griffin and images of local people surrendering to the Roman forces. Magnificent. What's more, it's absolutely wonderful to be able to approach it, touch it and sit on a stone next to it without all the palaver that usually comes with visiting such exquisite ancient ruins.

I saunter aimlessly and contentedly around the narrow streets of the souq until well after dark. One intersection of two alleys completely captivates me... the four corners of the buildings that form its edges are supported by worn Roman columns. Never have I seen such a natural integration of unpreserved history with everyday life. The last of the shops closes and most of the children that had been playing in the streets have returned home. I realise I've roamed the warren of overhung lanes for so long, completely absorbed in the general ambience, that I've become thoroughly disorientated. Normally I would find someone to ask directions, but I have another trick up my sleeve... literally. Feeling like a cross between a boy scout and a secret agent, I set my watch to compass mode knowing that if I head due north I'll come to the sea, near to which lies my hotel. It works superbly well. Ten minutes later I'm standing beneath an ornately decorated mosque, just a little way along from my accommodation, a self-satisfied smirk on my face. I like Tripoli immensely!

Day 18, Tripoli & Leptis Magna, Libya.
0 miles by motorcycle.

It's Friday, the first day of the weekend in Muslim countries. Over breakfast at the hotel, sadly a much blander affair than yesterday's, Essa explains that while mosques and picnic sites tend to be very busy on Friday mornings, businesses are generally closed. With time on our hands, I suggest we go to the Roman city of Leptis Magna some 120km east along the main coastal highway. Essa, who confirms that it's an absolute must-do for any tourist, readily agrees.

The conspicuous absence of wagons and cars makes the road tantalisingly empty. Bombing along with the accelerator pedal flat to the floor, I'm slightly disconcerted to read 150kmph on the Korean-made hire car's speedo.

"Everyone drives fast in Libya," Essa says with a grin as he catches my gaze. "You will need to be *very* careful on your motorcycle." As if to illustrate his point, within a few moments a car swings out from the right without pausing. We swerve around it before flashing past a gaping black hole in the middle of the road where a large rectangular manhole cover is missing. It's a suspension wrecker at best, but would be catastrophic for a motorcycle. Fair warning!

The radio emits some repetitive 90's Euro-pop and I ask Essa if he'd mind turning it down a bit.

"Do you want to listen to some real music?" he asks. "I have lots of CDs in the glovebox. You choose." Flipping the lid open, I extract a stack of at least fifty discs and begin thumbing my way through them. There's Vangelis, Vangelis and more Vangelis... Essa seems to have the complete back catalogue. I spot a title that stops my perusals and without hesitation, slip a recording of the *Blade Runner* film soundtrack into the player. It's a film I've watched with deep absorption several times, always finding that the strangely ethereal music adds considerably to its chillingly dystopian mood. As the futuristic, synthesized trumpeting of the title track reverberates around the car, I look outside at the uninhabited, barren desert that shimmers in dazzling sunshine... Libya couldn't be any further away from Ridley Scott's world of replicants, neon illuminated cityscapes and perpetual rain.

Passing through several villages, everything appears shut except for the mosques and the occasional police checkpost. At each of these, Essa has to hand over photocopies of various documents, including special paperwork allowing me to visit specific sites of historic or archaeological importance. This reminds me of a reason cited in my *Lonely Planet* book for the necessity of a guide. It's reported that in 2000, a group of Europeans travelling in a hire vehicle decided to take some ancient Saharan rock art, untouched for thousands of years, home with them. They weren't the first vandals to do this but at least this lot were caught with their booty at Tripoli airport, incarcerated for a couple of weeks, then deported. Almost immediately, the freedom for tourists to travel independently was withdrawn and the current system that requires an escort introduced. With Essa at the wheel, the white uniformed policemen simply glance through the documents, smile at me, then wave us on.

At the outskirts of Al Khums, the modern town that borders the old Roman city, we're forced to slow behind two open backed trucks filled with camels. It's incongruous to see these exotic and noble creatures, once the only certain means of crossing the Sahara, being transported through their domain in such relative comfort.

"Some rich man is moving his herd to a new location," Essa says. We turn left off the coastal highway while the trucks carry straight on, the dromedaries' heads gently bobbing in unison to the rhythm of the road.

Pulling into a small dusty car park, Essa immediately begins chatting to a posse of officials who seem to know him well. I buy a modestly-priced ticket and head into the complex, leaving him to smoke cigarettes and drink coffee with the local law enforcement chief. Viewed from the majestic Arch of Septimus Severus, the remains of the Roman city are awe inspiring. The huge limestone and marble arch was built in 250AD to celebrate a visit by the city's most famous son, Septimus. Chillingly called 'the grim African', he was a forceful military leader who battled his way to become Emperor by slaying all his rivals in great military actions across the Empire from Turkey to Britain and ultimately on to Rome. It's believed that the city was first founded by Phoenician colonists around 1,100BC but much of its current layout and buildings date from around 200AD when Septimus lavished his wealth on redeveloping it.

Despite the sweltering 36 degree heat and a searing, dusty wind coming from the south, I wander, mesmerised, among these incredible ruins for almost four hours. There are complete streets; Hadrianic baths; a nymphaeum (temple of nymphs); a forum; basilica; hippodrome; numerous imposing arches and the remains of a port, including the foundations of a once colossal lighthouse and loading docks. In the remarkably preserved theatre, where I pause for some time, it's easy to imagine gladiators at battle or criminals and Christians being mauled by lions. What fascinates me most, no doubt enhanced by the echoing dearth of other visitors, is an oblique sense that in the blink of an eye, the streets, markets and temples could come buzzingly to life with Romans going about their daily routines. I could almost be in a time-warp with Dr. Who striding round the corner at any moment.

Like just about every visitor before me, I perch my bottom on a long marble bench in the public toilet section of the baths. Each position has an appropriately shaped cut-out through which the Romans could defecate. Below are ingenious channels, once flowing with water, that flushed away the excrement and simultaneously allowed the Romans to wash their behinds and then their hands. I sit and contemplate for 10 minutes - as you do - and come to the conclusion that I'd seriously struggle to *go* in full view of 30 or so other people simultaneously doing their business. Standing to leave, I notice two teenage boys arrive. One reaches laughingly into his backpack and extracts a soft penguin toy, which he pops onto a marble latrine. I stare at the absurdity of it... what would old Septimus say? 'Surreal' wasn't a word in the semantic spectrum of his day. I whip out my camera and take a quick photo for posterity... or posteriority!

Speeding back to Tripoli, roads are beginning to get busy. Essa enlightens me.

"By mid afternoon, everyone comes out of their homes, goes for a walk, maybe has a family picnic or visits friends. Some businesses such as restaurants begin to open too."

Passing close to the coast, Essa, who's both knowledgeable and passionate about his country, tells me that much of the waterfront has been bought up for hotel developments.

"I think there's a move towards encouraging more tourism," he says. "My guess is that visa regulations will relax when all these big five star hotels are built." Looking at the shells of a couple of enormous complexes, I can't imagine there being enough able-bodied men available to act as guides.

In the meantime, accompanied by more Vangelis, we pass back through all of the police checkpoints with elegant ease.

Eager to find out if the pistons are on their way, we promote a visit to the internet café above our desire for food. Rex and Debb have sent an email that contains a TNT tracking number and I eagerly log onto the courier's website to check progress. They've left Leicester and are already at the international sorting hub in Liege, Belgium. Excellent.

After a simple couscous meal in a tiny back-street restaurant known to Essa, we look around parts of the modern city centre. Colonel Gaddafi's smiling face appears on a lot of billboards as well as in large framed pictures in shops, hotels and restaurants. He's celebrating forty years in power this year thus plenty of the biggest hoardings, several of which are over 15 metres wide, commemorate the anniversary. In many poses, he has both his hands clasped together either in front of his chest, above his right shoulder or high above his head to one side. I'm told it's a gesture of union, but it translates to my western gaze as the gesticulations of a Hollywood champion boxer.

Gaddafi has recently been keen to develop both Libya's and his own personal role in engendering African unity. Indeed, massive Libyan government financing is paving the way forward for Africa to become free of US and European control by leading the creation of an African investment bank, an African monetary fund and an African central bank with its own gold-backed African currency, developments which promise to end the continent's dependence on the IMF and the World Bank.

Spotting more hoardings, I can't help thinking that his sense of style is most unusual. His outfits are mainly generic African robes, however, in my opinion, the most intriguing pictures are where he dons one of his military uniforms. He appears younger in these images, and with his curly black hair, large Ray-Ban aviator sunglasses, colourful rows of medal ribbons and peaked military hat, I can't help but parallel his appearance to Michael Jackson at the height of the 'King of Pop's' gold-plated uniform phase. An unsettling, if understandable, sartorial comparison.

Essa maintains that he's not unpopular at home.

"In the last decade, things have become better here. The government has invested more of the profits from oil into projects that benefit everyone."

Libya has the largest reserves of oil in Africa and the ninth largest in the world.

"And don't forget," continues Essa, "it is a very safe place to live here because of Gaddafi, providing you obey the laws. Terrorists and drug smugglers don't do well... the regime has zero tolerance."

Over a light dinner - basically chocolate cake in a streetside café - we discuss some of the other monumental Gaddafi-led projects.

"Work is already underway to build a railway right across the country, linking Tunisia with Egypt," Essa begins.

I'd noticed several billboards showing a modern looking train engine on the way to Leptis.

"That's over 3,000 kilometres long and will completely transform how we Libyans and tourists get about."

In my mind, I automatically tabulate the route of a train journey across North Africa... amazing.

"And you must have heard about the Great Manmade River?"

Indeed I have, thanks again to Michael Palin in *Sahara* standing inside one of the giant water supply pipes. The project, which brings water from the enormous Nubian sandstone aquifer system, was dubbed by Gaddafi as 'The Eighth Wonder of the World'.

"It supplies water to Tripoli and cities like Benghazi and Sirte, some unreal amount like six million cubic metres a day," Essa adds. "I know it's in the record books as the world's largest irrigation system and cost the government around 25 billion US Dollars to construct."

After what amounts to a wonderful day's holiday, we say goodnight with a nodded resolution to dedicate tomorrow to Peggy.

Day 19, Tripoli, Libya.
0 miles.

Forgoing a drab breakfast at the hotel, I set off in search of Essa-style honey and chocolate croissants. The first place I try, just down the pedestrianised street, comes up trumps. Sitting under a large canvas umbrella at one of many outside tables, I devour two scrummy helpings and a double *espresso*. On my left is an elaborate Ottoman clock tower and the entrance to the Souq al-Ghizdir, a collection of small shops that reverberate with the musical clanking of artisans beating their copper wares. Across to my right, little more than 200 metres away, is Tripoli port and the rippling Mediterranean. Three mosques lie within a minute's walk and a little way behind the café is an imposing stone gateway which once guarded the entrance to the old city. Just beyond that sits Al -Saraya al Hamra, Tripoli castle. The whole place is steeped in history and simply oozes charm.

There's much evidence of the economic redevelopment aimed at attracting tourists which Essa spoke of yesterday. Buildings are receiving sympathetic facelifts that highlight their traditional regional architecture and even the pedestrian walkway is getting a makeover. The dozen or so labourers whose task this is, all black Africans, are an amusingly laid-back bunch. Their boss has obviously not yet arrived and they've tipped their wheelbarrows up so that the wheels are in the air. Smoking and chattering cheerfully while they listen to music on a ghetto-blaster, the men bask in the warm morning sunlight next to dormant stacks of terracotta-coloured paving bricks, making the most of the barrows as impromptu deckchairs. While I'm gazing in their direction, a man staggers past pushing a handcart, grossly overladen with gaily coloured embroidered goods, towards the souq, reminding me that the old ways of doing business still thrive despite the drive for Libya to become globally integrated and updated.

Essa, dressed in his usual attire of checked short-sleeve shirt and black jeans, joins me and we immediately head for the internet café. Passing a row of jewellery boutiques that seem to be open virtually 24 hours a day, he nudges me and nods his head towards an open fronted shop. A man in traditional Arab dress and two women clothed in vibrantly colourful Middle Eastern robes stand at the counter. The man has his hands deep inside a large trolley-type suitcase. They emerge holding great blocks of cash, which he adds to a substantial pyramid of notes already on the counter top. His hands disappear again, quickly appearing with more.

"That whole suitcase is full of money. How much is there, do you think?" asks Essa.

I've no idea, but Essa's guess is somewhere around $100,000.

"Many wealthy people from the Gulf States visit Libya, Gordon. But please do not be deceived, most Libyans are not rich, they live on very little."

We soon reach the internet café where I avidly check for progress. The pistons reached Dubai at 2am and are once again in transit. Superb.

Peggy's absolutely filthy so I decide she deserves a good wash. Furthermore, I'd hate any sand or dirt to get into the crankcase while replacing the piston. A car park opposite the Bantam's hotel is home to a motley bunch of car cleaners, all black African illegal immigrants.

"It is a very difficult situation for the government," explains Essa. "Most of these people walked across the Sahara from countries like Nigeria, Niger and Chad, hoping to find a way across to Europe and a well paid job. Many died in transit and a good number were ripped off too. The Europeans have really tightened up on illegal immigrants and all these people are stuck here. Still, they do at least work, happy to take any menial job."

We hire one of the men, armed with a bucket of hot soapy water and a couple of well-used sponges, to give Peggy a good going over. The job, which restores the Bantam to a presentable if not particularly shiny state, takes at least half an hour but leaves me feeling guilty about the black, oily state of the man's sponges... I'm sure he couldn't possibly use them on any of the cars in the car park, nearly all of which are white to counteract the heat of the sun. I just hope my tip covers the cost of replacements.

Next on the agenda is some much-needed maintenance. Essa helps remove the Bantam's rear wheel and we load it, my spare tyre and the bike's exhaust system into his car. After trying two puncture repair shops, neither of which is willing to tackle a tubed motorcycle tyre, I resign myself to doing the messy job back at the hotel. I've hardly seen a motorcycle or scooter ridden by a Libyan, so I'm very surprised when Essa finally pulls up at the doors of a chaotic-looking scooter repair shop. The mechanic at first agrees to change the tyre, then stops when he looks more closely at the wheel.

"Why?" he asks Essa in Arabic. "There's nothing wrong with this one."

I burst out laughing when Essa translates... it's practically bald! The mechanic is reluctant to use my tyre levers, preferring instead his own decrepit screwdrivers, but nevertheless completes the task in under five minutes. Pretty good considering it would have taken me at least a half an hour of sweating and cursing!

The exhaust presents a much bigger problem. A sizeable chunk of the brittle flange has snapped off the downpipe and there's no way I can now seal it properly against the cylinder head. We drive around for over an hour searching for someone capable and willing to attempt the welding job, eventually rolling up at the establishment of an Egyptian man who repairs car exhausts. He examines the downpipe from every angle then launches into a very intense debate with Essa.

"He thinks it will be difficult as the metal is very thin and might become more damaged with the heat," Essa explains to me. "But I am convincing him to try. He's a skilled man and it's our best chance."

With further encouragement from Essa, who doesn't seem to understand the meaning of the word no, the welder comes up with a solution. Finding a length of 5mm wire amongst a pile of rusty scrap metal in the corner of his workshop, he tells us he can try to attach a ring of it under the existing flange then build this up with weld.

What follows is a performance I don't think I'll ever forget. Wisps of tobacco smoke curl upwards into the Egyptian's eyes from the cigarette wedged permanently between his lips. In his left hand he holds the exhaust and in the right a pair of pliers gripping a rod of weld. The deadly gas welding torch is firmly trapped between his knees. Directly below the roaring blue flame are his feet, protected only by battered leather open-toe sandals. To top it all, his bare hands and absence of safety glasses give a perfect example of health and safety Libyan style... he'd be closed down on the spot in England! I watch in amazement as he sets to work, skillfully attaching the steel ring, which he bends into shape as it glows red. Once satisfied, he begins to fill in the gap with weld. His concentration is incredible as, despite all the risks and distractions, he chatters non-stop with Essa in a gruff voice. I watch from the open doorway, painfully aware that if he takes just one step backwards he'll fall into an oily six-foot deep car inspection pit. Yet his craftsmanship is superb and the finished job looks well shaped, robust and, to my relieved gaze, thoroughly wonderful. Although the flange will need to be ground flat, we now have plenty of metal to work with. I thank him gratefully, knowing that a serious stumbling block has been overcome.

Next we search for a workshop that will finish the job. The third place we try, which has an assortment of car crankshafts and cylinder heads stacked up on workbenches, agrees to give it a go. Standing at a bench that fronts the street, the business owner plugs in an industrial-sized grinder that requires both his hands to hold. It begins noisily spinning round and a shower of yellow sparks shoot past us and into the road when he presses it onto the exhaust. Almost instantly, the grinder cuts out and despite his best efforts, refuses to start again. This would be a perfect job for Derek, I think, remembering all the grinding he's done on the various modifications to Peggy.

Essa, who's proving to be immeasurably resourceful, suddenly recalls spotting a small business producing wrought iron gates on the road to Leptis.

"They're just beyond the missing man-hole cover," he tells me. "Shall we go?"

It takes 40 minutes to get there, 10 minutes to have the flange shaped up, then another half an hour back to our hotel. Essa seems to have unflagging energy plus a strong desire to get the job done, so much so that I have to remind him that we need to eat a late lunch before settling down to put everything back onto Peggy.

It's evening before we begin the task of replacing the rear wheel along with cleaning and oiling the chain. Then we try to fit the exhaust. The angle of the new flange is out by quite some way - when the downpipe's joined to the silencer there's a gap of almost 5mm at the top of the flange.

"Mmm," I say, "I think we'll have to take the motorcycle to the workshop tomorrow to have it ground to the right angle."

Predictably, my guide is unfazed by this.

"I will find a pick-up we can hire... it should be easy."

We leave Peggy's resting place and Essa leads me into the Medina along a cramped alleyway whose Arabic name he translates as the 'way of the wind'. It's easy to understand why... even though the city air is balmy and tranquil this evening, a strong cool draught seems to suck at my clothes from below as soon as we turn into it. Dinner tonight is at a more touristy restaurant, where the low level tables are surrounded by traditional woven carpets and cushions that we sit on. After saying goodnight, I head off alone to my favourite open-air café to drink mango juice and people watch.

Relaxing at an outside table well after 11pm, I'm drawn into conversation by a besuited, middle-aged Libyan man who asks if he can join me. We talk about my experience of Tripoli and travel plans, then move onto his and my family. Before leaving, I mention the omnipresent images of 'The Colonel'. He leans forwards,

"You know," he says in a hushed, almost conspiratorial tone, "that Gaddafi was always an American spy."

My response is little more than a mutter, neither hinting at agreement nor disbelief.

"Really," he rejoins, "think about it. The Americans and British, who both had military bases here, could easily have stopped his coup in 1969. They let him take power!"

Warming to his theory, my new confidante continues.

"Gaddafi wrote his philosophy for a socialist Libya in a book called *The Little Green Book*. You have heard of this, yes? Well, this was all part of their ploy to convince the Russians that he was bona-fide. We spent more than two decades running our country the Soviet way and it was such a waste of time and money. Just look around... any old concrete block buildings you see are Russian built. They're just about uninhabitable and are being torn down all the time."

By now he's unstoppable, talking with real passion.

"And why did we have this disastrous relationship with the Russians? Because Gaddafi was spying for the Americans all along. Truly, now that there are no communists left to spy on, he's free to be a capitalist, which you can see in how things have changed here recently. Believe me, he was a double-agent!"

I don't know whether I should laugh or look around for the secret police sitting at a nearby table. I shake his hand, telling him that I've very much enjoyed his company, and in a state of mild paranoia, beat a hasty retreat to my room.

Day 20, Tripoli, Libya.
0 miles.

An ever punctual Essa walks into the hotel's dining area at 8.30am, just as I'm polishing off my last slice of toast.

"To the internet café?" I ask, keen to check on the whereabouts of the pistons.

"Yes, it's here," replies Essa. Strangely, I only hear what I expect to hear and, it being a Sunday, misinterpret his words as 'yes, we'll check if it's here.'

"Okay," I breeze on, "how about we plan the rest of the day over an *espresso* once we've got an update on progress?"

Essa looks bewildered.

"But it's here already, Gordon. TNT sent me a text message an hour ago. Your parcel has arrived. We can go and collect it now."

This is just about unbelievable... only two and a half days from a village in rural England to Libya via Belgium and Dubai! Miss Thomas travelled in an era when there were motorcycle repair shops and BSA dealerships aplenty to assist with repairs and spare parts, but she wouldn't have been able to conceive of such an expeditious service from her homeland. We depart the hotel with my feet feeling as though they're floating on air.

A musical transformation has taken place in the car. After 3 days of non-stop Vangelis, Essa has switched to a different pile of CDs, this one comprising almost solely of Fleetwood Mac classics. It's comforting to hear such familiar and enjoyable sounds, my elbow hanging out of the open window catching the faintest of sea breezes as we negotiate light traffic past the port, then round the periphery of the old city.

We slow gently as traffic lights turn to red and are immediately nudged firmly from behind. I turn to Essa, who's showing no reaction whatsoever.

"Are you going to have a look for any damage?" I ask.

He calmly remains seated.

"What? Oh that, no, it's not important," he replies, his mind focused on remembering the route to the TNT office.

"But it's a hire car... won't there be penalties if the paintwork's scratched or the bumper cracked?"

"Look around, Gordon," he answers with a wry smile. "This happens all the time in Tripoli. Every car is scratched and dented. It's just how people drive."

The lights change and we move on without even a backwards glance at the offending motorist.

Although he's met him only once, roughly 12 months ago, Essa's greeted by the TNT clerk like a long lost friend. After handshakes and pleasantries, he signs for my parcel. Sitting in the car, as Essa jostles through the increasingly snarled up traffic, I stare at the Jiffy bag which is partially ripped at one end. With a certain amount of trepidation, I tear it fully open, extract the contents and do a stock take. Two pistons; two sets of piston rings; three sets of circlips; three gudgeon pins and a note from Rex and Debb wishing me luck... that should surely be enough to get me to Egypt! Essa looks across, registers the grin that's spread across my face and gives a satisfied nod. We're back in business.

The rebuild takes place in the hotel foyer where Peggy's spent the last three nights. Under the ever-watchful gaze of 'The Colonel' we remove the cylinder, then brace ourselves for the arduous task of extracting the gudgeon pin. I've already warned Essa about the freezer and blow torch tactics Keith and I were forced to employ when inserting it but we decide to give cigarette lighters a try before setting off in search of more serious heating tools. Attacking the piston from both sides in unison, we heat it for roughly a minute then Essa grips the con rod firmly and I tap the gudgeon pin with a hammer and wooden drift. It glides out at the first try. I jump up triumphantly, hardly able to believe we've achieved the task so easily.

"Hey, hey, Keith," I sing out loud. "You definitely won't believe this!"

Inspecting the pin under the bright overhead light shows the result of the heat it's been subjected to... the original shiny bright metal finish has turned to the mottled black-blue colour of a raven's breast. I pocket it as a memento.

Before fitting the new piston, I pull on the con rod to check all's well with the big end, which it is. I can't help but chuckle thinking about the first occasion Miss Thomas removed the barrel from Oppy, which was at the time suffering from loss of power. In a Vancouver basement with the help of a girlfriend and a library book entitled *Simplified Motorcycle Mechanics,* she undertook the task of decarbonising the piston and replacing the piston rings herself, in order to save money. With the barrel off, she became alarmed that the piston wobbled around on the rod. Hurriedly consulting the book, she found '...that this seemingly unnatural wobble was termed *normal play in the big end*. This sounded rather risqué, so we turned to other matters... there was hardly a finger-nail left between us when we had finished the revolting scraping task.' I think of relating the tale to Essa but decide that the school-boy nature of my amusement might be lost in translation.

The new gudgeon pin and piston are a perfect fit for each other, requiring just a smear of oil and no heat to aid their union. After a thorough clean of all surfaces, including the bore which seems to have survived the rigours of Tunisia with remarkably little ill effect, we begin reassembly. Essa's mission is to lower the barrel while I squeeze the rings closed one at a time. It's tricky, and we do work up a bit of a sweat, but within 20 minutes the gaskets are sealed and the head torqued down.

"I think you were teasing me," Essa says as we straighten up and stretch our backs. "This was not a hard job at all." If only he knew!

Over a late lunch, Essa spends time on his mobile updating his office on our progress. We pay our bill and leave, with Essa striking out in a different direction from Peggy's make-do workshop in search of a 'Man with a Van'... or at least Tripoli's equivalent. While he's gone, I finish attaching the tank and the saddle to the Bantam then do a quick check round for any loose nuts. Essa returns just as I'm about to wheel her down the stairs and onto the pavement. He's accompanied by a burly Berber, the size of a grizzly bear, who's the driver of a rattling, rusty pick up truck that's presently blocking access to the hotel. I don't know where or how Essa rustles up these characters but he's incredibly adept at it. With a heave from the three of us, Peggy's rapidly transferred into the back and secured by what appears to be domestic washing line. There's not enough room in the cab for all three of us, so Essa wedges himself one side of Peggy and I squeeze in on the other. The driver sets off as though he's in a race, spinning the rear wheels and mercilessly accelerating his jalopy until it's speeding flat out along the main coast highway.

Being mid-afternoon, the hot air blasts our faces as we weave competitively between lanes of equally ballistic vehicles. Our daredevil van-man, using a mixture of guile and brute force, more than holds his own... which is quite some achievement considering the wailing sounds coming from the engine and the almost total absence of brakes. Both thrilled and terrified, I laugh out loud; it's like being in the *Wacky Races* with Penelope Pitstop, Dick Dastardly and the Ant Hill Mob all in hot pursuit! There's nothing I believe I can do or say that will moderate our driver, so instead I search my memory for an appropriate character for him... it has to be Rufus Ruffcut in the Buzzwagon.

Half an hour of law-breaking, life-threatening four-wheel escapades later, Essa batters frantically on the cab's rear window, signalling for the driver to make a U-turn, which he does virtually without slowing. We come to an eventual halt, overshooting the doors of a motorcycle shop which Essa and I must have already unwittingly driven past several times. The two young men who run the business come outside to inspect our load. Essa animatedly explains our requirement, which they cheerfully agree to undertake. I glean from the conversation that they're honoured to have the chance to work on a Hitler bike! Peggy is promptly unloaded and wheeled onto a hydraulic bench within the shop. With the downpipe in my hand, I demonstrate the amount of grinding required to realign it to the cylinder head. The senior mechanic disappears into another room, returns with an electric grinder and in one fluid movement sets to work. Sparks shower our feet but the grinding disk proves too worn out to have any effect on the thick ring of weld. A boy is called into the shop, handed some money and sent off with the task of finding new discs.

Looking around, I notice there's only one complete motorcycle, a custom painted cruiser that belongs to the business owner. The place looks more like a wrecker's yard than a dealership, with several crashed or partly dismembered

Japanese sports bikes lined up against a wall, their bent chassis and partially stripped engines covered in unsightly layers of sand and crud. Making the most of the opportunity, I borrow a grease gun and give Peggy a good lube until the youngster returns with not only the new discs but four bottles of very welcome iced cola. Cigarette in mouth, the mechanic once again sets about the exhaust flange and after a few checks, the work is declared done. I fit a new exhaust seal and tighten everything up, mightily pleased at the result.

Back in Tripoli and under threatening skies, I recheck the ignition timing, fit a new spark plug and make ready to test the engine.

"Do you think it will work okay?" asks Essa, a hint of doubt creeping into his voice for the first time.

"She'll start first kick," I tell him with as much bravado as I can muster.

I go through the usual preparations, switch on the ignition then crank the engine. Right on cue, Peggy bursts gloriously into life. Essa guffaws heartily, simultaneously slapping me on the back as I rev the little 2-stroker loudly. Slipping into my jacket and helmet, I hop onto the saddle and make a short run along the seafront to the arch of Marcus Aurelius and back. All seems perfectly fine... we really can set off tomorrow!

The first drops of rain begin to fall as we wander contentedly back to the hotel. Once in my room, I open the huge arch windows that take up almost a complete wall and absorb the sweet smell of the heavy raindrops now tumbling earthwards... the cool, fresh air is exquisite. I begin to pack my luggage and make preparations for tomorrow's departure. Around 9pm it dawns on me that my riding trousers, kevlar-lined cotton cargo pants, which are great in the heat but have become filthy from many hours lying on Tunisian roads, are still at a dry-cleaners in the souq. Rushing out into the downpour to collect them, I get thoroughly and deliciously soaked. Life is such a relative thing.

Day 21, Tripoli to Al Khums, Libya.
76 miles.

The rain that fell heavily in the night has freshened the air but the sun's already high and burning hot as we prepare for our departure at 9am. Loading all my gear except for the tank bag into Essa's car, we stock up with ten litres of water and emergency rations of fruit from a nearby shop. Peggy once again fires up first kick, but this brings me little comfort... I've woken feeling petrified that she might seize again.

The tension I experience as we ride the first few miles east is just about unbearable. My shoulders lock and my hands and forearms ache from gripping the handlebars too tightly. What if the pinking and vibrations return or the piston seizes completely as it did so cripplingly on the first day of the journey? I can hardly breath for fear as these thoughts go round and round my head and after twenty minutes stop, walk away from the bike and calm myself. Essa, sensing this is a hurdle I have to overcome alone, relaxes in the car listening to Stevie Nicks singing *Gypsy* on repeat play.

We set off again but are soon halted by traffic lights at a major intersection. They seem to take an eternity to turn back to green, although I guess it's probably no more than two full minutes. The temperature's well over thirty degrees and my stomach knots even tighter as heat from the little Bantam's engine radiates onto my legs. When I accelerate forward, Peggy's response to the throttle feels woolly and there's definitely more engine noise evident than before. It's hard to decide whether I'm being over-sensitive and unduly mistrustful or if there's something genuinely amiss. I feel relieved when, having spotted a marine-equipment shop, Essa overtakes me and rapidly pulls up. We nip in to buy some much needed 2-stroke oil.

A pattern is soon established that's not dissimilar from the one in Tunisia. I ride for 10 to 15 fraught kilometres then sense that things are not as they should be. Becoming increasingly anxious about seizing, I reach the point where I can bear it no longer and pull up to cool the engine. During these stops, which usually last longer than the spells of riding, I vainly make the same set of checks and tweaks I'd tried day after day in Tunisia: points; timing; condenser; carburettor jetting and spark plug. None make any discernible difference to performance, which feels strained and unresponsive. The one comfort I have, however, is the absence of those destructive vibrations. Peggy may feel like she's riding the tightrope of near seizure, but it hasn't happened yet.

Throughout the hours of tortoise-like progress, Essa is patience personified. At many stops he sits by the roadside watching me perform the rote of adjustments and acting as a sounding board for my concerns and ideas. He has a book with him, *Islamic Architecture in Libya*, which he's studying to make himself more knowledgeable for tourists. He delves into it from time to time, but is mostly content to just sit and talk. When we're moving, he stoically follows 15 metres behind, hazard lights resolutely signalling to approaching vehicles that we're travelling at, by Libyan standards, a dangerously slow pace. And it's a good job for me that he's there... far from being embarrassed at such cosseting, I'm exceedingly grateful to have his protection. Cars and trucks are out in force, tailgating each other as they thunder along the unmarked lanes of the dual-carriageway at breakneck speed. The articulated wagons become especially menacing when the highway later changes to single lane. Thanks to Essa they give us a wide berth but still wreak havoc as they swing back over to the verge ahead of me, causing a vacuum that savagely sucks me along then tosses me around like a rag doll.

Sticking to the edge of the road has its fair share of dangers too. Often there's a faintly marked hard shoulder that's about a metre and a half wide, but in many places the superheated tarmac has melted and the wheels of countless vehicular behemoths have created great rifts and ripples in it. It's hard to spot them until virtually the last second due to the glare of the sun. Even when there's time for a cursory glance in my mirrors, I'm still afraid to swing out into the middle of the road in case I'm flattened by an unnoticed speed-freak. When Peggy's front wheel hits these vicious undulations, I have to cling on for dear life as we bounce and weave our way clear. I repeat over and over in my head, 'Jacques and Jane. Jacques and Jane', saying their names like a mantra to help keep my mind focused on defensive riding and staying alive.

Libya's population density is one of the lowest in the world, with a demographic statistic of three and a half people per square kilometre. However, as somewhere in the region of ninety percent of the country's 6,400,000 inhabitants live in the narrow fertile strip along the Mediterranean coast, it doesn't seem so. There are uninhabited stretches but it's mainly a case of hopping from one bustling village to the next. We eat our lunch in the empty car park of a multinational company's modern offices. An enormous bill-board, showing the company's logo and a picture of Gaddafi, has been erected. It's at least 30 metres long and proclaims, 'We wish this great and gutsy country, the great socialist people's Libyan Arab Jamahriya, on its 40th anniversary. We wish this great country congratulations and good wishes, prosperity and great achievements in the coming years.' As Essa and I discuss this blatant example of corporate sycophancy, a security guard arrives in a jeep. We must have been caught on CCTV. Time to move on!

Reaching the town of Al Khums at 6pm, we motor to a small budget hotel within a hundred metres of Leptis Magna's gates. Essa, predictably, is a friend of the owner whom he greets cheerfully. The three-storey concrete block building is rather shoddy, largely unoccupied and doesn't appear to have an area where I can safely park Peggy. Essa makes a request to the owner, who immediately tells me to push her into his own ground floor room for the night.

I'm concerned that petrol fumes might intoxicate him as his bed is only a couple of feet from where the Beeza's parked, but he simply waves me away, saying,

"No problem, no problem."

What brilliant service!

There's a huge release from stress now Peggy has survived the day. I sincerely thank Essa for his equanimity and support.

"Please stop," he humbly replies, using his hands to add gravity to his words. "It is my duty to help and keep you safe. And also I want to see you get this old bike to Egypt. It is my challenge now as well as yours. So, my friend, we will do what we need to do to make that happen."

Essa decides he would like to cook dinner for us tonight as he says he spends too many evenings in restaurants and misses being at home cooking for his family.

We drive into the centre of town, a sleepy place built around an expansive, gardened square. While he hunts down the ingredients for our meal, I phone Andy from the only internet café.

"She really struggled today," I begin. "Acceleration seems okay but there's little power once we reach the 30mph mark, which is the speed I'm cruising at to let the new piston bed in. It's almost as if there's a flat spot in the rev range and I'm sitting right in the middle of it. Every few miles I get the sensation that the power's falling away even more and she might be about to nip up, so I stop and let her cool."

Andy absorbs the information for a moment then responds with an answer that certainly sounds plausible.

"My guess is the engine's labouring doing that speed in top gear. I reckon you're going to have to risk going a bit faster and run it as it's designed to be run, which is at 40 plus. When you're going as slowly as you have been, it might be creating even more problems by not getting sufficient oil into the engine, which is critical in the heat you're riding through."

I agree to give it a go.

Checking my emails, I find one from Pete Rose in Southport which couldn't have arrived at a more serendipitous moment. It reads:

"Hi Gordon, so pleased that you're having a spell of better luck. Remember what I told you: ride that old bike like you are a teenager and have just stolen it! Seriously, keep the revs up in a low gear rather than let her labour."

"Excellent!" I call out, then look around to make sure no-one is looking at me.

Returning to the hotel I'm filled with renewed optimism.

The couscous dinner is delicious, wholly made from fresh ingredients Essa bought at a market... is there no end to this man's talents? He decides on an early night, but I feel restless so go for a stroll around the neighbourhood.

Close to the hotel is a large, subtly lit outdoor cafe situated within a manicured, potted garden. There must be at least fifty men seated at tables nestled within a maze of miniature palms, bushes and planters. The place is absolutely humming with a mixture of intense conversation, bonhomie and hilarity. Sitting at one of the few empty tables, I order a glass of mint tea and stare at the bright panoply of stars above, assimilating the sounds of the surrounding milieu. Nearly every man is smoking or sharing a sheesha pipe. The deep red glow of the coals as they're delicately manoeuvered with tongs, the sound of water bubbling merrily when smoke is drawn through the pipes and the heady smell of strong, flavoured tobacco is utterly enchanting.

As my second glass of tea arrives, the background music commences. It's most incongruous... instrumental versions of Elvis Presley songs played on what sounds like a Wurlitzer fairground organ. Everyone else seems oblivious to it, but I struggle to keep a straight face as 'In the Ghetto' merges into 'Teddy Bear'.

The perils of the Coastal Highway, Libya.

Day 22, Al Khums to Sirte, Libya.
206 miles.

After breakfast, another delicious cornucopia of fruity pancakes which Essa makes, we retrieve Peggy from the kindly manager's room. My nerves have now completely evaporated and I'm biting at the bit to ride the Bantam 'properly', anticipating higher revs and cruising speeds. Things, however, don't go to plan. The Al Khums town council has deployed an unnecessary plethora of traffic lights east of the centre, resulting in Peggy's engine being close to cooking by the time we finally get up to speed on the open road. Increasingly sensing subtle losses of power, my fears of impending doom return. After 14 kilometres we have to stop.

At our third cooling break, nearly two hours into the ride but with only 39 kilometres to show for it, I pull up just beyond a small village and find shade beneath a sprawling tree. Essa drives off in search of food and water whilst I flop back, rather glumly, out of the sun beside Peggy. A group of schoolboys walk past, cheerfully calling out the few phrases of English they know accompanied by much giggling:

"How are yoooou? ... I looooove you!"

The last boy to pass, who's probably around twelve years old, hollers,

"Where do yoooou live?"

"I live in England," I shout, employing the same jokey voice.

"Where do yoooou live?"

Expecting to hear the name of his village or possibly "Libya", I crack up when he cheekily rejoins,

"In a house!" and boldly walks on without looking back, his shoulders rippling with chuckles.

Essa returns and laughs helplessly as I recount the story, slapping me on the back and shaking my hand. Our shared humour lightens my spirits and we immediately hit the road.

Towards the end of the next short stint, riding at 65kmph along an empty straight with scrubby desert infringing onto each side of the road, I spot a fuel station in the distance. It's my favourite brand, mainly because it has a cool looking camel logo. Just as my brain's thinking 'slow down, stop, buy some petrol', I lose all power... it almost feels as though Peggy's been yanked from behind by an invisible hand. The engine cuts out and I drift to a halt under a lone tree at the front of the forecourt. Essa parks beside me and through his open window asks,

"Time to fill up?"

"She's seized," I reply then sit in the tree's shade on an abandoned truck tyre, head in hands, feeling completely crestfallen.

"No," he groans. "I don't believe this. What happened?"

I recount the experience, answer his suggestions that it might be something as simple as the spark plug or condenser in the negative, then wander off down the road to regain my composure.

Once the engine is cold, I try the kick-starter... more out of curiosity than hope. It turns with the usual amount of compression. 'Thank goodness,' I think, 'at least it appears to have only been a partial seizure.' I check the plug. Normally blacky-brown, it's now a shade of grayish-white, despite running with the carburettor needle in its richest position. I consider the problem and wonder if sand in the carburettor has caused a blockage resulting in a weakened mixture. Over the next hour we thoroughly clean the carb, finding quite a bit of sand inside the float bowl but no blockages in the jets. With everything back together and a new spark plug in place, I suggest to Essa that providing the bike will run, we should try to slowly reach the nearest town. Hopefully we can then find some shelter where I'll able to take the head and barrel off for a better look.

I stand beside the bike and tickle the carb. No petrol comes out.

"Come on Gordon," I say to myself with exasperation, "turn the tap on!"

Fiddling under the tank with my gloved fingers, it seems impossible to get a good grip of the fuel tap lever. I bend down and peer... the tap is already turned on. Tickling the carb firmly again, there's still no sign of fuel. Essa approaches and watches my confused fumbling. Just as I begin to wonder if I've not put the float back into the carburettor properly, he removes the tank filler cap and squints inside. Looking up, he starts to laugh and punches my shoulder. The new piston hasn't seized at all... she's simply out of petrol!

Essa can't speak for laughing. He doubles up holding his stomach, tears streaming down his face. The hilarity is infectious and I begin to laugh uncontrollably too. When we catch our breath, he removes his camera from his pocket, and without a word, flicks through a couple of images then hands it across. Angling the screen away from the sun, I see a photo of myself sitting under the tree approximately an hour ago, forehead in hands as I miserably contemplate my toes. Looking up, I catch Essa's eyes and we set off again, laughing until it hurts. With tears still damp on my face, I fill the tank and on the second kick Peggy ebulliently sparks into her normal and healthy, ring-ding-ding rhythm.

Resuming a modicum of composure, we continue the journey. I decide not to ride far, judging it expedient to check the colour of the new plug fairly soon... just in case. After ten minutes I see a tree and consider stopping. However, as a stiff, cooling breeze is getting up and the engine feels free, I decide to keep going just a little longer. Incredibly, we don't stop for 45 kilometres, when we spot a large air-conditioned roadside restaurant. It's the longest continuous stretch of riding since Italy. Essa's visibly chuffed and I'm ecstatic beyond words.

Depending on which direction the road takes, we have either a strong crosswind or buffeting headwinds throughout the afternoon. Both are great for

Wellington, New Zealand, 1997, with my first Bantam

brake cooling on the 2,160 M Grimsel Pass.

Above: A typical campsite, Switzerland.
Below: Peggy awaits collection in Portogruaro.

asket replacement, east of Grigno, Italy.

Friend and Bantam owner Derek Thom (AKA Mr. Bracket) shortly before the first departure for Egypt

Motoring through France at the start of the second ride, Peggy valiantly covers 812 miles in 4 days.

...h stop in Tunisia... just before we were stranded by the roadside for over 3 hours.

..., a land of friendly people, awesome scenery, excellent accommodation and terrible benzine.

The exhaust is skillfully welded, Tripoli.

Mr. Fathe and family, Tobruk.

With Essa's help, Peggy gets a new piston. Tripoli.

Essa at one of Peggy's many water stop

ing the desert to Tobruk. My right leg yet again positioned to allow extra cooling.

Another seizure... or have I run out of petrol?

ling light... who am I to judge! Libya.

Sunset on the road to Sirte, Libya.

Saying farewell to four wonderful Syrian truck drivers. El Alamein, Egypt,

Cooling stop for Peggy on the Desert Highway between Alexandria and Cairo.

hoto, moto!" Giza, Pyramids, Cairo.   A welcome patch of shade in the Sinai, Egypt.

pause while heading for the port of Nuweiba, Egypt. Peggy is running on fumes at this point.

Vadi Rum, Jordan. No sign of Lawrence.   Philipp with his favourite toothpaste, Aqaba, Jordan.

The 800 year old Krak des Chevaliers crusader castle. The Bantam has just made a 700 M climb.

Securing Peggy onto the AutoSlaap trein, Alessa

Above: Heading north from Damascus.
Below: Waiting for the ship's manifest, Venice.

Safely home with Jacques and Jane.

Peggy, keeping her engine temperature well within safety limits. In successive stages we cover 52, 87 and 106 kilometres. The last leg is done in the dark with Essa loyally following at the optimal distance, hazard lights persistently flashing their warning. My only real concern is that I might damage the front wheel on one of the many sharp-edged potholes that blight the tarmac but with Essa's full-beam headlights bolstering my own light, I manage to avoid all but a couple of the wretched things. Surprisingly, traffic is less of a problem in the evening as it turns out that trucks are banned after sunset, making the roads practically deserted.

Essa's concerned that we won't be allowed to enter Sirte, the birthplace of Gaddafi, as we don't have the appropriate paperwork.

"It's impossible to prepare for every contingency," he explains, "So generally, we arrange for permission to visit all the major places along the coast road that a tourist may want to see. Sirte is a modern, purpose-built city that one day may take over from Tripoli as the capital, indeed if Gaddafi has his way, as the capital of the United States of Africa! But we never thought you'd want to stop there... there's nothing of archeological, cultural or historic interest. We'll have to see if the police let us through at the last checkpoint."

Police inspections have been few and far between since Al Khums, and the last one before the turn off to Sirte fortunately only gives our documents a cursory glance. We make it into the city centre around 8pm, check into the *Hotel Africa* then head out immediately for food. While seated at a seafront café, and to change the subject of conversation away from bone-dry petrol tank 'seizures', about which Essa has teased me mercilessly, I ask him about Gaddafi's *Rocket Car*. Revealed at the 1999 *Organisation of Africa Unity Summit*, the Colonel's latest of many inventions was heralded as the 'safest car on earth'. Essa's never heard of it and is fascinated.

"I thought I'd see them everywhere in Libya," I tell him. "I've looked at photographs on the internet and the design looks extraordinary, with the elongated front and rear formed to sharp points like, er... a rocket. It's more of the *Thunderbirds* variety than NASA, but somehow manages to look both retro and futuristic at the same time. It's supposed to have an inbuilt electronic defence system and super-shock absorbing bumpers. You really haven't heard about it?"

"No," Essa answers, looking unusually nonplussed. "Let's make it our goal to see one before you leave Libya." We shake hands on it.

Once replete, Essa goes in search of an old friend he believes lives in the city. It's been fifteen years since they last met, but written in his diary is an address to try. I slowly wander back to our hotel, a journey around the edge of a market, then along a wide boulevard. It takes roughly half an hour and in that time, I'm greeted by at least twenty Libyan men who either say "*Salam Alaykum*" or "Hello", in a couple of cases shaking my hand. Libya certainly has a good vibe to it and not for the first time I feel safe, contented and very positive about being here.

Day 23, Sirte to Ajdabya, Libya.
258 miles

The only pre-departure preparations required today are a quick check round the Bantam for any fixings that have worked loose. Assisted greatly by the bulk of my luggage remaining in Essa's boot overnight, I attach the magnetic tank bag on top of the petrol tank, clip the Garmin into its holder and within five minutes, start her up. We're on the road by 8am.

We set off with purpose, buoyed by yesterday's good mileage. Assisted by a cooling cross wind, Peggy cruises the first 100 kilometres with just one break, which is for her rider to fuel up with coffee. Libyan cafés and restaurants serve the most flavoursome, rich *espresso* and it only costs half a dinar per cup, making my favourite addiction perilously affordable. Progress, however, slows in the late morning and afternoon. The onshore breeze that's so far helped the Bantam's engine to purr beautifully disappears when we turn away from the coast and head due south across a 90 kilometre stretch of open desert. Frustratingly becalmed, we once again stop every 10 to 15 kilometres, often without shade, to give the motor time to come down from melting point. Essa, who was intrigued to learn that the Bantam is a 2-stroke with no circulating, cooling oil, watches me spray 10 litres of water onto the head and barrel over the course of a couple of hours.

"You can tell people you have the only water-cooled 2-stroke Hitler bike that was made in England," he teases.

I'm reminded of Jack London's WWII thriller, *Dispatch Rider*. Carrying a top secret communiqué, the protagonist, Don R, is sent on a dangerous mission riding hundreds of miles across the Libyan desert to the stronghold of Fort Capuzzo near the Egyptian border. With the German Afrika Korps hot on his tail, he becomes lost in a sandstorm and spends several days stranded beside a poisoned well, boiling the water needed for his survival with the last of the fuel from his motorcycle tank. Best of all, his bike was a BSA.

"What I find most amusing," I reply to Essa, "is that Peggy consumes more water than we do. It's a good job we've got your car to carry it all."

Libya forms a large part of the North African plateau, which stretches from the Atlantic coast of Morocco to the shores of the Red Sea in Egypt, and more than ninety five percent of the country is covered by desert. The sand that surrounds us in the early afternoon is an arresting deep shade of red and is only sparsely broken up by tufts of pale green Saharan grasses and oatmeal coloured stones. Ahead, the road is completely straight and a heat-haze quivers on the horizon where the super-heated, translucent air rises off the tarmac. The occasional vehicles that drive towards us, with their wheels concealed by the distorted radiance, appear to be flying. It makes an eerie sight.

There are more police checkposts than usual today. Essa explains that they mainly scrutinize drivers for the correct ownership papers, insurance documents etc. He continually hands out an endless supply of photocopied documents and his cheerful but assertive manner with the authorities ensures we are rarely stationary for more than a couple of minutes.

At one checkpoint we rest under the shade of a giant concrete flagpost. Taking my watch off, I place it out of the sun and after a few minutes check the temperature... 36.7 degrees in the shade, which is about the average human body temperature. I recall Jane remarking, on a freezing cold winter's day, that one incredible feature of homeostasis is the universal stability of human body temperature. Relaxing here, sweat dripping off me, I make the unexpected observation that what's comfortable inside the body feels way too hot when it's on the outside. Essa and I sit opposite each other, our backs supported by broad reinforced columns. With no movement and hardly a sound except for the occasional buzz of a pesky fly, we both wilt. Essa puffs quietly on a cigarette and, comfortable not to have to talk, we contentedly let time drift for a while.

On the road again, we enter a region of beautiful white sand dunes. It's a must-take photo opportunity for me, although I can't help thinking skeptics might jokingly say I rode my bike to Southport beach and photographed it among the dunes there. On the opposite side of the highway, a herd of reddish brown camels with their adorable playful calves wander past.

"They can be very dangerous at night," warns Essa. "They like to stand in the middle of the road as the tarmac is warmer than the sand and it heats their feet. Crashing into them is common and causes a great deal of damage to cars and trucks." Not to mention camels, I think to myself.

Once underway again, we encounter another kind of desert driving menace, one I've already learned about through painful personal experience. A series of sand drifts have formed across the road... they're a magnificent sight but fraught with danger. On my ride to India, I found giant dunes across the road in the Baluchistan desert, some of which towered at least three metres high on one side dropping down to knee deep at their shallowest. With no sand riding experience but some vague notion that keeping up your momentum was essential, I'd simply dropped a gear and ridden into the sand at somewhere between 30 and 35mph. The result, somewhat predictably, was rather traumatic. I managed to cling on to the bucking machine until we reached the far side of the dune, but by then I was in a tank-slapper and found myself promptly flung off the bike, which, after bouncing a couple of times, landed squarely on top of me.

Since then I've read up on the subject and had a few opportunities to practice the skill of negotiating them. Chris Scott's excellent book, *Sahara Overland*, gives the best and most concise explanation of what can happen: 'If the dune is right across the road, two ruts are usually formed by passing traffic and to ride through successfully you must balance speed with caution. Although it's momentum that gets you through, riding into these sandy ruts at highway speeds will almost certainly knock you off. The sudden build up of sand under the front wheel will dramatically alter the castor effect of the steering and flip the wheel sideways, sending you over the bars.' Wish I'd read that before traversing Baluchistan!

The first drift of encroaching sand we meet today is quite shallow but its unexpectedness catches me by surprise. It's only at the last moment that I haul the brakes on hard, drop to second gear then accelerate through the dune... it certainly gets my heart pumping fast. The next two, a few hundred metres further on, are deeper. Forewarned, there's time to slow comfortably, retaining just enough momentum to steer when Peggy enters the drift. I hold the handlebars lightly with soft hands, allowing the front wheel to find its own course whilst the rear weaves around under hard acceleration through the soft sand. Success!

Serious progress is made when we turn east again and rejoin the coast. A stiff, chilling wind blasts in off the sea, allowing me to ride steadily into the evening, thoroughly enjoying motorcycling for long stretches without a break. As light fades I begin to shiver and have to stop to add layers of clothing, which I take as a positive... if I'm cold, so too must Peggy's engine be, all things being equal. Despite the threats of aggressive drivers, fiendish pot-holes, treacherous undulations of melted tarmac, impinging sand and errant gangly cud-chewers, I drift off into reverie for just about the first time in Libya, my fears of an engine calamity wonderfully in abeyance for now. It's bliss.

We reach an area where Essa suggests camping out in the desert. This has been at the top of my wish list for Libya ever since the journey was conceived, but with the difficulties faced on the ride to date, it feels prudent to clock up as many miles as possible while riding conditions are right. The wind tugs at my jacket and flaps my trousers as I reluctantly explain to Essa the meaning of 'making hay while the sun shines'. We continue heading east for another 85 kilometres, cutting through the vast blanket of darkness. At first Essa keeps his hazard lights flashing but eventually has to turn them off as approaching motorists, unsure of what the alien vehicle coming towards them might be, switch their lights onto full beam for a better look, blinding us in the process.

Arriving in the dusty city of Ajdabya after 9pm, we both feel worn out by over 13 hours of hard motoring but gladdened to have achieved such an impressive distance. The first hotel we try has room rates that would shock even the wealthiest of tourists, but our second attempt in the centre of town is much more reasonable. The foyer is accessed through giant plate glass doors that sit atop a broad flight of marble steps. In the surrounding streets are restaurants, open-fronted shops and a cinema. Keen to have us stay, the receptionist readily agrees to parking Peggy alongside plush sofas in their lounge. Between us, Essa and I manhandle the Beeza one step at a time upwards then push her to the furthest corner of the room, at which point I self consciously fiddle about arranging my dusty green bike cover in a vain attempt to blend her with the decor. Despite the challenges involved, it makes me realise just how handy it can be to travel on a 70kg lightweight motorcycle... no full size touring machine would ever have made it up those steps, unless, of course, its owner was an accomplished stunt rider.

After inspecting my room, I return to the reception and ask the manager for a towel. A few minutes later he brings it to my door.

"*Shokran*" (thank-you) I say as he hands it over.

"Have fun," he replies.

"No fun tonight, I'm having a shower then going to bed, thanks," I reply politely, not imagining he'll comprehend.

He looks quizzically at me then grinningly explains in excellent English,

"Actually, I said '*Af-whan*' which is Arabic for 'you're welcome'. We often say this in reply to 'thank you'".

Laughing heartily at my misunderstanding, we shake hands.

With two excellent days of riding under my belt, I feel highly optimistic about the 370 kilometre desert crossing to Tobruk tomorrow. After that it's only a couple of hours to the border and Egypt. It seems incredible that Peggy and I are now so close to our destination. Crikey!

Another cooling stop.

Day 24, Ajdabya to Tobruk, Libya.
125 miles ridden & 117 miles towed.

We're both so tired from yesterday's journey that we rise quite late, meeting for breakfast at 8am. I relate last night's conversation with the hotel manager to Essa. He thinks my misconstrued Arabic is priceless, repeating "Have fun" over and over between bites of gooey croissant.

"It'll be my new motto," he says, "and I'll tell it to all the tourists I escort in the future."

A fruitless search by car around all Ajdabya's motor factors produces no 2-stroke oil, leaving me with barely enough to reach Tobruk and delaying our departure until after 9.30 am.

I'd wanted to get underway early and make best use of the cooler hours to put a good chunk of the desert traverse behind us. However, as there's a howling wind swirling around the already busy streets, the air temperature seems less important.

Once we're on the desert road, I ride with my right leg awkwardly out at ninety degrees to the Bantam in order to get maximum air current, that screeches in from the south, onto the cylinder. I start to realise that I'd rather romanticised this part of the journey. Instead of an imagined sea of dunes and a boundless spectacle of inhospitable Sahara, the view on both sides of the road for the first half an hour is of endless litter. Unsightly polythene bags caught on rocks and stones flutter noisily and plastic drinks bottles, to all appearances in their thousands, roll in circles as gusts of wind spin them round and round. There's paper aplenty, abandoned clothes, shoes and furniture... even a couple of burned out cars. The desert here seems to have been used as one great open-air garbage dump.

The refuse thins out once we're far away from the city but my pleasure is short-lived as the blustery wind soon veers round behind us... not much good for cooling the tiny Bantam engine that's now obscured by my size 8s. The air becomes increasing stifling as the wind diminishes to a breeze, then dies to an occasional short-lived flurry that kicks up wisps of sand before completely vanishing. Resignedly, we revert to short hops. At the end of each engine watering hiatus, I kick Peggy back to life and briskly accelerate away, aiming to get up to speed promptly in order to cover as many miles as possible before being forced to stop again.

"I think you ride that motorcycle too fast Gordon," says Essa around midday. "You set off like a missile and it takes me some time to catch you up. Surely you need to accelerate more gently."

I try to explain how 2-strokes need to be revved, even relaying Pete's analogy of riding the bike like a criminal adolescent, but he still looks doubtful.

Around 15 kilometres into a stint, we power up a long incline at 65kmph to where the road straddles a craggy sandstone ridge. My mind is set on freewheeling down the far side then stopping to give Peggy's engine another dowsing. As I crest the rise, what I'd dreaded inevitably happens... without any warning, the engine tightens and the piston grinds to a cringing halt as it locks onto the walls of the cylinder. Instantaneously I haul on the clutch lever, to which my left hand's been permanently glued for the last couple of weeks in anticipation of this very event. The engine cuts out. Coasting downhill until we come to a standstill, I pull up, kick out the prop stand and step off feeling, once again, sick to the pit of my stomach. Essa joins me, thinking it's just a regular cooling interval. I tell him the news, but he just laughs, punches my arm and takes the cap off the petrol tank.

"Look, it's low! You were going downhill and the carburettor is starved of fuel."

"No, honestly, this is serious... it really has seized this time." I insist.

But after the last 'seizure', Essa is rightly dubious, jovially thrusting the spare fuel can into my hand.

"Have fun!"

Hoping against all logic that he's right, I let the engine become as thoroughly cool as possible, which takes more than half and hour, then turn her over. She starts and runs fine, but once under way with my left hand rigidly gripping the clutch lever, it soon becomes obvious that damage has indeed been done. Wretched Tunisian-style vibrations commence within a couple of kilometres and the distances we can cover before the piston begins to nip up rapidly shorten: 11km; 10km; 7km; 5km. After each soul-destroying spell of riding, we have to stop and cool the engine comprehensively before repeating the same tortuous routine all over again. It's very, very testing. We take a late lunch break on one of these stops, creating shade from the merciless sun by securing a large cotton sheet to the roof of the car and the top of a roadside cutting using several rocks. Sitting on a blanket underneath it, Vangelis back in favour on the car's stereo, we put Peggy right out of mind, sharing a picnic as we talk about life, the universe and everything but 175cc motorcycle engines.

The desert is stark and desolate with the only evidence of human existence beyond the narrow grey strip of asphalt an occasional truck tyre half filled with sand. The sun beats down like a tangible force and, without shade, I begin to feel light-headed... the unavoidable effect of its pulsating, unrelenting heat. Traffic becomes scant. The Libyan and Egyptian trucks I encountered in the morning have all but disappeared... they obviously have more sense than this Bantam rider. Even the grotesquely loaded Egyptian mini-buses have vanished. These madly top-heavy VW vans, full to bursting with passengers and crazily piled with so much luggage on their roof racks that their height is doubled, had both amused and amazed me. *Weebles* might 'wobble without falling down', but should one of these unbalanced death-traps pass their tipping point, calamity would be unavoidable.

There's one solitary petrol station cum service area on the desert road, logically situated quite close to the half way point. By 5pm we're still 20 kilometres short, with the stricken motorcycle only able to manage between 4 and 7 kilometres at a time. Reasoning it could possibly take another hour and a half to get there, which would be around sunset, Essa and I have a pow-wow. The best we can come up with is that he tows me, but we don't have a suitable length of rope. After 10 minutes, a colossal double-trailer truck approaches from the west. Essa takes his life in his hands and walks into the middle of the road to flag it down. Engulfed by the smell of burnt rubber from its screeching stop, we approach the cab with Essa making our request loudly, his arms wide open so that the driver doesn't feel threatened. Noticing for the first time my pink face and realising that I'm a foreigner, he opens his door and leaps to the ground, shaking both our hands with a crushing grip.

"He's happy to give us some rope, which he has lots of," Essa translates for me, "but his truck is empty and he's also offering to take you all the way to Tobruk for free."

I equivocate for a few seconds. It's a tempting offer and thoughts of Miss Thomas again flash through my mind. She'd broken down on a treacherous stretch of Mexican mountain road blighted by a dangerously wobbly rear wheel and a severe loss of compression. With nightfall rapidly approaching, a truck driven by a 'very Mexican-looking Mexican' who's appearance resembled 'a villain out of a Hollywood Grade B film' stopped and offered assistance. With the help of another lorry driver who fortuitously arrived on the scene, Oppy was hoisted into the cargo hold beside huge bales of paper and Miss Thomas and Matelot driven through the night to their destination, Mexico City. Our good Samaritan is anything but villainous looking and I decide that his offer is genuine and Peggy would be safe in his care. However, unlike Miss Thomas's rescuing vehicle, this dry bulk juggernaut is gigantic. Climbing up the ladder on the back of the first trailer, the driver winds the flap door open. Essa and I look at each other and laugh... it would be impossible for the three of us to get a motorcycle that high. Even if we all raised the Bantam onto our shoulders, the front wheel would still fall close to a metre short of the trailer floor.

Graciously accepting our refusal, the driver drags a heavy coil of thick rope to the open door, extracts a large hunting knife from a sheaf on his belt and asks Essa how much we would like. A 7 metre piece is then cut and thrown to us. The driver clambers down after it and, with his hand on his heart, firmly and generously refuses any compensation. Wishing us a safe journey, he warmly mangles our hands again, turns the monster's engine over and leaves.

Esa ties the rope to the rear of his car. I've never been towed before but know that in the UK it's illegal for a motorcycle to be towed by anything but another bike. Sagging in the heat, we begin to search for a stick to tie my end of the rope to. As we comb the wilderness, Essa finds the dried out husk of a small bird, its feathers still perfectly intact, which he picks up and hands me. Next he turns a few rocks over with his boot, keen to show me some of the indigenous scorpion population.

"There are sometimes green ones in this region," he shouts over to me with more enthusiasm than I feel is healthy. "They're the most dangerous ones."

Fortunately, I find a solid lump of wood before he unearths any predatory arthropods, green or otherwise. Returning to the roadside, I tie it to the tail of the rope and loosely wrap it once around the centre of my handlebars.

Libya's new-found answer to David Attenborough joins me and we agree some ground rules for the tow. Back in the car, he sets off as steadily as possible. Peggy jolts forward at first, causing the front wheel to momentarily shimmy from side to side. I use all my strength to keep the bars straight with one hand whilst taking most of the strain of the rope with the other as it slackens then tightens, causing more precarious jerking. As soon as we gather speed, however, the front wheel settles and I'm able to ease my grip, allowing the steering head to take the strain. Within 20 minutes, the petrol station appears like a concrete mirage on the horizon. Stopping is more of a concern to me than getting going was, so within 100 metres of the turn off I unwrap the rope from the bars and toss the stick as far forward as possible, hearing it hit the tarred surface of the road then rattle loudly as it's pulled along by the still fast moving car. In silence, I taxi to a halt just inside the service compound.

Under the shade of a line of well-irrigated bushes, I remove the exhaust header pipe and peer up the exhaust port with my torch. The top piston ring looks rough and shiny… not a good sign. I also strip and clean the carb, just in case there's sand lodged in it. Although I'm becoming quite proficient at this task, it still takes more than half and hour to reassemble and return Peggy to an operational state. We top up both car and motorcycle with fuel and make ready to leave. At the exit, we come to a stop and stare in awe at the sky. The sunset is magnificent… our star's translucent crepuscular rays fan out from behind a solitary cloud and the surrounding expanse of sky spans a stunning spectrum of purple and red hues. Juxtaposed with the dark and foreboding desert, the vista fills me with a rare feeling of euphoria. I lean towards Essa's open window,

"I feel so lucky to be here," I say "despite all the problems."

He doesn't need to say anything to let me know he's in accord with me... with smiling eyes he simply takes my hand and shakes it in friendship.

Against this phenomenal backdrop I crank Peggy back into a degree of life and slowly ride 3 kilometres to the only police check post on the desert road. Once through, the old Beeza immediately starts to struggle. Cutting the engine, I freewheel as far as possible. Out of sight of the police, unless they're peering through binoculars which I very much doubt, we rig up our towing arrangement again.

Over the next four hours, Essa steadfastly pulls us the remaining 168 kilometres to Tobruk. My greatest fear is that he'll have to brake suddenly and I'll be unable to avoid piling into the back of him. But never once does he touch his brake pedal, leaving me in reverence of his concentration as he somehow manages to keep the most impeccably constant speed on the seemingly interminable highway. We travel, strangely isolated, through the velvety indigo night, the car's lights and hypnotic flashing indicators the only illumination bar the horizon to horizon panorama of twinkling stars that exquisitely grace the vast heavens.

I'm immensely grateful that this section of highway, unlike any other in Libya, is completely devoid of potholes... it's as smooth and straight as an airport runway. Riding in eerie silence, I remain fixated on the rear of the car ahead, clinging to the rope and stick in fearful anticipation of the first glimpse of a red brake light or change in the angle of headlights caused by bumps in the road. It's very unnerving and almost too risky, but when needs must...!   Not sure whether I should be terrified or elated by the experience, I stop trying to think, narrowing my focus onto those two small red rectangles ahead.

We only stop twice. I let go of the rope on both occasions so that I can put on more layers to fight off the cold desert night and reassure a worried Essa that all's okay. We eventually roll into Tobruk at 11.20pm. Cruising down a hill, desperately trying to keep the tow rope taut, I see a ghostly outline of the city's famed harbour where many battles took place during the Second World War. Swinging round its edge, we climb into the town centre to the doorway of a hotel. I shake Essa's hand in both of mine as soon as he emerges from the car, offering him my most sincere thanks for aid far beyond the call of duty. He just smiles and says,

"Have fun!"

In double-quick time, we head off to find a bite to eat before the last of the city's few café's close.

Seized on the desert road to Tobruk.

Day 25, Tobruk, Libya.
0 miles.

I'm woken early by the sound of my window rattling noisily. A huge sandstorm rages around the streets of Tobruk, making the harbour almost invisible through a grey veil of dense, swirling dust.

"Do you think it's safe to tow me to the border?" I ask Essa over breakfast, aware that today is supposed to be the last one I have with him as my guide.

"No, not in this wind and poor visibility. And anyway, you must fix your engine so you can continue riding into Egypt. What I suggest is this: we will repair your motorcycle today. Tomorrow is my day off. In the morning, as a friend helping you in my own time, I will escort you to the border."

Sometimes there are no words to express the depth of gratitude we owe others.

Agreeing to Essa's plan, we need to find somewhere that's shielded from the wind in order to strip the engine. Our hotel, which fronts directly onto the street and only has a tiny carpeted reception, doesn't fit the bill. Essa, as usual, has an idea. A boyhood friend lives in Tobruk and he feels certain that the friendship will extend to using his home to work on the bike... if we can track him down. Essa's pal, Mr. Fathe, is in the army. Covering our faces with scarves against the stinging, surging air, we make a dash to the car and set out to look for the nearest army camp. It's surprisingly easy to find, perched on a hillside overlooking the deep water harbour from the south. Essa leaps out of the car and asks the soldiers on gate duty if they know his friend but draws a blank. Nearby is the German Afrika Korps war memorial, which we make a short detour to visit.

Commanding the top of a hill, the sandstone walled mausoleum looks more like a small medieval castle than a twentieth century structure, with imposing turrets dominating each corner. There's just one small door, which is locked. As we turn to leave, two cheeky looking youngsters, both with tousled hair and missing teeth, run towards us from a nearby house and unlock the door, earning a couple of dinars in the process. We briefly look around inside... it's extremely sombre and depressing. The fortress walls are clad with giant dark grey slate bas-relief sculptures depicting German soldiers and in the centre of the quadrant, four statues of black angels support a large iron bowl in which is supposed to burn an eternal flame. This has sadly been extinguished. Seeing the names of the thousands upon thousands of dead on austere recessed slate slabs is deeply disturbing.

Moving onto the next army camp, we hit the jackpot. Without hesitation, the guardhouse soldiers give Mr. Fathe's address to Essa. They even helpfully provide directions... so much for security.

"How did you manage that so easily?" I ask Essa in disbelief when he chirpily returns to his seat in the car.

"Oh, it's no problem here. I just told them we're from the same village and went to school together. They would do exactly the same as me if looking for a friend. That's just how it is in Libya."

I simply can't imagine the same scenario in the UK... lock him up and ask questions later would be the more likely outcome.

We quickly locate Mr. Fathe, who lives on the ground floor of an apartment block with his wife and five children. He's rather flabbergasted but obviously delighted to see Essa. Watching them together is amusing. I can imagine them as a couple of impish lads with sticky-out ears, the 'little terrors' of their neighbourhood. Mr. Fathe, as if reading my mind, points to a small scar on his face then indicates that Essa was the culprit. Within moments, the two old friends shed forty years and begin mock fighting. When they eventually settle down, Essa raises the problem of my motorcycle. Although there's a large communal entrance to the building, which in normal circumstances would be eminently suitable for stripping the Bantam, Mr. Fathe insists that I should bring the bike into his home as otherwise he fears I'll be pestered by inquisitive locals and over-friendly kids.

The storm seems to have abated when, after a quick cup of tea, we head out to collect Peggy. I finally get a clearer view of Tobruk... it's nothing like I expected. I'd imagined it to be a place of charm, with an atmospheric old town and a swathe of colonial buildings left by both the Italian and British occupiers. Far from it; the city's a wreck. There are piles of concrete rubble everywhere, broken, uneven pavements jut upwards at oblique angles and some side streets appear just about unnavigable with baked mud and scarred tarmac causing traffic to weave from side to side. There's no beauty in the buildings either, with many redolent of concrete block houses dating from the 1960s and 70's. Quite a few seem unfinished and those that are complete give the impression of being in very poor order. The city is messy too, with piles of litter and construction debris scattered randomly. I know that in 1941 it was under seize by Rommel's Axis forces for more than 8 months, a key battle in the Western Desert War. It must have been shelled and bombed constantly during this period, especially as the Royal Navy ships moored in the harbour not only provided Allied support but acted in turn as prime targets. Almost 60 years on and Tobruk looks as though it's still recovering.

The dismal sights are soon forgotten when Essa points to a car halted next to us at a red light.

"See that plastic tube sticking upwards from the top of the driver's window, Gordon? What do you think it is?"

I mull it over... the dirty-looking tube is about an inch in diameter and appears to extend quite a way into the car.

"My guess," I eventually answer some time after we're under way again, "is that the driver's a smoker. The lady in the back seat, his wife, doesn't like cigarette smoke in the car, so he has to blow it out through   that tube."

"Excellent. Really good guess," Essa says in between guffaws. "He's an illegal taxi driver and that's his sign, Look around, you'll spot lots of them. You see this only in Tobruk, nowhere else in Libya. The people are quite different here."

He's right... there are lots of tubes. Then I see another car that looks odd. The driver's stuck a coffee-coloured plastic cup upside down on his roof.

"He's an unregistered taxi too. That's their other sign. Only in Tobruk!"

By now I'm laughing like Essa. There are more cars with tubes and upturned cups than those without. Talk about improvisation!

Quickly rigging up the same towing arrangement as last night, we set off for Mr. Fathe's. It proves to be a far less effective towing system in the city than on the open road, especially with all the traffic lights, roundabouts and illicit taxis to negotiate. Just when I think we might escape without incident, Essa brakes hard on the downhill approach to a roundabout and the rope snakes on the road immediately ahead of me. I pull on the brakes but am unable to avoid running over it. Inevitably, the rope loops tightly around the front wheel causing it to lock up solid. It seems to be happening in slow motion but in reality takes only a fraction of a second... my poor, terribly abused motorcycle is whisked from underneath me and noisily dragged down the street.

I hit the road hard with my knees and palms but am on my feet in a flash, chasing after the toppled Bantam. Essa comes rapidly to a stop and so, just before jamming under his bumper, does Peggy. I catch up and immediately right her, hurriedly searching for any damage. Essa has by now joined us and is horrified at the accident, looking at my hands with visible concern.

"I'm sorry... really sorry, I know I braked too suddenly."

I dismiss his apologies as unnecessary and continue my worried inspection, pushing down on the handlebars with the brake on to check that the forks still freely move up and down.

"You are only concerned about your motorcycle," Essa says incredulously. "What about you? Show me your knees!"

I'm actually fine and Peggy's improvised front luggage rails have again saved her from any damage. He shakes his head in disbelief, totally at a loss to understand why a motorcycle, however treasured, can be more important than its rider.

Back at Mr. Fathe's, the family have already moved the furniture out of their reception area and we're invited to wheel Peggy straight in. The children are thrilled at this unusual event and all take turns to sit astride her and have their photos taken. With the help of Mr. Fathe's twelve-year-old son, who's responsible for holding my torch and safely storing the parts I remove, the Bantam is stripped for inspection. The piston comes off without protest,

157

showing seizing scars and a damaged top ring. The barrel, which seems to be made of kryptonite, looks to have escaped unscathed yet again.

Repairs and reassembly are postponed until after lunch. Mr. Fathe's two brother-in-laws and their families join us. The wives and children share a meal in one room and the men in another, as is customary. We five men sit in a circle on the lounge floor around a large bowl of couscous and a selection of side plates piled high with vegetables and fish. Essa recounts the tales of our crossing Libya and this morning's accident, to the amusement and concern of our hosts, whilst we all dig into the mountain of food from our respective sides. After washing our hands in a bowl of lemon water, a sugary dessert is brought out, followed by coffee which we drink on the green brocade settees that line practically every inch of wallspace. I'm too fidgety to sit and have a second cup, eager to get back to Peggy.

Deciding that the piston isn't beyond repair, I arm myself with wet and dry paper and set to work, painstakingly dressing off the score marks and replacing the rings. Then I lightly clean the bore before washing everything several times using washing up liquid and scalding hot water. With Essa's help, everything goes back together easily and just a couple of hours after starting, the job's almost complete. Torqueing down the head, I hope that the extra clearance created by dressing the piston will help prevent further seizures without losing too much compression... better to have a slapping piston in a fully working engine than a seized good fit, I reason.

We agree to leave Peggy where she is for the night and after a round of thanks to our wonderful and extremely accommodating hosts, say farewell. Locating a good restaurant for our evening meal proves problematic and we eventually settle on a pizza house. After a short wait, two oversized plates are brought to us, each laden with huge pizzas that spill over the edges. The waiter returns after a minute with two forks and two spoons.

"I think we'll need knives," I say to Essa.

He gets up and asks for knives from the manager, who sits beside an ancient cash register. A lengthy conversation ensues, then Essa returns empty handed.

"They don't have any knives... well they do, but they don't know where they are. In fact, the manager says he hasn't been asked for a knife in over a year."

While tearing our way through the pizzas, the manager arrives at the side of the table, a plastic bag in his hand full to bursting with grimy-looking steel knives. He hands us two as he chats good-naturedly with Essa, then disappears.

"His wife knew where they were. The rest will go back unused for another year. Only in Tobruk!"

With the pizza finished and Essa crunching his way through a bowl of eye-wateringly hot green chilli peppers - which he does several times a day - we discuss the remainder of my journey.

"I think you should only ride at night," he says, "when it's cooler. Set off at 7 in the evening and ride until 2 or 3 in the morning, then sleep late. It's the only way I think your bike will make it."

I can see his logic, but feel that prolonged night riding could be jeopardous.

"What you need is one of those yellow rotating lights like road workers have. Other motorists will be confused or intimidated by the light and they definitely cannot miss seeing you. That will keep you safe."

I agree to mull it over.

We wander the streets for a while but soon decide to call it a night. I lie awake in bed for quite a long time, unable to sleep as my mind frets about Peggy and contemplates tomorrow's journey to Egypt.

At the Libyan passport control office, Umm Sa'ad.

Day 26, Tobruk to Marsa Matrouh, Egypt.
89 miles ridden & 146 miles by truck.

Mr. Fathe is transformed when we knock on his door at 7am, with yesterday's attire of short sleeved shirt and casual trousers replaced by an olive green officer's uniform. However, his smile and the warmth in his eyes are unmodified as we wheel Peggy through his apartment's door and say goodbye. It takes three prods on the kickstarter to coax her loudly into life, then without further ado, we set off on the last leg of our journey across Libya.

Once clear of the city streets, I thank my lucky stars... the wind is still intense but no longer thick with sand. To my delight, the plucky little Bantam runs strong and smoothly. Our first break, for food at a roadside restaurant, is made after a solid 44 kilometres ride. I'd asked Essa if we could stop at the Commonwealth War Cemetery. Following the grimness of the German Memorial yesterday, it's not a visit I particularly relish but something inside makes me want to pay my respects. I enquire if we've far to go.

"I'm sorry, Gordon," he says. "I was so concerned with you being blown around by the wind, and also eager for you to keep riding while the engine is running well, that I completely forgot. The turn off is more than 30 kilometres back towards Tobruk." We decide the round trip's too far in view of the length of time formalities may take at the frontier and press on.

The wind veers round behind us... it feels as if I'm being pushed along by a powerful, invisible force. Peggy soon begins to sound as though she's running unevenly. I stop and do a few simple checks but, except for a very black and oily spark plug, have no idea what the cause may be so move off again. The engine's great when accelerating but as soon as we reach our cruising speed of 70kmph - at which point, because of the tailwind, the throttle's virtually closed - she begins to make an unpleasant chattering sound. Stopping once more, I recheck the plug and feel quite concerned... it's still very oily. Then it dawns on me that what we're experiencing must be what's known as 'four-stroking', most likely a result of the carburettor running too rich with the throttle closed. After weakening the pilot jet mixture slightly, we set off once more, whizzing along at an almost reckless 80kmph but content to have the throttle open and the engine performing sweetly.

Around 11am we arrive at the scruffy township of Umm Sa'ad, which turns out to be plagued by speed bumps, dawdling donkeys and impatient officials tearing around in plush 4x4s. Checking my mirrors, I see Essa flash his lights, so pull over at the side of a white walled office building.

"Perfect," he says once he's parked his car. "This is the place where you must return your Libyan registration plate."

While he sets about removing the gaffer tape that's held it securely to Peggy's back end since arriving in the country, I dig out my paperwork.

Together we enter the building, glad to get our heads out of the fiery sun. Essa takes charge of proceedings while I recline quietly on an old black leather sofa that's conveniently positioned beneath a slowly revolving ceiling fan. The hire of the license plate cost 135 dinar and I'm due a 100 dinar (approximately £50) refund. After some heated discussion, Essa walks over to me and says,

"There's a problem. The correct officer is not here to issue a refund. They say it will be another two hours before he arrives. Come on, let's go outside."

I follow him and stop beside Peggy, who's become piping hot in the direct sunlight.

"Do you think they'll pay up, or is it a ploy to keep my money?" I ask.

"Gordon, there is no question of not getting the refund," he answers.

"I know the system and the people very well. I will give you the 100 dinar and then return here with your paperwork after I've left you at the border. They will pay me this afternoon."

This sounds very unfair on Essa and what's more, is a bit of a blow as I'd planned to give the 100 dinars as a gratuity to him. I reveal my plan.

"Essa, that 100 dinars is for you, as a small thank you for how brilliant you've been with me. Several times you've made a seemingly impossible situation into an absolutely pleasurable one, you've always been patient and you've worked so hard."

Essa looks humbled and almost uncomfortable as I continue.

"But I want to make sure you actually do get the money, that it doesn't end up in the back-pocket of a corrupt official."

"It was my job to keep you safe and make your tour a good one," he steadily replies. "I have escorted several motorcycles border to border, but never an old one like this. I'm very happy it has made it and I have enjoyed myself very much too."

Before I can say anything else about the 100 dinars, he looks earnestly into my eyes and says,

"But I cannot accept any tips. It is strictly against company policy."

He brings out his wallet and extracts 100 dinars. I politely refuse to accept it.

"Essa, no-one at your company will know. This is just between you and me, and it's only a token amount relative to the effort you've put into the last ten days. You're even here with me on your day off," I conclude with my hands firmly planted in my pockets so he's unable to press the money onto me.

Impasse reached, he excuses himself, saying that while I prepare the bike he'll nip to a nearby petrol station in search of 2-stroke oil, which I'm desperately low on.

He returns after 15 minutes without luck.

"Sorry, they had none. I hope you can find some at the first town in Egypt."

"Me too," I reply, "thanks for trying."

I mount up and follow Essa for the last couple of sandy kilometres to the frontier post.

Once my passport is stamped, a simple formality, I load Peggy with all my luggage then Essa and I take photos of each other beside the Bantam while an elderly border guard waits patiently to one side. Essa eventually introduces us, explaining that he knows this man and has asked him to help me through the last stages of customs clearance for the bike. I feel choked as we stand opposite each other preparing to say our goodbyes. This charming, positive, enterprising, tireless and loyal man has been far more than a hired escort. Over the last ten days he's become a dear and true friend and I know I'm going to miss him.

"I didn't go to the petrol station earlier," he confesses to my complete surprise. "I really cannot accept a tip, it is not our way, so I changed 100 dinars into Egyptian pounds for you. I will get the money back in an hour when the officer returns to his office. Now you must take it," he says, pressing it into my hands adding "Have fun!" I'm lost for words.

Right at that moment, with truly synchronistic timing, an official stops his car next to us and gets out.

"Gordon May?" he asks.

I nod. He opens a folder, takes out a wad of 10 dinar notes and asks me to sign for them.

"I'm sorry I was not at my office earlier. I'm happy to catch you before you leave Libya."

Thanking him, he bows then returns to his car and I hand the money over to Essa.

We say our last farewell with a hug, then, accompanied by Essa's contact, I turn and begin to push Peggy towards Libyan customs and Egypt.

Everything starts well on the Egyptian side of the border, apart from being sent on a short detour to a mysterious 'quarantine' room, which I never find and which subsequently doesn't seem to matter anyway. My passport is stamped in the immigration hall within 10 minutes of my arrival. The adjoining building has a barred head-high window in its wall and turns out to be the conveniently situated bank. There's no queue and I'm efficiently served by a young man who, unlike everyone else I've so far encountered, is formally attired in a shirt and tie. From my research, I know I'll need to pay roughly £80 to an assortment of offices, so change enough for that and a couple of day's travel.

Next comes Customs. First I have to take all my stuff off Peggy so that it can be X-rayed, which is no fun in the sapping, motionless heat of the afternoon.

"Hey ho," I say out loud as I place the final piece, my worn spare tyre, onto the conveyor belt. Then the pantomime begins. Rubbings need to be made of the engine and frame numbers before my carnet can be stamped. I wait for half an hour while the rubbings 'engineer' eats, then watch him set to work with his pencil and paper. He's not happy with the clarity of the copy he takes from the frame, so scratches all the thick green paint off the surrounding area with a screwdriver and has another go. Disappearing, he returns with someone who can speak English.

"Your frame number is not correct," I'm informed as the carnet is slapped into my hand. He walks away and I lie on the ground and look in dismay at the newly exposed number. The final digit, which had looked very much like a '9' when coated in paint, now clearly resembles a '0'. Both my carnet and UK V5 ownership papers show it as a '9'. I'm completely baffled!

A bearded Egyptian man wearing threadbare jeans and a pink and white striped shirt approaches. I guess he's some kind of one-man private enterprise to help people through Customs. He explains, with his limited English, that this is a big problem... the Customs officers will not let it pass despite all the rest of the long line of digits being correct. Two inquisitive Syrian men come along, quickly grasp the extent of my difficulty from the Egyptian, and try to help. On their knees, they search the rest of the bike for another number, which entails wiping sticky oil and grime off large areas of frame. Like me, they draw a blank.

In the shade of a nearby inspection area I sit for over an hour ruminating on my predicament. As it's Saturday morning in the UK, I'll not be able to contact my carnet issuing body, the RAC, for two days. It's possible I'll have to pitch my tent and remain within the border compound until Monday. I look around at the parched and windswept area that's ringed by giant concrete blocks and razor wire fences... it's hardly conducive to a jolly weekend's camping. Egypt has the highest import duty rate for vehicles at 800% and I know from my research that there's very strict bureaucracy surrounding temporary imports such as mine. I decide that the only wise course of action is to remain extremely calm and patient and see how events unfold.

Out of the blue, the rubbings man returns with his senior officer and the Egyptian 'fixer' who'd tried to help earlier. Without introduction or hesitation, he wields a numbering tool and hammer and sets to work altering the Bantam's frame number from '0' to '9'. After a couple of thumps of the hammer I take a look... it's a pretty rudimentary job and I'm informed it'll cost me 100 Egyptian pounds *baksheesh*. But the fresh rubbing nevertheless passes muster and somewhat miraculously I'm free to move on with proceedings. I'm so overcome with relief that I can barely shift Peggy off her centre stand.

Following the 'fixer', Mohammed, to whom it would seem I'm now in some way contracted, I push Peggy next to a line of grungy cars that look as though they've been abandoned here for months. Sitting together on the kerb, he earnestly tries to communicate the procedures we need to follow and the costs involved. The numbers he scribbles on a scrap of paper seem greatly exaggerated and I feel more than a little concerned that I'm being fleeced.

We head to the office of the official who must stamp my carnet, passing the two Syrians who tried to help earlier. Waving my carnet at them as we pass,

I receive broad grins and thumbs up in return. In a cramped office with stacks of folders covering much of the floorspace, I hand money over to a suave man who shakes my hand and asks about my country as he examines the paperwork. He places my carnet at the bottom of a substantial pile and pleasantly waves us out of the room.

"Insurance... come," says Mohammed. "Money?" he asks, rubbing his fingers together. I know this should cost only 25 Egyptians pounds and am flabbergasted when he takes my pen from me and underscores 520 on his list. It's more than I have left, so we walk round to the front of the building to revisit the bank window. On impulse, I stall for time, asking the teller if there's a toilet I can use.

"No, not here. You must walk over to near the fence and make toilet there."

As I turn to leave, he has a change of heart.

"Wait. Come to the back of the bank. I will let you use my toilet."

Following his directions, I arrive at a formidable looking door which I assume belongs to the bank. Three large bolts are clunked back as soon as I knock and the teller promptly hands me a key and points along the corridor. Returning a few minutes later, Mohammed is still waiting beside the bank door. Knocking again, the teller opens up and invites us inside.

"Come in, please. It is very quiet today. Would you like coffee?"

Judging it would seem impolite to refuse, and realising this well spoken man may be able to shed light on the charges Mohammed is asking me to pay, I readily accept.

The teller, a lean man who introduces himself as Sami, makes a quick telephone call to order the refreshments, then perches on the edge of a desk while I take a seat. Mohammed excuses himself, promising to return for me shortly.

"I need to change more money... I think," I tell Sami.

"I can do that for you, it's no problem."

Tentatively, I raise the question of the costs I have to pay, showing him Mohammed's list.

"That is all correct," he tells me. "See these two at the bottom, the first is a thank you to the customs staff and the 150 pounds is what you must pay this man for working for you today."

I query the insurance, which is more than twentyfold the amount I'm expecting.

"Yes, you are right, it was 25 pounds but last year it was increased to this new amount. Ah, here is our coffee," he adds and turns away to answer a knock at his door.

The coffee, which is as thick as tar, is served in a small glass that scalds my fingers. While I'm blowing on the surface in between tentative sips, Sami asks me where I'm from.

"I live in the UK," I say, "near to Manchester."

Somewhat predictably, he immediately responds with gusto, "Manchester United!" Then, more contemplatively, he adds, "You come from a country that rapes other countries. For centuries your governments have invaded other weaker countries and stripped them of all their valuable resources. The British empire raped India and many other places. Now look at what they have done to my muslim brothers in Iraq and Afghanistan. I hate your country for how it acts."

I sit frozen, shocked by the strength and directness in his words and completely at a loss for what to say. To my surprise, his tone completely changes.

"But British people I like very much. They are always friendly and funny and very good to talk to. Yes, I like Britishers very much... it is just their government that I hate."

I'm mighty relieved he's able to make the distinction. Changing the subject as soon as possible, I ask about his home and family until Mohammed comes to collect me. After quickly exchanging more money, I proffer my gratitude for his hospitality and depart with smiles and a handshake.

Incredibly, it takes another two hours to buy insurance, which I'm now content is at the correct rate, secure a *carte grise* (a temporary driving licence) from the traffic police, have everything photocopied and then settle my debt to the frame number forger. Somewhat drained by the heat and the rounds of unintelligible negotiations with officialdom. we eventually return to the carnet man to have him stamp my paperwork. Last of all, we secure the hire of a pair of garish yellow numberplates adorned with incomprehensible arabic script from an office that has thousands of them lined up on the floor like dominoes. That done, I turn to pay Mohammed, feeling rather guilty for my initial mistrust, and thank him immensely for his help, which has been invaluable.

I pop out of the end of the Egyptian border controls like a cork from a champagne bottle... it's taken almost six hours and my pocket has been lightened by £170. Riding for half a kilometre along a straight sandy lane to the compound gate, armed with all the correct paperwork, I joyfully whistle The Bangles' *Walk Like An Egyptian* as loudly as possible. I'm dreadfully out of tune but really couldn't care... I've come a long way to experience this moment. Peggy has made it to Egypt!

It'll be soon be dark and I feel daunted by the ride to Alexandria. Even if Peggy's cleaned-up piston survives the heat, it could still take two to three days. The officer at the final gate asks me where I'm going, but cannot understand my reply. By and by it dawns on him that what I call *Alex*andria is his home city of Al-Iskendariyya.

"Iskendariyya?... Iskendariyya!" he calls out to his colleagues with delight and they all nod and smile. Just then, a line of five articulated lorries pull up. Two men jump out of the leading truck, walk over to me and vigorously shake my hand. They're my cheerful Syrian helpers... I hadn't realised they were truckers

"They offer to take you towards Iskendariyya," the border guard translates. "They don't want any money."

In total, six young drivers have now dismounted from the five trucks, forming a loose circle around me and Peggy. One of them with pale skin, fair hair, rosy cheeks and arresting green eyes could easily be mistaken for northern European. He points to his colleagues one at a time,

"Aleppo... Damascus... Aleppo," he says, indicating that they are all from Syria.

In his book, *Motorcycle Yoga*, Miles Davis contemplates his safety while riding alone in rural India: 'In a land that is strange to him, a lone motorcyclist must learn how to tell who is to be trusted - and how far. The price of a foolish and poorly calculated friendship can be a very bitter lesson. A quick decision about where confidence should be placed is the acquired skill of the savvy wanderer... To such as these I would advise that he who abandons his homeland must not assume an air of abandon.' That said, I instinctively know that I can trust these Syrian truckers and spontaneously accept their offer. Once through the compound gates, many willing hands hoist Peggy into the back of one of the empty trailers and she's soon made secure by suspending her with broad straps to the ceiling like a curious wheeled puppet. Checking her over, I'm concerned that she'll swing around too much once we're under way. Immediately, three whopping spare truck tyres are brought from the other lorries, the men working as a team to lug them into the trailer and wedge them against Peggy.

I climb into the cab of an early 1990's black Volvo rig with Abdullah, a dark skinned man who has cropped black hair, a beard and wears unblemished navy overalls. He speaks a few words of English and seems very happy to have me as a passenger. Sitting beside him, I think about what I've just so impulsively done and reach the conclusion that perhaps this is the only way I'll be able to complete the journey. Taking rides on trains, trucks and ferries to shorten the number of miles Peggy has to cover may still make the whole thing possible... it certainly seems like a less perilous option than riding through the night, with or without flashing yellow lights!

Positioned at the tail of our convoy, we head off along an otherwise empty belt of tarmac that's bordered by a vast limestone desert to the south and the Mediterranean, glittering like crushed sapphires, to the north. Within 15 minutes we come to a sharp bend in the road. Ahead is an enormous sheer drop of 600 metres to the town of Sollum, which nestles up against the shoreline of an idyllic horseshoe bay. The sun has just dipped below the horizon, casting the reflection of a flaming orange sky onto the still water and richly enhancing the encircling folds of golden desert. We begin to descend the cliff face, following a series of hairpin bends in low gear, the truck's air brakes shrieking and hissing under the strain.

Within half an hour we stop. The trucks parallel park on a stretch of empty land at the far side of Sollum and the drivers, who are returning from delivering tomatoes to Libya, set about preparing dinner. Suspended below each wagon are great steel boxes with flap doors. Once these are opened, the door serves as a large table while the inside is revealed to be a comprehensive mobile kitchen. There are shelves and cubby-holes full of grains and pulses, glass jars of spices, neatly stacked trays of plates and a strapped-in saucepan set. One end of the cupboard is taken up by an industrial looking gas ring that's fuelled by a butane bottle. Buzzing with effervescent conversation and a pleasant levity, all six drivers set about the task of preparing a meal. One makes cups of tea, another deftly handles the frying pan, three prepare vegetables and Abdullah appears to be gathering the cutlery and plates we'll use. I join in, peeling and chopping a pile of courgettes.

With the food steadily simmering in a large cooking pot, I'm given a towel and block of soap then led to the side of another truck where there's a tap. The man who accompanies me, one of four called Ahmed, washes his face and hands and gesticulates for me to follow his example. As I dry my face, two drivers converge from opposing angles, both with bottles of shampoo in their hands. Laughing at their synchronised arrival, they gesture that I should wash my hair. I feel rather confused about the necessity for this as my hair is cut short and already reasonably clean, but assume it's a kind of ritual so do as asked. Once tousled dry, they encourage me to wash my feet. I'm unsure whether this is a cultural practice, of religious significance or if mine are simply on the whiffy side, but go with the flow. Removing my boots and socks, one driver crouches down and immediately begins to lather my feet, then rinses them with cool, clean water from a plastic teapot. Being bathed in such a way by a stranger while I lean against the wheel of a Syrian truck at the top of Africa is a most peculiar, if not humbling, experience! The other driver returns within a minute carrying a pair of sandals and his leather jacket for me to wear against the increasingly chilly evening air, picking up my boots in the process and stowing them in a locker under his truck.

Back at the 'kitchen', the atmosphere is wonderfully amiable. Everyone is sharing jokes, leaning on each other with a hand placed on a friend's leg or shoulder in the way that's typical of the male bonding I've witnessed since arriving on this continent. The lively conversation switches to me and we somehow manage to trade information about my journey and their lives, which includes one of the older drivers phoning home so that his wife, who speaks some English, can ask me questions. I find the way I'm welcomed into their group and made to feel completely at ease truly extraordinary.

Dinner is served on a tarpaulin spread over the grubby wooden floor of one of the empty trailers. I was dreading this part of the evening, certain the food would have meat in it. Apart from eating fish on the advice of a naturopath to help my body recover from an attack of meningitis I developed in India in

2005, I've been vegetarian for over 24 years. That withstanding, it would be highly ungracious of me to refuse to eat the meal and I would hate it to be seen as an affront to my hosts' incredible hospitality. I decide that when the time comes, I'll simply try to spoon out as little of the flesh as possible. When a plate is handed to me, I'm gobsmacked to see a stew consisting of tomatoes, garlic, onions and my courgettes but not a morsel of meat.

Sitting in the cave-like trailer, the smell of dust and oil mingling with a slightly musty organic odour from the goods they've recently delivered, I relax deeply. Illuminated by two candles that reflect their flickering light in the hard pressed steel roof, I observe the six drivers treating each other with respect, fondness and humour in a truly enviable team spirit. I can't make out whether they always travel together or simply meet up from time to time, but they interact like the best of friends, even the best of brothers. Being among them, in this extremely shoddy environment, I can't help noting how rich their lives are, and by comparison, how impoverished are the multitudes who strive for material wealth and acquisition, placing so little emphasis on such intrinsic community and humanity. I wonder if, ironically, they're unaware of what real treasure their camaraderie is, and, influenced by the spread of the the global media's 'must have' message, they covet the consumerist 'pleasures' of the shopping mall... I suppose I'll never know.

Everyone pitches in good naturedly with the washing up and packing away, then the drivers scale the short ladders up to their cabs. I'm told they'll drive as late as midnight then park up until morning. Abdullah clears everything off the bunk behind his seat, puts a clean cover on the pillow and indicates I should climb into his bed. I don't want to offend his generosity by turning down the offer but am conscious that as a driver he'll need a good night's sleep. I try to protest but he is resolute, pointing high and signalling that later he'll sleep above me in the smaller top bunk, which to my eyes appears more like a luggage shelf. In the end I yield and climb into the secure comfort of the bed.

As the truck sets off, Abdullah puts on a tape of the Quran. The musical modulations of the voice make it sound like a folk song rather than a holy reading. Wrapped in a cosy blanket, I'm lulled off to sleep by the rocking movement of the truck and the rhythmic, devout Arabic voice on the cassette player.

Day 27, Marsa Matrouh to Alexandria, Egypt.
124 miles by truck & 81 miles ridden.

I sleep incredibly well despite being awakened in the wee hours by a used gudgeon pin sticking into my ribs... I have absolutely no idea how it got there. Above me, Abdullah stirs. It's 7am. He quickly rouses himself and joins the rest of the team who are already chatting outside. Pulling on some clothes, I hop down and find the group gathered round one of the fold-down canteens. To my surprise, I see that there are now only three trucks, all parked on a strip of scrubby land close to Marsa Matrouh. Two of the truckers decided to continue on through the night, hoping to reach Cairo before dawn.

Breakfast is the same communal affair as dinner. I proudly contribute some organic Colombian ground coffee that I brought on the journey to drink while camping but which I hadn't opened. However, I quickly sense that the Syrians are only making a show of drinking it, as one asks if it's Nescafe! I understand why when they brew a second round of drinks using some of their own beans. The Syrian coffee, prepared the Turkish way with the grinds left like thick claggy mud in the bottom of the cup, is at least twice as strong as mine. I contentedly relax on a folding chair and, accompanied by the sound of waves breaking on the nearby foreshore, eat unleavened bread smeared with sticky, dark honey,

We set off east in bright sunshine, staying on the quiet coastal main road. It feels odd to sink comfortably into the Volvo's hydraulic seat, secure in the knowledge that Peggy's safely ensconced in the back of the artic we're following. The four drivers swap around from time to time so that one can rest and after a while one of the younger Ahmeds takes over Abdullah's steering wheel. For almost an hour he sits cross legged on his seat, the truck running on cruise control. Thankfully we have the roads almost completely to ourselves... I can't guess how long it would take him to untangle his legs and hit the brakes if a heavily laden overland motorcyclist were to cross his path!

Around midday, I notice that the views on both sides of the road have been obliterated by colossal holiday apartment complexes, most of which are little more than shells awaiting confirmed buyers before windows, internal walls and in many cases roofs are added. There appear be tens of thousands of partially completed residences, a state of affairs which I guess must be largely due to the global economic downturn of the last couple of years. As we roll by the huge concrete skeletons for nearly an hour, it seems increasingly likely that no more than a small percentage will ever be finished.

We eventually reach El Alamein, renowned for two pivotal battles during WWII. It's a nondescript place, with no immediate signs of where Montgomery's Eighth Army battled the panzers of Rommel's Afrika Korps. At the end of the second decisive battle in November 1942 and with the Axis forces in full retreat, Winston Churchill notably said, 'Now this is not the end. It is not even the

169

beginning of the end, but it is, perhaps, the end of the beginning.' Recalling this speech as the trucks brake to a halt, it feels like today will mark pretty much the same phase for Peggy and me.

From here, the Syrians will take a short cut south east to join the desert highway to Cairo. We park on the roadside a hundred metres ahead of the turn off to a petrol station and all four drivers pitch in to unload Peggy, who's survived the 260 mile journey in the cavernous tomato wagon without so much as a scratch. Once she's down on the tarmac, Abdullah removes the petrol cap and peers into the tank... it's almost empty. There's a group discussion before they enquire, mostly by gestures, if I have enough Egyptian money to buy fuel. I reach into a trouser pocket and pull out a modest amount in notes to show that I have some local currency. Abdullah shakes his head and makes it clear that this is not enough. He gets out his wallet and tries to put a couple of large denomination bills into my hand. The willingness of these men to help me, to share virtually everything they have, is so estimable that I'm knocked sideways in gratitude to find there are still people with big, kind hearts like these four Syrian men gracing our planet. Finally, to end their insistence that I take the money, I have to climb into the cab to retrieve my motorcycling jacket and show that I have a couple of hundred Egyptian pounds in reserve. As we prepare to say goodbye, I'm lost to know how to convey my feelings and thanks. Taking each of their hands in both of mine and looking directly into their eyes, I say "*Shokran*", but it somehow doesn't seem enough.

As the other three drivers return to their trucks, Abdullah earnestly says,

"Tell people... your country... muslim man, good man. No terrorist... good man."

I nod vigorously to impart that I'll do exactly that and feel sad as they drive away, knowing that I'll never see them again. Their rich camaraderie, openness, community and hospitality have moved me deeply.

With my luggage strapped back on, including a bag tied to the handlebars to assist airflow on the engine, I push Peggy onto the petrol station forecourt. Puzzlingly, it only sells 92 and 90 octane fuel, which is useless. Firing her up, I ride half a kilometre to the next fuel stop, an Esso which sells 90 and, to my horror, 80 octane... what on earth can run on that, I wonder? It takes two more attempts before I find 95 and I really don't mind that it costs one Egyptian pound more per litre than the 92. I'm able to stock up on 2-stroke oil at the same time, thank goodness. The bottle has a picture of a speedboat on the side of it, but I have to trust it'll work just the same.

The ride to Alexandria takes almost five hours. At first I look in my mirrors almost expecting to see the white car of my guardian angel, Essa, sitting at our tail with flashing indicators, but as the miles pass, slowly become used to his absence. Peggy gets seriously hot and I'm forced to stop every 10 to 15 kilometres to let her cool... what's new! Traffic builds as we get closer to the city, and it's no fun. Trucks and large expensive cars bully me out of their way, pulling up behind with flashing lights and blaring horns. Why they can't overtake on the dual carriageway's second lane is beyond me but I'm forced again and again onto a narrow hard shoulder. This is somewhat problematic as not only is it covered with patchy sand, it's also populated by numerous people flagging down lifts, obstructed by temporary plant shops and littered with broken chunks of concrete at each of the turn offs to the countless stalled building sites. There are even a couple of burst sewers that I'm forced to motor through, my face screwed-up and my lips sucked-in tightly!

Alexandria has a population of over four million and is spread for many miles along the coastline. With night falling, I navigate using the small scale map in my Egypt guide book, the sat nav set to compass mode and a bit of dead reckoning. For 7 kilometers I get trapped on a 6 lane highway, which is rather perilous as I'm by far the slowest vehicle and my fellow road users once again seem decidedly lacking in tolerance. At last I pass an enormous chemical plant, its towers spewing flames and noxious-looking gases, then thankfully take an exit heading north towards the city centre.

The final stages of the journey, through swarming streets, are exceedingly challenging. There are no lane markings and vehicles try to drive three abreast where there's really only room for two. Bustling yellow and black Lada taxis zip in and out and battered minibuses tear along at breakneck speed before making what's effectively an emergency stop as they contemptuously swerve across my path to pick up passengers. Local motorcyclists astride 100cc machines fantastically illuminated by scores of blue or red flashing LEDs recklessly zigzag around, their bare armed and bare headed riders seemingly oblivious to the risks of a crash. As we near the shopping district, pedestrians spill into one lane of the road from the overflowing pavements and trams bulldoze their way down the middle, clearing their path with hoots worthy of a ship's fog horn.

Throw into the mix gaping potholes; inverted speed breakers; slippery tram lines that trap Peggy's front wheel and nearly have me off; sleeping policemen built like ramps in a skateboard park; street hawkers; children chasing either each other or a football onto the road... and it's a roller-coaster of a ride! I go slowly over one speed hump that resembles a concrete log. It's so tall yet compact that the Beeza's alloy sump guard grounds and the centrestand graunches as it digs in. I have to frantically stab my feet on its apex to stop us falling over sideways then, with cars bouncing over it on both sides of us, rock Peggy forward to free her. I'm bathed in sweat from the concentration required to stay safe and aching from the exertion of navigating the ever-changing obstacles, but Peggy mercifully keeps running for half an hour non-stop.

We finally come to a chugging halt next to the legendary Cecil Hotel at the edge of the city's famed Corniche. The Cecil was built in 1929 on the site where a pair of 3,000 year old red granite obelisks, known as *Cleopatra's*

Needles sat, before being relocated to London and New York in the 19th century. In its heyday, the hotel's guests included the likes of Winston Churchill, Noel Coward and Somerset Maughan. It's even said that in the 1930s the British Secret Service operated out of a first floor suite.

At over $300 a night, the Cecil's a long way out of my price range. Removing my sat nav and tank bag, I leave Peggy fully laden next to the pavement and nip down a side street in search of a more affordable alternative, The Crillon, which comes highly recommended. I soon find its entrance but the ancient lift, accessed through a concertina wrought iron gate, is frustratingly slow. By the time I've found the third floor reception, been shown a couple of rooms and legged it back down the stairs in preference to waiting for the antique elevator, I've been away from the Bantam and all my luggage for a good 15 minutes. As I run round the corner, heart pounding, I see crowds walking past her with a few pedestrians pausing for a closer look, but nothing has been touched... phew!

I wheel her round to the hotel building's entrance, but there's no way to haul her up several flights of stairs to the safety of the Crillon's landing. A young curly-haired Egyptian with humourous eyes and a smile as wide as his face comes to my rescue. Introducing himself as Bebo, he leads me to his tiny pavement hut, which is no more than one and a half metres square. From this spartan establishment, he manages all the cars parked on the street. He shows me a board on which hang all their keys and tells me that his job, between watching football on the miniature TV that's wedged into a corner, is to wash the vehicles when required, move them around to maximise space and keep them safe. We lift Peggy onto the sidewalk and park her next to his shack, which Bebo somehow manages to sleep in... he must have mastered the exacting skill of vertical slumber! For a very reasonable fee he will keep Peggy secure. I wrap a chain round the front wheel, shroud her in the bike cover and head for a shower.

One of my favourite black and white movies is the WWII drama *Ice-Cold in Alex,* starring British silverscreen greats John Mills, Anthony Quayle, Harry Andrews and Sylvia Syms. From the comfort of my armchair I've often watched the tale of their escape from Tobruk in an Austin K2 ambulance and the daring journey they make east across the formidable Qattara Depression towards the British lines and Alexandria. Throughout, Mill's character, Captain Anson, dreams of knocking back a pint of ice cold lager at his favourite Alexandria bar, which after many trials and tribulations is how the plot ends. Tonight I wander the lively streets of Iskendariyya, which to all appearances retains a great number of buildings from before the war, and find a restaurant that does indeed serve chilled lager in frosty glasses. I don't think the film's protagonists can have enjoyed their beer any more than I do tonight... and though she's out of sight in Bebo's care, I toast Peggy as I down the icy deliciousness.

Day 28, Alexandria, Egypt.
0 miles.

The Crillon has charm aplenty. The snug lounge, with woven rugs spread on top of beautifully grained polished wood floors, is lined with classy furniture and interesting collectables. Armchairs and sofas are covered in vermillion and gold brocade and are so thickly padded that when I stop to test one, I feel blissfully cocooned and don't really want to move. Rather idiosyncratic is the array of stuffed exotic birds that are perched here, there and everywhere. They're obviously very old and give the feel of an eccentric colonial ornithologist's drawing room. Best of all, however, is the outlook from the hotel's restaurant where I eat breakfast. Viewed through open floor to ceiling windows that let in a cool salty breeze, the uninterrupted vista of Corniche and harbour is truly grand.

In need of a day off, I leave Peggy completely untouched.

"Morning girl," I say as I stride past her, wave into the adjacent custodian's shack and set out to explore Alexandria.

The city's lively and energetic... there seems to be a vibrancy generated by its inhabitants who appear to do everything both purposefully and vigorously Many young people are dressed in fashionable Western clothes that wouldn't look out of place on the streets of any European capital, but what I notice most are the women. In Libya I didn't speak to a single female and except in Tripoli, never even saw one on the streets alone. Here, women confidently walk on their own, some wear a headscarf, as is customary in Islamic countries, but many don't. I even see a female police motorcyclist on duty, directing traffic through a junction where water spews onto the road from a burst main. Compared with Libya and Tunisia, Alexandria feels decidedly modern and cosmopolitan.

Wandering along the crescent shaped Corniche, I admire views of the stunning cityscape that curves around the gently ebbing waves of the harbour. It amazes me to think that a settlement was first founded here by Alexander the Great and the sunken remains of the ancient city of Cleopatra lie beneath these blue waters. Indeed, divers have recently found obelisks, red granite columns and a diorite sphinx complete with the face of Ptolemy XII, father of Cleopatra, in a submerged area now dubbed *Cleopatra's Palace*. One of the Seven Wonders of the Ancient World, the Pharos lighthouse, was a towering landmark for the early port. The tallest manmade structure on earth for many years, it safely guided mariners along the tricky coastline for more than 16 centuries before being destroyed by two powerful earthquakes in the 14th century. The Pharos's former site, which is within walking distance, is occupied by an impressive fortress that was constructed using the wrecked lighthouse's huge, recycled blocks of masonry.

Lunch is easily solved by visiting a popular fast food outlet called *Gad.* I usually stay well clear of convenience food but this place is different... it serves the most amazing, healthy falafels crammed into pitta bread with fresh salad, a squirt of lemon juice and a sizeable dollop of tahini. Better still, as the saying goes, it's as cheap as chips. I take mine to a small park and sit on a bench in the sun, happily munching my way through it. It's so good, I have to go back for more, receiving great big, if somewhat knowing smiles from both the cashier and the falafel maker. The city centre is packed with cafés and teahouses, including a great chunk of the landward side of the cornice that's taken up by an almost continuous string of ahwas (coffeehouses). Having already had more than my fair share of caffeine for the day, I pass these and get a freshly pressed mango juice from a backstreet juice shop. It's run by a lively, ebullient man with blazing ginger hair who talks and laughs non-stop. Like the food, one's just not enough, so I indulge in another, which judging by the reaction of the jolly juicer seems to be a normal occurrence.

Almost next door is an internet café, reminding me that I need to catch up on mail. Whilst waiting for my webmail programme to open, I see a news item outlining the coalition government that's been formed in the UK. Two weeks have passed since I last saw any news updates and it makes me smile that I've been so out of touch with events. It also reminds me that often, when travelling, the world refreshingly shrinks to one's immediate horizon and what's required on a minute by minute, day by day basis. For me, it's highly liberating.

Back on the streets, I find taxi watching greatly entertaining. The city's overflowing with identically painted Lada Rivas that resemble automotive bumble bees. These simple, utilitarian Soviet-made cars, based on a 1966 Fiat 124 sedan, seem to be omnipresent on Alexandria's roads. Their drivers are somewhat cavalier when it comes to road safety, making radical U-turns in the middle of a nearby intersection and recklessly weaving in and out of lanes. But it's not their crazy antics that amuse me... it's the after-market badges they've attached to their radiator grills. Many sport Peugeot lions and I spy a few Toyotas together with a couple of Chrysler emblems. My personal favourite, however, is the aspirational owner who's proudly glammed his decrepit old Lada with the four circles of an Audi. There's lifemanship for you!

Beat-up trams trundle along the lines that were so nearly my undoing last night. As I cross one set of tracks heading inland, a horn blasts from behind so loudly that I jump about six inches off the ground then frantically look around, heart in mouth, expecting to see the imminent approach of a thundering tram. Unbelievably, it's a bicycle. There's an 18 inch brass contraption attached to his handlebars that looks like an antique pump action plant watering device but is, in fact, an ancient klaxon capable of decibels way beyond its size. I watch the man pedalling strongly down the middle of the road, scaring the bejesus out of any pedestrians that dare cross his path.

Most of the motorcycles whizzing around are 2-stroke MZs or Vespa scooters. It really bothers me that they seem able to cope with the heat whilst Peggy, despite all the care and skill used in assembling the rebuilt engine, has had the toughest of times. I can only reason that these bikes are simply run for short, unstressed spurts, not at constant speeds hour after hour... and must have flat topped pistons to cope with the ridiculously poor fuel! I'm brought to a halt by the sight of a parked motorcycle the likes of which I've never seen. It appears to be some kind of Chinese copy of a Honda 125, but I can't say for sure as it's impossible to see the tank emblem... the whole of the top of the machine is covered in a made-to-measure carpet! Gaping, I slowly make my way round the bike, studying from every angle the well-worn patterned rug that bedecks petrol tank, seat, side panels and rear mudguard. Best of all are the golden tassels, each at least 10cm long, that hang from every edge. It's a splendidly bizarre work of art.

The moment I turn onto the Corniche I'm stopped by the driver of a tourists' horse and carriage taxi. With jet black bodywork and canvas hood contrasted by large scarlet spoked wheels, the cab is arrestingly eye catching. The glossy-coated bay mare, with her head deeply buried in a sack of oats, looks well cared for and I'm rather tempted to go for a ride. However, the cabbie immediately puts me off with his pushy attitude. He hops out of his seat and follows me, aggressively shouting and wildly gesticulating, pressing hard for me to hire him. Trying to keep things lighthearted, I smile and lightly shake my head, then turn to continue walking. This only seems to goad him to further intensify his pitch. Taking my life in my hands, I dart across the busy road in-between the hectic rush hour traffic and make my escape. It's a shame, I think as I sit on the sea wall to take in the view, that the likes of this man give Egyptians a bad reputation for hassling tourists... everyone else I've encountered has been polite and supremely helpful.

Indeed, returning to my hotel I have another experience of Egyptian courtesy. I open the antiquated lift doors too early, causing the lift to stop with its base still a good 40cm above the ground. I try closing them to see if the elevator will finish its descent, but nothing happens. A lady, who's obviously a resident of one of the building's many private apartments, steps around me, pulls the doors open, hoists her two bags of groceries into the lift and promptly follows them. She pulls the gates closed, pushes a button and disappears upwards, leaving me standing open-mouthed.

"Charming!" I mutter under my breath.

I hear the lift stop but before I can push the call button it begins to descend again. The gates are opened by the occupant, who to my surprise is the lady that had just left me stranded on the ground floor.

"When stop," she says in broken English, "you climb in and up, not down. Please, come."

Lesson learned... on more than one level.

After dinner, I wander around some of the city's characterful backstreets, taking in an odd mixture of buildings ranging from preserved victorian grandeur to dilapidated 20th century structures that are teetering on the edge of collapse. My attention is caught by a pyjama shop selling the most garish and, to my taste, ludicrous nightware imaginable. I'm tempted to buy a lurid pink frilly dressing gown for Jane as a joke, but refrain in case she thinks I'm being serious. Taking a circuitous route back to the Crillon, I come across an area where several alleyways are crammed full of tables and chairs, the overspills from working-mens' teahouses and sheesha shops. On impulse, I walk down one and take an empty table next to a group of men who are engrossed in a game of backgammon. Ordering a pipe, I select the first of the many choices of tobacco I'm offered. It feels odd to draw the flavoursome, thick smoke through the cooling water and take it into my lungs. Then it hits me with a wham. I make a great show of adjusting my coals to hide the fact that I've turned red and am desperately trying not to choke! The following tokes are less challenging, but after a couple of minutes I can feel my chest tightening and stop. The waiter is rather confounded that I'm leaving so early, my pipe unfinished... I'm just glad to be able to walk away without retching and coughing helplessly.

Before bed I repack all my bags. Most spare parts containers are full of sand from the numerous times they were open in Tunisia and Libya, but it's a good feeling to have everything properly organised again. I desperately hope they won't be needed on tomorrow's ride to Cairo.

Lada taxis on the Corniche.

176

Day 29, Alexandria to Cairo, Egypt.
146 miles.

"It's a BSA!" exclaims a passer-by, an Egyptian man in his sixties who's stopped to watch me load Peggy. "I remember these motorcycles. There were once many BSAs in Egypt and there are still some left, mostly in Cairo."

This comes as a bit of a surprise as I'd imagined nearly all the wartime machines would have been scrapped many years ago. Unfortunately, the man reveals no more information, turning his attention instead to chasing a mange-ridden cat down the street.

We're rolling by 9am and are immediately in luck, finding a main road out of the city which, by chance, runs past the strikingly designed *Bibliotheca Alexandrina*. This amazing library, with shelf space for 7,000 000 books, was built to commemorate the *Library of Alexandria*, the greatest library of the ancient world which was sadly lost to antiquity, thanks in part to Julius Caesar supposedly setting fire to it by accident. Turning inland, I stay on a busy four lane road, stopping just once to check my bearings with a policeman before spotting the first overhead signpost for Cairo. There are two routes we could use but I elect to follow the Desert Highway as I've been told it's in better condition than the alternative Nile Delta road. Furthermore, it approaches the city via the Giza pyramids, which I aim to reach before sunset.

The day's typically scorching and within 15 kilometres I have to stop for the first engine dampening session, which coincides nicely with a petrol station that sells 95. At our next break, 13km further along, I exit onto a baked earth track, heading for the shade of a tree at the edge of a small holding. With Peggy leaning on her sidestand, I idly watch two school-age boys harvesting leafy vegetables with a small scythe before loading them into a wooden wheelbarrow. Once full, the smaller boy, who's probably five or six, hops onto the barrow whilst the older boy cheerily pushes him towards the Bantam and me. As they wobble to a halt, the younger one smiles and shyly offers me a tomato from a small pile nestled between his legs. I decline his generosity with thanks, conscious that their crop is quite small and will most likely be precious to them. They both wave goodbye and continue on their way.

As the humidity intensifies, so the frequency of our stops increases and we're soon into our habitual 8 to 12 kilometres ride, 20 minutes break pattern. During the morning, these interludes are used to considerable gain. I tighten all fastenings on the bike, put a little air into the rear tyre with my foot pump and adjust the rear chain. Even the gearbox oil is changed, utilising a plastic bag to collect the used lubricant. Several cars and pickups stop as they see us by the roadside, the owners winding down their windows and using the same universal sign to ask what I'm doing and whether I'm okay. Keeping their right hand open, they quickly twist it round at the wrist from pointing downwards to facing up. It's hard for me to communicate back other than by smiling, looking upbeat and sticking my thumb upwards. In every case, they pleasantly acknowledge my response and drive on.

The roadsides are largely devoid of habitation and there doesn't seem to be anywhere to buy lunch... I guess it's because the non-classic 2-stroke traffic has little problem covering the distance between the cities in just a couple of hours. Suddenly, I spot a huge pyramid of shiny dark green skinned watermelons partially shaded by a tatty makeshift canopy. I'm never convinced that the sweet and juicy red pulp of the watermelon, succulent as it is, is safe from bacteria. However the lady running the stand also sells water, chocolate bars and peanuts which I gratefully devour, squeezed into the tiniest triangle of shade between Peggy and the neatly stacked fruit.

During our next spell of riding and at full speed, I hit a smooth but fearsome hollow that's disguised by the sun's shimmering reflection on the tarmac. It's probably 2 metres long by half a metre deep and ends in a wickedly steep slope. The front of the bike is airborne for a moment then pounds into the far side of the depression, bouncing me off the seat and throwing me forward well over the handlebars like a bucking rodeo bull. Somehow holding on, I thrust my weight backwards and shakily regain the saddle and my balance. My hands and wrists still feel the strain ten minutes later when we stop. I inspect Peggy. There's quite a lot of grease oozing around the bottom of the right fork leg where the seal has been damaged by the force of the impact. I reflect that failing to spot the trough until the last moment was a blessing in disguise... if I'd seen it a couple of seconds earlier and applied my front brake, the forks would have been fully compressed when we hit, most likely resulting in more serious damage. Far worse, I'd probably have been hurled off headfirst in the process. It's a lucky escape.

The road is in the process of being widened to an 8 lane super highway and the roadworks become exceeding tricky to negotiate, with repeated 2 lane contra-flow systems where the speeding traffic jostles crazily for position. Entering and exiting these reverse direction areas is darned dangerous, with trucks and cars not braking until the very last moment. Then, at risk of destroying their suspension or wiping Peggy out, they jounce over speed breakers and sections of the demolished central reservation into which are wedged whopping patches of shattered concrete and slippery shingle. On one such contra-flow, with a line of fast cars bombing past in the outside lane and a frustrated minibus sitting just inches from our back wheel, I encounter some shed vegetables strewn across the road. Most of the tomatoes have already been squished but many of the onions, being much harder, remain intact. With nowhere to go, there's no option but to take my chances and ride through the debris, a nerve wracking and hazardous experience.

Traffic remains generally intolerant of our modest tempo, with huge articulated rigs overtaking one another whilst careering along, passing us three abreast. Even the occasional bulbous fronted Bedford TJ truck, a relic from a bygone era that on another occasion would make me smile with nostalgia, bludgeons its way past us. Most of these late 1950's wagons carry dry goods piled into an open, wood-sided cargo bay. However, we slowly catch up to one such vehicle that's massively overburdened with very fine grey gravel. It's obviously not suited to the job as every time it hits a bump in the road, a shower of hard stones fly out of a gap at the bottom of its tailgate and painfully strike us.

Twisting Peggy's throttle three quarters open, I accelerate hard, swinging out into the third lane to give the old truck a very wide berth. Returning to the inside lane and our normal cruising speed, I focus my attention ahead. A cursory check in my mirrors shows the Bedford has speeded up, pulling into the second lane in a charge after us. The driver is tenaciously hauling us in inch by inch. I go a little faster... so does he, now pulling up alongside us but barely able to make any headway as the highway begins to climb a gentle incline. I take a hurried glance up to the cab... the driver scowls at me, determination written all over his face that he's not going to be outdone by this little green pipsqueak of a motorcycle. Eventually, nudging a couple of metres ahead, he throws the truck across to the inside lane and sprays another painful fusillade of tiny sharp stones all over us. I give up, hitting the brakes until he's almost out of sight before returning to our normal measured pace.

During the afternoon's cooling stops, I resort to reading a secondhand WWII Ken Follett spy novel, *The Key To Rebecca*, which I picked up in Alexandria. It helps distract me from the constant drone of passing vehicles and the exasperating flies that crawl indefatigably over my perspiring face, neck, hands and up the legs of my trousers. I bought the book simply because it's set in Egypt during the war and to my delight it proves to be a gripping tale about a British GHQ officer tracking down a German spy who's feeding secrets to Rommel's advancing forces. As the afternoon light begins to soften towards evening, I reach page 47 and simply cannot believe what I'm reading. The pursuing British agent, Vandam, sets off across Cairo on a fast, army issued motorcycle. It's a BSA 350! I'm tickled pink.

We reach the outskirts of Cairo around 8pm, just as it becomes dark. Traffic is pandemonium. Engulfed by choking fumes and surrounded by hot exhausts, the road is so densely packed that our jerky stop-start advancement becomes painstakingly laborious. It takes at least half an hour to cover 4 kilometres and I feel completely overawed by the experience. Edging my way to the gutter, which is in itself no mean feat, I bounce Peggy onto a strip of cracked sidewalk and turn her off. Perched on the kerb, just a foot away from the moribund wall of traffic, I feel very low. We've been on the road for over eleven hours and have only covered a derisory 132 miles. Bemoaning the constantly overheating engine for making the journey so woefully prolonged and taxing, I attempt to push Peggy 30 metres towards a streetside snack stand and lose my balance. She falls over. The luggage cushions her landing, but to cap it all, while trying to right her, the centrestand scrapes up my shin bone. Close to tears, I hobble the rest of the way to the drinks seller, kick out the sidestand and flop down.

With half an hour's rest and fortified by the intense sugar fix provided by a Snickers bar and Coke, I press on, following signs for the city centre. Traffic is so crammed that Peggy becomes repeatedly wedged in between larger vehicles and I fear to fully plant my feet on the tarmac in case they get run over. Many of the great mass of drivers are utterly unpredictable, cutting across blocked vehicles with just inches to spare so they can try their luck down the numerous side streets. The joy of seeing so many white VW Type 2 Kombi vans, the mainstay of trendy campervans the world over, being used as collective taxis is spoilt by the impetuousness of their drivers, who make the Alexandria minibus operators look like *Advanced Motorists*. Several times, these wonderful old air cooled buses, often with sagging suspension and packed to bursting with passengers, come to a slewing and abrupt halt right in front of me so that people can climb on or alight. On top of all that, every action of every motorist seems to be accompanied by the blast of a horn, creating an almost impenetrable din that's exceedingly wearing.

We continue to make stilted and sometimes heart-stopping progress and I begin to fear for Peggy as the gearbox becomes decidedly clunky and neutral increasingly awkward to find. I also worry that the clutch could easily burn out under this level of abuse. But against all the odds, the engine miraculously keeps running with virtually no airflow to cool it. My hands, wrists and arms ache and lose their strength from overuse, making me a far less effective rider. Pausing in a stationary queue, I look right and catch my breath. Almost alongside us, illuminated by the waxing moon, is the majestic outline of the Great Pyramid. This morning I'd envisioned parking up beside it at sunset but the challenges of the protracted day's ride had wiped this dream from my mind. Despite the horrendous, tormenting traffic and our miserable pedestrian progress, I'm filled with elation... so thrilled in fact that I slap Peggy's tank and shout,

"You're at the pyramids Peggy. You've done it!"

My joy is short lived. In a temporary reprieve from the jam that lasts for only 30 seconds, cars, buses and taxis erratically chop and change lanes all around and I can't really look again for more than a brief glimpse. Reaching the back of more congestion, I again haul on the clutch and brakes, slogging forward a foot or two at a time before our movement is further arrested. It's impossible to ride smoothly or nurse Peggy whille surrounded by so much chaos.

By and by we swing right onto a wide bridge and cross a broad expanse of dark, still water. Peggy gets another gleeful slap on the tank and, feeling only a little off-beat at communicating with a motorcycle as if it were a sentient being, I cry,

"The Nile Peggs! We're crossing the Nile!"

On the far side, the roads are thankfully less congested but I stop once more to give us both a rest, this time buying a bunch of stubby, ripe bananas for the energy I need to cover the final few miles. Underway again, we pass the imposing Egyptian Museum, then take the first wrong turn of the night. I instinctively realise what I've done but because of the one-way system, it's impossible to back track. Pulling up, I check my bearings with some pedestrians then climb off and push Peggy against the flow of traffic for two blocks before cranking her over and following a new direction.

At 10.35pm, we pull up outside the Windsor Hotel. I'm bathed in sweat, completely done-in but exultant. The two white uniformed policemen who sit at the hotel entrance instruct me to park Peggy close to them as they're on duty all night and will ensure there are no problems. As I prepare to walk away, I unashamedly stroke her headlamp and whisper,

"Thanks for getting us here safely."

Rather wobbly, I enter the welcome sanctuary of the hotel, a venerable Cairo institution that hasn't changed one jot since I stayed here on my only other visit to Egypt in April 1987. The building was erected at the turn of the last century as the baths of the Egyptian royal family, then for many years served as a colonial British officers' club before being purchased by a Swiss hotelier. The antiquated reception desk and ancient telephone switchboard, a tangled spaghetti of wires and plugs, are just as I remember them. So too is the courteous and friendly demeanour of the staff. I choose a room and then, with the help of a porter, unload the Bantam and transfer everything to the lift. This too is gloriously dated, with iron gates securing its front and back. I climb in with the porter, who clunks a long brass lever a couple of notches to operate the lift. We rather splendidly rattle upwards, completely exposed within the open shaft which forms the centre of the hotel's winding staircase.

After blasting my tired muscles in a long hot shower, I descend to the lounge. It's still decked in colonial décor that incongruously merges with an Alpine bar area which features seating made from cut down wine barrels. I order a pizza and a cold beer. The label says Stellar, however it's not the renowned Belgian brew I'm familiar with but Egypt's own brand. After my 13½ hour endurance test to get here, such a detail doesn't matter.

furthermore

Day 30, Cairo, Egypt.
0 miles.

After a surprisingly restful night's sleep on my boingy wrought-iron bedstead, I spend the day tucked away in the lounge of The Windsor, recuperating from yesterday's Herculean ride. The peculiar ambience created by colonial elegance mixed with 1960's Swiss kitsch is almost comforting... snowy Alpine mountain scenes on Tourism Switzerland posters look fabulously out of place in sweltering Cairo and I can't help but beam each time I see them. For several cosy hours I contentedly loll around, drinking pot after pot of fresh coffee while reading the rest of *The Key To Rebecca*, which concludes with the hero chasing a southbound train across the desert on his BSA. How marvellous!

The hotel staff, who all provide exceptionally cordial service, are old hands at their jobs. They include two motherly waitresses who've been employed for 13 years apiece and the wiry, chirpy barman who's clocked up 24 years. He's as delighted as I am when we work out that he must have been here during my 1987 visit. The manager, Philip, an urbane gentleman who's worked his way up through the ranks in over 30 years of service, is interested in my exploits on Peggy. He confesses to loving classic cars, confiding that the one which presently sits in his garage, an armour-plated 1980 Mercedes Benz, has a rather curious history. It's the former bullet-proof limousine of a Gulf State sheik which, although luxurious, is exceptionally heavy and thus guzzles petrol.

Opposite The Windsor is a café specialising in tea and Sheesha. At 5 o'clock I stroll over to meet a young English couple, Scott and Alice, who've followed both this ride and last year's aborted attempt online. The pair are enthusiastic teachers working their second year in an Egyptian school with over 2,000 fee paying students. Neither are motorcyclists but were switched onto Peggy and our journey by Scott's father, Kevin Allsop, a classic bike rider from Buxton, England, whom I'd once met during a motorcycling event. After a customary mint tea at an outside table, they offer to take me on a tour of some of their favourite parts of the city which are, happily, all within walking distance.

We meander along Mohamed Ali Street to an establishment where *ouds*, a type of ornate Arabic pear-shaped wooden string instrument, are hand crafted. According to the vocal business proprietor, they're the best in Egypt. There's also a cluster of furniture shops where I spy - and it would be impossible to miss it - the most garish three-piece suite I've ever seen. Mounted on curved alloy feet, the fantastically lurid scarlet arms and base are shaped like a capital 'C'. In striking contrast, the seat cushion and cupid's bow back are covered in an arresting black and white zebra pattern. Bursting out laughing, I wonder how anyone could accommodate it without developing acute eyestrain... and instantly fall in love with its outrageous vulgarity.

We eventually arrive at the magnificent gate of Bab Zuweila, a medieval entrance to the walled old city.

"Look up there," points Scott. "That's where they poured boiling oil onto invaders."

He also highlights another feature of the gate: hanging iron balls, explaining that in times past a family member could pay for these weights to be tied to the feet of people being hung, thus shortening their suffering. Some comfort!

There's a large mosque with a towering minaret next to the gate which Scott tells me is the Mosque of Sultan al-Muayyad.

"The story behind this place is fascinating. The future sultan was imprisoned for many years on this site in a dungeon. He vowed that if he was ever released he would have his gaol demolished and build a place of worship there, which is exactly what happened in 1415."

Entrance for tourists should have closed two hours previously but Scott notices that the gate's still open and, with a fistful of baksheesh, encourages the custodian to let us in. We climb to the top for a breathtaking panoramic view. At this height, the cacophony of Cairo's ceaseless traffic is greatly muted and the sky illuminates a grand scene as the descending sun filters through heavy smog. This softens the outlines of buildings and minarets which, in the distance, blur into the golden brown hues of a faded watercolour painting. I gaze down at the domed and flat roofed structures of the higglety-pigglety old properties immediately below. A young man unselfconsciously dances to the Egyptian pop music that's emitting from a silver ghetto blaster and a little further away, on another rooftop, a pregnant woman hangs a rainbow of washing onto a line stretched between two air vents as a group of small children play chase around her.

After clambering down the narrow stone stairway, we wander along the alleyways of Islamic Cairo's shopping district, where a long stretch of walkway, surrounded by shops selling vividly coloured materials, has been deeply excavated to lay sewerage pipes. This doesn't prevent people either walking along it or even trying to trade from its depths.

"What's incredible is that there are no archaeologists at work here," says Scott, who's passionate about history, the subject he teaches. "The government simply won't allow them in, missing out on an incredible chance to unearth ancient remains."

Along this particular alley we visit a fez workshop which claims to be the oldest in Cairo. Despite the presses used in the hat-making process resembling some ancient form of torture equipment, the owner and chief fez maker could not be more hospitable. I know that variations of the fez have been worn throughout the muslim world for centuries and have, until quite recent times, had just as many military wearers as civilian. Nonetheless, I struggle to disassociate the tasseled, bright red hat from the British comedian, Tommy Cooper. In the immensely popular comic's TV shows, where everything seemed to go wrong, Cooper was inseparable from his fez. I'm sorely tempted to don a hat and do a quick, "just like that!", his catchphrase, but manage to restrain myself reasoning that the owner must be sick to the back teeth with foreigners' terrible impersonations.

A busy road separates this local shopping area from Khan El-Khalili... tourist shopping central. We cross over a footbridge and stepping down on the other side, instantly feel the atmosphere change. The friendly, relaxed looks and occasional "Salam Aleykum's" of the shopkeepers that we recently passed have evaporated. Stall-holders on this side of the four-lane divide intensively peddle Egyptian memorabilia. Sphinx t-shirts hang next to Pharaoh papyrus paintings, stuffed camel toys, silver jewellery and faux silk prayer carpets.

Although it's nearly closing time, hawkers are aplenty and an absolute treat to listen to. First, with a highly trained ability to flick seamlessly from Japanese to German to Swedish, they take a guess at our mother-tongue. Once ascertaining that we come from the UK, the men begin to fire some great one-line sales pitches at us. Over my shoulder I hear,

"I don't know what it is you're looking for, but I'm sure you'll find it in my shop."

One adopts a cockney accent.

"Watcha! Come and 'ave a butchers... here... 'av a shufti."

It's really quite hilarious.

As we delve deeper into the market's tight and partially covered alleyways, Alice reveals her personal favourite to be,

"I'll give you Asda price."

Joining in, Scott tells me about the more honest approach he heard recently:

"Come into my shop and spend all your money."

He goes on to say that since the start of the recession, he's noticed an increasing air of desperation amongst the traders as they vie for business from the steadily diminishing number of visitors. Nevertheless, the merchants' antics make for lighthearted entertainment.

We dine in an elegant restaurant before taking a cab back towards the Windsor for a Stellar nightcap. Walking through eerily hushed streets for the last couple of hundred metres, Scott explains that two rival Cairo football teams, Ahly and Zamalek, are involved in a make-or-break dual. Looking through open doorways and shop windows, we see large groups of men huddled around flickering TV screens. Suddenly, the city's ambient noise level soars with a rich mixture of cheers and groans as one of the teams looks like scoring... but misses. In the Windsor bar, the hotel staff, including the manager, have formed a semi-circle around a TV set in one quarter of the lounge and are similarly intent on watching Egypt's national sport.

All too soon my terrific hosts have to depart as they've an early start in the morning for their long bus ride to school. It's been a brilliant evening... I've been shown sides of Cairo life that I wouldn't have experienced so fully on my own and I also feel I've made two new friends.

Day 31, Giza and Saqqara pyramids, Cairo, Egypt.
49 miles.

Rising early with a plan to get across Cairo before the anarchic rush hour commences, I begin to load Peggy with a view to photographing her in front of the pyramids at Giza. It feels like a really momentous day, the culmination of a huge amount of effort. After all, reaching the pyramids was the original objective of the journey when first conceived with Derek. The hotel staff, once I explain my plan, are remarkably trusting and allow me to ride off on my laden bike without settling the bill or even handing in my key. I depart, feeling like the shepherd boy in Paulo Coelho's *The Alchemist* on the last day of his momentous journey to the pyramids, but hope that, unlike him, I'm not robbed and beaten when I get there!

Traffic is relatively thin on the ground at 7am and it takes less than 45 minutes to reach our destination. Ahead I can see the upper half of the Pyramid of Cheops, undoubtedly one of the most recognisable man-made structures on the planet and for almost four millennia, until the construction of Lincoln cathedral in England, the tallest. Jubilant, I ride through the outer gates and into the ticket booth compound, track around a small one-way system and park near to the ticket windows. Before I've even removed my helmet two stroppy policemen make a beeline for us and tell me in no uncertain terms that I cannot park here. Seemingly, no motorcycles are allowed. I look around at the cars, taxis, mini buses and coaches pulling up around me and cannot understand what's wrong. I quietly call their bluff when I see a young Egyptian moped rider buzz straight through the car park and carry on unhindered towards the pyramids. They wait beside Peggy as I go to buy my ticket.

On my return to the Bantam, ticket in hand, I climb back on, kick her over and, giving the two cops a wide berth, head towards the main entrance along with a taxi and a plush Mercedes. Another policeman jumps out, arms windmilling as he blocks my path. I stop. An agitated member of staff wearing a baseball cap hurries over and tells me I cannot take the motorcycle inside. Furthermore, I must immediately leave with it. I'm nonplussed... do they think I've got a bomb in my baggage? I ask why all the other vehicles are allowed inside but not my motorcycle. No explanation is given, I'm simply told again that I must remove it. Now.

A third policemen approaches. I ask if he can help explain the problem. He motions me to follow him to an office where he speaks in Arabic to a smartly dressed civilian and a police officer he refers to as "Captain". The latter looks up from his newspaper, appraises Peggy and myself in a flash, then declares in clear English,

"No way!" He looks down and begins reading again.

"Please can you tell me why?" I ask.

I receive no answer. I've clearly been dismissed.

Resigned to leaving, I get out my camera, step a few paces back and aim to take a shot of Peggy. Two of my tormentors immediately jump in front of her, blocking my view... that's not allowed either!

"No foto, moto," one of them loudly repeats. Fearing that strong arm tactics will be used on my camera if I persist, I heed their instructions. As I put my helmet and gloves back on, I somehow keep my equanimity. Around me, hundreds of tourists walk, drive or bus into the site, their cameras and video cameras in constant use.

"Come, you can get your money back," suggests the man in the baseball hat. At least he's polite, I think, as I thank him and rather dejectedly walk back towards the ticket booths.

I leave feeling both disappointed and bewildered. All I can think is that foreign motorcyclists have previously shown up with the intention of photographing their machines against this iconic backdrop and that some kind of problem occurred. Without making a fuss, I ride away hoping others will have better luck than me in the future.

On impulse I head south, following signs for Saqqara, necropolis for the ancient capital of Egypt, Memphis, and site of the stupendous Step Pyramid of Djoser. It's only a 25 kilometre ride but Peggy gets predictably hot so I stop beside a dried out irrigation channel to let her cool. Some time later, I approach the entrance to the Saqqara archeological site and with considerable trepidation halt in front of a police control barrier. The two officers on duty seem fascinated by the old BSA. They walk around, pointing to the suspension then the tiny engine while jovially talking to each other.

"Is it okay for me to come in and take photos of my bike in front of the pyramids?" I ask in the most sanguine voice I can muster.

They reply in unison,

"Yes, please. Which nationality are you? Welcome to Egypt."

The barrier is raised and I'm cheerfully waved through. As I ride on, just one word enters my mind... bizarre!

After buying a ticket, I check out the crumbling monoliths close up then take some snaps of Peggy... conclusive proof, I muse, that the sand and palm trees I'd backdropped her with en route were not taken at a British seaside resort. The Step Pyramid itself, Egypt's earliest remaining stone monument dating from approximately 2,650BC, looks to be in a state of utter ruin, with rickety stacks of bamboo scaffolding encasing its lower levels. The sky turns a murky brown, a warning sign of an approaching sandstorm, and dust swirls around my feet as I walk up to the remains of a mastaba, a flat topped burial tomb that seems to be in even worse condition than the pyramid. Time to go, I think, before the air becomes choking or the police have a change of heart... or shift. I restart Peggy and head back towards the city.

Traffic has built up substantially, so for both our sakes I take a break part way towards the Windsor and buy a freshly pressed mango juice for myself plus a bottle of water for Peggy. The drinks vendor is very typical of other Egyptians I've encountered. He's interested in where I'm from and what I think of Egypt. We shake hands and our conversation is accompanied by smiles and earnest warmth. I feel blessed that all the people I've met, apart from the police at Giza and the Alexandria tourist cabbie, have treated me exceptionally well.

"Egyptian people are very good... very kind," I say. He looks pleased.

Back at the hotel in time for a late lunch, I first unload Peggy then cover her up. The rest of the afternoon is spent in a state of deep soul searching. I'm acutely concerned that given Peggy's propensity to overheat, it could possibly take another couple of months to ride her all the way back to the UK along the route I'd originally hoped to follow. The little Bantam is simply unable to run for any reasonable period once the air temperature rises above 30 degrees. Nearer to 40 degrees, she feels as though she'll seize at any moment. I have neither the money nor the time to do this and certainly don't think the idea of doubling the length of my trip will be well received at home.

I reconsider Essa's suggestion to ride in the cool of night with a flashing amber light fixed to the luggage racks but for a second time, dismiss it. However after the first failed attempt to get here, I'm utterly determined that I'll return Peggy to the UK with dignity, riding her wherever possible. Moreover, I want to avoid the humiliation of having to be recovered again, reasoning that I owe it to all Bantam owners, not just myself and those people who've supported me, to achieve what I set out to do one way or another. I start to look online for trucks, boats and trains that will bring our journey back within its original timeframe and give the best chance of completing the ride with Peggy still running.

My first port of call is the website of *The Man in Seat Sixty-One*. Although primarily aimed at international rail travellers, this amazing site is packed full of up-to-the-minute travel information. What I particularly love about the approach of the website creator, Mark Smith, is his never-say-die attitude towards finding a way from A to B, whether it be by route C, D, E or any conceivable combination of night trains, ferries and, where a rail service has ended, buses. Ensconced once more in the bosom of the Windsor's lounge, I begin to explore rail options through Syria, Turkey and Greece. The chances of loading Peggy into a freight carriage don't look very hopeful.

I know, from research at home, that ferries stopped plying between Athens and Alexandra via Rhodes and Cyprus around 2001, so I all but choke on the handful of peanuts I'm munching when I open a page entitled *UK to Egypt without flying*. There, bold and bright, is information on catching trains to Venice from where a new ferry service, operated by Italian company Visemar Lines, will carry you to Alexandria via Tartus in Syria, or in my case, vice versa. I follow the link to the Visemar website and check the sailing times. It seems that the service is only one week old and the ship, Visemar One, brand new. The cost of sailing from Tartus to Venice, a journey of four days and nights, including a berth for Peggy, is an extremely doable 335 euros. It's the answer to my problem and, spurred on by my memory of Miss Thomas catching a steamer from Veracruz in Mexico to New Orleans, I decide there's no shame in doing something similar to ensure our journey's success. With a bitter-sweet sense of relief, I make the reservation.

At dinner, I'm served by a young waiter who spotted my return from Saqqara with Peggy.

"I like your moto very much," he says while taking my order for an omelette. "Did you see mine? I parked it next to yours."

I have to confess that I hadn't noticed it. As I'm his only customer, Aziz takes time to tell me all about his love of motorcycles and his own machine in particular, which is a Chinese made 150cc Yamasaki.

"I bought it one year ago and only yesterday had to take it in for a service. My home is more than 60 kilometres away, so every day I ride here and back home twice, once for breakfast and again for dinner. Many things have worn out already, but I love riding this bike. One day I'd like to make a trip like you."

I give him as much encouragement as possible, thinking that this mild-mannered young man must have nerves of steel to travel so regularly through Cairo traffic, let alone cover a total of 240 kilometres a day for work.

Staying up late, I explore *Motorail* travel from northern Italy to Holland, which offers a further option for ensuring Peggy will make it home under her own steam. Putting the fiasco of Giza firmly out of mind, I finally look online at photos of the wreck of the *SS Thistlegorm*. Over dinner last night, Scott and Alice had avidly told me about this shipwreck, which they'd recently dived on. The Thistlegorm is a British freighter that was bombed and sunk by German warplanes in October 1941 whilst moored in the Red Sea. Her cargo included consignments of Bedford trucks, Bren guns and Norton and BSA motorcycles. Although all of the bike's speedometers and badges have been prised off by divers, the machines themselves are still clearly visible secured to the deck of the ship. I drift to sleep with eerie images of these barnacle encrusted wartime BSAs swimming around in my head.

Day 32, Cairo to Ras Sudr, Egypt.
146 miles.

Like Burlington Bertie, I rise at 6.30, aiming to make best use of the light traffic while everyone's at Friday prayers. Breakfast and two cups of coffee are rapidly downed then I return to my room and set about some final packing. My mind wanders from the job at hand.

'What if I stay another day?' I think. 'Just imagine how relaxed I'll feel after a further 12 hours unwinding in the Windsor lounge.'

Flopping into a chair under the steadily whirring ceiling fan, I study a road map. My desire to stay longer in Cairo is intense but I gee myself on, rationalising that I can always unpack essentials should I decide to stay. Eventually, I wander downstairs to the lounge. It's closed and through a side window I see cleaners beavering away. Just as I motivate myself to get going, one of the dining room staff spots me and leads me by the arm into the restaurant for another coffee. I finally get up, extract the luggage from my room and begin to load Peggy. Even now I work in slow motion.

Philip comes outside for a farewell chat, asking where I'm heading today. When I tell him the Sinai, he gives me directions to the Suez highway and encourages me to leave soon before traffic builds. At 10.30am, with Peggy ready for the off, I saunter across the road to a cafe where two lone patrons sip tea and lazily inhale from bubbling pipes. Buying myself a chocolate ice cream, I sit on the pavement next to the Bantam and ponder. It's been nearly 4 hours since I got out of bed but despite detecting a sharp increase in the volume of car horns on adjoining streets, I continue to linger.

Idly working my way around the melting chocolate cone, an understanding of my odd behaviour dawns on me. After the trial of crossing Tunisia and Libya, followed by the mammoth journey from Alexandria, I feel utterly daunted by what lies ahead on a bike that's struggling so badly. I laugh at myself. Recognising my delaying tactics for what they are somehow frees me up, so I pull on my riding gear, get on to Peggy and, looking rather wistfully at the Windsor in my mirrors, hit the road.

Sticking to Philip's instructions and following signs for Cairo airport, we merge onto the Suez road in under ten minutes. After a brief stop to fill up with petrol, we clear the city limits, heading out into flat, windswept desert. Forging on, I hang my right leg out at right angles to allow the maximum blast from a strong cross wind to hit the engine. I'm surprised to find that our first precautionary cooling stop, which I take immediately after being processed slowly at a police check post, is almost 40 kilometres later. Encouraging!

Our ally, the southerly wind, persists and we continue to make real progress, reaching the outskirts of Suez by 2.30pm. I stop at the first fuel station and ask for 95 Super. They have none. Following instructions that lead us to a larger petrol station produces the same results. Then onto another and yet more, but to no avail... there's nothing better than 92 octane on offer and some places have only 90. After an hour trawling around the suburbs and port area, and by now at our seventh garage, a motorist who speaks English overhears me asking an attendant for help. He immediately offers to lead us to the centre where, he informs me, we will find the only 95 octane pump in Suez. It's hard to comprehend that a city of half a million people, with oil refineries and an immensely busy port, has such limited choices. However, I gladly accept his assistance and within 10 minutes motor onto the forecourt of a Miso garage. Hopping off Peggy, I approach my guide and gratefully shake his hand through his open window.

"Welcome to Egypt," he says with a huge grin then drives off.

I fill the tank and spare 5 litre fuel can to the brim, anticipating that there might be problems locating more 95 before reaching Jordan... I only hope I'll have enough to get there.

Construction of the Suez Canal began in 1859 and remarkably, took only 10 years before becoming operational, shaving weeks off travel around the Cape of Africa for shipping. It's been lengthened, widened and deepened several times since and is currently used by up to 60 ships of all shapes and sizes per day. Apart from the numerous small ferries that ply backwards and forwards across its 193km length, there are two major road crossings. I'd love to ride over the Egyptian-Japanese Friendship Bridge to get a spectacular view of the canal, but that lies 70km north at El Qantara. Instead I head just 10km out of the city to the only tunnel that connects Africa with Asia, the 1.6km long Ahmed Hamdi Tunnel.

There's little activity at the entrance, with a lone car or truck passing through the toll booths every 5 minutes or so. Nonetheless I play it safe, allowing Peggy to thoroughly cool while I munch cheese and bread under the token shade of a potted palm. With no other vehicles in sight I approach the entrance, determined to keep my revs up and blast through the tunnel as quickly as possible. It takes between eleven and sixteen hours for ships to navigate the canal in convoy, with the average toll exceeding $250,000. Having been waved through the toll booths without the need to pay, our crossing lasts just 2 minutes. Peggy gets another slap on the tank as we emerge out of the dark depths into glaring sunlight.

"You're in Asia now, Peggs," I gleefully tell her.

Within a kilometre we halt at a fork in the road. To the left is the straight and flat highway that leads to the town of Taba at the Israeli border. From there we can track down the Gulf of Aqaba to the Egyptian port of Nuweiba and a ferry to Jordan. The right fork offers a much longer route along the Red Sea shoreline in the direction of Sharm el-Sheikh at the southern tip of the peninsular. To reach Nuweiba, we'll have to head inland just beyond the half way point, crossing the mountainous desert of the Sinai. As usual, I've left decision making until the last minute and still cannot decide which is the best route to follow... the shorter route to the north or the more scenic one to the south. Common sense says I should limit Peggy's mileage and take the quickest and flattest way but acting purely on intuition, I turn right and head south, praying that a sea breeze will aid the journey.

It doesn't. Within sight of the shimmering Red Sea it completely dies. All too soon I sense a familiar tightening of the engine and come to a swift stop. Plonking down beside the smouldering bike, I gaze out to sea where several giant dry-bulk container ships and oil tankers lie at anchor, waiting their turn to sail along the canal. Our next stop, no more than 10 kilometres further on, is by the electronically locked gates of a large package holiday complex. Roughly the same distance again brings us to a checkpoint. A heavily armed policeman, after inspecting my passport and enquiring about my destination, tells me there's just one hotel that accepts casual guests in the next town, Ras Sudr, then no other for at least 70 kilometres. With the Bantam's engine sounding like a bag of nails, I set off in search of it.

It's surprisingly hard to find. The town, with a busy centre comprising half a dozen shops and the same number of eateries, seems to have risen out of the desert very recently. It consists of a mixture of new and half-complete apartments and some grandly gardened holiday villas, which a passer-by informs me are owned by the wealthy of Cairo. Further along the shoreline, he says, are a couple of large complexes for tourists who stay for weekly holidays. When I finally locate the hotel, it looks so beautifully laid out, with tranquil swimming pools and large canopied seating areas, that I'm sure it'll cost a fortune. I'm amazed to find that it's a mere 100 Egyptian pounds, approximately £12.50, for a an en-suite air-conditioned apartment with a separate lounge and satellite TV.

With the help of a gardener, Peggy is hoisted up several steps and parked in front of the reception window. As usual I lock and cover her up, hiding my rather threadbare spare tyre on the front luggage bars. When night falls, a giant projector screen is erected next to her. I go in search of something to eat and return to find the hotel's front garden packed with local men sitting in rows. They're all watching WWF wrestling on the big screen. My instinct is to feel concerned for my motorcycle's safety, but none of the 50 or so viewers show any interest in her... she's completely upstaged by the larger-than-life macho action. I leave them to it and go to bed.

Day 33, Ras Sudr to St. Catherine's Monastery, Egypt.
152 miles.

I bump an unladen Peggy down the garden steps and onto the road, then ferry all the luggage across to her one piece at a time. We're ready for the off by 9.30am and with the sun virtually overhead there's absolutely no shade. One of this Bantam's best assets is her ease to start, indeed, I'm so confident that this'll happen on the first or second kick that I put on all my riding gear before even attempting to crank the engine over. I turn on the fuel, prime the carburettor then flick on the ignition. The horn blares loudly causing me to visibly jump. I try fiddling with the switch but it won't be silenced. Turning the ignition off and back on makes no difference so, sweating profusely, I remove my gloves and take the switch apart. When it's reassembled the din persists. Wilting, I shed my helmet, jacket and back protector and proceed to unpack some tools. It takes more than half an hour to track the break in the horn lead insulation, which is as deeply buried under the petrol tank as it's possible to be, and remedy it.

A staunch wind blasts off the Gulf of Suez. To ride in a straight line I'm forced to lean Peggy constantly over to the right, but it's worth it to have a well ventilated, free spinning engine. The road soon takes an inland route and begins to climb steadily up the side of a sandy rock escarpment. Sheltered from the wind, I have to pull up short of the summit to give Peggy her first breather. A glance at my Garmin provides cause for celebration. It shows we've progressed 52 kilometres, our best single stretch of uninterrupted riding since Libya!

In Cairo I'd received two emails suggesting ways to help Peggy cope with the heat. The first, from Pete Rose, was to increase the amount of oil in my petrol. Accordingly, I've changed the mix from a ratio of 24:1 to 20:1. The other came from Richard Ross at *Hitchcocks Motorcycles*. It read,

"In the old days, when I used to ride 2-strokes for long distances at constant speeds, we'd pull in the clutch every minute or two and give the engine a really good rev. It helped deliver a burst of cooling and lubricating oil to the cylinder."

I've applied this technique unfailingly for the last couple of days and it now seems to be paying dividends.

Some 20km later we commence a hair-raising freewheel down an alarmingly extreme gradient of road while being battered by a howling headwind that's funneling furiously between the rock faces which tower on each side of us. As I breathlessly reconnect with the coast, the colour of the sea changes from a deep aquamarine to a turquoise so vibrant it appears somehow virtual. Pulling up briefly to inhale the fresh air and watch the waves breaking against a narrow sea wall, I then continue south, once again precariously leaning into the blasting air current.

In the heat of the afternoon we turn east and head into the heart of the Sinai. There's a lone petrol station just beyond the junction, but as anticipated, it only sells 90 octane. I pour every last drop of fuel from my spare canister and feel quite concerned that Peggy's tank is barely half full... our only hope is that there'll be plentiful opportunities for coasting downhill on the far side of the peninsular.

The barren splendour of the craggy, red stone desert encourages me to stop several times for photographs of Peggy amongst its magnificent volcanic topography. The frequency of our stops is also governed by the need to cool the engine, with the average run somewhere around 8km. But as we're constantly climbing, I feel reasonably philosophical about these distances. One memorable halt is caused by a pair of free ranging cocoa brown camels sauntering down the middle of the road. As we slow to a crawl and edge nervously around them, they stand stock still, their dark glassy eyes regarding us indifferently through fluttery eyelashes. It's an extraordinarily exotic moment.

The triangular shaped Sinai Peninsular is named after its best known landmark, Mt. Sinai, which is described in the Hebrew and Christian Bibles and Quran as the place where Moses received The Ten Commandments. Many of its coastal towns are popular tourist destinations but its crowning glory is undoubtedly the mountain itself and the Greek Orthodox Saint Catherine's Monastery which is nestled at its foot. The monastery is believed to be one of the oldest working Christian churches in the world and is a sacred place for pilgrims of all three faiths as well as for tourists to visit.

Climbing past 1,200 metres, the frequency of police inspections increases. At each one I'm questioned about my destination. I always reply that it's the monastery, which isn't entirely true as I haven't yet made up my mind whether or not I'll try to press on and cover the remaining 140 kilometres to Nuweiba in the cool of the evening. There's a checkpoint and fuel stop at the fork in the road where I'm forced to make my decision. The petrol station is closed and glancing at my watch I guess that three hours of daylight remain. The ticket office where I can book myself onto tomorrow afternoon's sailing to Jordan closes at noon, so I decide on the spot to stay at Saint Catherine's tonight and make an early start for the coast in the morning.

After following a single track road for a few kilometres, I come to a small settlement and the final turn off for the monastery. As usual, it's guarded by police and a wooden barrier.

"Where are you going?" asks a policeman in an interrogative manner.

Instead of replying seriously, I laugh then say,

"Timbuktu," as it seems a ludicrous question when halted at the start of a 300 metre lane that leads to nowhere except the monastery and mountain.

From the stern look on his face, I immediately know that it was the wrong thing to do; this is a man who obviously takes his job very seriously. He chides me for my flippancy. I try to explain my humour, but it's lost on him. Instead, and no doubt as a reprimand, my bags are emptied and searched, my passport inspected closely and I'm asked questions about the reason for my journey over and over again. I resolve to keep my lips well sealed with the police in the future, no matter how fatuous their questions.

Half an hour later we're released and slither along the shingle lane that leads to the monastery gates and courtyard. To my relief, there are still some reasonably priced rooms available and the tariff includes both dinner and a packed breakfast. Peggy gets a parking spot next to my door and I begin to unload her straight away, receiving a queer look from the room attendant as I pat her on the tank and thank her earnestly for the great day's ride.

"You and me, girl," I unashamedly say... and really mean it.

Half an hour later I join other pilgrims and guests in the dinning room for a fabulous four-course communal meal served by members of the monastery. Once replete, and with the sinking sun casting dramatic shadows from the surrounding rock formations, I walk around the back of the complex to where a number of Bedouin men sit in a group smoking. Their rather rank smelling, cud-chewing camels languish in a circle, waiting for mountain-bound customers to emerge from their beds in the small hours.

On the spur of the moment I run back to my room, throw my sleeping mat and bag along with some food and water into a daypack, grab a torch and set off for the summit. The monastery is situated at around 1,400 metres and according to my guidebook, the mountain's top peaks at 2,285 metres. It takes close to 3 hours to walk up the easier of the two available routes, Siket El Bashait, 'the camel path', but I feel energised by the good ride today and the promise of a stunning sunrise over the desert. The way is remarkably clear and the footing good, but as my second set of torch batteries begin to give out, I'm more than pleased to reach a small flat area where a handful of others are spending the night. Just 750 steps remain to reach the summit in the morning.

In the blackness, lying in my sleeping bag with the buzz of whispered conversations carried around on a gentle breeze, I feel utterly content. It's a privileged experience to be surrounded by millions of celestial bodies and to look down onto stars which are actually below us on the horizon. Mesmerised, I find it hard to fall asleep.

Day 34, St. Catherine's Monastery to Aqaba, Jordan.
80 miles.

Left to my own devices I'd have slept deeply on through daybreak. The sound of my companions rising and the arrival of quite a few other travellers, both on foot and camelback, brings my deep slumber to an abrupt end and I rouse myself. After a bleary final climb to the peak, where a small mosque and the Greek Orthodox *Chapel of the Holy Trinity* have been erected, I share a panoramic dawn spectacle with pilgrims and a group of backpackers. There's an awed silence as the sun's blazing orange orb edges its way over the rocky skyline and illuminates, in hues of vivid ochre, the surrounding mountains, gorges and plains.

I don't hang around for long and as the majesty of the sunrise fades, head downhill, taking the much shorter and more direct route, Siket Sayidna Musa. It's known as the 3,750 Steps of Penitence and was carved into the bare rock by monks. Quickly gathering speed, I find myself bounding downwards with a boyish carefree energy... although three quarters of an hour later at the bottom, painfully puffed and with aching thighs and knees, I'm forced to question the wisdom of such enthusiasm.

A swift shower is followed by a quick breakfast and I'm on the road by 7am, more immediately concerned about the diminished petrol level in Peggy's tank than reaching the ferry port in time. We take the fork for Nuweiba past the still closed fuel stop and head out into the desert. The beauty is spellbinding, with crusty sedimentary rock outcrops wildly projecting skywards from the sandy and stony plateau that we motor along. Occasionally, the intensely yellow and red landscape is broken by a dry gravel wadi where a lone acacia tree somehow clings onto life and once, in the distance, I see a young Bedouin boy herding a small flock of scraggy goats. Without the faintest flutter of a breeze, the only noise is the peppy buzz of the BSA engine zooming along. In spite of two stops for photos, the fresh morning air and frequent downhill gradients, where I freewheel to preserve every millilitre of petrol, ensure a cool engine and thus excellent progress. Just one car comes from the east, a battered old pick-up truck that struggles up a steep incline. The sense of isolation, the desert's untamed, ragged grandeur and our unhindered advancement grant me the most peaceful and joyous riding.

The main descent to the coast, defined by my sat nav as being 800 metres below, is almost straight and wickedly steep. Sheltered by precipitous banks on both sides of the road, I slip into neutral and switch off the ignition. Peggy rapidly gathers momentum, streaking along at what must almost be her terminal velocity, 107kmph. It takes under 10 thrilling minutes of rushing air and ghostly silence to reach the bottom and glide into the outskirts of Nuweiba. I pause to look in the tank... there's barely any petrol left, less than a finger's depth swilling around in the bottom. Nonetheless, with just an hour to spare before its advertised closing time, I decide to head straight for the ferry port and the notorious MB Maritime ticket office.

To my surprise I encounter no huge queues, no surly staff and minimal red tape... so much for believing the worst of online reports. I pass a wad of US Dollars and my passport through a shoulder-high window and within ten minutes the passport's returned, together with a ticket for the slow boat as the twice daily fast boat cannot take vehicles.

My endeavours to clear passport control and Customs are a different affair. The process is so overly complicated by procedural correctness and an unfathomable order that it's hard to know what to do first. Once through the port gates, I park Peggy next to officials collecting and counting stacks of battered yellow number plates. They don't want mine as I haven't yet amassed all the relevant pieces of paper and stamps that allow them to accept it. Walking away in frustration, I rationalise that my passport needs stamping at some point and now is as good a time as any. As soon as I enter the vast hall I realise why purchasing my ticket had proved so easy... the other passengers already have theirs and are well ahead of me in the process of exiting Egypt. Hundreds of men plus quite a few families stand crowded in noisy lines, three to four bodies wide. At the front only four out of ten passport control booths are operational. After half an hour's wait in the airless hall I become increasingly anxious as the columns of travellers inch forward at a snail's pace.

A tall policeman, dressed immaculately in a dazzling white uniform and sporting a tremendous moustache, which stretches almost from ear to ear, stops next to me. There's a large patch on his shoulder which reads '*Tourism and Antiquities Police*'. Being the only Westerner in the hall, and most likely on the ferry, it seems that I'm his only customer.

"You have moto?" he asks, looking at my crash helmet.

I nod and smile.

"Come," he instructs, setting off for the front of the line without looking back.

When he reaches it and sees me hesitating half way down the queue, he waves his hand vigorously, signalling for me to move right to the front. I feel acutely uncomfortable. A privileged foreigner queue-jumping seems so unfair and even though I guess it'll take an hour or more to get processed under my own steam, which will make clearing customs with Peggy just about impossible, it simply feels wrong. I look straight ahead as I walk the remaining 30 feet to the front.

Once I have an exit stamp in my passport, my personal policeman, who merely shrugs and motions for me to follow him when I ask his name, leads me outside then marches across the enormous compound to an office that deals with my *Carte Gris*. This is the start of the Customs clearance process. Over the next hour and a half we undertake 13 distinctly separate stages at a number of open office windows, booths and portakabins randomly placed around the enclosure. Twice we return to offices we've already visited to get additional stamps and signatures, slips of paper, a photocopy or make nominal payments of a few Egyptian pounds. There are no signs, not even in Arabic, and still, to my eye, no discernible logical order of events. At first I feel lighthearted, amused by the nutty complexity which seems to do nothing but keep a lot of people gainfully employed, but in the midday sun and still lugging around my valuables and riding gear, I become thoroughly fatigued and my mirth evaporates. The increasingly sullen policeman utters hardly a word during the whole process, simply relieving me of papers or money then signalling to follow him 300 to 400 metres to the next queue at another nondescript window.

We eventually make it back to the licence plate collectors who appear lost in the midsts of a confused stocktake. My heart's in my mouth as one of the staff takes a pencil rubbing of Peggy's engine and frame numbers and my relief is enormous when it's simply stapled to a document without scrutiny... phew! I say a hugely grateful thank you to the Tourist Policeman, without whom I'd still be wandering around among the throngs. He proffers his biggest shrug to date and, gaining further respect from me for not asking for *baksheesh*, departs towards the air conditioning of his office.

Free from the clutches of the paper-shufflers, I ride around the docks past a small line of trucks. Each has its contents, a multicoloured cornucopia of household furnishings, clothes and personal possessions, spread over an area the size of a basketball court. People in the process of moving their homes are awaiting Customs inspection... after my bewildering ordeal they have my heartfelt sympathy.

Our ship, the *Pella*, is a battered old crate that's sailed for almost 30 years under two different names in both Japan and the Greek Islands. As I'm waved straight on, Peggy falters, only just making it onto the flat cargo deck. Things soon gets worse. I'm directed up an even steeper ramp to a higher deck deep within the boat's bowels. This time the engine simply can't make it and cuts out. I kick her over and start again with the same result. To save her from further mechanical abuse and allow the driver of the humungous Hummer that's following us to complete his upwards journey, I hop off and walk beside the labouring bike, revving furiously and wincing as I slip the clutch to get to the top.

Flummoxed by the sudden loss of power, I hoist the Bantam onto her centrestand and check the spark plug. It's clean and the gap is fine. I do the same with the points. They're completely closed when they should be wide open. Somehow, on descending from St. Catherine's, they've inexplicably slipped firmly shut. It's one of the easiest repairs of the trip.

With Peggy safely strapped to a handrail next to the silver Hummer, our only vehicular companion on the voluminous steel deck, I head up a flight of stairs and hand my passport over to a Jordanian immigration official.

"Collect it when you arrive in Aqaba," he dismissively orders me. I find some shade on the stern deck, perching myself on top of a large steel box which, judging by its constant vibration, is probably the air vent for a generator. The deck's crowded to bursting with hundreds of Egyptian migrant workers, all young men heading for jobs in Saudi Arabia and the Gulf States. As the ferry slips her moorings and edges out of port, I remove my boots and socks and settle down to eat a St. Catherine's Monastery packed lunch.

Once at sea, a bearded man rises from a group near the stern of the ship and sings out in a deep voice,

"*Allahu akbar. Allahu Akbar,*" (Allah is greatest. Allah is greatest).

He continues reciting the *adhan*, the call to prayers. At least half the men seated on deck rise and begin to form lines straight in front of me. The man who will lead the prayers stands just to my right and begins. As a complete outsider, I'm uncomfortable to be within touching distance of the front row of at least a hundred men who repeatedly prostrate themselves in humble dedication to their god. Fidgeting, I don't know where to look and equally, don't know how to angle my feet to avoid pointing their soles at the worshippers. Fortunately, the young man who's squeezed next to me on the steel box has not joined in and is contentedly eating some pieces of chicken. His nonchalance helps me to relax.

The published two hour crossing takes four and a half hours and the sun is already sinking below the darkening waters of the gulf as we reverse slowly into port. I chat to the only other driver on the ferry, a somewhat paradoxically intrepid Iraqi businessman whose fear of flying has forced him to drive across Saudi Arabia to Egypt for a single meeting. He's now on his way home.

"Getting into Jordan is easy, not like Egypt," he tells me. "But if there is a problem for you, I will help," he adds with unquestionable sincerity.

First stage in the proceedings is an X-ray. In a vast hall I park Peggy beside the Hummer and an artic. Climbing a flight of stairs, we take sanctuary in an office while the X-ray machine runs end to end along the roof of the building.

"What are you looking for?" I ask the operator. His companion, a police officer, replies on his behalf.

"We look for humans, for people traffickers."

He says it so seriously that it's a struggle not to erupt into laughter. I know Peggy's heavily laden but can't conceive how it could be imagined that I have illegal immigrants stowed in her pannier bags! Solemnly accepting my X-ray clearance certificate, I ride round to the Customs hall for the carnet to be filled in. The queue is short and within 10 minutes it's my turn. The official starts work, then asks for my insurance document.

"I hope to buy insurance here," I tell him.

He points to a window across the hall.

"Please buy it now. I must see the certificate before I can complete formalities with your carnet," he replies.

There's a problem. Around 150 men and 20 women have formed lines in the Customs hall while I've been waiting for the carnet to be processed. They begin prayers just when I need to cross it. There's no way around the lines, except by walking through the smaller rows of women at the back of the hall, which I think would be inappropriate. Trapped in front of worshippers again, I stand with my hands respectfully crossed in front of me. Some of the older men in the front rows are so beautifully attired in flowing robes and white turbans that I find it hard to stare into space and not watch them.

Prayers last 20 minutes. At their conclusion it becomes apparent that my presence hasn't gone unnoticed. A couple of elders at the front stand up, smile at me and wave me through the mass of people who are now collecting themselves and putting their shoes on. One shakes my hand as I walk past and a couple of others smile and say, "*Salam alaykum*".

I reach the insurance desk, hand over my documents and ask for a quote. A hand lightly taps me on the shoulder. I turn to see one of the worshippers, a gigantic bearded man in Arab dress, looking down on me. He's at least 6' 6".

"Hello. I am Mohammed from Beni Suef in Egypt. Please accept this from me as a gift."

He presses a small bottle of cologne into my hand. The Hummer driver, who has just joined me, says,

"It is a present for you. Please take it."

I accept the cologne, shake the man's hand then thank him with my right hand on my heart. He smiles and walks away. I then realise that I have forgotten my manners... I've read that in Arab countries it's polite to initially refuse a gift, accepting it only when the offerer insists. Mohammed has disappeared from sight and I'm left hoping that my demeanor and obvious pleasure at his kindness have alleviated any rudeness caused by my eagerness to accept.

Part way through the completion of formalities, my name is called out by a uniformed official. I raise my hand.

"Here is your passport," he says with a smile. "I have given you a month's visa and stamped you into the country. Welcome to Jordan." he adds, shaking my hand as he departs.

"Now that's service," I mumble to myself.

I flash my torch into Peggy's petrol tank before reattaching the tank bag. All that's left of the petrol I bought in Suez is roughly a saucerful at the back... the front is bone dry. I set off along an unlit dual carriageway, praying we can make it to the city, some 10 kilometres north, on fumes. Halfway there we come to a stop at traffic lights. Ahead, spread like a fairy tale of twinkling lights, is the city of Aqaba. Further along the raven blackness of the bay is the Israeli city of Eilat, its waterfront illuminated by rows of large tourist hotels. As a young man, I earned much needed travelling money by doing 5 weeks of construction work in Eilat. Back then, I'd stared across the water at Jordan wondering if one day I'd ever visit it. Now that I have, I peer at the Israeli resort and wish I could return and see what, if anything, I recognise. I know that it's impossible on this trip as I won't be allowed into Syria with an Israeli stamp in my passport.

The lights turn to green. As I open the throttle, Peggy's engine cuts out, the final splash of petrol used up. Damn. I look up the steep road to my right and can hardly believe my eyes... the only building within sight is a petrol station. Elated, I get off and push.

Fully tanked on 95, I venture on to the city, find its centre and stop to ask a man directions to a hotel I've read about. He smiles and points to a large building on the opposite side of the road. My luck continues, as it's only 50 metres away. The reception clerk takes one look at the old Beeza and suggests I wheel her into an internal courtyard for safekeeping. My room's decor, which would have been at the height of fashion in 1975, is strangely charming and the floor to ceiling picture windows allow a great view of the bay. Heading out for dinner, I smile remembering that the third and most well loved king of this interesting country, King Hussein I, a great peacemaker and undoubtedly the most steadying force of modern times in the troubled region, was a fan of British motorcycles and a BSA rider to boot.

Egyptian Customs, Nuweiba.

Day 35, Aqaba to Wadi Musa, Jordan.
73 miles.

Even at 9am my thermometer reads 38 degrees. Peggy's engine was melting hot when I stopped last night so I reluctantly come to the conclusion that more remedial work is required. Ruminating over breakfast, I decide on a decoke and the umpteenth ignition timing check. Leaving the table, I walk to the courtyard and roll her into the most shady corner to start the checks.

I remove saddle, tank and cylinder head. I'm now so proficient that it takes less than 5 minutes. Unsurprisingly, the head and piston crown are thickly coated with a new layer of the dreaded black stuff. I'm about to reach for my trusty decoke tool, the blunt end of my plug spanner, when a man crosses the courtyard, a look of complete disbelief on his face.

"Wow. Is that a DKW?" he begins, coming closer. "No, it's a Bantam," he says, crouching down next to me. "I can't believe what I'm seeing. I have a DKW-engined bike too, an old MZ, but I never thought I'd see one of these here!"

With that we fall into a cheerful conversation about our favourite subject.

Philipp, a genial chap who's around my own age, is a teacher from Bavaria specialising in motorcycle mechanics. He explains that he's holidaying with his wife, using local buses to get around. In the past he's ridden his MZ to Russia and back and I quickly discern that he is a font of knowledge on all things 2-stroke. Before long we're companionably working side-by-side on Peggy, with Philipp teaching me useful new tricks along the way.

"You can use toothpaste and soil to rub the carbon off the piston. I've had to do that several times by the roadside or on campsites" he advises, before rushing to his room to grab a tube.

"The American brands work the most efficiently," he laughs on his return, brandishing a tube of a popular make. "I think they must put extra whitening compounds in the formula and whatever creates that Hollywood white smile seems to help dissolve carbon."

We scoop soil from a large plant pot onto the piston crown along with a squirt of toothpaste and start rubbing. Within moments, the centre of the piston is shiny and spotless... without the scratches I usually make!

Once the timing is checked and everything reassembled, we squat under a palm and discuss my overheating problems.

"Why not take off your front mudguard? It will help airflow," Philipp suggests. "Let's face it, I don't think you are going to have problems with rain here."

It takes about 15 minutes to remove the deeply valanced mudguard. Peggy looks rather naked and vulnerable at the front end but Philipp's idea makes such good sense that I'm willing to give it a go.

"Hey, it looks like an old Indian racer. I like it!" he enthuses.

At that point his wife, Sigrid, joins us. I look at Philipp's blackened, oily hands and realise that he's spent virtually a whole morning of his holiday with me and Peggy. I immediately apologise to her.

"Oh, please don't worry. He's very happy doing this and it's given me some relaxing reading time as well."

We clean up and head off for a quick lunch at a nearby cafe. The grilled halloumi, a Middle-Eastern mixture of sheep and goat's cheese, is superb, as is a drink that Philipp and Sigrid introduce me to... chilled lime juice blended with mint leaves. It's remarkably refreshing. All too soon we wander back towards the hotel, enjoying the cosmopolitan feel of Aqaba, then say our farewells. The pair are off on a coach tour for the afternoon and I'm also keen to get moving.

It's 42 degrees by the time I load up, strapping the redundant front mudguard onto the back of my Ortlieb rack bag. It looks mighty odd to see the front wheel clearly spinning round as I ride up an enormous steep hill out of the city, but it seems to help as Peggy copes brilliantly with what feels like an interminable climb and we reach 1,100 metres above sea level with just two precautionary stops. On both occasions I sit in shade beside the Bantam, eating melted chocolate.

Miss Thomas rode Oppy across the Sonoran Desert from California through Arizona, New Mexico, Texas and into Mexico. Before setting off, she reflected on advice she'd been given about desert travel.

'...I had sifted it into three categories: exaggerated, helpful and obvious.

'Exaggerated' were the statements that I wouldn't find petrol stations or water for two hundred miles at a stretch, that my little engine and tyres would never stand the heat and that I would collapse physically and in all probability mentally too, from the hot sun rays of July.

'Helpful' was the suggestion to wear something on my head and not have Matelot clipped, because his coat would help insulate him against the heat.

'Obvious' was the advice to drive at night if the heat became too unbearable.'

As it transpired, Miss Thomas and Matelot's most challenging desert encounters were with a sandstorm, torrential night-time rain and having to use a shower in the room of an amorous male motorcyclist who'd accompanied her on part of the ride. Apart from a worn rear wheel bearing which had been replaced in Tucson, her Bantam had handled the trial admirably.

Peggy, as indefatigable as her namesake, continues to resolutely plod on despite it being the hottest day of the journey so far. Soon we come to the turn off for Wadi Rum, an area increasingly popular with tourists, many of whom do rock climbing, camel safaris and camping in the desert. Populated by Bedouins, the region first became notorious as the base from which T. E. Lawrence, Lawrence of Arabia, ran his operations against the Ottoman army during the Arab Revolt of 1917 and 1918. All around, the desert is windswept and stony but towards the nebulous horizon I can just discern the sandstone and granite mountains that make the wadi.

Crassly whistling the famous theme tune from the David Lean film masterpiece, *Lawrence of Arabia*, I keep going, passing several 'beware of camels' roadside warning signs and a sea of exotic white sand dunes. We reach a collection of a dozen or so small houses centered around a solitary shop and stop for refreshments. Heading straight to the refrigerator, my eyes almost pop out of my head. There on the top shelf sits a shining row of *Vimto* cans. It's a cordial that originated in Manchester and was my firm favourite drink as a boy. I didn't even know that it's still made, let alone available in a one-horse-town in the Jordanian desert! I grab two cans, which instantly become covered with condensation in the intense afternoon heat. After paying for them, I slug both back, my thirst quenched by the sparkly cold fruitiness and my soul touched by memories of childhood.

Back on the highway, burbling along at a steady 60kmph, I reflect on the way that it's so often smells or tastes which evoke the most vivid and sometimes most poignant memories. Heading steadily on, my nostrils now catching familiar whiffs of 2-stroke fumes as a tail wind begins to blow strongly, we come to a road closure sign and have to take a diversion that runs for 30 kilometres off the main route. The road climbs even higher and, as the plains are now well behind me, the air temperature dips. I ride through a series of sleepy villages. At the outskirts of one, upon hearing the sound of my approaching engine, a boy dressed in his school uniform jumps nimbly off the outhouse roof he's been reclining on. In one fluent movement he scoops a stone from the ground and takes aim at me. I've read that cyclists visiting Jordan need to beware of children, who seem to find rock throwing highly amusing. I haul on the brakes and with the implied threat of me possibly catching him, he drops his arm. The moment I accelerate away, however, he launches straight into his throw. He's a good shot, catching me squarely in the middle of my back and I can understand how cyclists have been seriously hurt. Thankfully, I'm wearing a back protector.

Peggy seems to be the only vehicle on the road and I stop at the next village to ask a fruit seller directions. When I leave, my pockets are stuffed with juicy nectarines and peaches. I soon pass through a village where the road narrows and see a woman walk out of a house with a large bucket in her hands. I've no time to react as she throws the full contents, a dirty grey liquid, onto the road. I ride straight through it. With no mudguard protection, a jet of slimy water, pungent with detergent, sprays vertically off the exposed front tyre and soaks my jacket front and face. Yuk.

In the cloudless early evening we climb to 1,400 metres. The change in landscape is amazing. Gone are the sand, enormous rock formations and all-encompassing heat haze of the desert. Instead we're surrounded by rolling grassy moorland. If it weren't for the occasional fields of high pasture wheat haphazardly running along contours on the heath, it could easily be mistaken for the Highlands of Scotland on a summer's day.

I track down a modern but friendly hotel in the hilly town of Wadi Musa, the Valley of Moses, so named as it's purported to be one of two possible locations in Jordan where Moses struck a rock with his staff and water sprung forth to quench the thirst of the Israelites. Peggy rests outside the reception area, close to two locals who, sitting upright on folding chairs, are deep in congenial conversation. They smile at me as I start to unload the Bantam and say,

"Welcome to Jordan. Welcome to Wadi Musa."

Reassured by the Jordanian reputation for honesty and hospitality, I leave several bags strapped on for the night, hidden below the bike cover. Sometime later, as I drift off to sleep, my mind ruminates over today's progress. Just 73 miles. I relax, because the truth is I really couldn't have done much more before nightfall and more importantly, aided by Philipp's knowledge and intuition about the front mudguard, Peggy is somehow soldiering on. I feel sure we can still make our ferry from Tartous in a week's time.

The awe-inspiring Wadi Mujib, Jordan.

Day 36, Wadi Musa to Madaba, Jordan.
145 miles.

With eyes that struggle to open, I rise at 6.00am, keen to visit the ancient city of Petra and hopefully make an escape before packed tourist coaches arrive en masse. I laugh at myself... the things we do for a photograph that makes us look like intrepid, lone explorers in these remote and exotic locations! The gates open at 7.00am and I'm amongst the first in the ticket queue. A meandering path leads between gift shops, then makes its way downhill towards a ravine where three colourfully dressed Beduin offer horse rides further into the site. There doesn't seem to be much business available at this time as the other early risers, cameras at the ready, are striding forth with as much sense of purpose as I have.

The walls of the ever narrowing gorge, known as the siq (the shaft), have intrinsically beautiful discolourations that run horizontally in flowing contours along their smooth rock faces. Walking on unusually pink sand, it takes 15 minutes to reach the canyon's narrowest point, which is just over 2 metres wide. In front of me, between the shadowy rock walls, appears a brilliant crack of light filled by the distinctively sublime shape of Al Khazneh, the Petra Treasury building. In my mind, it's the unmistakable film set from the final search for the Holy Grail in *Indiana Jones and the Last Crusade,* and I wonder just how many others, like me at this point, attempt a crooked Harrison Ford grin while humming the trilogy's theme tune.

Dragging myself out of bed has certainly paid off because there's no one in front of me as I walk the last few paces along the siq and only five people in the natural amphitheatre that hosts the Treasury. I quickly lean against the back wall, extract my camera and join the others in taking my own 'I'm the only one here' shots. Beyond The Treasury, I'm surprised to find that a whole city exists carved out of rock. I'd assumed that Petra was all about the one building, a kind of archeological one hit wonder. Not so... for the next couple of hours I amble in awe around the complex, which has some exceptional tombs, houses, monasteries and even a theatre which in Roman times could seat 8,500 people. For some places a guidebook is particularity edifying, such as the Temple of the Winged Lions, the High Place of Sacrifice, the Street of Facades and the Tomb of Sextius Florentinus.

First constructed by the Nabateans, a nomadic Arabian tribe, from around 600BC, the city was at its zenith during the rule of King Aretas, 8BC to 40AD, when around 30,000 people lived there. Incredibly, these included hydraulic engineers who created dams, channels and reservoirs to protect the city from annual floods. Over the following years, Roman, then Muslim rulers commanded the city but from the twelfth century onwards it became a forgotten backwater, in effect, a lost city. It wasn't until 1812 that it was rediscovered by Europeans. Swiss explorer extraordinaire, Johann Ludwig (AKA Jean Louis and then Ibrahim) Burckhardt, having heard tales of a wonderful ancient city, persuaded his porters and guide to lead him there, whilst journeying to Cairo. He wrote about Petra in his book, *Travels in Syria and the Holy Land*, and since publication in 1822, it has been one of the most desirable travel destinations... in recent years becoming one of the New Seven Wonders of the World.

As I retrace my steps up the siq, the volume of traffic heading down is quite unbelievable. In the space of 15 minutes I pass at least 30 tour groups, all either following an umbrella toting guide or standing around in a tight semicircle listening keenly to information on rock formations and waterways. Between them weave independent visitors travelling by camel and, more alarmingly, groups of four riding in careering horse drawn carriages driven by Beduins who don't spare the whip.

Back at the hotel, my thoughts turn to the ride ahead. I've three options. The first is a modern four lane course to the capital, Amman, known as the Desert Highway, which I dismiss immediately. The second entails riding north east to the Israeli border. From there I can track due north along the Dead Sea shoreline on the quiet Dead Sea Highway. The appeal is strong as riding below sea level next to such a renowned body of water and paralleling the border of the Palestinian West Bank would be amazing. Finally, we would continue north to Bethany In The Jordan where it's believed that John The Baptist taught and baptized Jesus. I'm sorely tempted... but the third alternative is just as enticing.

The King's Highway lies just a few miles east of my hotel and heads north through the heart of Jordan. It's an ancient trade route that originally started in the long lost Egyptian city of Heliopolis at the apex of the Nile delta, crossed the Sinai then headed north to Damascus and the Euphrates river. The highway is believed to have been in existence for almost 5,000 years and also has biblical connections, this time in the book of Numbers of both the Hebrew Bible and the Christian Old Testament.

Still undecided, I begin to load Peggy. One of the men I met last night walks up the street then squeezes tightly next to me in the tiny pocket of shade that the side of the hotel offers. I ask him about the two roads. Both, it would seem, are beautiful.

"But the Dead Sea Highway is very hot," he says. "I think you will find it too hot to be enjoyable."

It's not me that I'm concerned about. My decision is duly made for Peggy's sake... I'll take the cooler King's Highway.

Wending my way around the twisting streets that climb steeply through Wadi Musa centre, I'm unsure how to join it so stop to ask a bus driver who's parked beside an open-fronted shop.

"Follow me," he says, starting his engine. Kindly, he leads me to a petrol station then along a small one way system. After 10 minutes we reach a roundabout that leads to the Highway, now officially deemed Route 35. He goes full circle round it, giving me a big wave through his open window before heading back towards Wadi Musa. The road climbs steeply again before levelling out at 1,200 metres and is a delight to follow, as for miles it's lined with shady trees and fields sprouting verdant green crops. I hear bird song, smell the roadside wildflowers, watch butterflies aimlessly gliding in and out of dappled shadows and ride along in a state as close to bliss as it's possible to be.

Yesterday I'd struggled to understand what was happening to my engine. On the flat it had developed a slight misfire when travelling at low revs, although for most of the day this had been overcome by the necessity to rev hard when climbing. I was nonetheless still concerned. The problem returns this morning whenever I begin to cruise for long periods on level ground. A momentary loss of power makes my heart flutter but within a couple of seconds Peggy resumes running sweetly. A minute later it recurs, then again and again. Thankfully, the sensation feels completely different from the slowing, awful tightening I've experienced on so many occasions when the piston was about to seize.

I again observe, while climbing, that the problem once more disappears. At the top of a rise in the road I stop to let Peggy cool. As usual, I briefly touch the cylinder and head then flick a few spots of water onto their fins to gauge how hot they actually are and monitor their rate of cooling. My splashes are not very accurate and I hit the carburettor by mistake. It instantly hisses, pops and produces steam. I touch it with my bare hand. It's piping hot, so hot, in fact, that it's impossible to tell if it is any cooler than the engine itself. It dawns on me that my new misfire is related to the carburettor. Without a front mudguard, sufficient air is reaching the engine to cool it, thus avoiding seizure. However, the increased volume of hot air being blown backwards is heating the carburettor to the point where petrol is evaporating before it gets into the cylinder. When opening the throttle nearer to the half way point, for example when climbing in a lower gear, the fuel/air mixture is sucked through much faster and has no time to evaporate. I feel pretty chuffed with myself for this analysis and even more pleased that it's not ride threatening. The solution is easy too... more revs!

Riding through a village where the road forks, I stop to get help with directions.

"King's Highway?" I ask several people. All seem puzzled... it's obviously not a term, especially when spoken in English, that the locals are used to hearing. Eventually I consult my map and get the name of the next major town on the Highway, Al Karak. Instantly I'm directed along the right fork. Within half an hour I need to check my bearings again, this time in the shadow of a beautifully preserved fortified crusader outpost with a footprint that's hardly bigger than a large house.

The Lonely Planet guide book for Jordan tells anyone wishing to travel the King's Highway by public transport of the difficulty in crossing the vast dammed canyon, Wadi Mujib, which has perilously steep sides. Apparently, local communities to both the south and north are served by minibuses, but there isn't a cross canyon service as nearly all through traffic follows the Desert Highway. Crossing the Wadi will certainly be a challenge for the Bantam, and as I approach what I believe to be the staggeringly steep descent into it, I park under some trees to have lunch and assess what lies ahead. It looks absolutely formidable!

Two Jordanian men taking a break under the shade of an olive tree wave me over. Both are in their forties and dressed in worn suit jackets, baggy black trousers and clean white shirts. They speak no English, but respond warmly to my salutations and motion for me to join them around a small stove they're using to boil a kettle. Deftly they prepare super-sweet black tea in simple little glasses and offer me one. It's so sugary that I find it hard not to grimace as I sip it. Struggling to communicate, I point to the edge of the Wadi, say, "Wadi Mujib," stretch my arms as high and low as possible to mimic its great depth and make corresponding "phew" sounds. Their reaction takes me completely by surprise. Shaking their heads, they say in unison,

"Wadi al-Hasa", then pointing to the other side and demonstrating a further distance with their hands, "... Al Karak... Wadi Mujib.".

Blimey, I think, if this towering gorge is not even mentioned in the guide book, what must the deeper Wadi Mujib actually be like... poor Peggy! As I stand to leave, both men shake my hand, their faces shining with kindness. From my diminutive reservoir of Arabic words, I avidly repeat "*Shukran*" (thank you) and "*Ma'a as-salaama*" (goodbye).

Freewheeling to the depths of Wadi al-Hasa is a speedy affair and on a number of switchbacks I have to use my right foot to aid braking and get us round the bend... it becomes exceedingly hot through the sole of my boot. Without encountering another vehicle, we sweep across the dam bridge at the bottom. I flick on the ignition switch, click the selector lever downwards into second gear and Peggy joyfully responds. We begin the vertiginous ascent. It takes 15 minutes of shuffling between first, second and third gears to reach a patch of gravel half way up on which I give Peggy a well-earned rest, followed by another 20 minute slog of revving and relentless gear changing to mount the top. I'm amazed that she's made it in just two stints and as well as a grateful caress on her tank, I give her another break at the summit.

The road is now flat and flanked on both sides by a vast, chalky desert. Keeping our speed up, the Bantam whizzes along at a cracking 70kmph... poultry in motion! Soon we reach the outskirts of Al Karak with its majestic Crusader castle dominating the skyline. I stop at the roadside and crane my neck upwards, imagining Saladin's armies laying siege to the fortress just over 900 years ago. But I have little time to explore. Ahead lies the daunting challenge of Wadi Mujib.

Once at its edge, I switch on the sat nav and set it to altimeter mode. We start at 1,050 metres and within a very short time, to the sound of Peggy's squealing brakes and my jacket sleeves and trousers flapping in the rushing air, come to a halt at the bottom. At an elevation of just over 200 metres, the atmosphere is oppressively hot, and from here, because of the steepness and curvature of the sandy cliff faces, it's impossible to see the top. After a minute of scrutinising, we begin the climb.

"Come on girl," I encourage repeatedly as, packhorse-like, Peggy toils slowly up the side of the canyon.

The hairpin bends are the worst as it's so easy to lose our momentum and I have to, inevitably, drop from second to first gear to rev our way out of them. Inch by inch we stoically continue upwards, only stopping once for me to photograph the scale of the test she's being put to. Sounding and smelling markedly hot, we eventually crest the summit, which is close to 1,100 metres. I'm delighted.

On reaching Madaba an hour later, we quickly find accommodation at *The Black Iris*. There's no parking available outside the hotel but the owner's family home is just 50 metres away on the other side of the road. I push Peggy across and, under the guidance of a teenage boy, lock her up in their garden. It's too late to visit Madaba's fascinating Greek Orthodox church but I enjoy an evening of wandering around buzzing city streets, alive with visiting pilgrims, shoppers and restaurants. I have dinner at a pizza shop called *Mystic Pizza* which turns out to be a woeful choice, with the dough base overcooked and the cheese tasting rancid. Half its contents gurgling unsatisfactorily in my stomach and feeling very un-mystically moved by the experience, I give up on it and cross the road to a small café that serves chocolate ice cream. As I'm the only guest, I spend a relaxed hour with the night manager who, as well as serving huge dollops of dessert, loans me his laptop to access the internet. In the course of our conversation, he tells me he has two university degrees yet is unable to find work in Jordan and would love to get a job overseas. It's a story I hear often when travelling. After polishing off a second helping, I wish him good luck and happiness and depart into the warm night.

Day 37, Madaba to Damascus, Syria.
143 miles.

I'm woken not by the sun, which is streaming into the bedroom through thin curtains, but by the sound of choral singing from the open window. It's enchanting and I spend a good half hour drifting in and out of sleep to the accompaniment of soaring *a cappella* melodies and recurrent alleluias. After breakfast I walk to its source, St. George's Church. The godly ensemble has ceased its liturgy by the time I walk though the gates but I'm in for a different sort of treat as the church is home to the oldest surviving map of Palestine, an incredible mosaic spread out on the floor like a giant jigsaw puzzle. Dating from AD560 and written in Greek, the enormous map, patchy from centuries of being vandalised, burnt and buried under the rubble of the old Byzantine church, is nonetheless breathtaking. It shows all the major biblical sights in the Middle East and amazingly, when complete, was made up of more than two million pieces.

Returning to *The Black Iris*, I find it hard to get under way. There are so many small maintenance jobs to do on the Bantam that I eventually run out of shade and find myself lying on the dusty road in the baking sun, tightening nuts and bolts, changing the air filter and spark plug, re-tensioning the rear chain, tweaking the brakes and adjusting the clutch which is slipping with increasing regularity. Consequently, by the time we eventually rejoin the brilliant King's Highway it's after 11am.

The initial peace and our unhindered progress turns to custard once we're forced to commence the battle required to circumvent Jordan's capital, Amman, a task exacerbated by the city's ring road being closed for roadworks. Within the maelstrom of fast and aggressive traffic, we're diverted through nondescript suburbs towards the centre of the city. Using dead reckoning, it takes over half an hour to work my way back around to the road north. Shortly after rejoining it, I halt at the front of a large set of traffic signals in the inside lane of four. Instantly, buses, trucks and cars squeeze in tightly around us. The lights turn to green and we all tear off in typical Jordanian boy-racer fashion. Catching movement out of the corner of my eye, I sense, more than see, that the car next to me has slammed its brakes on. A large white Mitsubishi Animal, its tyres squealing under hard turbo-charged acceleration, wildly cuts from the third lane across two rows of traffic to make a sharp right turn.

Horns blare as I stamp on my foot brake and haul the front lever back to the bars. Peggy's little front brake plate is made of flimsy pressed steel and even without my luggage is not the sharpest stopper on the block. The Mitsubishi screeches across our path, missing the front wheel by a whisker. I come to a shaky halt, my heart beating hard. Cars try to force their way around us so I unsteadily drive 100 metres forward then park up by the side of the road to recover my equilibrium. It's the nearest miss of the trip by far... just as well I adjusted the brakes this morning!

We descend almost 700 metres into the sweltering Jordan Valley then begin to climb again in the direction of Jerash. Stopping at the top of a long incline, I sit on the verge and press my back against the trunk of a juniper tree. A lizard scurries away from my feet and in the nearby bushes, pied wagtails and strikingly coloured sunbirds dart this way and that. As I gaze into the distance, where Griffon vultures gracefully soar, I digest the stunning beauty of the vast valley with its mixture of desert plains, olive groves and small agricultural hamlets, all hemmed in by a great border of bare rock mountains. It's tremendous.

From some distance, I see the Roman walled city at the edge of Jerash, the giant Hadrian's Arch dominating one end of the ruins. Riding round the back to a car park, I ask two policemen in a wooden hut if they'll keep an eye on Peggy. They're happy to, so I throw the cover over her and head for the entrance. After roaming around the superbly complete baths, nypmhaeum, temples and theatres, I'm thrilled to come across a Hippodrome. A man at a desk informs me that mock gladiator battles and a *Ben Hur* style chariot race are held daily. I look inside, imagining what it must have been like tearing around the race track. It serves to emphasise one of Jordan's charms. As a visitor you repeatedly come across places of great historic interest: biblical sites; Byzantine churches; Crusader forts and Roman cities, just a stone's throw from the roadside, easily accessible, hassle free and either inexpensive or without charge.

On the far side of Jerash, I stop at an undistinguished row of shops and buy some snacks to use up the rest of my Jordanian coins. As I walk back towards Peggy, another customer leaves the shop and approaches me. He's dressed in plain white robes and wears a traditional red and white check *keffiyah* headdress.

"Welcome to Jordan. What can I do to help you? Whatever you need, you must ask... it is my duty to make you welcome." All is said in a very dignified and sincere manner. With a lot of handshaking and smiles, I manage to convey that my only need is confirmation that I'm on the right road to the Syrian border, but the encounter exemplifies the gracious and hospitable reputation for which Jordanians are renowned.

Half an hour later, with less than 15km to run to the border, I halt at a set of traffic lights. A deep rumbling sound approaches from behind. I look over my shoulder as a Suzuki Intruder, piloted by a muscular man wearing black leathers and a stars and stripes bandanna, pulls up next to me.

"Hey man," he exclaims in a deep bass voice as I subject my hand to his bone-crushing grasp. "Your motorcycle's famous. We had a text from a friend that an old BSA 2-stroke bike was riding north through Jordan... but I didn't believe it!"

Just as I begin to shake the hand of the flaxen haired woman on the pillion seat, the lights change and we both lurch forwards. At the next set we pull up alongside each other again and I ask where they're from.

"Austria... been on the road for seven months, mostly around the Caucasus. Isn't this place great?"

"How long's your trip?" I enquire, with one eye on the signals in preparation for our next spurt.

"As long as we want... I'm retired... living the dream!"

The lights turn to green, they both call,

"Take it easy," then roar ahead, quickly exiting the small town on their much faster machine.

I watch them vanish into the distance, the fluttering collection of rainbow coloured flags on their top box giving a last metaphorical wave.

With no warning, in the middle of a busy street in the town of Ramtha, we reach the frontier. Exiting Jordan is just as easy as entering and proceedings are done with in less than 20 minutes. I ride to a Syrian checkpost and am waved straight through, entering a narrow track that resembles a hedgerowed English country lane. One kilometre passes, then another. The notion that I'm riding across no-man's land begins to dissipate as I clock up kilometre number four. 'Maybe I'm actually in Syria? Doesn't anybody want to see my documents?' I wonder as I keep on in a straight line. Then, round a slight bend, the road opens and I approach a neat row of white buildings that contain the immigration hall.

Verifying my visa and having my passport stamped takes ten minutes. I then proceed towards the Customs inspectors, three men who lounge on wooden chairs. They're preoccupied, shelling seeds whilst deep in the middle of an obviously humorous conversation. With hardly any interruption to their repartee, one of them points to a small building behind me and says,

"Insurance."

I lean Peggy on her sidestand and walk over to the hut. There's no one visible until I approach the first counter. In the back of a tiny office, a man dozes in a chair. I cough politely and he jumps to his feet and bustles over.

"*As-Salamu alaykum,*" I begin. "Carnet? Insurance?"

"*Wa alaykum salam,*" he replies, then points to another counter. "Please, go to the money changer. He will help you with everything."

I follow his directions to a window where a gruff sounding man now waits for me. Without introduction, he types the number of Syrian pounds I'll need for the transaction onto a calculator.

"Can I use Jordanian dinars?" I ask, aware that I have a few notes still in my pocket. He takes the proffered 26 dinars from my hand, splits them into two unequal piles, asks for my carnet, which he duly completes, puts one pile of Jordanian notes into his till and thanks me for my payment. Under his guidance,

I take the other, smaller pile of notes back to the insurance desk, where the required paperwork is efficiently filled in. As I walk out of the room, I feel a jolt of uneasiness that I've possibly been slightly duped, but I'm really not sure so let it go.

The three customs officials are now playing cards and drinking tea. I approach with my carnet and passport in hand. The same man as before looks up as I get nearer, waves my paperwork away and points towards the exit gate,

"Welcome to Syria."

I'm free to leave without anything being checked... it's the most pleasantly *laissez faire* approach to customs control I've ever experienced!

Just one sentry box remains to be passed. A soldier steps out as we ride towards the barrier, raises his hand and requests my passport. With an expressionless face, he opens its pages and carefully studies the writing.

"What is your father's name?" he asks in a serious, interrogative tone.

I tell him.

He scrutinises my passport as if checking that I'm telling the truth.

"And your mother's name?" he questions.

Again I give him the answer, which he double checks with my documents. After more careful thought, he continues probing.

"Please tell me your profession."

He's already examining my passport by the time I reply,

"Website designer."

"Okay," he says after a final flip through its pages, seemingly now satisfied that I'm bone-fide and that my answers match all the written details.

"Welcome to Syria," he adds in his unchanging dead pan voice.

I try to keep a straight face as I tuck the passport back into my pocket and prepare to ride on... none of the information he'd requested and carefully corroborated is written in its pages!

Avoiding the fast highway, I take the old road to Damascus, approximately 120 kilometres to the north. It's practically deserted and apart from the occasional village or small town, I hardly see any other traffic for the first half hour. It would appear that there are more motorcycles here than in Jordan and there's even a special lane reserved for them on each side of the tarmac. I keep within its yellow striped borders for a while, but as I only see a battered old truck, spewing clouds of diesel smoke every ten minutes or so, and the occasional worn-out Peugeot 404 at roughly corresponding intervals, I soon decide to take my place in the middle of the road.

Light is fading as I near the capital and traffic begins to build then slow with congestion. There are few roadsigns in Damascus and I struggle to find my way towards the old part of the city. Halting next to two men, I ask directions. An in-depth conversation in Arabic that lasts at least 4 minutes ensues between them, at the end of which they look at me, smile and shrug their shoulders in apology. Rather frustrated, I kick Peggy into gear and set off again, my temper quickly quelled by the realisation that their honest reply, although the result of a painfully protracted debate, was far better than a false lead given to save face.

Soon stopped by traffic lights, I ask a motorcyclist next to me if he knows the way to the souk. He's a middle aged business man on a 100cc Chinese Honda copy. The bike looks as though it's been in at least 20 accidents... all 4 indicators are broken off and the headlamp glass is missing, the tank and front mudguard are dented and scuffs and scratches run down its side. The battered briefcase strapped onto the rear rack appears to have seen plenty of spills too. I laugh to myself, as with Peggy's mudguard strapped onto the back and her front luggage carriers bent from our various tumbles, it's possible the man is looking at us and thinking along the same lines!

"Please follow me," he says. I do, praying that we're not going to be led into an accident as he threads his way along lines of impatient, snarled-up cars and nips through a red light to turn a corner. Within ten minutes we pause at a busy intersection. He points across the road to the edge of a medina.

"I think this is where you mean, but if you cannot find the hotel you seek, you will find many others here," he says.

We shake hands and he sets off at speed, narrowly avoiding being flattened by a thundering, overcrowded bus.

I quickly locate the hotel that's been recommended to me. Unfortunately the entrance, which resembles a wooden beach shack, is at the top of a steep flight of stairs. I count a dozen on my ascent and there's nowhere on the congested road or pavement where I would feel happy to leave Peggy. The hotel is owned by three brothers who are all in the reception area when I venture inside. Out of a window they take one look at her and without hesitation set off en masse down the steps. I remove most of the heavy luggage then all four of us lift her up high, not stopping until she's safely planted in the hotel lobby.

Following a map given to me by the receptionist, I walk through Souk Saroujah then head for the city centre and a main road teeming with both pedestrians and cars. Half way along I find Al-Kamal restaurant. Actually, it'd be hard to miss as its the most brightly lit eatery I've ever seen, with enough 100 watt light bulbs to qualify for a place in the *Blackpool Illuminations*. Sitting inside, served by smart suited waiters who outnumber patrons by approximately two to one, I feel like the proverbial goldfish in a bowl as hundreds of people walk past and look in. Fortunately the outstanding mezze, comprising salads, humous, tahini, olives and breads, justifies the radiant exposure.

Day 38, Damascus, Syria.
0 miles.

The hotel proves to be very noisy and the toilets leave a lot to be desired so straight after breakfast I take a walk, keeping my eyes peeled for an alternative. I fall an instant victim to the charms of Damascus... it's a city with something of interest around every street corner and whose inhabitants seem exceedingly relaxed and likeable. I come, by chance, to the old Hejaz train station, the terminus for a historic narrow gauge steam railway that once connected Damascus with Medina in Saudi Arabia. Inoperative for a number of years now, it's a service that many train buffs hope will one day be resumed. Walking inside the grand entrance, I take in the scene of simple tiled floor, decorative wooden balcony and a dazzling technicolor wall ablaze with stained glass windows brightly illumined by the morning sun. As I peer out of the back, I see that where there should be tracks, there is an enormous hollowed out pit, easily big enough to take the foundations of an entire tower block. Approaching the ticket office, which sells tickets for a modern service that runs from the city's other railway station to Amman in Jordan, I ask the sole occupant,

"Do you know if the steam train will ever run again?"

"*Insha'Allah,*" (if it is God's will), he replies with a look of amusement... I somehow think it's a question he's been asked more than once.

Opposite the station lies the Orient Palace Hotel, a grand relic of the 1930s with heavy Deco influences in its design. I quickly fall in love with its faded grandeur, stylish architecture, peaceful lobby, fancy dinning room and the simple bedrooms that are filled with period, if somewhat knocked about, furniture. Better still, it's quiet, each room has a balcony and there's space aplenty for the BSA. I hastily return, pay, pack my bags, bounce Peggy down the flight of stairs to the road, and ride the half mile to our new and rather splendid lodgings. Peacefully watching scores of swallows weaving and swooping around, I spend the next 30 minutes on my balcony sipping a large orange smoothie bought from the juice shop across the road.

Setting off for the old city, I head straight into a labyrinth of covered medieval souks. The huge, dark arched roofs, made of blackened corrugated iron, have hundreds of tiny holes in them, supposedly bullet holes made by the machine guns of French aircraft in 1925. The rays of intense sunlight which pour through each of them give an unexpectedly magical ambience. There are shops galore, selling all manner of goods from flamboyant silks and brocades, rich hand knotted carpets, exquisite wooden, copper and brass handicrafts and ornate jewellery to children's fancy dress clothes, World Cup footballs and everyday household consumables.

Beyond the souk, the back streets of the old city, too narrow in many places for a single car to travel along, is a higgledy piggledy warren of lanes and alleys. In places it's impossible to look up and see the sky as the buildings, several of which are propped upright up with huge wooden stakes, lean crookedly over. I become fascinated by the doorways. Some are intricately carved of aged hardwood while others are superbly fabricated from iron. There are even a few covered in bright and vibrant enamelling and one with a star shaped entrance. Slinking backwards and forwards across the front of several homes are silky slim cats, presumably waiting to be admitted... or fed.

When I walk along the alleyways that are wide enough for cars to navigate I encounter a motley collection of parked vehicles, all bashed and beaten up by countless collisions in Damascus's perpetual nose to tail traffic. There are dented VW Beetles and a couple of badly scarred Kombi vans, various maltreated 1970's Dodges and V8 Cadillacs (I think of these as *Kojak* cars), a rickety Citroen Light 15 fitted with modern bucket seats and an Austin Cambridge masked with so much brown dust that it's hard to make out what colour paintwork lies beneath. Next to the Austin is a street cleaner who's sitting on a doorstep savouring his cigarette break. We're the only two people in the very long lane.

"Where are you from? Welcome to Damascus," he utters with a toothy grin.

I attempt to strike up a conversation but he doesn't understand a single word I'm saying and just laughs mirthfully. Figuring these are the only two English phrases he knows, I realise they are meant sincerely, shake his hand and walk on.

The Umayyad Mosque is Syria's greatest Islamic structure and in sanctity is considered one of the most revered mosques in Islam. Little wonder, then, that it's packed with crowds of visiting Muslim and Syrian tourists. An extensive white marble open courtyard, which burns my feet as it lies mainly in direct sunlight, contains a fountain and a rather curiously shaped building called The Treasury. I rest in its shadow for a while close to a group of fifty or so people who sit in an attentive circle around an imam who's holding audience.

Continuing my amble through a grand prayer hall bedecked with swathes of rugs, I enter the room that is the mausoleum of Saladin, the notorious adversary of the Crusaders, who died in Damascus in 1193. Finally, I view the marble covered shrine of John the Baptist who's known as Prophet Yehia to muslims. My guide book explains that during the building of the mosque in the 8th century, a casket was unearthed from under the old basilica floor (the mosque is built on top of the Roman Temple of Hadad-Ramman which was converted in the 4th century to the Christian Cathedral of Saint John). It supposedly contained the biblical character's head, complete with skin, hair and all. The book goes on to qualify this quite humorously, indicating there are so many claimed resting places for the cranial relic that if all are to be believed, the saint must have been endowed with multiple heads. I laugh out loud as I read this, images of Douglas Adam's whacky character, Zaphod Beeblebrox, the most ludicrous example of polycephaly I can think of springing up in my mind. It feels most unseemly to be chortling away to myself.

As I re-enter the expansive covered section of the souk, feeling slightly guilty at the irreverence of my laughter in such a holy place, I notice a steady stream of people walking along licking huge white ice cream cones that are covered in little bright green objects. Approaching an animated crowd that's gathered around a shop window, I move in close to see what the attraction is and find it's an ice cream shop called *Bekdach*. Working in the window, a man wallops a half metre mound of white ice cream with big wooden paddles. Next he flips chunks of it into the air before pounding it back into the pile. Finally, he scoops an enormous dollop from the top and in one skillful, choreographed movement, flings it behind him onto the spatula of another white clad member of staff. This chap sets to work rolling the ice cream into a cylinder shape the size of a long french bread stick, then covers it in thousands of chopped pistachios. Four more men are constantly at work behind the counter slicing the rolls into segments that are either served in silver bowls or scooped onto cones.

What's most amazing is the crowd inside the shop which resembles a rugby scrum! Upwards of 30 people push and shove five or six deep trying to make their way to the counter and through them weave a pair of harassed waiters who carry trays overladen with brimming silver bowls. I can't imagine it being more frenetic if they'd been giving money away! I enter but avoid the mob barging their way to the counter and instead join at least a hundred others in long rows of tables to grab a bowl from a waiter. My verdict... worth the struggle.

Leaving *Bekdach* feeling well indulged, I walk along the remainder of the throbbing Souk Al-Hamidyya in the direction of my hotel. A large banner, at least 10 metres wide, is in the process of being strung across it. I stop to read what is catching everyone's attention:

'Thousands of Greetings and Salutations to the Freedom Fleet. The Syrian People Console His Excellency, the President of Turkey and the families of all the martyrs, and highly admire the sacrifices and efforts they have offered.

Where is the Security Council & The United Nations From all that is happening? Victory is coming, God willing at the hands of his excellent president Bashar Al-Assad.'

I don't have any idea what it means, but soon spot a very large group of roughly protesting outside the Hejaz station. Vociferously chanting slogans and waving similar banners to the one in the souk, they receive lots of encouragement from the passing cars. Most beep their horns but in some cases passengers and drivers alike hang out of their windows and shout their support. Public demonstrations, no matter how interesting they appear, are always best avoided, especially when you're an outsider with no clue to what's going on, so I walk by on the other side of the road and enter the hotel.

"What's the demonstration for?" I ask the receptionist.

"Last week, Israeli commandos stormed a Turkish aid ship that was sailing to Gaza as part of the Gaza Aid Flotilla. The ship was in international waters and only on a humanitarian mission. They shot nine people dead and injured many others. You know that Syria and Israel have been at war before, and that they occupy the Golan, and that they have murdered and abused our Palestinian brothers? So the people in Syria do not like Israel very much."

It serves to underline just what a volatile hotbed of conflict the Middle East still is.

In the evening, as I walk out of the hotel's front doors in search of dinner, preferably in a more subtle environment than last night, I'm hit by a revolting stench. A sewer has burst at the side of the Hejaz station and effluent is freely pouring down the road in front of me and into the gutter. Worst still, the cars that drive through spread streams of it in five or six directions along roads adjoining the intersection. A motorcycle policeman, thankfully equipped with knee length black leather boots and wearing a token surgical face mask, stands in the middle of the rippling brown lake. He's fighting a losing battle to slow traffic down and divert it away from the worst of the sewage. Thinking that I wouldn't fancy the task he'll face polishing his boots, I carefully stick to the far edge of the pavement until well clear of the square and mercifully avoid being sprayed by the wheels of passing cars. After 100 metres, the odious smell vanishes and I thank my lucky stars that my room is situated a good distance away at the back of the large hotel.

It gets busy in the Bekdach ice cream shop, Damascus.

218

Day 39, Damascus to Qala'at Al- Hosn, Syria.
135 miles.

Peggy needs attention before I can depart Damascus as she's sounding more and more like a bulldozer. I take off the exhaust down pipe and immediately see the cause. The welded ring from Tripoli is still in place but the rest of the original flange has disappeared and the area below the weld is badly perforated. I use two new copper gaskets, one each side of the remaining flange, as a wishful repair, aware that the only real solution is a new exhaust.

Last night's broken sewer pipe makes escaping the hotel tricky. City engineers have stemmed the flow during the hours of darkness but the road is as yet unwashed and there are still patches of foul gooey liquid, the consistency of melted chocolate, which without a front mudguard would be pretty catastrophic for me! The muck has been spread far and wide, so to avoid stinking tyres... or worse, I sweatily heave Peggy fully laden onto the pavement and push her three blocks past the central Post Office before finding a sidestreet which is completely clear.

Once again I've timed my exit from a capital city to perfection as, being Friday morning, the streets are devoid of virtually any other vehicles. Searching for the road north, I pause beside a huge car yard which catches my attention. Having seen the battered state of the majority of most Damascene cars, I'm amused to note that you can, most pragmatically, buy a complete front or rear bodywork shell as a direct replacement. The new exterior includes either bonnet or boot, with wings, windows and doors... the whole half caboodle! Piled high on top of each other, in an automotive house of cards, are hundreds of these takeaway bodywork kits.

We join the major four lane highway north, a motorway designated M5, which leads to the city of Homs. Almost immediately, I ride under two bold road signs... a turn off to the left is signposted Beirut and to the right, Baghdad. Awesome. There's a beat up narrow road that runs almost parallel, the old route 5, and I take to it in search of a petrol station. My obsession with finding the optimum fuel for Peggy is eased in Syria. I try three garages to check for the highest octane benzine and conclude that only one option exists... *Go Tiger*. It's the product of the state owned oil company and is exactly the same petrol, at the same price, wherever I stop. Although I can't see an octane rating, I'm assured it's 95 which will do nicely.

My map shows that the old road runs in a snake like fashion backwards and forwards across the path of the motorway. With Peggy's tank full to the brim, I decide to use it and thus avoid the stress of travelling with high speed traffic. Leaving the petrol station with an unexpected sense of freedom, I cheerfully accelerate past the motorway entrance and keep going. Although I can hear the muted drone of the nearby fast vehicles, the winding road weaves its way through the middle of rough and rugged farming country and I'm able to really soak up the landscape. Loose rocky cliffs with towering boulders are enveloped by fields covered with thin grasses upon which flocks of long legged sheep feed. Going is slow as the road's in a poor state of repair and has many blind bends, but despite Peggy's growling baritone exhaust note, a sure sign that the new gaskets haven't made one jot of difference, she dependably motors along.

Within 5 kilometres, the road rejoins the motorway. Infuriatingly, I can see it continuing northwards far across on the other side but with a concrete central reservation and speeding cars belting down the southbound lanes, there's no chance of reaching it. The old route 5 reappears as a turn off after a quarter of an hour and without question I take it. However, 500 metres of gravel and sand later it rejoins the motorway! A few kilometres on, the same occurs and this time we get around 2 kilometres before once again being forced to do battle with speeding articulated trucks. It then disappears for so long that I cease looking out for it.

A gusting headwind develops making it possible for us to ride long stretches without cooling stops, although I can't resist taking a breather under one of several roadside pictures of the president, Bashar Al-Assad. One side of the poster shows him looking very suave in a Savile Row suit. The other side is an illustration of his father, Hafez al-Assad, who ruled Syria for the 29 years before him. An urbane man who studied to become an ophthalmologist in London, Bashar is married to a sophisticated English investment banker of Syrian descent. In TV and newspaper interviews he comes across as a firm but moderately progressive leader who's nevertheless an outspoken opponent to the occupation and destabilisation of neighbouring countries, including Iraq, Lebanon and Palestinian Territories, by what he calls colonialist powers, notably the United States, the UK and Israel. As a visitor buzzing through the country on a motorcycle, it's impossible to know if the branding he's received as an iron fisted dictator and culpable member of the so-called *Axis of Terror* is valid or whether that's all part of the Western propaganda that he speaks out against. I take photos of Peggy under the posters and move on, none the wiser.

The motorway has a hard shoulder that I use with increasing frequency during the afternoon to avoid being an obstruction, or worse, run off the road. But this has its dangers too as the narrow strip of tarmac is in places badly rippled, pot holed and festooned with shards of windscreen glass and truck tyres. There are two broken down cars, both surrounded by a pool of steaming water from burst radiators and a serious crash where a truck has run into the rear of a coach. Unnoticed, because of the gentleness of the incline and my concentration on these dangers, we ascend to over 1,000 metres. The descent, however, is much steeper and with Peggy's motor in neutral, we fly down.

I make my lunch sitting on a rock some distance back from the road. Peggy has the afternoon sun on her which only serves to highlight just how oil stained and dusty she's become. With the front mudguard suspended from the back and the yellow tank panels misshapen due to my knees rubbing the green paint from around them, she looks decidedly tatty. It reminds me of a passage in a book, *Desert Taxi*, by Michael Marriott, which relates the tale of a couple driving a veteran 1930's London taxi from the UK to Kano in Nigeria in 1953. Towards the end of the expedition, they appraised the sorry state of their cab, which had a cracked cylinder head, a missing bonnet, a smashed windscreen, numerous dents and several rough modifications, all of which served to change its former prim appearance beyond recognition. Well, I decide, at least Peggy's not in that bad a shape, and as if to prove a point, she perkily starts first kick when it's time to depart.

Taking the ring road south of Homs, we head due west. A turn off to what appears to be a derelict house comes into view and across its entrance is parked a white van with the side folded down to reveal a café. We're in the middle of nowhere, so I briskly stop, more out of curiosity than hunger. To my delight, the van boasts a sizeable *espresso* machine which in a jiffy conjures up a fortifying shot of full strength arabica. The cost... 16 Syrian pounds, less than 20p!

Some 20 Kilometres later I spot the sign for Qala'at Al-Hosn and turn off. Since Homs, the road has been completely flat and mainly surrounded by brush and desert. Quite unexpectedly, it begins to climb and within moments the surrounding countryside becomes distinctly arable. I stop to savour the scene, a panorama of fields of golden wheat, hedgerows and shady oak trees. Drawing in a deep breath, I realise it could be Home Counties England on a summers day, except for the smell, which in some indescribable way is wrong. My illusion of an English rural idyll is completely broken as a tractor trundles past towing a trailer loaded with wizened looking peasants listening to loud Arab music which booms through a ghetto blaster. The men wear patched up, faded suit jackets and threadbare trousers and the women are dressed in black with gaily patterned headscarfs. I wave and instantly receive a reciprocal salutation before the tractor plods round a corner and out of sight.

We start to climb in earnest. The air cools and the surrounding countryside becomes much greener. The road's so steep that on a couple of hairpin bends I struggle to keep the Bantam from stalling, even in 1st gear. Thankfully the incline eventually shallows and we surge forward into 2nd then 3rd gear. Peggy feels incredibly small as we labour ever higher, which endears her to me even more.

"Come on Peggs, you can do it," I holler as we creep forwards at less than 10mph around another tight bend.

In under 30 minutes, stouthearted Peggy hauls us from close to sea level to about 700 metres without stopping once.

Turning a corner, we are greeted by an awe-inspiring sight... Krak des Chevaliers, an 800 year old crusader castle so perfect that it could easily appear, from this distance, as a Warner Brother's creation. The pale white stone outer walls, which are over 9 metres high, have archers' slits and are topped with battlements. Round turrets and arches complete the fortifications. Of the castle, T. E. Lawrence wrote that it was 'perhaps the best preserved and most wholly admirable castle in the world.' I concur, and immediately search for somewhere to park Peggy so that I can photograph her against its magnificence.

The castle sits on the top of a rather steep mound, towering above the surrounding valleys and plains. I head away from it to the top of the opposite valley, along a dirt track, and locate a hotel with uninterrupted views. Indeed, my room has a private balcony that faces it. For the next couple of hours, I sit watching the colour of the castle walls change in the sunset and am so smitten, I ignore my rumbling belly. Only the cloak of darkness, which descends as a solid black mass, gets me out of my seat, but I set my alarm for 4.30am compelled to witness the sun rising from behind it.

Ships queuing to access the port of Tartus, Syria.

Day 40, Qala'at Al-Hosn to Tartus, Syria.
44 miles.

I wake around sunrise anticipating more spectacular views of the castle. There is fog so thick that I can't see more than five metres in front of the balcony. Hey ho, back to sleep. When I do rise, the sky glows a vivid cerulean without a solitary cloud to smudge its brilliance and I head off for a closer look at the fortress.

Located in a strategically important position, known as the Homs Gap, the castle was used to control the flow of goods and people from the Mediterranean ports into the interior of Syria and beyond. Financed by the Emir of Homs, construction began in 1031 but it wasn't until the arrival of the Crusaders that fortifications were erected to the impressive standard that's still visible today. Indeed, so commanding is its position and so thick and tall its walls, the castle was never truly conquered. Despite numerous attacks and sieges, it was only relinquished to Muslim armies in 1271 when, after a one month siege, the severely reduced garrison of 200 knights departed having been given safe passage.

The man who collects the modest entrance fee greets me like a long lost friend, pumps my hand vigorously and says,

"Welcome, welcome."

I head down a long cobblestone tunnel that climbs into what was obviously an accommodation area. Four young men walk ahead of me. They all have large black bags and are either busy emptying rubbish bins or picking up the bits of litter dropped by yesterday's visitors. I'm whistling loudly as I catch them up. A couple of them immediately start to whistle too, then the others join in, creating a tuneless melody akin to a cats' chorus. As our whistling turns to laughter, one man signals for me to follow him and leads me into a large cavern-like room that I suspect was once a chapel. Leaning backwards into an alcove, he starts singing,

"*Allahu Akbar... Allahu Akbar*".

His voice echoes loudly and I'm amazed how the sound magnifies and multiplies as it bounces off the old walls and arched roof in surprisingly musical resonances. Grinning, I give him a thumbs up. He responds with a big smile, obviously pleased that his party piece is appreciated, returns the thumbs up then leaves to rejoin his co-workers.

I spend an hour sitting on top of one of the castle towers, absorbing the expanses of the surrounding plains. This will be my last day in Syria as tomorrow we'll catch the ferry to Italy. I've mixed feelings about sailing past a sizeable chunk of the journey home. When I made the ferry reservation in the lounge of the Windsor Hotel, I could never have imagined that Peggy would have made such sterling progress crossing the Sinai and travelling north through the Levant. Without question, it's been the best and most stress-free part of the whole journey. But whether our good fortune would sustain for another 3,000 miles riding back to the UK is another matter altogether. The desire to make it home without succumbing to a long journey in the back of an RAC recovery van remains dominant. Deep down, I know the ferry has to be, on balance, the right choice.

Walking back to the hotel, a group of crouching teenagers roar past on new 100cc motorbikes. Fearlessly, they don't touch their brakes on the approach to the sweeping uphill bend at the rear of the castle but lean hard over, their feet and knees almost touching the verge to get safely round before zooming noisily on. I guess they're all riding at full throttle which reminds me of once being a carefree teenager myself, loving the thrill of blasting around on my first bike. A few moments later comes another, altogether different biker. An elderly man steadily rides a machine that's certainly been around for awhile and is clearly his everyday transport. Sitting on the petrol tank with her hands gripping the centre of the handlebars is a girl in a pretty frock. I estimate her age to be around four and think she could be the rider's granddaughter. With a cigarette hanging from the corner of his mouth, the helmet-less man takes his left hand off the handlebars, gives me a wave, then gently curves his way around the same bend the teenagers have just negotiated. A greater contrast in riding styles I can't imagine.

It doesn't take long to reach a restaurant near the top of the hill. It's the only place to eat that boasts elevated views of the castle and has a large car park which I'd used yesterday in order to take some photos of Peggy. I wander inside to buy a bottle of water. The airy dining room is enormous with enough rows of tables to comfortably accommodate coach loads of sightseers. There's no one around except for a member of staff who's tidying behind a counter, so I approach him and ask the price of water.

"Fifty pounds."

I look knowingly at him, aware that the going rate is much less.

"Okay, I saw you on your moto yesterday. You're not a real tourist, not rich like the people who come here. You can have it for thirty five."

His commonly shared perception that all foreign tourists are rich isn't strictly true - except in relativity to the majority of Syrians - but I leave feeling happy about both the distinction he's made about me and the price of my drink.

On the track back to the hotel, I meet a boy leading a large grey donkey by its halter. On it are perched two children, a lad of roughly eight years old, and a girl a couple of years younger who shyly covers her face as I get near to them. Then I notice that trailing the donkey, attached by a length of rope, are two enormous bulls crowned with solid, menacing horns. They placidly follow on and pay me little attention as I rather nervously edge by. It's a true picture postcard scene.

After an hour working on the Beeza's clutch and exhaust, I set off for the coast, enjoying the scenery as we glide down the steep hills that had proved such an effort to climb yesterday. On the highway to Tartus, it's blowing a Hooley. Fortunately we don't have far to go, which is good as a procession of monstrous port bound trucks overtake us constantly. That said, the Bantam keeps up a steady 40mph for almost an hour, maintaining this even on the last long rise before reaching our destination. Close to the top I give Peggy my usual encouraging slap on the tank, feeling really proud of her, only to have my bubble burst by a tiny 100cc bike carrying three young men who all act with utter nonchalance as they zip past us! Arriving in the town centre at lunchtime, we head straight for the seafront and ride up and down the quiet - except for Peggy's exhaust - promenade in search of a hotel.

Tartus has a population of 90,000 people, although where they are today is a mystery. All the shops are closed and the streets look like a scene from an apocalypse film in which nefarious aliens have beamed the inhabitants up. The only places open are ice-cream cafés, so I spend a good deal of the afternoon sitting alone at pavement tables sampling some of the best ice-cream on the planet. In all, I try seven scoops from three different establishments and come to the conclusion that ice-cream making is one of Syria's best kept secrets.

I can't help noticing that there are Syrian flags and photographs of Bashar al Assad everywhere. He seems to be a popular leader. As well as framed pictures in shops and my hotel, I spot several cars with semi-transparent rear windows sporting his Presidential noggin, including one across the back of a rather smoky but splendid Mercedes Benz fintail that's seen better days but is somehow still going. In many ways, Syria seems a very relaxed and modern place, with the manifestations of state control far less apparent than in any other country I've passed through after departing Italy. I've not encountered a single police checkpoint since clearing Customs and there's a laid-back approach to formalities when checking in at hotels or changing money in banks. As a predominantly Muslim country (Christians make up approximately 10% of the population and Druze 3%), Syria has also been far from what I expected. My guide book explains that since 1971, legislation has guaranteed Syrians the freedom to practice any religion they choose. Women are visible everywhere and are not necessarily covered up, with the hijab headdress a less common sight than in many other Arab countries. Indeed, at the seaside, women are to be seen everywhere in typical Western clothing.

As afternoon turns to evening, it's as though the aliens have suddenly released their captives. Tartus is swiftly transformed, now thronging with thousands of people enjoying the cool of the evening. All the cafés and restaurants are open, including a number of sheesha joints where men partake of their evening pipe. The promenade's fountains and trees are illuminated with colourful fairly lights and a miniature railway, also lit like a Christmas tree, runs along the seafront. Locals sit on chairs outside their homes or shops, talking or playing backgammon while others mill around and pack the restaurants to bursting point. I find a small table in one busy streetside establishment, where a waiter produces a great mezze dinner: pickled peppers; roasted aubergine; smoky babaghanoush; tangy yoghurt: tabbouleh rich with mint and parsley; marinated olives; unleavened bread and a glass of Lebanese red wine.

Back at the hotel, standing on my balcony, I peer down into the car park where Peggy sits chained to a railing, then look out to the sea. There, defined by their navigation lights, sit at least a dozen ships moored in a long row waiting for access to the port. One of them, I assume, will be carrying us to our next destination.

Peggy's berth on the Visemar One.

Days 41 to 44, Tartus to Venice, Italy.
At sea.

In the half light of early morning we travel the short distance to Tartus port. The gate staff look blankly at me when I ask for Visemar Lines, our ferry operator, but thankfully allow us in to the huge compound and point us in the direction of the Customs hall. Parking Peggy right next to the entrance doors so that I can keep an eye on her, I'm met by a rather harassed looking shipping agent. There are only 11 passengers boarding but, as he explains, the Customs staff are still not up to speed with clearing privately owned vehicles and due to a last minute change of plan, the ferry is now leaving 4 hours ahead of schedule. No pressure then!

I start by getting an exit stamp in my passport then join the other three vehicle owners, including a pair of German diplomats, who are each trying to press their paperwork onto a lone Customs officer. If the shipping agent looked stressed, this chap appears to be right at the end of his tether. He takes the papers that are being foist upon him, scrutinises them and, turning redder and sweatier by the minute, hands them back with a look of uncertainty.

Time passes. The ship is due to sail at 10am and with an hour to go none of us have yet had our carnets completed. The agent attempts to intervene. The hapless Customs officer reluctantly takes all our documents back and walks into a nearby office where he's simply waved away by a superior. He returns to his counter, looks through all the pages again and then walks away, leaving the carnets behind. He talks to the passport officer, who shrugs, then walks back past us looking worried. It's at this moment that I realise he simply hasn't a clue what to do. Taking action, I approach a younger man who's completing freight paperwork. I explain that time is getting short and ask him to help. He walks over to the struggling man who's once again ineffectually clutching four carnets. Taking them out of his hand, he rapidly stamps them. We're clear!

The agent escorts me to Peggy and suggests he leads us through the port as it's a fair way to the ship. He's not kidding. We travel around 2 kilometres before coming to the end of an exceedingly long pier against which the gleaming Visemar One is moored. I ride straight up the ramp and park up. With the help of two efficient Italian crewmen, we secure the bike to the deck using four brand new sets of ratchet straps. I remove only the bags required for four days at sea and after briefly checking that the seamen's backs are turned, discreetly murmur,

"You've made it, girl," and pat her saddle.

I set off walking across the bold blue decking. Apart from half a dozen articulated trailers that have been shunted on, the Bantam is the only vehicle on the main cargo deck. There are two more internal freight decks, both of which are empty, and a huge open air car deck housing just three cars. It's like a ghost ship.

An impeccably groomed purser, the spitting image of actor Harvey Keitel, greets me. With his white shirt and black tie, it's really difficult for me not to think of him as Mr White in the film, *Reservoir Dogs*. Handing over a key, he directs me to my cabin which comprises a four bed room with a plush carpet, wooden table, seriously comfortable berths and a bathroom with a shower. The room's so immaculate that I suspect it's never actually been used before. It certainly smells brand new. The ship runs on Italian time, so I reset my watch then head off to explore my home for the next few days.

Visemar One is a roll-on combined freight and passenger ship with a capacity of 200 articulated trailers, 70 cars and 325 passengers. Its 126 metre length is painted a striking combination of scarlet and brilliant white and the decks are a deep blue. Every single part of it is shiny and pristine, not surprising considering this is only its third voyage. Owned and built by an Italian shipping company, the vessel follows a weekly triangular route between Venice, Tartus and Alexandria, with the Alexandria to Venice journey the longest leg.

I stand on the rear deck as we glide out of Tartus. It's about the size of half a football pitch and I have it all to myself. Once we're at open sea, I climb onto the top deck, complete with helicopter pad, pull out a sun lounger and settle down for a day of reading. Life on board, it soon transpires, consists of relaxing, eating and sleeping. I make my own breakfast and have one of the chef's excellent pasta dishes with basil, tomato and buffalo mozzarella for lunch followed by an even simpler gnocchi for dinner. On both occasions I am the first diner, so hungry that I'm at the restaurant door waiting for it to open. No one else arrives for their meal until I've finished and am about to leave.

The most exciting part of the day is the lifeboat and lifejacket test. All 13 passengers, including two who have sailed from Venice, are summonsed on deck by 'Mr White' who instructs us, in his best gangster voice, to put on our life jackets. I'm not sure if any of my shipmates have made the link with the hard man in *Reservoir Dogs*, but we all jump to attention and pull the life vests over our heads at the double.

Sunset is undoubtedly the best time to be on deck. There's something which stirs us in the place where the skyline meets the ocean, especially when, like this evening, it's aglow with golden and crimson vapours. The cool air and idle rocking motion of the ship soon lull me into a welcome torpor.

The whole of day two is spent in Alexandria docks. First thing after breakfast, I make overtures to 'Mr White', showing him my passport with its recent Egyptian exit stamp and asking if he can arrange some shore leave. I watch him approach the Egyptian shipping agent, who's sitting beside a Customs officer. Both firmly shake their heads at his request. Disappointed, I head for the sun deck to read my book but it's hard to relax with such an alluring city so close, especially when I can smell it and hear its sounds.

Instead, I look down on a Kingston-registered freighter that's unloading paper at the bow and being painted by her crew at the stern. Across to my right are vast stacks of containers and on the quayside is a large white van that contains an X-ray machine which meticulously scans the small amount of freight coming onto and off our ship. Along the side, spaced at 30 metre intervals, are policemen sitting on small stools, each holding an umbrella to stave off the effects of the hot sun. They seem to be guarding us, but from what I can't imagine.

With 'Mr White's permission, I head down to check Peggy over. As I take a couple of photos of her, I'm chased away by a policeman who thinks I'm photographing his temporary desk made from a packing case. What is it with Egyptian authorities and my camera! I drop it off in my cabin, return to the cargo ramp and ask another Egyptian officer if I can walk along the quayside. I'm clearly instructed to leave the cargo deck... immediately. I return to the passenger area.

The ship's officers and technicians are all Italian, but the service staff, the men and women that clean the cabins, serve the food and carry out all the general duties around the passengers, are Honduran. Two in particular, Francisco and Alan, are very friendly. In a long conversation they divulge that they are on a six month contract. I'm gobsmacked when they explain that this means six months on the ship, without any leave whatsoever! They tell me it's common but it sounds unbearable. That said, I once travelled on a sleeper train in Thailand where my carriage attendant, a delightful Thai woman in her mid-twenties, revealed that she had lived on the train for almost a year. It's a powerful reminder of how fortunate I am to lead the life that I do.

The highlight of the day is the arrival of a further 10 passengers. All head straight for their cabins but one emerges quite quickly. He's a young American man with a battered acoustic guitar slung over his left shoulder. His long hair and predilection for colourful hippy clothes make him look like someone returning from a visit to India in the late '60s. I invite him for a coffee in the café and it turns out that he's worked on a Kibbutz in Israel for several months, spent a few weeks travelling around Egypt and is vaguely heading for northern Europe in search of casual work.

Apart from the rise and fall of the sun, the regular calls for food are the best markers of time on board. I have dinner, another excellent pasta dish, and then head to the highest point for a last view of Egypt. And what a spectacle it is. The water reflects the final radiance of the day's sun, illuminating the shipping containers and transforming them from dowdy, rusty boxes into vibrant yellows, reds and blues. They look like giant glowing Lego blocks. I say farewell to Egypt for a second time on the journey and retire to my cabin in the hope of another very long night's sleep.

Day three is the hardest as there's very little to do and I've finished both of my books, an excellent John Le Carré spy novel and John Wyndham's sci-fi classic, *The Day of The Triffids*. I pace up and down on the open cargo deck, deep in thought, occasionally pausing to look for dolphins. The two diplomats, who've positioned themselves on the top sun deck, seem to have a great deal of luck, or perhaps sharper eyesight, yelling out joyfully every half hour or so that they've seen another school of dolphins. I always somehow miss them, but to be honest, my main thoughts are on the maintenance I could do if I was allowed below deck.

I seize the opportunity to talk to some of the people who boarded in Alexandria. The first group comprises a German family travelling in a 1984 Man truck which, with its high suspension and off-road tyres, resembles an ex-military vehicle, although I'm told it was actually used for pipe laying. The cab has two rows of seating and onto the back is attached a sturdy steel box with shuttered windows, that's used for sleeping and cooking. I wonder how intimidating the vehicle must appear to locals, especially in areas away from the main tourist centres. The couple have three children under five, the youngest of whom is just 18 months. Their trip, which they began in the early spring, had taken three months and was mostly centred on camping in Syria, Jordan, Israel and Egypt. They are now on their way home to resume 'normal' life.

Another family, again German, has been on the road for more than two years. Over the course of a couple of hours, their precocious 12-year-old son, Andreas, tells me about their travels through South America and from Cape Town to Cairo by public transport. He's remarkably self-assured and is interested in motorcycles, especially since an Austrian biker took him for a ride around the Sudanese port of Wadi Halfa on a KTM adventure bike. His sister's now four... I can't begin to imagine how tough it was for his parents coping with her as a toddler in South America.

"But my mum is a teacher," explains Andreas, "so she has been teaching us for an hour or two a day. I'm really not looking forward to going back to real school in Germany."

The change in conditions once we pass the heel of the boot of Italy on the fourth morning is noticeable. The Adriatic Sea becomes tranquil, although it is pockmarked by floating litter and smeared with oily deposits. We can easily see both coastlines at the same time, with Albania to the right and Italy on the left. Ahead, the blue sky melds into an unpleasant nicotine stain of smog on the northern skyline yet behind, off the stern, the enormous wake from the ship's twin propellers foams white all the way to its vanishing point on a crystal clear horizon. We parallel other northbound ships but none of them can match our speed.

In between my habitual wanderings on deck and the regulated visits to the restaurant, my thoughts increasingly turn to riding Peggy again... I'm biting at the bit. Rather than staring at the Montenegro coastline and wishing I was riding up it, I get out my maps and focus on making the most of the ride across northern Italy.

Day 45, Venice, Italy.
15 miles.

Early in the morning I'm packed and on deck, hankering to be reunited with Peggy. Although we'll be docking at Venice, the city of Marco Polo and a place that I've never visited, I know that the string of islands on which most of its renowned architecture and canals are built can't be accessed by motorised private vehicles. I'd like to look for a campsite and travel in by train or boat, but as that could easily waste a major chunk of the day, I've come up with an alternative plan. Roughly 150 kilometres north west is the city of Verona, noted for its Roman and medieval architecture and the Arena di Verona, an amphitheatre famous internationally for its open air opera performances. I'll spend the night in the city and the following day ride to Alessandria. From there, I've decided to catch the *Motorail* car train across the Alps to Holland. Jane has told me that Greg, her father, has gone into hospital, which is very distressing for her. This news, combined with Peggy's continuing problems, makes taking the train feel like the correct thing to do.

We soon enter a wide channel and join a slowly moving line of freighters, four ahead and two behind. Marker buoys gradually narrow the shipping lane until we're sailing within 50 metres of the shoreline. Speedboats and water taxis skim along beside and between the steadily advancing line of ships. Many are heading across to Venice, whose superlative spires and fine rooftops gradually emerge from the early morning mist to the east. A campsite, occupied by a smattering of tents and a disorderly row of mobile homes, comes into view. I grab the Garmin, which is conveniently cosseted inside my crash helmet by gloves and scarf, and switch it on. By the time the maps have loaded, we've sailed 100 metres past it. Despite being offshore, I mark our position.

'Mr White' lets me down into the cargo bay a few minutes before we dock. The air's so hot and muggy that it resembles a sauna and the deep vibrations of the loud engine serve to compound the unhealthy atmosphere. It's an almost unbearable place to be... no wonder I wasn't allowed down here while we were at sea! Once we've reversed to the quay and the giant loading door is lowered, I climb on board the little green Beeza. It only takes three kicks to start her up and I'm first off the ferry to meet the Italian officials waiting at the quayside. Sitting on the bike at the head of the short line of vehicles that have disembarked, I have to wait, becoming increasing cooked by the overhead sun, until the ship's manifest is handed over by a member of the crew. While we linger, the immigration officers, a man and woman both in their thirties, chat about Peggy and my trip. As soon as the paperwork arrives, they tick my name off the list and we're free to leave, entering Italy and therefore Europe without a passport or vehicle registration check, let alone a customs search... astonishing. I must have an honest face!

We set off with a roar that turns the heads of several stevedores.

Reverberating against the sides of Visemar One and a stack of nearby shipping containers, Peggy's exhaust sounds more like a vintage racing machine than a humble lightweight commuter bike. The sat nav leads us out of the docks and several kilometres along a series of leafy back roads. Heading towards my marked spot in the sea, I feel liberated to have the wind in my face and the fresh smell of vegetation rushing into my nostrils as we twist and turn along the narrow lanes. Just 100 metres short of coming to a rather soggy end in the Venetian Lagoon, I see a sign for the campsite, *Camping Fusina*, and turn in. Spot on.

After paying our pitch fee of 18 euros and depositing valuables such as my laptop in the reception safe, I ride round the grounds and find a smooth patch of lawn with a clear view of the water's edge. Unloading Peggy, I quickly pitch my tent and have a bite to eat. By 11.30am I'm on a small motorised boat known as a vaporetto heading for Venice, laughing at myself for whistling 'O Solo Mio', proof that years of Cornetto ice cream advertisements have left their indelible mark.

The 19th century Russian writer, Alexander Herzen, wrote, 'To build a city where it is impossible to build a city is madness in itself, but to build there one of the most elegant and grandest of cities is the madness of genius.' As I walk across the ornate and, in some cases, truly magnificent bridges that crisscross the numerous small waterways, I fully understand what he means. That so many homes, civic buildings, art galleries and spectacular churches are constructed on top of huge alder piles that have been submerged for centuries, with the waters of the lagoon lapping constantly above their foundations, and often on a spring tide even higher, renders me incredulous.

Immediately swept up in the procession of tourists, I follow a well beaten path around all of the major sites: Ponte di Rialto (Rialto bridge); Ponte dei Sospiri (Bridge of Sighs); The Grand Canal (effectively the main street of Venice) and Basilica di San Marco (St Mark's Cathedral). The queue to enter the latter is considerable, stretching a long way across one side of Piazza San Marco. On reaching the doorway, like the man directly in front of me, I'm refused admission as my daypack is too large. My observation that women with significantly bigger handbags are being allowed through falls on deaf ears, and we have to walk round a corner of the square and down an alleyway to deposit our packs in a lock up. To make matters more irritating, Gunnar, the Swedish fellow offender, and I are made to rejoin the tail of the queue. Once inside, we realise it was worth the hassle as the cathedral's beauty is dazzling.

On the upper parts of its walls and ceilings are glittering gold and bronze mosaics but I spend most of the time staring down towards my feet, amazed by the coloured geometric marble patterns. Were I still making neckties in New Zealand, I'd definitely want to photograph metre after metre of this remarkable underfoot mosaic to try and replicate the intricate artwork on fabric.

Everything about Venice is so incomprehensibly splendid yet I somehow feel underwhelmed. Walking to a quiet piazza, which boasts none of the architectural highs of the main attractions, I sit on the wall of an unpretentious fountain and observe the multitudes marching past, heading in the direction of the railway station. I realise that it's the visitors, which of course includes myself, that spoil Venice. There are literally tens, if not hundreds of thousands of us milling around, and the majority of local businesses, whether they be gift shops, fashion outlets, jewellers, bars or restaurants, seem to exist solely to meet our immediate wants and needs.

I recall watching Michael Palin spend a day in Venice at the beginning of *Around The World in Eighty Days*, which was filmed in 1988. His morning revolved around helping the city's garbage collectors load up their refuse boats, thus providing him with a rather unusual and humorous view of Venetian life and us viewers a more down-to-earth - or water - insight into the workings of the city. Maybe, like me in this instant, he could think of nothing to say about the beauty, grandeur or history of the place that hadn't already been eloquently said. More than that, I realise that Venice in 2010 feels like a fabrication. The gondoliers appear bored and uninterested, the impersonal shopkeepers are run off their feet and although a number of house windows are open, their occupants seem to be missing. Perhaps the best time to visit Venice is very early in the morning, when the locals are out and about but before the sightseers arrive in their droves. That said, I can see that couples who come here for more romantic reasons, in many cases taking a Gondola along one of the canals, seem to be having an altogether different experience. Each to his own, but for me, it's too much like being in an expensive and overcrowded museum. Give me the living, breathing, quotidian streets of Alexandria, Tunis or Damascus any day.

I rush to catch my vaporetto, which leaves on the half hour every two hours, making it with less than a minute to spare. I don't look back towards the smoggy, yet unquestionably splendid, skyline. Instead, I look forward, past the cruise ships, towards my campsite. Once there, I head straightaway to the water's edge and sit on a boulder with tiny waves lapping inches from my feet. In the next hour, two ships pass, heading for open water. I had hoped to see Visemar One as it left on its way to Tartous, but begin to think I've missed it. Just as I'm about to head back to the tent, get out my stove and heat up a meal, I spot a red and white shape slowly growing larger at the dock's entrance. Five minutes later the familiar outline is upon me, heading down the Adriatic towards the Med. I wave furiously, but none of the crew I've come to know is to be seen on deck. At the very back of the upper car deck, however, stand a line of half a dozen new passengers. I continue to wave and they wave back, completely unaware of the significance this holds for me. In my mind, I wish them wonderful journeys, wherever their ultimate destinations may be, and profoundly yearn to be heading south once again myself.

Day 46, Venice to Redaville, Italy.
180 miles.

I sleep through the night with the tent door open which allows a deliciously cool breeze to waft over me. Watching giant cargo ships sail past at daybreak, with the silhouette of Venice just visible in the hazy distance, I feel rested and ready for whatever the day may hold. After a bowl of muesli - it's amazing just how far two 1kg bags can be made to stretch - I break camp and prepare Peggy for departure.

Following a grass track round the campsite heading towards the exit, a Dutchman, Roel, who spotted the Bantam last night, emerges from under an awning and flags us down. It's impossible to refuse the offer of joining him and his wife, Marjon, for a steaming mug of coffee. Travelling in a huge mobile home which looks as though it could easily sleep six adults, the pair are at the southern point of their month-long trip and will soon, like me, begin their northbound journey home.

Once clear of the campsite, I begin to notice just how green Italy is. Following weeks of barren sand and bare rock the change in flora is wonderfully refreshing for my eyes. I pass through a couple of small villages where roadside gardens are in full bloom and the smells, most notably the potent scent of jasmine, are exquisite. It's also a relief to buy European 98 octane petrol, although the cost is quite a shock.

There isn't a direct route to Alessandria except by taking a couple of Autostrada. This option is completely out of the question as Peggy is just not suited to motorways, so I hop from town to town, always aiming for the next westerly *comune* or municipality, rather than looking for a specific road. Another exhaust bodge, carried out last night, holds for almost an hour but Peggy soon resumes bulldozer mode. I leave well alone, recognising that there's nothing more to be done as it's affixed as tightly as humanly possible. Of far greater concern is the engine, which is vibrating more than usual and the clutch, which is slipping with increasing regularity. Passing fields verdant with tobacco and sugar beet, I enter the town of Legnago around lunchtime having covered only 85 kilometres. Slowing for a roundabout, I tap the gear change to drop a couple of gears but the lever slips uselessly and, stuck in top, I have to kill the engine. It's the third time this has happened on the journey and on closer inspection, I'm amazed it hasn't been a more frequent occurrence as the splines are completely worn. I set to work, hammering the ring to create as tight a fit as possible on the shaft. Thankfully, the bashing is a success and the lever, when refitted, bites and holds firm.

Making our way along the SS10, a busy single-lane road that passes through village after village, I become incredibly tense. The early afternoon heat, which registers as 34 degrees on my thermometer, is once more wreaking havoc with Peggy's engine and a misfire develops that no amount of revving will cure. Just as I'm beginning to think it's time to stop and do some investigation, not to mention resting hands virtually numb from the vibrations, the engine cuts out and I coast to a silent halt. Learning my lesson from travelling with Essa, I lift off the tank bag and peer into the fuel tank... in my desire to hang on for another station selling 98 octane, I've run out of petrol again. Fortunately, my Primus fuel canister is full to the brim with fresh Italian benzine and its 600ml is just enough to get us to an automated Texaco station 12 kilometres down the road.

After riding through the red tiled town of Mantova, a charming place with gorgeous Renaissance architecture and a grand piazza, we once more head out onto the open road. Zooming along beside vineyards, I'm attacked by hordes of small flying insects. The little pests are swarming in their thousands, making it terribly difficult to stay focused. They become stuck in my beard, tickling my skin as they wriggle around in search of freedom. With a lorry close behind and a fuel tanker being overtaken by a car heading towards us, a couple of these little mites squirm around in my right ear, another makes serious headway up my left nostril and several more promenade across the front of my goggles. Aaaagggghhhh!

Situated on the banks of the Po River, which snakes its way across most of the breadth of northern Italy, the Lombardy city of Cremona is surrounded by ancient red stone fortified walls. Poking above them I see the roofs of several beautiful municipal buildings, old church spires and a great cathedral. Traffic is heavy on the ring road we follow, with a particularly long tailback caused by a distant roundabout. I pull out from the back of the queue and, following the white line down the middle of the road in second gear for a couple of hundred metres, slowly overtake the almost stationary file of cars. Approaching the roundabout, I squeeze the front brake lever. For a fraction of a second I feel something give, as though a couple of fine strands of wire are letting go, then the lever limply pulls all the way back to the handlebars. The brake cable has snapped!

I stamp down on the rear brake pedal as hard as I can and press my right boot onto the tarmac trying for every ounce of extra stopping power possible. Peggy's rear brake is pretty ropey at the best of times and the roundabout, which has a constant stream of cars moving around it, gets closer and closer. We come to a wobbly stop less than 2 metres short of it, my right hand still desperately clamping the useless brake lever against the handlebars. The car driver next to me sets off and the following vehicle shoots through at speed. I manage to release my right hand and wave it up and down. The next car stops, allowing me to hop off and push Peggy to the roadside. I'm rather shaken, as it's the first time a brake cable has ever given way on me, but feel immensely grateful it happened when I was travelling at relatively low speeds and not in an emergency situation. Fishing my spare cable out of a pannier, I do the necessary and we're soon underway again.

As afternoon fades into evening our route takes us through the centre of several large towns as well as the city of Piacenza. Peggy's clutch slips repeatedly and her engine is searing hot. Then begin a series of jerks, which I'm unable to interpret as either seizures or lack of fuel caused by worsening carburettor evaporation. My anxiety levels soar. Riding along busy streets, the engine repeatedly misses. My tightening shoulders and thighs ache and I begin to get a headache. Stopping at traffic lights, I ask a dapper man astride a silver Vespa if I'm on the right road for Alessandria. He points ahead, repeating three times,

"Road... broke."

Blooming Nora, what next?

What actually comes next, without any broken roads, is the *comune* of Castel San Giovanni. We bounce along its shiny cobbled alleyways as I follow my nose in search of our onwards route. Just when I think we're clear, I miss a turn and have to retrace our path around the long one way system, going right through the town centre again. After a short spurt in the countryside we enter another charming town, Stradella. Rather than taking the ring road exit at a roundabout, I head in a straight line up the main street, the setting sun acting as the perfect navigational aid. It's a lively place, with crowds on the pavements and cafes and bars full to bursting. I cruise slowly while looking left and right for a hotel, but my search is unfruitful so I emerge within ten minutes and rejoin the SS10.

Roughly 70km short of Alessandria, I pause at crossroads next to the small village of Redaville. On a stone wall are several signs pointing to a church, a couple of hilltop vineyards and the local post office. Below them is another simple hand-painted one advertising Bed & Breakfast. I turn and ride through the quiet village streets then head down a narrow lane, past a dilapidated barn, and locate the house that offers accommodation. An elderly Italian lady with subtle purple streaks in her hair welcomes me in then locks the garden gate behind us.

Viewed from my bedroom window, the rambling vineyards which cling to the hillside opposite are lovely and as soon as I'm showered, I set off on foot in search of a restaurant that, my landlady informs me, serves locally produced wine. Despite having the restaurant's business card, I walk up and down the main street past the telegraph office and church three times. After 10 minutes I'm forced to concede that I can't fathom the restaurant's line drawn map. Under an open first floor window from which the sound of much hilarity and clapping bursts forth, I stop a pedestrian, the first soul I've seen since departing my quarters. I hand him the card but unable to read it, he leads me to his house some 50 metres away. After a minute he emerges from a side door with his daughter, a raven-haired ten-year-old who smiles at me. In excellent English, she explains that her dad is Lebanese and cannot follow written Italian. When she reads the name on the card out loud, they both point down a dirt track that leads away from the main street and across a field in the direction of the highway.

I set off only to be brought to an abrupt halt after 100 metres. To the left is a solitary limestone walled house and ranging in front of it, a very unfriendly dog. It barks fiercely then takes up position in the middle of the track. I try the trick of pretending to pick up a stone to throw but the mutt appears to be naive, brave or stupid. Instead of backing off it charges towards me, abruptly halts, and then barks furiously, undaunted by this foreigner. I yell at it, hoping that an owner will come out of the house to investigate, but to no avail, so I have to resort to real stones with which I aim to just miss. These keep it at bay long enough for me to retreat and regain the safety of the village. I find a detour which adds an extra 15 minutes' walk to the restaurant.

The local wine is served in a carafe mixed with sparkling water. I've no idea why, but it's pleasant enough. Wandering out into the night, I don't risk the shorter route but choose the long way back... two weighty stones still in my hand.

Village hopping en route to Alessandria, Italy.

237

Day 47, Redaville to Alessandria, Italy.
45 miles ridden & 720 miles by train.

For once I have time up my sleeve as the *AutoSlapp Trein*, as it is known, doesn't leave Alessandria until 5pm. After a perfunctory check round Peggy for anything that may be working loose, I decide to go for a stroll along the lane to assimilate the peaceful mood of the hillside vineyards. The neighbouring property, a large house with a shoulder-high mesh fence, is protected by my close-on nemesis in the form of two fierce guard dogs that jump at the wire and scare the living daylights out of me. Just a few metres further along I gaze across a steeply climbing row of vines and spot a Rotweiler playfully chasing another large dog. Their presence, after last night's encounter, is reason enough to quit canine-ridden Redaville without delay.

The SS10 seems especially quiet on a Saturday morning. Satellite navigation isn't required for directions as my map shows the road leads straight to and through Alessandria. However, I have it switched on as Peggy's speedo gave up the ghost within 300 miles of starting out from England and the Garmin has performed as both speedometer and odometer with complete reliability ever since. I glance down and see that it's trying to guide us along a fork off the SS10, which presently arches away to our left. On impulse I follow the suggested detour which in a short time leads us straight through the centre of a silent village before rejoining the SS10. A few kilometres later the same thing happens. It dawns on me that the unit's programming is set for the shortest route, and that lies directly through the centre of communities built upon an older, and obviously more direct, incarnation of the road.

On one such foray through a small hamlet, without a single person in sight, I stop to photograph Peggy beside a field of red poppies in full bloom. Atop of spindly stalks, their wide open crimson petals undulate gracefully in the morning breeze. With no real pressures and such a short distance to ride, my spirits soar and I relish, absolutely and utterly, every single moment of motoring westwards. Each gentle curve in the road is a delight, a pause or halt becomes a golden opportunity to exuberantly accelerate away and throughout, there's the accompaniment of that distinctly characteristic Bantam 2-stroke popping sound which emanates rather loudly from the silencer.

We arrive at Alessandria station just as the *Motorail* train pulls in at the end of its overnight journey from the Netherlands. Coming to a halt, I stay seated on Peggy and watch a handful of classic cars, as well as more mundane family saloons, drive off... an MGB GT, an E-type Jaguar and a Jaguar XJS all catch my attention. Then come the motorcycles, a mixture of Japanese sports bikes and BMW tourers. Within five minutes, all have departed and silence ensues. The train staff explains that there are still five hours before loading commences for the northbound leg so I kick Peggy over and ride off in search of a café to while away the time.

There's an empty table outside a *paninoteca* (a sandwich bar) that's adjacent to a large central square where a weekend market's in full swing. Sipping my second *espresso*, I feel a gentle splash on my face and look skywards. Within seconds, the heavens open. A sharp, intense shower sends me scurrying away in search of shelter under nearby trees. I can't help but wonder about the coincidence of this downpour... the last time I experienced a single drop of rain was on the ride through this very city while racing south to catch the ferry to Tunisia! Thankfully, unlike the battering storms and flooding experienced then, today's skies clear to sunshine within 10 minutes.

With steam rising off the cobbled streets, I take a spin around the city. The inner ring road holds no appeal as it's mostly lined with modern office buildings but off the main square I find a series of charming lanes. Most of the shops are closed, however one that's open is an ice cream parlour called Naturalia. It's hard to find any flat tarmac on which to park Peggy so I simply lean her against a wall, our luggage providing cushioning. At home, apart from the occasional *Feast*, I hardly ever buy ice cream and it's surprised me just how addicted I've become on this ride. The day manager, a stylish young man who could easily feature in any magazine as a designer clothes model, is both gregarious and helpful, guiding me through a choice of over thirty flavours before finally dolloping three colourful scoops into a carton. I sit on the bench outside and slowly make my way through the bowl, with the pistachio frozen yoghurt most definitely my pick of the three. Once finished, I go inside to give feedback, which is all positive, and say cheerio. The manager continues to work as I talk and with a certain amount of ceremony, hands me another tub containing three more varieties.

"These are for you to try... my favourites. They are *gratis*... how do you say in England, on the house?"

It's such an unexpected gift that I struggle to know what to say. After expressing my thanks, I return to the seat in the sun and devour blobs four, five and six. By the time I'm finished, lunch is redundant.

Returning to the railway station, I park Peggy next to a temporary information point erected by one of the train staff and head for a supermarket across the way to stock up on provisions, most notably, a bottle of *Nebbiolo* to enjoy during the evening. Back at the station, the time comes to load Peggy. Along with a dozen or so other motorcyclists, I loop four fasteners onto the Bantam's frame then ride up a ramp and onto the freight wagons, ducking low to avoid decapitation on the overhead steel framework. Peggy's the final bike onto the carriage and as soon as I halt and climb off, three burly railway workers set to anchoring her securely to the car deck beside a British registered Yamaha R1. More than at any other moment on the journey, juxtaposed with this sleek, black speed-machine, Peggy looks like a relic from the distant past. Within two minutes the railwaymen have completed their task and with broad ratchet straps have pulled the Bantam down so tightly that her suspension appears to be completely compressed. I walk around her, double checking that all the luggage I've left on is equally sturdily secured, then feeling rather nervous about leaving her, head for my berth.

With my riding garb and overnight bag safely deposited in the couchette, I walk the length of the train which fully fills the platform from end to end. For reasons unknown, the bold writing along the tops of all of the couchettes really tickles me... *slaapwagen*, which I guess must be Dutch for sleeping car. Returning to my room, I discover that I have an English roommate, Philip, the owner of the R1 that Peggy's parked behind. We immediately fall into conversation about motorbikes. His, it transpires, has been less than reliable, which comes as a great surprise. On a ride around Italy the previous autumn it had suffered major engine failure. Still under warranty, the bike was left at an Italian Yamaha dealership for repair, a process that took several months and included a new cylinder being specially freighted from Japan. It's only now, almost 9 months later, that Philip has had the opportunity to collect it, making a holiday of the task by riding around northern Italy for a couple of weeks before catching this service home.

"It's not as big a deal as it sounds," he adds at the end of relating his saga. "I've another bike at home that I've ridden through winter, so it's not as though I've been without transport, and the R1's going like a dream now."

After a sudden lurch, the train edges forward and gradually builds speed as we head north east, through Milan, then north west to the Italian town of Domodossola in the Pennine Alps. After a brief stop at the station, where smokers are allowed off for a short reprieve from their enforced abstinence, we depart towards the town of Varzo and its 3 kilometre long spiral tunnel, believed to be the longest loop tunnel in the world. Through the train windows there's nothing but pitch darkness and it's impossible to perceive that we are in fact travelling in a full circle. Upon completion of the loop, we promptly enter the straight, 20 kilometre long Simplon Tunnel, which for 75 years prior to the 1982 opening of a tunnel in Japan was the world's longest railway tunnel. As we rattle along, rocking rhythmically from side to side, it's hard to forget that above us lies up to 2 kilometres of solid rock!

Once through the tunnel and firmly in Switzerland, the call goes out for diners to take their tables in the restaurant car. The meal's a three course gourmet affair accompanied by a selection of regional wines. It costs nearly ten times more than most meals I ate in North Africa and the Levant, so I relish every morsel. However, it feels like money well spent if only to have the chance to eat while enjoying, in the fading light, magnificent views of rivers, lakes, picture postcard mountain villages and the Lepontine Alps. I may not be travelling in quite the opulent style of the Venice-Simplon Orient Express, I tell myself, but I can enjoy a relative indulgence while journeying on, at least for now, the same route.

Each time we pass another train at speed I can't help thinking of Peggy being pulled along at the tail of the last carriage. It's there that the violent effects of bends and suction created by these high-speed passes will be felt the most... I hope she makes it safely through the night without suffering any mishaps. Savouring the moment by dragging out the last spoonfuls of pudding and final mouthfuls of wine, I watch the headlights of an isolated car dancing around on the twisting mountain road beside the rail track. Half wishing I was doing the same on Peggy, I weave my way along several corridors and return to the couchette. The attendant has made up my bed and Philip, who's chosen to sleep on the opposite top bunk, is already snugly settled in. Over a glass of wine we talk about... motorcycles! When we eventually turn the lights off, the gentle rolling motion of the train gradually woos me deep into the arms of Morpheus.

241

Day 48, 's-Hertogenbosch to Zeebrugge, Belgium.
155 miles.

During the night we pass through Basel, Freiburg and Bonn. Opening a crack in the curtains sometime after dawn reveals that we have stopped in the German city of Köln. I nod off again and the next time I take a peek, see that we're passing through an empty German suburban station. We cross the border into Holland and rattle through Venlo. Dead on schedule at 9.50am, the train pulls into Den Bosch (the commonly used Dutch abbreviation for 's-Hertogenbosch, meaning 'The Duke's forest') railway station. I'm keen to get underway as soon as possible because our ferry to England leaves from Zeebrugge this evening. Frustratingly, the last bike on is also the last off and I have to wait, almost hopping from foot to foot, for 20 minutes before Peggy can be released from the train.

Today of all days I need my sat nav as there's little room for slippage. But when I switch it on, I discover that it's not mapped for Holland or Belgium. I instantly realise that prior to departure I'd never envisaged travelling this far north. The background map shows nothing more than an approximation of cities and major highways, so with just my compass and small scale European map book, I ride south east on minor roads heading towards Tilburg.

As soon as we join a dual carriageway and start to motor faster, the Bantam begins to misfire. Dam it, this is the last thing we need. It's so bad I'm forced to stop immediately. I swap the spark plug for one I cleaned and correctly gapped in Italy. It makes no difference and a couple of hundred metres further on I have to halt again, this time changing the condenser. Within a kilometre the misfire returns. Now I change the points but, on setting off once more, the engine cuts out, restarts with a lurch then judders forward towards a pedestrian who's trying his luck crossing a junction with the lights against him. I don't know who gets the biggest fright, him or me!

Deeply worried, I park up for a fourth time and on this occasion sit back from the kerb to consider my options. The coil seems the next logical electrical component to check. I probe underneath the petrol tank with my fingers and immediately find the problem. The nut that secures the lead from the points to the coil has worked loose, most probably the consequence of the rollicking train journey Peggy has just endured. The resulting poor connection is the cause of the misfire.

I'd have thought I would be better at this by now; the episode has cost us an hour. My concern about reaching Zeebrugge on time intensifies, as the ferry sails at 9pm and the reservation states we should check in 2 hours in advance. The road we're on goes through Tilburg city centre, which I fear will delay us further. After a quick check of the map, I bear left onto a motorway that bypasses the city. Riding as fast as I dare, we belt along at 75kmpg.

Nonetheless, traffic races past us at shocking speeds and I spend more time watching my mirrors than the road ahead. Thank goodness it's a Sunday morning rather than a busy weekday, as cars travelling in excess of 120kmpg simply cannot gauge our pace and more often than not don't pull out to an overtaking lane until the very last moment. It's frightening. Mercifully unharmed, we exit after 18km and take a southerly back road towards Belgium.

While travelling through dark woods that seem to crowd in on us from overhead as well as both sides, I'm somewhat reassured to see a blue road sign bearing the word 'Belgique' surrounded by a circle of gold stars. It's 12.40pm and at last we're beginning to make meaningful progress. Passing through a series of small towns and villages, we encounter few cars but the bicyclists, whose silent approaches from all directions catch me off guard several times, demand an extra degree of vigilance. Proper horns rather than little tinkle bells on their handlebars would certainly be more helpful.

The biggest impediment on our journey appears to be the city of Antwerp. There's a motorway around it but after this morning's hairy experience and with city bound traffic rapidly multiplying, I default into other options. Dog-legging in small stretches of a kilometre or two at a time, we go from village to village in a squiggly anti-clockwise direction around the busy urban centre. Often we follow narrow lanes or pass through housing estates and once even go down a dirt track that's so long, I'm convinced that the directions given by a farmer are wildly inaccurate. Fortunately I persevere for a further 10 minutes and to my delight the shortcut turns out to be a godsend. Pulling onto the forecourt of a petrol station to the west of the city, I grab a sandwich, fill Peggy's tank and consult my blackened, dog-eared map. The road we've just joined should lead us directly to the coast, with no more major obstacles. I check my watch... it's 4.50pm and there are still 60 miles left to ride.

We set off and without warning, the national grade road becomes an Autoroute. Then we come to a halt at a highly unusual sight - a set of traffic lights smack bang in the middle of a motorway. On the approach I'd seen 'Motorway Ends' signs, yet straight across the junction there are 'Motorway Begins' symbols too. It's certainly uncommon, if not bizarre. My map shows equally confusing road numbers, as N49 and E34 are both written along the same line. I can only guess that it's in the process of being upgraded, although there are no obvious indications such as road works.

Peggy's once more running terribly hot and I'm too apprehensive about her seizing to maintain our maximum of 70kmph for long periods. Running parallel to the highway is a succession of narrow pathways used by bicycles. Fearing a breakdown that I'm not able to fix quickly enough on a motorway hard shoulder, I decide to give the empty cycle paths a go and turn off. At times they're only a metre wide and every few kilometres they either peter out, turn off into a village, cut across a farm track or rejoin the motorway at more traffic lights. On one occasion they simply terminate abruptly with a steel barrier. It makes riding a real seat-of-the-pants affair. I constantly check the handlebar mounted clock. Time is getting short and our much slower parallel route is eating away at the last of our safety margin. Just 25km from Zeebrugge, under fast approaching rain clouds, I rejoin the motorway and ride as fast as my nerve will allow.

At a roundabout I see signs for the car ferry, a routeing which leads off to the south rather than heading straight through the town centre. Dithering, I go full circle round the roundabout while making up my mind. Second time around I follow the ferry signs which proves to be a mistake as the detour, designed to keep heavy goods traffic out of the town centre, just about doubles the distance to the port.

But the Bantam doesn't let me down, battling resolutely against a cross wind which blasts off the nearby sea. Sweating and stiff-necked from the stress but overwhelmingly happy, we motor into the port at 7.35pm. Peggy's still running and my delight, mixed with an appreciable release of anxiety, is immense. Slapping her repeatedly on the tank and punching the air several times, I follow signs for P&O Ferries. With almost an hour and a half to spare before the ferry sails, I've no doubt whatsoever that I'll soon be on board, showering then eating my first square meal of the day.

I steer Peggy to a halt in front of a check-in area which seems surprisingly deserted, then spot several trucks in the process of boarding a small ferry. Riding to the P&O gate which leads to that ship, I dismount. Having travelled all day without any real break except for brief petrol stops, my legs feel like jelly as I walk towards the gatehouse. I enter and ask where to board the ferry to Hull. The lone official looks at his watch then says in halting English,

"The ferry to Hull sailed half hour before. It goes at seven... always."

I stand with my mouth open, unable to speak. It gets worse.

"But this week one of the ships in dry dock, so no ship to England tomorrow."

"What about that ship?" I ask, pointing through the window to the dark blue ferry with P&O boldly painted in white along its side.

"Sorry, this is for freight only."

I'm speechless.

Eventually I recover sufficiently to remonstrate that I have a reservation which clearly says the sailing time is 9pm. The official looks skeptical. With heavy feet I return to the Bantam and retrieve my laptop. Back in the office I boot it up and show the reservation emailed to me by my travel agent. It plainly says 21.00hrs. The official is somewhat perplexed and telephones P&O's head office. Within a couple of minutes he has an explanation.

"The agent made a mistake. He give you the time of the Rotterdam ship. I am sorry, but you must wait here two days or go to Rotterdam tomorrow. You can sail to Hull from there."

Before I set off in search of a hotel I have to phone home and relay the news. I'm close to tears as I tell Jacques. He's been so excited about my imminent return and his disappointment is painfully evident down the echoing phone line. After the jubilation of finally reaching the Channel, my spirits plummet to undoubtedly their lowest ebb of the journey. I find a nearby hotel, another plastic Formula One job, where, as I'm checking in, two Brits, a father and son, arrive on a Honda and a Suzuki. They're at the start of a week long ride, mostly around Germany. Landing at the port earlier in the day, they've spent a few hours looking around the nearby town of Brugge.

"I hope you're not hungry," one of them says. "We've just trawled around the local restaurants and they're either closed or frightfully expensive."

The hotel manager corroborates their warning.

"I'm sorry, there is nowhere good to eat in Zeebrugge. You can ride to Brugge, where there are many restaurants, or maybe the Texaco petrol station around the corner can sell you sandwiches."

Instead, I rummage in a saddlebag and produce a *Travellunch* packet, the last of the 6 instant camping meals I've carried from home. After last night's indulgence, I can make do with its simplicity and the manager is very amenable when I ask for boiling water.

Before climbing into bed, I telephone the travel agency that had arranged the ferry, leaving a message on their answerphone that outlines the problem and asks them to call me in the morning. I struggle to fall asleep, undecided about whether to wait 48 hours or head for Rotterdam, the pros and cons of both options going round and round in my head. Still focused on ensuring Peggy makes it all the way home under her own power, it's hard to know whether to risk another day's ride or wait in safety for Tuesday night's crossing.

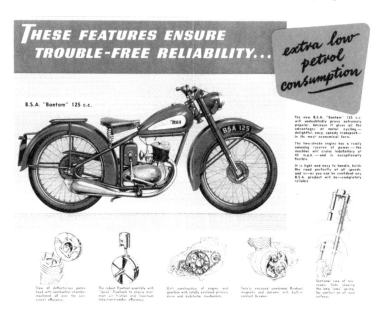

Day 49, Zeebrugge to Rotterdam, Netherlands.
120 miles.

Until now I've taken a far more judicious approach to the return journey than the outward one, but this morning there's absolutely no doubt in my mind about what I want to do. In William Shedd's often cited words: 'A ship in harbour is safe, but that is not what ships are built for.' The journey will soon be over and I simply cannot resist the lure of another day of Bantaming, whatever it may entail.

I programme '*Europoort*' into the sat nav. Just like yesterday, there's no depth to its map but the suggested route does give me a sense of where to head when checked against the detail of my paper map. The most interesting route also appears to be the most direct one, crossing many of the acclaimed Delta dam works that connect the islands of Zeeland and protect much of low lying Holland from flooding. The morning air is sharp and there's the bonus of a truculent northerly wind that should blow directly onto the Bantam's engine once we're under way. Peggy, as though champing for an additional adventure, starts first kick. With good cooling guaranteed, I set off feeling curiously unperturbed about the ride ahead.

We travel north east for an hour, quietly crossing back into Holland in the process and, without any mechanical or electrical complications, reach the small town of Breskens which sits on the edge of a wide estuary. I follow signs to its tiny ferry terminal, park up and head for the ticket office which is located in a foyer at the top of a flight of stone steps. As I begin to climb, two women lift their bicycles and carry them up the stairway beside me. The queue for tickets is short and in no time I'm in front of an efficient young man at the counter.

"One motorcycle and one passenger please."

"I am sorry," he replies, looking perplexed, "but this ferry is only for foot passengers and bicycles."

He gets out a regional map and points to a spot in the middle of the estuary 30 kilometres to the east.

"There is a tunnel here, just before Terneuzen, that you must take."

"My motorcycle is very small," I respond in vain hope. "Can't I push it on like a bicycle?" I add while having no clue how I could possibly hump Peggy and all our accoutrements up the steps.

He shakes his head. The sat nav is jammed into my helmet, so I pull it out, explaining that it brought me to this ferry crossing.

"That is strange," says the ticket seller. "There hasn't been a car ferry here for eight years, not since the tunnel opened!"

It's another valuable lesson... if you're going to rely on a sat nav, make sure the maps are up-to-date maps. With two ferry foul-ups in less than 24 hours, I walk back to Peggy hoping that tonight's sailing will prove to be third time lucky.

Following the N255 towards Terneuzen, we release strings of articulated lorries and cars that repeatedly build up behind us by again riding impromptu stretches on immaculately trimmed bicycle paths that are hemmed between the road and deep dykes. Locating the Western Scheldt Tunnel entrance in under an hour, I pause for a while to ensure the Bantam's engine is cool as a sign indicates the subterranean crossing is more than 6km long. Satisfied, I restart Peggy and make the short trip to a toll plaza. A woman leans out of a window, takes my proffered 2 euros, and, as I'm about to set off, cracks into a big smile and says,

"Hey. You look like someone out of Mad Max!"

I can't think of a suitably witty reply and, with cars in a small queue behind me, just smile and wave before roaring forwards towards the tunnel mouth. However, I chortle to myself at the thought of a gun-toting, black leather-clad Mel Gibson tearing around on a D1 Bantam.

I travel through Middleburg then continue north east towards the first Delta dam. Peggy's buzzing along nicely, the sun breaks through the clouds and the air feels sharp and fresh. Passing hedgerows and fields that smell strongly of manure, I momentarily catch the hint of a black spot directly ahead which, within the blink of an eye, slams painfully into my neck. Being hit in the face by insects or stones is unquestionably one of the drawbacks of riding with an open face helmet and it's only to a small extent that my beard offers a degree of protection. I'd sometimes wondered, especially after a near miss, if it would be possible to be stung by riding into the backside of a bee or wasp. Today I find out that it is... and how much it hurts. Braking rapidly to a halt, I check my neck in the mirror. A large red welt has already sprung up. As well as the pain, it's tormentingly itchy.

The first dam we cross to the island of Noord Beveland is fairly small, but ahead lies 'the daddy' of the Delta works, the 9km long Oosterscheldekering. It's a spectacular feat of engineering, a procession of sixty five enormous pillars between which are secured giant sluice doors that allow water through the dam when the tides are favourable. Although the dam-top road is partially protected, the wind howls savagely off the North Sea, bringing with it the salty smell of sea air. It's exhilarating, if a little scary, as huge gusts tug menacingly at the Bantam's front wheel. The rear however, under considerable weight, remains firmly pinned to the tarmac. We reach the manmade island, Neeltje Jans, in the middle of the estuary and I stop to take some photos. Looking backwards, the long line of white pillars stretch as far as my eye can see, resembling the spine of a giant science fiction monster rising from the depths. As we recommence our journey across the dam's final 4km, I cogitate further on yesterday's bodged ferry booking - and decide that maybe it has its bright side.

Back on solid ground, we continue north before heading out over another magnificent flood barrier, the Brouwersdam, then onto the island of Goedereede, which boasts a great number of campsites. We skirt around a couple of small, red tile roofed villages before motoring out onto the 5km Haringvlietdam dam. It's the last we have to cross today and by far the windiest, causing me to lean Peggy precariously over to seaward in order to maintain a straight line on the road. On the far side, I take a break by riding onto the central lawned area of a roundabout, so large that I'm happy we can't be seen by the encircling traffic. Drawing the heady aroma of freshly cut grass deeply into my lungs, I lie back and stare at the sky whilst close to my right ear, Peggy's cooling engine tunefully crackles.

After a couple of bridges I spot the first sign for the Europoort. Similar to last night, I feel an upswell of elation but this time, as I pull up at the tail of a long line of motorcycles waiting to board the enormous P&O ship, feel for sure that Peggy and I will soon be sailing for England. Within moments of dismounting, a man leaps out of an elegant, burgundy-coloured vintage car that's parked in an adjoining lane. He bounds over towards us.

"That's never a Bantam," he exclaims with a mixture of disbelief and pleasure. "I had an old Post Office 125. It was my first motorcycle... I remember it cost me just £5."

I'm intrigued by the gentleman's car.

"It's a 1938 Bentley straight-6," he reveals with obvious pride. "We're just coming back from a classic car show in Germany where it won best in its class."

The man removes his camera from its pouch and begins to take photos of Peggy. I wander over to admire the sleek lines of the Bentley, then through the open passenger window strike up a conversation with his wife, giving her a brief overview of our journey. After a pause in which she intensely engages me with penetrative but warm eyes, she says,

"You remind me of my brother. He's always going off travelling too."

Then, with a certain gravitas, she adds, "Whatever you do, you must keep making adventurous journeys on your old motorcycles."

Continuing to look deeply into my eyes, she urges,

"Really. You must. It is very important for you."

I'm not sure whether it's the woman herself or the timing, but her words really strike a chord.

Before we can talk further, the waiting cars begin to edge forward and board the ferry. I hop onto Peggy and follow approximately 30 bikes, most of which are returning from a classic racing event at Spa-Francorchamps in Belgium. Peggy, by far the smallest and oldest of them all, is also the most raucous courtesy of the blown exhaust, but by now, I really couldn't care.

Once on the ship's cargo deck, two motorcyclists who have just stepped off sports bikes help me secure Peggy with some ancient ropes and straps. As we work, they tell me they both have classic bikes at home but think I'm mad for attempting such a journey on one. Then the taller of them, who introduces himself as Brian Thompson, says,

"I'm in the Vintage Motorcycle Club. We've got a guest speaker booked that you'd be interested in. He's coming to our section in August to give a talk about riding an old Royal Enfield all the way to India."

I laugh so hard, I can hardly get the words out to explain that I am that very man. The biker's world is a small one!

At sunset the ferry leaves port, heading for the east coast of England. After dinner, I sit in a bar with a glass of wine, watching container ships and oil tankers crashing into steep waves as they too sail away from Rotterdam. It feels unreal that tomorrow will mark the last day of my travels with Peggy.

Day 50, Hull to Romiley, UK.
99 miles.

At 5.30am the passengers' wake-up call blares through the previously unnoticed speaker in my cabin. Redolent of *Hi-de-Hi!* 'Good Morning Campers!' but without Gladys Pugh's dulcet Rhondda Valley tones, it comes as a shock to the system. When, 10 minutes later, it reverberates around the tiny room again, repeating all the breakfast choices available during the next hour and a half before we berth, I bury my head under the pillow, realising that it's a restaurant sales pitch rather than a warning of imminent disembarkation.

Preparing Peggy for departure, riding off the ferry and clearing UK immigration and Customs seems to go by in a flash. In something of a daze I find myself riding in English rush hour traffic, with a couple of careless Hullensian motorists coming close to knocking me off the bike. As if that wasn't enough to contend with, I also have to think very carefully when negotiating road junctions and roundabouts after more than 6 weeks of motoring on the right.

I follow signs for the Humber Bridge. Opened in 1981, for over a decade it was the world's longest single span suspension bridge. I've admired it several times from a distance but never actually crossed it. Easily keeping up with the flow of cars and vans ahead, we slow to pay the £1.20 toll then begin to motor up the gentle arch that spans the centre of the Humber Estuary. There's a 40mph speed limit in place which is perfect for a Bantam and as the following traffic can't press us to go any faster, I have time to enjoy the views and take in the bridge's superlative design.

Once across, I turn down a narrow country lane, park up beside a field of spring wheat and take some photos of Peggy against the back-drop of the bridge's flowing lines. Mounting up, I head back along the road, which is on a steep uphill slope and has a succession of blind bends. I cruise round a couple, power along a short straight then set myself up to round the next one. In horror, I suddenly realise we're on the wrong side of the road! Intensely thankful not to have caused a head on crash, I throw Peggy hard over onto the left lane, telling myself over and over to concentrate.

Our route cross country is undemanding, a series of 'A' roads that enable us to bypass Scunthorpe and Doncaster. However, there's no avoiding Barnsley and I have to ride slowly through its centre. Once free from a depressingly long string of traffic lights, I heave Peggy onto the pavement at the edge of a housing estate and phone home.

"All right, love?" asks a woman walking her dog as I finish my call. I ask her if there's a café nearby where I can get some lunch.

"Round 'ere? I dawn't reckon," she replies.

Pointing ahead, she adds,

"Papershop ont' corner 'as none. There's a bakers downt' rawd thet'll make thee a butty."

Her dialect, rich, strong and, to my ears, lovely, is one that I've grown accustomed to in recent years since attending many autojumbles at Rufforth, near York. Feeling comforted by the familiarity of her accent and its proximity to home, I thank her warmly, crank Peggy over and go to look for the bakery.

Three and a half hours after departing Hull, we reach the start of the A628, the road which crosses the Pennines over the notorious Woodhead Pass. I've travelled along this route many times by car when heading to and from the M1 motorway and am familiar with its barren, windswept beauty. In winter, it's also treacherous and prone to closure because of snow, high winds or fog. Knowing the steepness of the incline and feeling especially vulnerable to the fast and heavy volume of traffic that uses it, I want to ensure Peggy's engine is stone cold before commencing the sharp climb to its 450 metre summit. Waiting in a layby, slowly sipping a cup of instant coffee bought from the portakabin transport café, I watch a large articulated Marks & Spencer lorry pull up in front of me. The driver, a Scot, climbs out and admires the Bantam. For a couple of minutes, I summarise our journey, the seizures Peggy has suffered due to overheating and my desire to make it over this final obstacle and safely home.

Without answering, he steps off the pavement, stands next to Peggy and with his back turned towards me, begins speaking to her.

"Listen here," he says, leaning close to the petrol tank. "I want you to get this laddie home in one piece."

He then wags a finger at her and concludes,

"Come on now, you can do it."

"You're a man after my own heart," I tell him as he remounts the pavement.

Shaking his hand, I continue,

"I think I've talked more to this bike than I have to other human beings over these last few weeks."

As I secure my helmet strap, he directs a last word towards Peggy,

"Now remember what I've told you," then wishes me luck as I climb onto her saddle.

Bracing myself, I rev hard the whole way to the top, determined to make plenty of cooling oil reach the engine. But after all my concerns and preparation, the ascent is almost an anti-climax as, in 3rd gear, we easily crest the highest point in under 10 minutes. Indeed, traversing The Pennines seems a stroll in the park compared to some of the mountains we've scaled in the Alps, the Sinai and in Jordan. I begin the descent without even pausing to let her cool.

"Come on, Peggs, nearly there," I encourage her as we glide round a long series of downhill bends towards the Longdendale valley, past a chain of four reservoirs then through the village of Tintwistle.

Near Mottram, I stop to phone home again. Jane answers, her voice drowned by Jacques's excited questions,

"Where is he mum? Is he here yet?"

The last few miles take 30 minutes. Roads become increasingly familiar, the sun comes out and the butterflies in my stomach grow.

Jubilantly descending the short hill that leads into the village of Romiley, I prepare to turn left but have to pull the brakes on hard. Jane and Jacques are standing on the corner, watching avidly for our arrival. Jacques runs across and throws his arms around me, then sets off up the lane as fast as his legs can carry him, racing Peggy to his front garden.

After a long round of hugs and kisses, I find my camera, set it to self-timer and take several photos of the four of us. Jane then takes a picture of me with my head resting on Peggy's tank, my face split by an enormous grin. It's hard to believe that in spite of all the problems we've had, the little Bantam has kept going, and most importantly, made it home in one piece... popping, banging and blue smoking in her inimitable true 2-stroke spirit.

We spend much of the afternoon in the garden and I leave Peggy there throughout, almost as if I can't quite put her away. I'm aware of two strangely amorphous states within me. One relates to the necessary transition from my travelling experiences and freedoms to the welcoming, loving, but restricting nature of life at home. The other is the poignancy which overrides any sense of achievement best described by Robert Louis Stevenson, 'To travel hopefully is a better thing than to arrive'...

Epilogue

On my return to the UK it was hard to settle back into a daily routine, complicated by the demands of being a parent and travelling virtually every weekend with my work. As time progressed, I was able to recapture my enjoyment of the journey and began to write this book. However, two stumbling blocks prevented the manuscript from being published. The first was the war in Libya and my deep concerns for the safety of Essa and Mr. Fathe and his family. The second was my unresolved quest to find Miss Thomas, which became something of an obsession.

In writing this book, I can only give a personal perspective based on the brief encounters I had with some truly wonderful people. It's almost impossible to decipher the whole truth in world affairs as so much that is reported is either subjective or edited, especially when big business, arms sales and oil are concerned. Subsequent events in Tunisia, Libya, Egypt and Syria, the 'Arab Spring', have brought with them a reportage declaring oppression and brutality that were not evident during my visit to these places. Although only passing through, I always took time to listen to people, to ask them about their lives, hopes and aspirations. The impression I was left with was of countries where there were problems, largely economic, but a distinctly greater level of optimism than I experience in Britain.

No more so was this the case than in Libya where, despite his past label of 'mad dog,' Muammar Gaddafi appeared to me to be improving the general living conditions of the Libyan people. Certainly I saw none of the extreme poverty that one readily sees in places such as India, Bangladesh, Indonesia and even some of the poor inner city areas of many European nations. And there was no evidence of the violence, overt or tacit, by individuals or gangs, that is commonplace in the majority of Western countries, including Britain and the United States. Instead, I met people who were, in the main, content... certainly as content as most people I know. As far as I could see, their lives had a stability and richness that was rooted in family, culture and religion, and much less defined by the fever-pitch consumerism and financial accumulation which life in the Western world has largely come to embody.

Once NATO began to fight on behalf of the rebel forces rather than adhering to the UN mandate of protecting innocent civilians by keeping the air space free, it became obvious that there was only one inevitable outcome to the civil war. I wanted to ensure that nothing I wrote, even though it was far from being radical, would have implications for Essa and Mr. Fathe, yet at the same time I didn't want to alter or attenuate any of my experiences.

For eight months I sent emails and text messages to Essa but received no reply. I tried not to fear the worst, reasoning it was most likely that mobile phone networks were down and internet access blocked. On 5 October 2011, some time after the fall of Tripoli but before the killing of Gaddafi, I finally received word that he was safe. I guess that I hadn't really acknowledged to myself how great my fears for his safety had been, for such was my relief on reading this I began to cry. He has not been able to work for over nine months as there were no tourists to guide, however his communications seemed positive. I very much hope that I will be able to keep a lifelong friendship with this upbeat, sincere and hugely generous man.

My search for the 'real' Peggy resumed very soon after returning to the UK. I tried the original publishers once again. My intensity and dedication finally struck a chord with one of their staff... or maybe she simply wanted to end my perennial calls! Not only did she supply Miss Thomas's last known address in Copenhagen, which she thought was circa 1979, but also the names Percival and Ursula Thomas in the UK, whose joint bank account had received the author's royalty payments. I immediately looked online in fascination at a block of Copenhagen flats where Miss Thomas had apparently lived but on checking the address register found no one likely to be a match.

Sometime later I discovered that since 1968 all Danes have to be registered with a central body, know as the CRS (Civil Registration System), and are issued an ID card. Moreover, the CRS database is open for other Danish citizens to view. In a fine example of the way that technology has speeded up our lives and shrunk distances, I phoned Hilda, a dear friend in New Zealand. Her brother, Peter, has lived in Denmark on the island of Jutland for over thirty years. She gave me Peter's Skype moniker and in under an hour I was engrossed in a video call with him. He instantly agreed to help and forthwith sent me an email that offered real hope.

'My neighbour is a policeman. Not only can he access the national database, he can do a police search too. If your lady is in Denmark, we're sure we'll be able to find her.'

Days turned to a week, then two, without any news. Eventually another email arrived which I read with bated breath.

'Had a long chat with the policeman today and he does not think that Peggy ever had a CRS number. The address you gave has never had anybody there of that name or any viable combination of names. He said maybe it was a c/o address. His colleague helped him and they checked everything from 1975 into the 80s. They also did another type of check which the police sometimes use but that was also negative. Sorry and good luck, Peter.'

With Denmark now ruled out, I searched telephone directories for other Scandinavian, then north European countries. I found a Peggy Sorensen living in Norway and a Peggy Iris in Germany, but none panned out. I lay awake at night in frustration, tormented by the difficulty of locating someone who may have been been divorced or widowed then remarried. I didn't even know her true birth name or place of birth to give me a proper starting point! However, the names Percival and Ursula had opened a potential new avenue of enquiry. Unsure if they might be parents or offspring, I set about searching the UK births, marriages and deaths register in the hope of locating a birth certificate. Nothing looked likely as it's necessary to know a mother's maiden name to have any real chance of success... all I had was a possible christian name. Day after day I searched through lists of Peggy, Margaret, P I and M I Thomas's born between 1920 and 1930. I eventually ordered three copy birth certificates but, to my dismay, two proved to be Peggy Irenes and one a Margaret Ida.

A couple of years earlier, when Jacques was struggling to build a Lego set designed for children much older than him, I told him about Winston Churchill.

"During the Second World War, this man was the Prime Minister and inspirational leader of Britain. He was invited to go back to his old school, Harrow, and give a speech. What he said was 'Never give in, never, never, never, in nothing great or small, large or petty, never give in.'"

Jacques has shortened this to his motto, 'Never give up, never give up, never give up!' and much to both Jane's and my consternation repeats it in his regular attempts to acquire new toys or cram down excessive junk food. One evening, while relating to Jane my day's unproductive search efforts and wondering if I should give up as I'd already put several weeks of work time into the quest without any notable success, Jacques came into the room and listened attentively.

Fixing me with a level eye, he said,

"Remember that Churchill man... well, never give up, never give up, never give up!"

The following morning I got straight back into my search.

I bought copies of the electoral register. One Peggy Thomas, registered in Plymouth in 2002 looked hugely promising as searches for Ursula and Percival Thomas, on the chance that they were children not parents, revealed an Ursula living 4 miles away, a Percival 46 miles away and incredibly, a C. Sorensen just 2 miles away! I was ready to jump in my car and make the 500 mile round trip the next day but was fortunately persuaded by Jane to write a letter instead. A reply came back within a week saying sorry, I'd got the wrong person. Then I discovered a Peggy I Thomas living in Somerset. This lady was on the 1998 register but not evident on any more recent ones. Still, I spotted her in the telephone book and she also had an Ursula Thomas living in close proximity. Again I sent a letter, which I followed up a week later with a phonecall.

"Sorry love, I received your letter but it's not me. I'm Peggy *Irene* Thomas."

I thanked for her time and bid her farewell.

"How many blooming Peggy *Irenes* can there be!" I blurted out in exasperation as soon as I'd hung up.

Concerned that my search was becoming a fixation, I nevertheless diligently reread every page of *A Ride In The Sun.* If Miss Thomas had made friends with people on her journey and they were still alive, then perhaps, I reasoned, they'd kept in touch. Certainly when crossing Canada she had stayed as a guest of people whom she'd been given introductions to and also as a result of impromptu roadside meetings. I followed each name and locale up online but with zero success.

When I moved onto the United States, I read about Dick and Jo Anne Feringer of Seattle. Miss Thomas had first met them in a Norwegian Youth Hostel in 1950 and they had exchanged addresses. I typed Frederick Feringer into the *Seattle White Pages* search facility, patiently waited a few seconds while invisible cogs turned, and nearly fell out of my seat when a screen emerged announcing that F. Feringer, aged 87, related to Joanne Feringer, lived at an address in Puget Sound that was consistent with the one described in the book. I waited a couple of hours until it was 10am on the west coast of the USA then made my call.

"Of course I remember meeting Peggy and her visit here. It was such a long time ago, but they are great memories," echoed a strong, male, mid-atlantic accent down the phone line. For a while Mr. Feringer reminisced about the European bicycling holidays he and his wife had made in their youth, then I brought him back to the subject of Miss Thomas.

"Oh no, I'm sorry but I don't think we've heard from her in at least thirty years. Call back after six tonight. My wife will be home then and she may be able to help."

Seattle works on Pacific Daylight Time which is eight hours behind GMT. That night I set my alarm for 2.30am and, cold and bleary eyed, phoned Mrs. Feringer.

"Oh, we have Peggy's book and loved it, but you know how things go sometimes, you just lose touch with people. It's been so long that I couldn't even guess to the nearest ten years when we last heard from her. But if you do find her, please put us in touch, she was such a lively and fun person."

Much to my surprise, a few months later a blazing ray of hope was offered from an English motorcycle parts trader residing in France. In an email he wrote:

'... if you are going to send me a couple of books would you be so kind as to make one of them personalised to Peggy Iris Thomas? She holidays over here with friends and has been gracious enough to sign two of my *Bantam Banters* for me. She is a lovely lady.'

Over the moon, I typed a reply so fast that my fingers tingled as I hammered on the keyboard, explaining my quest to find Miss Thomas. A couple of nervous days later I received a reply,

'Hi Gordon, sorry, I can't help with any further info, I met her through a friend of a friend who lives over here a couple of k's down the road. I wouldn't call her a friend, we are not going to be exchanging xmas cards, she holidays over here once a year for a couple of weeks. All I can say is I had the privilege of meeting her and it was cool. If you send me a book over I will make sure she gets it. If she then decides to contact you at a later date then so be it. At this time she has said no.'

Left feeling bewildered, frustrated and thwarted, I wrote again, asking if instead he would forward a letter to Miss Thomas. He eventually agreed, replying,

'I can assure you that I will forward any correspondence through my third party contact.' A couple of days later I posted a letter and a copy of *Overland To India* to his address, along with 6 euros to cover onwards postage. He acknowledged receipt and informed me that it would be taken to his friend's house that night.

The first week waiting for a reply was easy, after all, I had to allow time for my letter to reach Miss Thomas, wherever she lived. The second week was harder. With ever increasing anxiousness, I looked out for the postman to call. By the third week, I was waiting by the front door for letters to drop through my box but nothing arrived. Finally, in week four, feeling rather sad, I got back onto my lists of Percival and Ursula Thomas's recorded on the UK electoral roll and started a whole new round of letters, confused as to why, at worst, I hadn't even received a polite refusal to my correspondence.

Jane sometimes says that there are times in life when you simply have to 'show up'. When things get tough, you're feeling low or unmotivated... just do the work. For two and a half years I'd put a huge amount of effort into finding Miss Thomas and was now feeling really disheartened. However, 'showing up' one evening in early October 2011 to check for emails about a new missing persons search facility, I noticed a message from the *Overland To Egypt* website. With one click of the mouse, the whole tapestry shifted and the vibrant, colourful threads of Miss Thomas's life emerging in ways I could never have imagined. The correspondence was from her lifelong friend, Marjorie Marshall, who'd spotted a simple tribute page about the intrepid traveller that I'd created in 2009.

Transfixed, I read:

"I found you on the internet as I was trying to locate my friend's book *A Ride in the Sun*. We knew each other from when we were about sixteen, when we used to 'Dig for Victory' every year. She went into the WRNS and we had many holidays together - cycling round Cornwall on sit-up-and-beg bikes and walking in the Lakes in November, when sometimes we found the Youth Hostels were closed! She wanted me to accompany her on her travels, but I got married, so she bought Matelot. As you will know she was sadly killed in a road accident on her way back from her beloved cottage in Donegal. I still wear her favourite coat!'

Thrown into a mixed state of bafflement because of the recent misleading communications with the man in France and the gut blow from hearing such news about Miss Thomas's death, I immediately began to panic that I wouldn't be able to get back in touch with Marjorie, as in the past many people have filled in the contact box on the website but omitted to write their contact details. Thankfully, she'd left her email address at the bottom. I hurriedly typed a reply. One came back almost immediately and our written correspondence soon became a joyful daily occurrence as she related her memories. After a week of these communications, I was able to build up a picture of Miss Thomas's life.

In the words of Marjorie:
'Peggy grew up in a house in Ewell, Surrey, called the White Cottage and attended a private school for the 'Daughters of Gentlemen'. She was raised in an atmosphere of charming, impoverished gentility as her mother's family had lost all their assets in The Crash in the Thirties. As a young woman Peggy often went as au pair to German or French families who lived in castles, managing hordes of children! She was bi-lingual in French.

Mrs Thomas, (Ursula) had been a senior Army Nurse in the First World War - I think she may have been decorated - and Mr. Thomas, (Percival) was one of her patients. She used to cook weird things for supper, well it was in the War, which we used to eat rather nervously. At the end she would announce triumphantly, "You have eaten WHALE!". On another occasion, my fiancé, who soon became my husband, disappeared into another room and reappeared without his army moustache. Mrs. Thomas took me aside and said that was a dangerous sign!

Once, when Peggy and I went off around Surrey on our sit-up-and beg bikes, we were cycling down a hill near Oxshott and Peggy disappeared. She had crashed over the handlebars and was unconscious. I stopped a Canadian army jeep and they took her to hospital. She had broken both her wrists and they always remained slightly out of shape.

When we used to go Youth Hostelling I carried as little as possible but Peggy always had onions and potatoes in her haversack and we of course shared the load. I once bent down to tie up my shoelace and was dragged over onto my back! When we arrived at a hostel, Peggy would immediately start frying onions and we thought there would be a new rule about cooking 'after hours' as we were always late. When we sometimes found the hostel closed we would throw ourselves on the mercy of some unfortunate villager to let us stay the night! We used to hitch-hike all over the place, which was safe then, but we were very fussy about which lorry we chose.

And of course every year we went Digging for Victory. Mostly we were under canvas and then taken off in lorries to pick apples up tall wobbly ladders, or sometimes picking up potatoes. When on an apple farm we had to take turns in the packing factory and had a wonderful time talking and laughing and doing the automatic actions which I can still do! We generally went with the same 'gang' every year.

I remember Peggy buying the Bantam and she had to ride around the

BSA garage forecourt to learn how to drive it. She never settled down with Carl Erik after returning from America - they were divorced quite soon after the marriage. But she continued to use his name, Sorensen. After her adventures a motorcycle company gave her a huge bike - really for publicity as I think she appeared in several advertisements. When it fell down she could not pick it up! My son thinks it was a Douglas Dragonfly. But most of my memories are of pre-Bantam days as in the 1950's I was bringing up my children, so there are gaps in my knowledge of Peggy's life from then.

Later on, Peggy lived in a house in Hampton, Middlesex. It was in a row of gentrified artisans' cottages. She did most of the maintenance herself and could often be seen up the ladder in her bikini, decorating the outside or making some repair! During the summer Peggy had her own little business, trimming and clipping dogs as well as 'having them to stay', from which she made enough money to go off to exotic places in the winter. I don't think any of her other adventures were on a motorcycle though. She used to fly off I think - sometimes to South Africa, though not always. Tony (my husband) and I were once in Cannes on our motorbike, probably the Sunbeam 350cc. Suddenly we heard someone screaming 'Marjie' and it was Peggy! Neither of us knew that the other was in France. Peggy was on a push bike, pulling a little trailer, and in it was a Frenchman. Tony spoke no French and the Frenchman spoke no English and they did charades throughout the evening. At night we went down to the beach and Peggy and I swam. When we came out of the water Tony and the other guy had done a brew-up and we drank coffee with lumps in. Then we looked into the sugar tin with a torch, and it was a solid mass of ants!

Peggy also had a very traditional cottage in Donegal that she was restoring to its original condition. She had this battered old Ford Cortina station wagon - she regularly went off to Ireland, loaded with odd bits of furniture for her cottage. An official of some kind rang me about her death as they had seen my name in her diary and in her address book. What a shock. Her car was hit by a cement-mixer when she was returning from Donegal. She had several small dogs with her at the time of the accident, but they were eventually found. Peggy's funeral was quite bleak - just in a crematorium in the Hampton district.

Peggy was such a brave, indomitable person, always so brimming with enthusiasm, always the first out of the tent when we were camping! She had such a strong personality and it was impossible to realise that she would never breeze in to our house again, like a whirlwind!'

Like a skilled sleuth, Marjorie soon got herself online and helped find crucial missing pieces. With ingenuity she led me to the record of Miss Thomas's (Mrs. Sorensen's) death and I was then able to order a copy of the death certificate. Upon its arrival I viewed the spot on Google Maps where the crash occurred and felt an intense sadness. The accident happened at a staggered crossroads on the Isle of Anglesey, just a few miles from the ferry port that serves Ireland. It's easy to see how a driver, approaching the junction at an acute angle, could easily have missed spotting a fast approaching vehicle. I can't help thinking that for someone who survived such an enormous journey through the Americas on a crazily overladen motorcycle, complicated by a weighty pillion with a penchant for chasing cats, to come to such grief on a quiet Welsh road seems not only ironic but somehow wrong.

Within two weeks of our first contact I was able to meet Marjorie at a motorcycle show.

'You won't believe this,' I wrote in an email, 'but I'm at a show next weekend and its only a few miles from your home.'

A reply came back overnight,

'And I have another coincidence too, as we are all going to the same motorcycle show!' To hear this from a lady of 86 was not only a surprise but a great delight.

I immediately guessed it was Marjorie when she approached my stand. There was a vibrancy and buoyancy in both her face and her demeanour that had come across so brightly in the emails she'd written to me. From her handbag she produced a selection of photographs of Miss Thomas before and after she was Mrs. Sorensen. Some had been taken in her garden and some during parties at Marjorie's home. There was even a faded black and white shot of their coincidental meeting in Cannes.

"Look," she said, as she was able to close her bag. "I still use Peggy's purse. I think she bought it in Mexico... it's so old now but it reminds me of her."

Finally, Marjorie was able to put me in touch with Pamela, Miss Thomas's older sister. It had always been my hope that one day I would be able to reprint *A Ride In The Sun*. Its limited availability and the high cost of the rare editions that do show up on Amazon and eBay have made it into one of those cult books that many people know of but few have been able to read. It's such a cracking good story! Thanks to Pamela, and of course Marjorie, my aspiration to republish the book has become a reality.

At this time neither can remember what happened to Matelot... or, for that matter, Oppy. I think that most classic motorcycle enthusiasts dream that one day they'll unearth something rare and exotic that's been left abandoned in a barn or garden hedge for decades. Vincent or Brough Superior V-twins immediately come to mind. I have that dream too, but my wish is for a 125cc Bantam registered as OPE 811. Knowing just how many people have bought dilapidated Bantams and put them away in their shed to restore when they retire, I live in hope that one day this little hero will see the light of day again.

As well as being asked "why?" I am now frequently asked whether or not I would make another overland journey on a Bantam. That's a tricky question to answer. I've mapped out in my mind a series of long distance journeys that I want to undertake. I lie awake at night running through the routes, imagining the bikes, all classic, that I would ride, dreaming about the chance to have more adventures and meeting wonderful people like Essa along the way. But on

Peggy... I'm sorry to say probably not. I don't for a moment regret taking her on this ride as she gave me a unique experience and I learned an awful lot about both myself and motorcycle mechanics along the way. But undoubtedly my limited time and the testing geographical and environmental conditions exposed the fragility of her design. As my future dreams are for even longer rides, I believe that taking her would prove just too taxing for motorcycle and rider alike. If I had 18 months like Miss Thomas, that might be another matter!

Peggy has taken up temporary residence in my garage. The scratches and dents, oil stains, dust and sand that she collected on our ride to Egypt are for now preserved. Derek, as ever true to his word, has allowed me to keep hold of her. It's my hope to display her, fully laden, at a few choice classic motorcycle events. After that, I would love to give her nothing more than a good clean, return her to standard road trim and ride her locally. Derek also thinks he would one day like to use her for a charity run, which sounds like a splendid idea.

There's just one loose end from the whole Overland To Egypt project... my promised ride on NEL 906, the *Friday Afternoon Bantam*. But that's one of the joys of motorcycling... it always gives you something more to really look forward to.

Chain
I used a German-made **Iwis Megalife** chain supplied by **Sprockets Unlimited**. This chain has a silver coloured coating that ensures it does not rust and special bushes which are sintered. This means it can be run dry or with minimal lubrication and therefore not easily pick up dust or sand. The chain only needed a few adjustments and has thousands of miles of life left in it. Sprockets Unlimted are chain experts and have over twenty years experience of supplying chains for both classic and modern motorcycles. They also provided new gearbox and rear sprockets for the Bantam.
Contact: Sprockets Unlimited, www.sprocketsunlimited.com
Tel: +44 (0)1386 831341

Carburettor
We attached a new **Amal 626 MK1 Concentric carburettor**, sourced directly from the manufacturers, **The Amal Carburettor Company**. Exceedingly well made yet reasonably priced, the transformation in steady idling and ease of starting was remarkable. As you can customise your carburettor when you order it, we chose a puncture-proof 'stay up' float and a brass throttle slide. Amal's service and spare parts back up is excellent and they provided a major repair kit, including jets, needle valve and clip, o-ring and gaskets, for the journey.
Contact: The Amal Carburettor Company, www.amalcarb.co.uk
Tel: +44 (0)1722 412 500

Tyres
D1 Bantams take a hard to find 2.75 x 19" tyre. Fortunately, tyre and wheel experts, **Wheel House Tyres**, stock a suitable tyre with a classic tread pattern... **Cheng Shin C117 Universals**. These tyres did a sterling job in keeping the heavily laden Bantam safely on the road in snow, torrential rain and sand. Their sister company, **Central Wheel Components**, who specialise in wheel building for classic and modern motorcycles, provided Dunlop inner tubes, spare spokes and rim tapes for the journey.
Contact: Wheel House Tyres, www.wheelhousetyres.co.uk
Tel: +44 (0)121 7480000
Central Wheel Components, www.central-wheel.co.uk
Tel: +44 (0)1675 462264

Engine Rebuild
For the second journey, the engine was carefully restored by classic motorcycle engineer, **Andy Berry**, of Preston, UK. Andy restored my 2008 'Overland To India' Royal Enfield engine which proved so reliable. His attention to detail and workmanship are top class and his knowledge of motorcycle engineering invaluable to this project.
Contact: Andy Berry, eMail: ajb1962@hotmail.co.uk
Tel: +44 (0)1772 788077

Engine Bearings and Seals

Rex Caunt Racing specialise in high quality Bantam engine parts and ignition conversions. All of our replacement engine bearings and seals came from Rex. The inner crank seals that failed on my first ride were replaced with Rex's top quality **Viton rubber seals** for greater durability. Rex's advice on the engine rebuild was invaluable.

Contact: Rex Caunt Racing, www.rexcauntracing.com
Tel: +44 (0)1455 848212

Crank, Ignition and Clutch

Bantam engine specialist, **Peter Savage**, did a smashing job of assembling our crank. His renowned **big end conversion** includes a wider big end bearing and crankpin. Peter machined a recess in the flywheels to accept the new assembly. A tough MZ con rod was used. We also fitted one of Peter's neat contact breaker conversions, which employs a robust VW **contact breaker backplate** and made the points much easier to adjust. The original clutch outer cover was distorted by my first journey. We fitted a superior Peter Savage **clutch conversion** with a thicker pressure plate and a deeper outer cover machined from alloy.

Contact: Peter Savage, Email: p.savage56@btinternet.com
Tel: +44 (0)1827-874015

Pistons

The original high-compression Hepolite pistons proved unsuitable for the job, especially when used with low octane fuel. **Rex Caunt Racing** provided a replacement flat-topped, lower compression **D7 Bantam piston**. Although it seized on the road to Tobruk, it dressed up nicely, made it through the rest of the journey and is still used in the bike today. Rex also provided numerous gasket sets and vital advice on keeping the engine running in the heat.

Contact: Rex Caunt Racing, www.rexcauntracing.com
Tel: +44 (0)1455 848212

Cables

We used braced scrambles bars on the Bantam, which resulted in none of the standard cables fitting. **Carrot Cycles,** a UK web-based business specialising in made-to-order control cables and other quality classic motorcycle consumables, came to the rescue. They provided me with custom-made cables that fit perfectly. They also supplied a new BAP fuel tap and classy braided fuel hose for the bike.

Contact: Carrot Cycles, www.carrotcycles.co.uk
Tel: +44 (0)1522 595975

Gearbox Oil

The gearbox oil drips onto the main bearings on late Bantam engines such as the D14/4 I retro-fitted to Peggy. **Penrite** oil did a fantastic job preserving my engine on the 2008 ride to India and so I used their 20/50 multigrade in my gearbox for this journey. Even in the hottest temperatures, it did the job superbly well.

Contact: Penrite Oil, www.penrite.co.uk
Tel: +44 (0)1962 732601

General Bantam Parts and Consumables
Many of the missing or replacement parts for Peggy came from **Bournemouth Bantams.** These included a **Wassels** exhaust downpipe and silencer, clutch plates and springs, wheel bearings, spark plugs, centre-stand return springs, rubber parts and a selection of specialist nuts and bolts. The business is now under new ownership.
Contact: **Bournemouth Bantams, www.bournemouthbantams.com**
Tel: **+44 (0)7517 160388**

2-Stroke Oil
I found **Rock Oil Road 2 Stroke** best suited for use with the Bantam. It's a high performance mineral oil with excellent film strength which proved very easy to pre-mix. I felt quite vulnerable when my supplies ran out in Tunisia and I had to resort to local 2-stroke oil.
Contact: **Rock Oil, www.rockoil.co.uk**
Tel: **+44 (0)1925 636191**

Charging System Improvements
To improve charging, especially when using lights, we fitted a single phase **120W alternator stator** (Lucas RM21 pattern) supplied by classic bike electrics specialist, **Paul Goff.** We connected this to one of Paul's single phase **12V regulators** which replaced the Zener diode and the rectifier. Finally, to keep track of the charging system and battery status, we fitted a **BSM (Battery Status Monitor).** The BSM's bright LED changes colour according to the state of the battery, showing critically low, normal, charging and overcharging. It proved an excellent tool until it failed! It has since been replaced by the manufacturer and I will certainly use it again.
Contact: **Paul Goff, www.norbsa02.freeuk.com**
Tel: **+44 (0)1494 868218**

Air Filter
My ride to India taught me to value a good air filter. I encountered sandy and dusty road conditions en route to Egypt, which were dealt with admirably by my **Ramair pod filter**. It has a unique multilayered Aeriform material that ensures both maximum filtration and airflow. I carried two spares and rotated them daily, washing and drying the used ones overnight.
Contact: **Ramair, www.ramair-filters.co.uk Tel: 44 (0)1980 623401**

Throttle Twist Grip and Fuel Filter
The standard Bantam throttle twist grip leaves the throttle cable hanging in open air, making it susceptible to snagging. **AJS Motorcycles** sell the solution, a **Gunnar Gasser** side pull twist grip which the keeps vulnerable throttle cable out of harms way. Poorly stored, contaminated petrol can be an issue in Africa. I used an **In-Line Alloy Fuel Filter** also supplied by AJS. This has a replaceable micro mesh filter and is far more robust than the more commonly available glass bowl type filters.
Contact: **AJS Motorcycles, www.ajs-shop.co.uk**
Tel: **+44 (0)1264 710 074**

Mirrors

I tried to use stainless steel fittings on my bikes where possible. **Halcyon Design & Manufacturing**, famous for their aviator and motorcycle goggles, produce beautiful stainless handlebar and bar-end mirrors. I fitted a pair of their **Stadium 850** handlebar mounted mirrors which look authentically classic and were surprisingly untroubled by vibration. They also manufactured the excellent stainless tax disc holder that I used.
Contact: Halcyon, www.classicpartsltd.com
Tel: +44 (0)1992 537546

Horn

Horns are used hundreds of times a day in some countries. I broke 2 horns riding to India. For this ride we installed a superior **Stebel TMN80 air horn**. Supplied by Stebel's sole UK distributors, **Mountney**, the horn is compact, robust and VERY loud.
Contact: Mountney Ltd, www.mountneyltd.com
Tel: +44 (0)1525 383055

Clocks

I always seem to be checking my watch whilst riding, which is a risky operation. The solution was to fit a **Formotion Signature Series stainless steel clock** on this trip. The timeless styling, with a black face, looks very much in keeping with a classic bike. It's waterproof and the hands are luminous for night use. Formotion also supplied a handlebar-mounted compass which proved very handy whilst trying to follow a map around city streets.
Contact: Formotion, www.formotionproducts.com
Tel: +01 415 331 0400

Battery

I chose a **Yuasa** battery as engine-builder Andy Berry swears by them. His experience is that they hold their charge far better than other battery makes he has tried. I concur, it was excellent on the ride. We upgraded the Bantam's electrics to 12 volts, so I fitted a **YB9L-B** model. The Yuasa website is well worth a look as it has some useful information on battery maintenance and how to select a battery for your bike.
Contact: Yuasa, www.yuasa-battery.co.uk Tel: +44 08708 500257

Indicators and Light Bulbs

I'm usually very happy to use hand signals whilst riding my classics. However, for this journey it seemed prudent to fit indicators; especially for use in Europe.
Paul Goff provided a pair of **bulls-eye indicators** and a matching relay. As I wanted to run the bike all day with good lighting, I chose an **LED tail light.** Not only is it brighter than a standard lamp, it also lasts longer and uses very little current. At the front, I employed a quartz halogen 12V bulb in the pilot light hole as a daytime running light. For the main beam, I installed a British pre-focus **quartz halogen 12V 35W**. These were also supplied by Paul.
Contact: Paul Goff, www.norbsa02.freeuk.com
Tel: +44 (0)1494 868218

Carburettor Tuning

Tuning a carburettor is not my strongest point. I have found the **Gunson Colortune** kit very useful. Colortune allows you to see into the combustion chamber of the engine and to adjust the mixture simply by colour. A light blue flame is weak, a yellow flame rich and a bunson burner blue flame spot on.

Contact: Gunson, www.gunson.co.uk
Tel: +44 (0)1926 815000

Bantam Parts and Manuals

At the last minute I needed some additional Bantam consumables and a parts book. Happily, a long established BSA parts business that's now under new ownership, **Lightning Spares**, was close at hand. The owner, Brian, provided a helpful, over-the-counter service.

Contact: Lightning Spares, www.lightning-spares.co.uk
Tel: +44 (0)161 9693850

General Motoring Supplies

Last minute purchases such as fuses, rolls of electric wiring, cable-ties and even specially ordered spare sets of points and condensers came from my local automotive supply shop, **Castrees Autobar**. More convenient than a trip to an automotive supermarket and with far more personal service, it's a bonus to use such a helpful local business. Every town and village should have one!

Contact: Castrees Autobar, www.castreesautobar.co.uk
Tel: +44 (0)161 4307439

Suppliers: Rider Equipment

Jacket

I was really proud to wear my **Barbour International jacket**. Made from 100% waxed cotton, the jacket has been in production since the 1930s when it was used by a succession of British teams in the Olympics of motorcycling, the International Six Days Trial. Barbour kindly provided me with a new sandstone coloured jacket for my ride to India. Its light weight and breathability was perfect for the hot climates I rode through. The same jacket, now rewaxed, made it to Egypt and back and is still going strong!

Contact: Barbour, www.barbour.com Tel: +44 (0)191 455 4444

Neck Brace

I used a **Leatt Neck Brace** on the journey, supplied by UK distributor **KP Racing Services**. These braces are a safety device that, in my opinion, are just about as important and a helmet. It helps prevent hyperflexion, hyperextension, lateral hyperflexion, axial loading and posterior hypertranslation. Best of all, I wasn't the slightest bit aware of wearing it when riding. Business owner, Karl, is a very knowledgeable fellow too.

Contact: KP Racing Services, www.kprservices.co.uk
Tel: +44 0845 4595409

Helmet

I entrusted my head protection to a **Cromwell Spitfire.** Now made in Italy, these beautifully designed helmets are light, comfortable and exceed the latest EU standards. - it even has a stainless steel outer shell. It looks in keeping with my bike and I've been thrilled with it! Mine was sponsored by **Barry Vincent**. Barry has many years of experience working in the crash helmet industry and is a regular sight at major UK motorcycle shows, where he sells his well-known motorcycle storage line, **Vac-Bag**, which I also highly recommend. Barry is a friendly and helpful chap who offers great service as well as excellent prices.
Contact: Vac Bags, www.vac-bags.co.uk
Tel: +44 (0)1832 733 115

Body Armour

I've tried hard-shell armour in the past and always found it too stiff and uncomfortable. I simply couldn't believe just how light and easy-to-wear **Forcefield** gear was when I first tried it on; I could hardly tell it was there! And unlike any other armour I've encountered, it's even reusable after an impact. I used a **Forcefield *Sport-Lite L1* back protector**. It's soft, light and breathable. I also used **Forcefield performance upgrade inserts** which I slipped into pockets sewn into my jacket's shoulders and elbows and also in the knees of my trousers. I always feel reassured to be wearing such high quality protectors.
Contact: Forcefield, www.forcefieldbodyarmour.co.uk
Tel: +44 (0)1933 410818

Boots

I used **Alt-Berg Original Hogg Lites.** They were absolutely superb. They're designed as a dual purpose bike and walking boot, making them ideal for touring. The beauty of these boots is that they are made to measure, so the fit is perfect. For a fitting you can visit Alt-Berg, as I did, at their premises in Richmond, Yorkshire. It's a bonus that their shop is surrounded with great motorcycling countryside. Alternatively, you can see their stand at one of the UK's major bike shows. I was very impressed to meet a fellow biker in their shop who had brought his 6-year and 120,000-mile-old Alt-bergs in for a resole. Now that's longevity! Incredibly, mine stayed absolutely waterproof riding through storms in Northern Italy.
Contact: Altberg, www.altberg.co.uk
Tel: +44 (0)1748 850615

Goggles

I've been riding with **Halcyon** goggles for roughly 18 years... they are comfortable and allow great peripheral vision. In my opinion, the style of their split lens goggle compliments a classic bike perfectly. For the trip I used a pair of soft leather **MK49 Deluxe goggles** with tinted lenses to cope with the bright sunshine. I removed the visor from my helmet and wore my goggles all the time as they provide great protection from dust. After 6000 very tough miles, there's still not a scratch on the lenses.
Contact: www.classicpartsltd.com
Tel: +44 (0)1992 537546

Gel Pad

I was so stiff and sore on the ride to India that I estimate I must have ridden at least 10% of the journey standing up. On my return to the UK I set about solving the problem. The result is the **Supreme Comfort Seat Gel Pad.** Made from medical grade gel (a hi-tech viscoelastic polymer that prevents friction between the seat and skin, distributes weight evenly, gives a floatation effect and reduces vibration), the pad simply clips on top of the existing seat. Although most gel pads are shaped for modern bikes and dual seats, I used one on the Bantam that's specially made to the shape of a classic bike sprung saddle. The result... no numb bum on the ride to Egypt!

Contact: Supreme Comfort Seats, www.motorcyclegelpad.co.uk

Gloves

Lewis leathers have a proud heritage of making leather clothing for aviators and motorcyclists and their quality is just as legendary as their styling. I've always owned thick, chunky biking gloves, which would have been far too hot for this journey. The Lewis gloves are unlined and made from the softest hide imaginable. Now I know what it means when people say 'it fits like a kid glove'. Surprise bonuses were the increased sense of feel and control of the handlebars and how easily I could get them off, even on the hottest days. The company has now opened a specialist shop in London, which sounds like a great place to meet other motorcyclists as well as checking out their classic riding gear.

Contact: Lewis Leathers, www.lewisleathers.com
Tel: +44 (0)207 4020863

Riding Clothes

I wear **Icebreaker** pure New Zealand Merino wool clothes just about every day, summer and winter. They're just so practical and exceedingly comfortable. The beauty of Merino wool is that it's super warm when layered, yet remarkably cool in hot climates. It naturally breathes and resists body odours so you can wear it day after day without getting whiffy! I wore a **_BodyFit 150 t-shirt_** under my biking gear with a **Go Tiger 220** top to layer when necessary. These are great biking tops as you can zip the neck up and pull the sleeves down using thumb loops on colder days. I went for days on end in 32 - 40 degree heat wearing the same BodyFit t-shirt. Not once did I detect a hint of body odour. Amazing!

Contact: www.icebreaker.com
(list of UK and international dealers available on the website)

Bike Trousers

I went straight to **Draggin Jeans** for my motorcycle trousers. Leather trousers would have been too hot and I don't like wearing synthetics all day, which ruled out nearly all Enduro pants. I chose a pair of Kevlar-lined **Draggin cargo pants**, the perfect combination of safety with easy to wear trousers. They look great, are supremely comfortable and were cool to wear in the extreme heat of North Africa. They also survived the tumble in Tobruk surprisingly well.

Contact: www.dragginjeans.net
Tel: +44 (0)1732 834 888

Travel Clothes

I only had enough room in my luggage for a couple of changes of clothes. **Rohan** travel clothes were inimitably suitable. They are extremely rugged yet very packable and easy to care for. They also look smart however tough the conditions. I took a pair of **Bags**, Rohan's iconic multi-function travel trousers. They weight just 335 grams and have a lightning fast drying time of 3 hours. Rohan specialise in very well-designed travel accessories too. I wore an **All Terrain Money Belt** that from the outside looks just like an regular belt for holding your trousers up.

Contact: www.rohan.co.uk
(list of UK stores available on the website)

Rain Suit

I packed a **Jofama Wet Stop Rain Suit** just in case the weather turned against me. Thank goodness I did! The suit is exceedingly well designed, with zippers that come up to the knee for ease of getting it over boots and a main zip that runs diagonally across the chest, almost down to the knee. The large Hi-Vis stripes that run across the sleeves, back and chest area are a very nice touch. Jofama are made in Sweden to the highest standards and much of their gear looks in keeping with classic motorcycling.

Contact: www.jofama.se
(list of UK & international dealers available on the website)

Earplugs

I use **Pro Guard** plugs custom made for my ears by experts **Enhanced Listening**. An appointment was made for me at a local specialist who took impressions of my ear canals. The resulting earplugs are fabulously comfortable and I was able to wear them all day (once I learned not to push them in too far!). Small filters were added so I can still hear the sounds I want to hear.

Contact: www.enhancedlistening.co.uk
Tel: +44 (0)208 1440370

Hydration System

Some days I drank up to 6 litres of water whilst riding the bike. Finding room to carry that volume of liquid, as well as stopping frequently enough to drink it, could have been problematic. UK distributors **Zyro** supplied me with a **Camelbak 3 litre Classic** hydration pack. It's simple in design and style and didn't look too out of place on the back of a classic motorcyclist. With my open face helmet, it was very easy to drink on the go.

Contact: www.zyro.co.uk Tel: +44 (0)1845 521700

Suppliers: Equipment

Tools

After years of fiddling around with secondhand tools of average quality, I now have a set of the best, thanks to British manufacturer **Britool**. The Bantam has

Whitworth fixings and the Britool combination spanner set and 6 piece socket set covers every nut and bolt on it. I have never used such superbly made tools and they feel as though they will last a lifetime. I spent countless hours spannering by the roadside on the ride to Egypt and it was extremely reassuring to have such fine tools to do it with.

Contact: Britool, www.britool.com
Tel: +44 (0)1142 917266

Bike Cover

A good cover not only protects your bike from the elements, it can act as an extra deterrent to prying eyes and hands. Being able to securely cover up when you want to explore a new place gives peace of mind and makes for a more enjoyable trip too. I used a bike cover from **Specialised Covers** on my ride to India. It was superb. The company produce excellent made to measure bike covers, but the Bantam easily fits inside one of their standard size designs. The cover is waterproof, ultra light and clips under the bike front and rear for added security.

Contact: Specialised Covers, www.specialisedcovers.com
Tel: +44 (0)1943 864646

Tank Bag

For stability I tried to keep as much weight forward as possible. My super magnetic **BSA tank bag** came from Redditch-based **Classic Bike Shop**. I carried heavy items such as guidebooks and useful things such as a mobile phone, camera, essential tools and sun block in it. There's also a handy clear map pocket in the top. For a low cost item that's not expedition quality it performed outstandingly well, far exceeding my expectations.

Contact: Classic Bike Shop, www.classicbikeshop.co.uk
Tel: +44 (0)1527 454158

Rack Pack

Another success from Overland To India was the **49 litre Ortlieb Rack Pack** from **Lyon Equipment**. Ortlieb make superb outdoors equipment, tried and tested by travellers for over 25 years. It has a full-width roll closure which allows fast access and is guaranteed to keep water and dust safely on the outside. Mine's now covered over 20,000 miles and still looks like new.

Contact: www.lyon.co.uk/ortlieb.html
(list of UK dealers available on the website)

Saddlebags

Hard luggage is far too heavy for a Bantam. I used featherweight **Ortlieb Motorcycle Saddle Bags**, again supplied by **Lyon Equipment**. These fully waterproof panniers have roll top closures and are secured to the bike with wide Velcro fastenings and tension straps. The individual bags can be used as shoulder bags using removable shoulder straps. With practice, they took 2 minutes to remove and 5 minutes to fit. I'll use them again and again.

Contact: www.lyon.co.uk/ortlieb.html
(list of UK dealers available on the website)

Water Filtration

Until now I've bought bottled mineral water when travelling. The amount of plastic bottles used to provide this water is a real environmental hazard. For this trip I used a **Pure Hydration Aquapure Traveller** purification system that produces safe, clean drinking water from taps, stand pipes, rivers and mountain streams. It's simple, highly effective and affordable too.

Contact: Pure Hydration, www.bwtechnologies.com
Tel: +44 (0)333 6007000

Satellite Navigation:

My **Garmin Zumo 550** is now 4 years old and remains totally reliable... a great piece of kit. It fits easily on the bike and draws a maximum of 15W which is important when your old bike has limited power output! The unit came with street-level maps that were very useful on the ride south through Europe. A world map to cover main roads for the rest of the journey was relatively inexpensive. A really great feature of the Zumo 550 is that it comes with a car mount and speaker so I get maximum use from the equipment year round.

Contact: Garmin, www.garmin.com/uk

Luggage Straps

I've tried many ways to hold awkwardly shaped odds and ends on bikes in the past with limited success. **Rok Straps** do the job superbly as they're specially designed for motorcycles. The larger **Motorcycle Stretch Straps** I took can hold up to 40KG. I also used several pairs of smaller **Adjustable Packs Straps** which were a neat way to add extra items onto my bars. The product is excellent and the company great to deal with.

Contact: Rok Straps, www.rokstraps.com
(list of UK and international dealers available on the website)

Lock

The **Grip-Lock** from **K-Lock** securely clamps both the throttle and front brake lever. It's compact, highly visible and easy to use. It's also ideal for a classic bike like the Bantam, which has a drum brake and therefore cannot use a disc lock. It's strong yet lightweight with 3 hardened steel inserts made to deter hacksaw blades. I used it every time I parked up as it's a clearly visible deterrent.

Contact: K-Lock, www.k-lock.co.uk
Tel: +44 (0)1797 367527

Trailer

Moving the Bantam around to have work done to it was made easy using a **Motolug** collapsible trailer. Superbly designed and constructed to a high standard in the UK, the **Motolug S7** folds away into the boot of my car or garage when not in use. I'll be displaying Peggy at several classic bike shows over the next couple of years, courtesy of the Motolug.

Contact: Motolug, www.bikelug.co.uk
Tel: +44 (0)1386 841506

Pump and Tyre Sealant

I needed a compact but efficient foot pump. **Bike It** produce a **Mini Foot Pump** which, weighing in at just 300 gms, fits the bill perfectly. Before setting off, we also injected **Slime tyre sealant** into both inner tubes. Guaranteed to instantly seal punctures of up to 1/4 inch, it gave peace of mind from roadside puncture repairs. Both were supplied by Brendan Layton of **SS Direct**. Brendan has a large stall selling a plethora of motorcycle accessories at most of the UK's major bike shows and is very helpful.
Contact: SS Direct, www.motorbikebits.co.uk
Tel: +44 (0)7914 783197

Travel Adapter

On my travels I carry a digital camera, mobile phone, laptop and GPS. A quality worldwide travel adapter is essential and the **Lindy All-in-one Mains Plug & USB Travel Adapter** strikes me as the best. Charging my phone and camera straight from the mains socket via USB without carrying their individual chargers was a great bonus.
Contact: Lindy, www.lindy.co.uk Tel:
+44 (0)1642 754000

Thread Locker

Old British bikes are notorious for losing nuts and bolts due to vibration. I liberally used **Loctite Lock N' Seal** on all fixings and didn't lose a single one. On visiting the Loctite website I was very surprised to see the company make everything an overland motorist could possibly wish for in a emergency repair kit. Manufacturer, **Henkel**, very kindly provided me with a whole range of products including **Duck Tape**, epoxy glue, instant gasket, chemical metal, silicone sealant and even a magic metal compound that would plug a hole in the crankcase if necessary!
Contact: Henkel, www.henkel.co.uk

Camping

Tent

Weighing in at just 2kg, the **Vango Banshee 200** lightweight tent was perfect for my journey. It accommodated all my bike luggage and riding gear and was even tall enough for me to sit upright inside. Ventilation was excellent for hot climates and it proved a cinch to pitch in just 5 minutes.
Contact: Vango, www.vango.co.uk
(list of UK dealers available on the website)

Dry Bag

I used two **Ortlieb Dry Bags** on the ride. Heavy duty and fully waterproof, one tube-shaped **PS490 Dry Bag** carried heavy spare parts and oil. The other carried all my camping equipment, which weighed in at under 4.5KG. Undeniably great pieces of kit.
Contact: Lyon, www.lyon.co.uk/ortlieb.html

Stove

The **Primus Omnifuel stove** can run off virtually any fuel - LP Gas, naptha, gasoline/petrol, diesel, kerosene, aviation fuel and even a Bantam petrol & 2-stroke oil mixture!Designed to work well in the most demanding conditions including extreme altitudes and high or low temperatures, it's a real gem. The 600ml of petrol carried in its fuel bottle ensured Peggy made it to a petrol station on several occasions. Mine came from UK importers, **Rosker**.
Contact: Rosker, www.rosker.com

Mattress

A self-inflating mattress is essential for insulation and a restful night's sleep. UK based manufacturer **Multimat** make the best! I used a **Summit 25/38** mat that's a comfy 38mm thick at my torso, weighs just 895g and packs into a very compact fleece lined sack that doubles up as a pillowcase. And as lightweight camping shouldn't be without its comforts, I also carried a **Multimat Chair Converter** so that I could use the sleeping mat as a seat. Its weighs just 495g and packs to the size of a small folding umbrella.
Contact: Multimat, www.multimat.uk.com
(list of UK dealers available on the website)

Sleeping Bag

I needed an affordable down sleeping bag that was lightweight and would pack really small. The **Vango Venom 300** fit the bill perfectly (880 gms and 25x16 cm before compression). With a comfort range of 0 to 25°C, it certainly kept me cosy throughout the two journeys.
Contact: Vango www.vango.co.uk
(list of UK dealers available on the website)

Multi-tool

I've found **Leatherman** multi-purpose tools invaluable in the past. The **Leatherman Blast** has a saw, scissors and bottle/can opener tools and is ideal when camping. The file and needlenose pliers came in handy on my bike too. An essential piece of kit.
Contact: Leatherman, www.leatherman.co.uk
(list of UK dealers available on the website)

Camp Food

I took a tasty selection of **Travellunch** high energy, freeze dried meals on the ride. Made in Germany by **Reiter**, each meal weighs just 125g before adding boiling water... even my humble Bantam was able to carry half a dozen packs! Mine came from UK importers, **Rosker,** but they are generally available in good camping stores.
Contact: Rosker, www.rosker.com

Cookware

I used a lightweight but durable **Vango stainless steel cook kit**. These are manufactured tough to provide years of use with little or no maintenance - perfect for me! The 1 person set includes a frying pan, 2 pots and a cup that all nestle into each other to save space.

Contact: Vango www.vango.co.uk
(list of UK dealers available on the website)

Essentials

The BSA Bantam Owner's Club

A club for riders and enthusiasts alike which aims to encourage members to get the maximum use of, and enjoyment from, BSA Bantams. The club now has more than 800 members and produces a superb magazine, the *Bantam Banter*. You can see the club stand at a variety of classic bike shows in the UK and the shared knowledge, helpfulness and friendliness of its members makes it an absolute must for owners and would-be owners alike.

Contact: The BSA Bantam Owners Club, www.bsabantamclub.org.uk
Membership enquiries, Tel: +44 (0)1529 497304

The BSA Owner's Club

This long-established club, with several international affiliations, provides information and support for all BSA owners, including technical support, machine dating, events to attend and a network of branches where you can meet fellow BSA enthusiasts. Club members receive a 40 page monthly magazine, *The Star.*

Contact: The BSA Owners Club, www.bsaownersclub.co.uk

Horizons Unlimited

A website that is so much more! **Horizons Unlimited** is dedicated to the overland motorcycle traveller and is packed full of useful information. Its forum, **The Hubb**, offers great support to travellers, including information on overland bikes, travel equipment, safety, border crossings, paperwork etc. The website organisers and members also arrange several meetings around the world where you can get together with like-minded motorcyclists. There's even a regular inspiring ezine. It's a highly useful and comprehensive resource for any traveller.

Contact: Horizons Unlimited, www.horizonsunlimited.com

Motorail

I travelled from Italy to Holland on **Motorail**, Motorcycles and cars travel securely strapped onto special carriages while you sleep comfortably in a couchette compartment. It's a cost effective way to travel long distances, especially when you're short of time (or pistons!). My reservation was made through UK booking agents, **Railsavers**, who've been transporting bikers this way for over 25 years.

Contact: Railsavers, www.railsavers.com Tel: +44 (0)1253 595555

Libyan Travel Agency

To enter and cross Libya with your own vehicle you need the assistance of a local tour company who will provide a mandatory guide and arrange your visa. I used **Temehu** and found them to be completely reliable, fair and committed to helping me have an enjoyable and successful journey. The escort I was allotted was exceptionally friendly, helpful and accommodating. The Temehu website has a large amount of up-to-date and interesting information about Libya, including Sahara routes, prehistoric art and an excellent travel guide.
Contact: Temehu, www.temehu.com

Ferry to/from Italy, Syria and Egypt

The long standing ferry service between Greece, Cyprus and Egypt ended almost a decade ago. Launched in 2010, **Visemar Line** run a weekly Ro/Ro freighter between Venice, Tartous and Alexandria. Cabins are comfortable, your motorcycle is secure in the hold and it's a relaxing and inexpensive way to reach North East Africa.
Contact: Visemar Line, www.visemarline.com
Tel: +39 (0)41 2712505

Research Material

I found a lot of information on Peggy Iris Thomas as well as period Bantam advertisements thanks to **Pig Farmer Bike Magazines.** Run by Keith Batten (of replacing the piston on Day One fame), Pig Farmer stock tens of thousands of motorcycle magazines dating from the 1930s to modern times. Their website is excellent, with an indexing system that allows you to search for articles by motorcycle make and model.
Contact: Pig Farmer Bike Magazines, www.pigfarmerbikemagazines.co.uk
Tel: +44 (0)7908 706671

Accommodation

One of the best travel bargains ever is access to the **Hostelling International** network. You join your own country's **Youth Hostel Association** (in the UK that costs a paltry £15.95 per annum) and you automatically can stay at more than 4000 youth hostels in 80 countries. Members can be of any age and prices are more than reasonable, especially in city centres. Youth hostels are clean, safe and a great place to meet fellow travellers.
Contact: Hostelling International, www.hihostels.com
UK Youth Hostel Association, www.yha.org.uk

Motorcycle Insurance

'How do they do it?' is the question I ask myself every year when I renew my bike insurance with **Carole Nash**. Fully comprehensive classic bike cover, including a take-you-home breakdown recovery service from anywhere in the EU, costs an astonishingly low price. Their assistance when the engine failed on my first attempt at riding to Egypt was faultless.
Contact: Carole Nash, www.carolenash.com
Tel: +44 0800 8047952

Carnet De Passage

It's not only the rider that needs a passport... for some countries the bike needs one too! To temporarily import my motorcycle into Syria, Jordan and Egypt I required a Carnet De Passage. The ever-helpful Carnet team at the **RAC** arranged this document for me. In summary, I paid a fee, a deposit and an insurance premium to guarantee I would not sell the bike. 100% of the deposit and 50% of the insurance was refunded on return of a correctly completed Carnet.

Contact: RAC, www.rac.co.uk/driving-abroad/carnet-de-passage
Tel: +44 0800 468375

Travel Insurance

Most insurers don't provide travel insurance for overlanding on a motorcycle. **Carole Nash** insurance offer a comprehensive motorcycle travel package that's just the ticket and only costs about the same as regular worldwide travel insurance without motorcycling. They even fly your panniers, leathers and helmet home with you in the case of a serious accident.

Contact: Carole Nash, www.carolenash.com/other-insurance/travel
Tel: +44 0800 8047952

For further information, photographs and links to all of the suppliers on these pages, visit www.overlandtoegypt.co.uk

Guest Speaker

If you are a member of a motorcycle club, motoring organisation or any group that would like Gordon to give a talk and slideshow about this journey, or the *Overland To India* ride, please get in touch by email: speaker@overlandtoegypt.co.uk

Also by Gordon G. May

A total of 8,400 miles from Manchester, UK, to Chennai, India, in just under seven weeks. A challenge on most vehicles, but on an antiquated 1953 Royal Enfield...?

"Your bike belongs in a museum, not on the road," was how one doubter tried to discourage Gordon from undertaking this journey. Despite intense heat in excess of 40°C, a crash in the Baluchistan desert and some of the worst roads and driving standards on the planet, Gordon's old Royal Enfield Bullet did indeed make it triumphantly to Chennai.

In his first travel book, Gordon describes in detail the restoration of his motorcycle and the build up to departure, the larger-than-life characters he met and the many challenges he faced. He also recounts the more personal highs and lows of life on the road. Above all, *Overland To India* is a heartwarming book that illustrates human kindness and hospitality and encourages other riders to take their own motorcycles on a long-distance journey.

234 pages including 8 pages of colour photographs, £9.95 from
www.overlandtoindia.co.uk

By Peggy Iris Thomas

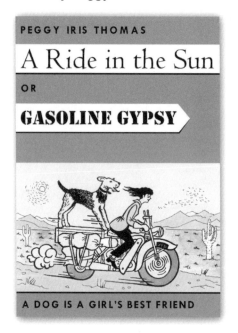

PEGGY IRIS THOMAS

A Ride in the Sun

OR

GASOLINE GYPSY

A DOG IS A GIRL'S BEST FRIEND

"So many people have dreams like mine," the author writes. "Dreams of satisfying that inner voice that says 'Go on, quit that job, take the plunge and see if it really is greener on the other side of the hill.'" Here is the refreshing story of someone who did take the plunge; who landed in Halifax in the spring of 1951, with her BSA motorcycle, Oppy, and her Airedale, Matelot, on the pillion, and set off to explore Canada, the United States and Mexico. Loaded on Oppy was camping equipment, food, a variety of clothing and a typewriter – everything she needed to secure complete independence. Before they turned homeward once more Peggy and Matelot were to pitch their tent in such strange places as a vacant lot in downtown Los Angeles, a Mexican village bar room, a mosquito-infected Louisiana swamp, and on the heights of New Jersey's Palisades.

She was travelling on a strict budget, so from time to time she worked – typing night telegrams, making plywood (backbreaking work this), serving milkshakes, acting as a 'car-hop' at a road-house. And everywhere *Senorita Motorsicilista* went she met curiosity and great kindness. She tells of her experience in a cheerful and likeable book, full of infectious enthusiasm, which will appeal to everyone who warms to a tale of real-life adventure.

226 pages including 4 pages of photographs, £9.95 from
www.gasolinegypsy.co.uk

278